ESTES KEFAUVER

A Biography

Estes Kefauver

A Biography

By Charles L. Fontenay

The University of Tennessee Press : Knoxville

Clothbound editions of University of Tennessee Press books are printed on paper designed for an effective life of at least 300 years, and binding materials are chosen for strength and durability.

Library of Congress Cataloging in Publication Data

Fontenay, Charles L   1917–
    Estes Kefauver, a biography.
    Bibliography: p.
    Includes index.
    1. Kefauver, Estes, 1903–1963.   2. United States
—Politics and government—1945–   3. Legislators
—United States—Biography.   4. United States.
Congress. Senate—Biography.   I. Title.
E748.K314F66   973.9'092'4 [B]   79-28299
ISBN 0-87049-262-4

Only those remembered best by the heart are privileged to be written of honestly at the time of their death.

—Will Muller

Contents

Illustrations

Foreword

This book is designed to be an accurate and reasonably complete biography of the late Senator Estes Kefauver of Tennessee. Ordinarily, the only kind of introduction to such a book that I would consider justified is the kind made unnecessary by the general nature of the first chapter of this one. The kind I certainly would not consider justified, normally, is a narration of "how this book came to be written." Writing a book, good, bad or indifferent, is not so exceptional an accomplishment that the reader usually is fascinated by a blow-by-blow account of the gestation and birth of this marvellous creation.

The present case, however, I must concede reluctantly to be an exception to this very good rule because of a peculiarity it exhibits, which might be labeled "falling between two stools." The casual reader, interested only in a cracking good story and perhaps an attached moral, may be a bit irritated at being distracted by numerous markers for footnotes. On the other hand, the scholarly reader, concerned with reliability and the accessibility of source materials, may be equally irritated to find some of these notes vague as to time and place, or absent altogether. I can sympathize with both breeds of critic, having been in both positions under different circumstances. But this introductory foreward is in the nature of an explanation as to how this ambiguity occurred.

I met Estes Kefauver early in 1948, when he visited the city room of the *Nashville Tennessean*, which had incautiously employed me as a reporter about a year and a half earlier. He was in the initial phases of his campaign for the United States Senate, and the day after I met him, I was assigned to accompany him and cover that campaign for the newspaper. During that campaign, we became friends and I learned to admire Kefauver, even though I continued to disagree with him on some basic philosophical principles. When he ran for President the first time in 1952, I was disappointed not to be assigned to any phase of the campaign as a reporter, but in my spare time I edited a campaign newspaper for him and, if I recall correctly, took a week of vacation so I could watch every minute of the 1952 Democratic National Convention on television; I know that I bought my first television set for the purpose of watching it.

In the spring and summer of 1955, I researched and wrote a biography of Kevauver. The research involved going to his birthplace and boyhood home, Madisonville, Tennessee, to interview his family and those who had known him during his boyhood; to Chattanooga to interview those who had known him during early adulthood, before and after he entered Congress; and to Washington to interview Kefauver, his family, his staff, and his congressional colleagues and former colleagues, and to study the voluminous papers and scrapbooks in his office. I am not sure whether the biography was originally my idea or his, but in either event, Kefauver hoped for publication of the book in time to aid his forthcoming 1956 presidential campaign. He attempted to place it with one of the publishers of his own two books—an unfortunate effort because they were uninterested and my agent could have possibly sold it to another publisher. But, with time running out before his campaign opening, he approached me with the proposition that columnist Jack Anderson had a publisher interested but no manuscript, while I had a manuscript and no publisher. So I sold the manuscript to Anderson, who rewrote it into a concise campaign biography, adding some material of his own, and it was published in 1956 as *The Kefauver Story*, under the byline of Anderson and his colleague, Fred Blumenthal.

As I recall, my original manuscript had been rather fully footnoted as to sources and documentation, but *The Kefauver Story*, being a campaign biography, omitted this. I assumed that the publication of *The Kefauver Story* marked the end of a Kefauver biography as a project of mine, although I was disappointed that it was not the thorough and detailed kind of biography I had had in mind. During the next fifteen years, in the course of a divorce and remarriage and five changes of residence, my copy of the original manuscript of that biography disappeared, along with notes and other research materials. When I took up the project again in 1970, Anderson graciously granted me permission to use any material from *The Kefauver Story*, which included his contributions as well as that drawn from my research. Although I drew on memory for some facts that were in the original manuscript but were not in *The Kefauver Story*, I have fallen back on it as a citation in some cases when I could not remember precisely, or could not locate, the original source of the information. In most cases where this book is documented as a source, the reader may assume legitimately that the source behind the footnote is my own research in 1955. (That research, in fact, as publicized in *The Kefauver Story*, was the original source of a great deal of the biographical material on Kefauver that appeared in newspapers and magazines during his 1956 presidential campaign.)

After 1956, due to developments in my personal life, my contact with Kefauver became more tenuous than it had been during the previous eight years, and I was only peripherally aware of the exceptional record in antitrust investigation he built up in the years just before his death. It was not until six and a half years after Kefauver died that an unexpected letter from an editor for a New York publishing firm apprised me that "the Kefauver story" had not yet run its course for me. He asked me if I were willing to research and write a definitive biography of Kefauver, and of course I was. Many of my sources for the original biography, including both Kefauver and his wife, were dead by then, but I spent several months in further research. I took considerable time to study the papers and records of the Kefauver Collection at the University of Tennessee Library in Knoxville; I interviewed all three of his former administrative assistants; I talked with key members of his Antitrust and Monopoly Committee staff; I questioned two of his children and one of his most trusted secretaries; and I spent a day and a highly alcoholic evening in Chicago with a key figure in both of Kefauver's campaigns for the presidency.

The manuscript that emerged from this intensive research, although it exceeded wordage agreements by approximately 100,000 words, was inadequate for my editor. I did further research, visiting both Madisonville and Chattanooga, among other cities, in search of veracity and completeness, and was well on my way to a three-to-five-volume biography of Estes Kefauver when my editor and his publisher came to a parting of the ways. The eventual result of this development was the decision by the University of Tennessee Press, which previously had published a philosophical work of mine, to publish the Kefauver biography.

At the time I wrote the original version of the current biography, and subsequently its expansions, my study was piled with thermofaxes, notebooks, and other reference materials. But the New York publisher wanted only the minimum of documentation for this "popular biography," and when the manuscript was completed, I disposed of most of the research material in order to be able to get around in the room. Later, when the University of Tennessee Press became interested in the biography, I was told it needed to be documented thoroughly and accurately.

I have done the best I could. In addition to researching the files of the *Nashville Tennessean* exhaustively again, I went to Chattanooga to research newspaper files for references to Kefauver's early adult life; I spent some days in Knoxville going through the massive Kefauver Collection again in search of material that I remembered being my original source; and I spent additional time re-creating research at the Joint University Libraries in Nashville. But the notes are necessarily less complete than they would have been had the original manuscript—not just this later one, but *The Kefauver Story* too—been documented while the original research material was still in hand. At the time I first researched the Kefauver Collection at the University of Tennessee Library, the papers were still being catalogued, and I know of a few cases in which material has been shifted to different boxes since then. Inevitably, the categories into which the mass of material has been organized overlap, and this second time it has been impossible to locate some letters and other reference material I remember having studied originally in that collection.

Of course, it has been impossible also to recall exact dates of interviews done for the predecessor of *The Kefauver Story* nearly a quarter of a century ago, or even those done nearly a decade ago, because my notes on them were destroyed. The objection has been raised that I must have taken very careful notes or taped conversations in order to quote different people so precisely. To that, I can reply only that I have been a newspaperman for more than forty years and have gained a reputation for quoting sources accurately, even when they are political opponents who do not expect me to; and my notes were adequate.

One of the reasons this book is written and documented as it is, is that I am a newspaperman in my fundamental approach to a story, rather than either a fiction writer or an academician. It is organized and written very much as I would write a long and exhaustive newspaper series on Kefauver's life and his significance on the national scene, this many years after his death, with, of course, certain necessary adjustments to the requirements of the particular literary vehicle.

Since my repertorial career for many years was largely in the controversial area of politics, I also have a tendency to recheck my work for accuracy when possible. Therefore, Kefauver's cousin, Allen Cox Jr. of Memphis, very kindly read all of the chapters dealing with Kefauver's childhood and early life, up to his marriage, in the original manuscript of this book. A. Bradley Eben of Chicago, a key figure in both of Kefauver's presidential campaigns and a prime source of information on those campaigns, read the manuscript chapters dealing with those campaigns. Various other chapters dealing with different aspects of his career were read by his last two administrative assistants, Charles A. Caldwell and Richard J. Wallace, and by one of Kefauver's former colleagues, Paul H. Douglas, and the entire original version was read in manuscript by Carol V. Harford, who was Nancy Kefauver's personal secretary after Kefauver's death.

I owe a debt of gratitude to these individuals, at least one of whom is now dead; and I also owe thanks to many others who provided information and cooperation, sometimes unsolicited, toward making this a better and more factual account.

When I contracted to take up the project of a Kefauver biography for the second time, in 1970, Richard Kluger, the editor who was interested in it, said that he would like for the work to be a "definitive biography," as none had been done previous to that time. Nor has such a biography appeared in the interim since then, dealing with all phases of his personal, professional, and political life; only works dealing with fractional aspects of it. Although this book is less than half the length it was at one stage of its preparation, it does attempt to deal with the man himself, as I knew him, and not just with the senator, the candidate, or the investigator. As I knew him, he was worthy of at least such an attempt.

CHARLES L. FONTENAY

October 1979
Nashville, Tennessee

PART I

An Honest Man, Politically and Personally

—Prentice Cooper, 1955

Chapter 1

You Have Always Stood for the Folks

He walked into the Senate Chamber alone. Into that marble-columned hall that has reverberated to the voices of Henry Clay and Daniel Webster, most members of the United States Senate enter in casual groups of three or four, or more, chatting and laughing, before dispersing to their desks. But, during the fourteen and a half years that he served as United States senator from Tennessee, Estes Kefauver ordinarily walked in alone, slowly but with a firm, heavy step and a preoccupied expression that conveyed an intangible sense of purpose.

He would go straight to his desk near the front of the chamber and sit down, his long face impassive, his big hands folded in his lap. It would not be true to say that a hush fell upon the chamber at his entry, but those of his colleagues who had legislative plans for the day were aware immediately that he was there and that his presence was a factor to be calculated.

"They were afraid of him," said John Blair, whose long association with Kefauver as chief economist for the Antitrust and Monopoly Subcommittee (and before) acquainted him intimately with Kefauver's thinking and methods. "They knew he couldn't be bought, and they were afraid of him."[1]

Big, raw-boned and slow-moving, Kefauver was almost clumsy, but not quite. In the decade of the 1950s, when that rather peculiar name needed no further identification all across the nation, he seemed almost handsome (as the young Kefauver had been) and yet, paradoxically, almost ugly. A reporter wrote of him during the 1956 presidential campaign that he "looked like an overly alert horse who was getting dexedrine in his oats."[2]

1. Personal conversation, John M. Blair, Washington, May 15, 1970.
2. Jim Bishop, *New York Journal-American*, Aug. 18, 1956.

A Yale graduate, *cum laude*, he was almost a cold-blooded intellectual. A warm family man, an inveterate hand-shaker, and arm-around-the-shoulder greeter, he was almost a typical politician. He was almost a liberal, almost a rabble-rouser, almost a clownish folk-figure—but not quite any of them, ever. He was almost President of the United States. In his mind, a mind that no one really knew in all of its complexities, that last "almost" haunted him throughout many years of his life. Yet his failure twice to achieve that deliberate goal may have been of less consequence to the nation than his partial successes as a single individual working his way persistently past an intricate complex of political barriers in several fields of legislative endeavor.

Kefauver was a native of Tennessee's eastern mountain country who practiced law in Chattanooga and participated actively in the city's civic life for a decade before entering the U.S. House of Representatives just as World War II exploded in Europe. In just under another decade, he advanced to the Senate, gaining a name for himself as a giant killer in the process by participating in the overthrow of the long-established political dictator of Tennessee, the colorful and shrewd Edward Hull Crump. He had not been in the Senate long before he rocketed to national prominence through his conduct of the partly televised Senate committee investigation of organized crime in America.

Entering the 1952 presidential race, he swept most of the state primaries but fell short of the nomination when the incumbent President, Harry S Truman, took a hand. Kefauver tried again four years later but withdrew after his defeat in two key primaries by the 1952 nominee, Adlai Stevenson. At the 1956 Democratic National Convention, entering the vice presidential contest almost as an afterthought, he defeated John F. Kennedy in a close battle to gain a place on the ticket.

After the defeat of the Stevenson-Kefauver ticket in the 1956 election, Kefauver retired from the national political lists to devote the remaining six and a half years of his life to several major legislative projects, one of which—the Kefauver-Harris Drug Control Act of 1962—brought him a final flare of nationwide fame.

His 1952 presidential campaign provided all of the basic elements of what became known in his lifetime as "the Kefauver legend." It appeared for a while as though this one determined individual might achieve the incredible feat of overturning the organized power of the incumbent Democratic party leadership by a simple, direct appeal to popular sentiment. Ever thereafter, whenever the public became aware that Kefauver was prominent in a political or legislative fight, it was assumed that he was struggling against the massed obstructionism of The Establishment; and the assumption was usually right.

Kefauver's near-decisive string of primary successes in 1952 was attributed variously by the political wiseacres to the publicity derived from the Senate crime investigation, to popular disillusionment with the Truman administration, to his lack of opposition by any candidate of major stature except in the two primaries he lost. All of these things undoubtedly were factors, but both the "experts" and the party leaders apparently failed to recognize another, deeper influence, in spite of the warning signals raised by the emergence of two major splinter parties in the presidential election four years earlier.

People all over the country had a vague feeling that something basic was wrong with American society. In the joyous reaction to the end of World War II, they had anticipated that the nation soon would settle back into a peaceful, normal environment—only better. With the war won, and the United Nations to guarantee the peace, great strides in technology promised a rich future.

What people expected was something of a qualitative improvement upon that "normalcy" that older people remembered of an era when the United States was largely a rural nation, and nationwide industrial and communications networks were just beginning to develop. Not everything was perfect in that America, but the country remained hospitable to the individualism and free enterprise that had been traditional since the nation's founding.

These concepts were still traditional in the hearts of the people as World War II ended, yet a subtle atmosphere was thickening in America that increasingly made individualistic nonconformity suspect and the time-honored definition of free enterprise questionable. It was an atmosphere that bred Joseph R. McCarthy and the Red witch-hunts of the 1950s, pointing ultimately to Richard M. Nixon and Watergate, an atmosphere that seeded the violent social and ideological conflicts of the 1960s and early 1970s.

As Kefauver remarked in a speech in 1954, "I doubt if there is a half-century in history in which men have been more abused by conflicts and collisions within the societies they inherited." And he added, pointing up the root of an increasing popular exasperation: "Paradoxically, I do not believe that men in any other period have created such tremendous potential for the ultimate benefit of mankind."[3]

This discrepancy was a source of frustration to vast numbers of people, who expressed their dissatisfaction with the programs and leaders of both major political parties. They were looking for a leader with fresh solutions, such as most of them still believed they had found in Franklin Delano Roosevelt. Many of them saw this new leader in Estes Kefauver. Hundreds of thousands of television viewers and newspaper readers knew him as the man who had exposed the ugliness of organized crime, and they believed that he would devote himself with equal intelligence and integrity to the task of conquering other evils that undermined the nation.

As a popular repository of such confidence, Kefauver was a peculiar mixture of the traditional and the progressive in his own thinking. Grounded philosophically in the principles upon which the nation was founded, he was devoted to the concepts of individual rights and civil liberty. Yet he was always ready to accept changes, even radical changes, in government and society if such changes appeared to offer a more practical means of realizing the democratic principles he treasured.

The roots of Kefauver's populism rested in that combination of conservatism and progressivism. Senator Dennis Chavez of New Mexico wrote him once: "Like Andy Jackson, you have always stood for the folks."[4] Kefauver's own rationale of standing "for the folks" was outlined in a talk at Etowah, Tennessee, in May 1948, when he was running for the Senate:

"In the United States today, there is some division and some conflict in point of view. On one side there is the belief that we should put a lot of water in the top layer and let a little of it trickle down to the people underneath. Others believe that if this country

3. Speech before a luncheon meeting of State Jaycees, Oklahoma City, May 15, 1954. A copy of the speech, entitled "Youth's Challenge Today," is in the Estes Kefauver Collection, Univ. of Tennessee Library, Knoxville, Series 10, Box 4.
4. Letter, Dennis Chavez to Estes Kefauver, March 25, 1954; Kefauver Collection.

is to be kept great, the little man must be given an adequate opportunity and a reasonable standard of living. I'm on the side of the latter people."[5]

This commitment to the average man—"Joe Smith," Kefauver called him when he was campaigning for Vice President in 1956—explains why, though he was an internationalist and essentially liberal, the core of his popular strength in both his presidential races lay in the conservative, isolationist, but individualistic Middle West.

Kefauver was sometimes labeled a Populist, after that political party that occupied a fragment of the nation's stage in the late nineteenth century. Philosophically he was related to the Populists, but practically he was a Democrat. Kefauver's brand of democratic thought, however, did not appeal to the intellectual liberals, who were strong in the Democratic party since Franklin Roosevelt. Pitted against Truman, Senator Robert S. Kerr, or Senator Richard Russell, Kefauver could command substantial support from that somewhat abstruse element of the party, but Adlai Stevenson, witty, learned, and appealingly modest, wooed them from Kefauver with ease.

Without the intellectual liberals, Kefauver was lost, in terms of his practical ambition. However qualified their influence might be on voters in the actual election, they were important in terms of convention delegate votes in the North and East. Always disliked by the party pros, always anathema to the Southern conservatives, Kefauver had to have the support of the intellectual liberals as a supplement to his base of popular strength to win a party nomination. Because Stevenson trumped him on this count, Kefauver's unique brand of populism—though it won him sensational primary victories and a substantial scattering of near-fanatical adherents throughout the nation—never won him public office outside his home state.

Yet his campaigns were not without their own importance to the American political process. All presidential races and many congressional races since 1952 have mirrored the impact of the tall, easygoing Tennessean, with his engulfing handshake, his slow smile, and his grave manner of discussing issues with individual voters in simple, familiar terms. And Truman's comment about New Hampshire in 1952 that primaries were but "eyewash" proved to be the

5. *Nashville Tennessean*, May 28, 1948.

somewhat embarrassing valedictory for that pragmatic attitude: presidential primaries alone still cannot guarantee a nomination, but since Kefauver in 1952 no serious presidential candidate has felt that he could ignore them—Jimmy Carter being one of the outstanding recent examples.

Although his political fame rested in his personal campaign touch, Kefauver's substantial contribution to his time was nevertheless primarily legislative. He focussed his legislative attention on relatively few areas, changing his major focus from time to time but pouring a great deal of energy and study into each area that commanded his attention. These principal legislative interests may be listed briefly as the Tennessee Valley Authority and public power, governmental reorganization, action against organized crime, Atlantic Union, and antitrust activity.

Of all the legislative works that justified Kefauver's reputation as a friend of the common man, his long battle against monopolistic practices in a wide area of the nation's economy was the most significant. An anonymous business lobbyist, while Kefauver was in the House, is said to have coined the phrase, "In Kefauver we antitrust."[6]

A successful corporation lawyer who became interested in antitrust legislation through a chain of fortuitous circumstances after entering the House of Representatives, Kefauver met with meager success in the field as a congressman, but still he was a persistent gadfly to big business lobbyists and their congressional allies. After he reached the Senate, however, and especially after he rid his bonnet of the presidential bee, he plunged deeply into antitrust activity. During the last years of his life, as chairman of the Antitrust and Monopoly Subcommittee, he made the legislative investigation a weapon to be feared by those who trod near the edges of the antitrust laws. He led the subcommittee in probes of numerous economic areas—notably electrical equipment, steel, and prescription drugs. His final major legislative accomplishment, the Kefauver-Harris Drug Control Act, while more a safety measure than an antitrust law, was an outgrowth of this subcommittee's investigation.

"The sociological basis for my belief in antitrust," he said in an

6. J. Lacey Reynolds, *Nashville Tennessean*, Dec. 11, 1949; Jack Anderson and Fred Blumenthal, *The Kefauver Story* (New York: Dial, 1956), 96.

address to the American Economic Association in Chicago in 1947, "is my conviction that standards of human welfare tend to be higher in communities which are characterized by the existence of a large number of independently owned and operated enterprises than in comparable communities in which most of the economic activity is carried on by a few large plants owned by distant and outside interests." In the same talk, he gave the fundamental political basis for his antimonopoly philosophy: "Is there not some real merit in the argument that a great concentration of industry would inevitably lead to some type of collectivistic state in which our democratic liberties and political rights would cease to exist? . . . Certainly, the pages of recent history lend little comfort to those who would stake their hopes on a wise, humane and judicious exercise of a great centralization of political and economic power."[7]

Kefauver was therefore a "liberal," but in an old-fashioned way. Far from a leader on either side of the civil rights battles that raged while he was in Congress, he stood firmly and publicly for racial segregation until the Supreme Court's 1954 decision declaring it unconstitutional, when he accepted the principle; and he consistently opposed a Fair Employment Practices Commission. On the other hand, he favored abolition of the poll tax from the beginning of his career in Congress, turning most of his Southern colleagues against him, and further offended the Southerners by opposing the filibuster, the principal weapon of the Southern minority against civil rights legislation.

Civil rights was a difficult problem for him politically, both in Tennessee and nationally. He might be, as both *Time* and *Pageant* magazines said of him, "the Senate's most effective symbol of the South's new progressivism"[8]; but being a political realist, he told a reporter once, "I don't want to be a dead statesman."[9] He preferred to talk softly on such ticklish issues, on the theory, as he expressed it to me, "Well, Charlie, you know, you have to get elected before you can do any good up there."[10]

But in the somewhat less tangible area of civil liberties, there was never such a tinge of equivocation. He was alert to infringement of

7. *Press-Scimitar*, Memphis, Dec. 30, 1947.
8. *Time*, April 3, 1950; *Pageant*, Sept. 1951.
9. Irwin Ross, *New York Post*, May 11, 1956.
10. Personal conversation, Estes Kefauver, Nashville, Spring 1954.

civil liberties in all legislative areas, and his vulnerability to "pro-Communist" charges stemmed from the fact that the greatest pressure for ignoring civil liberties while he was in Congress was a product of the "great Red scare" of the late 1940s and early 1950s. When anti-Communist hysteria combined with partisan politics to bring to the floor an extreme Communist control bill in 1954—an election year for Kefauver—he cast a lone Senate vote against it.

Partly as a consequence of his extensive presidential campaigns in his leisurely, familiar way, probably more people throughout the nation felt they knew Kefauver personally than any other public figure in his time. He encouraged that feeling by following up the most casual political contacts with correspondence. He was so assiduous at maintaining mail contacts that at one time his Christmas card list exceeded 50,000 annually.

Kefauver's warmth in dealing with people was genuine. He was a man who could stop on his way to the airport to telephone a secretary on his staff and apologize for speaking sharply to her. He was a man who could be told by Lyndon Johnson, never one of his ardent admirers, "If a vote were taken on the Floor of the Senate as to who is the most considerate and thoughtful member, I believe that the name of Estes Kefauver would be right at the top of the list."[11]

Yet that warmth never touched the core of his being, which remained unassailably and secretly his own. The outgoing friendliness of his greetings, sometimes dropping a big arm around a shoulder or enveloping an acquaintance in a great bear hug, was not exactly a pose, but it was a phenomenon of the "exterior" Kefauver.

In private, and occasionally in public, he was an aloof, introspective individual whose mental processes were a mystery even to close friends. Jac Chambliss, a Kefauver law associate in the 1930s, described his reserve as "a disengaged manner that makes it hard for people to know what's going on inside him." Theodore H. White, one of the nation's more perceptive political observers, called him "a lonesome man, elusive, abstracted, wrapped in his own thoughts," with "no intimates." Former Senator Paul H. Douglas of Illinois, who was allied with Kefauver in numerous legislative battles and was his most devoted backer in the 1952 presidential

11. Note, Lyndon B. Johnson to Estes Kefauver, Aug. 11, 1958; Kefauver Collection, VIP File.

race, said: "I was a great admirer of Estes, but the truth is, I did not feel close to him. Everyone thought I was, but I think no one was intimate with him."[12] His wife, Nancy, said once: "Even in the family, it's hard to tell what Estes is thinking."[13]

Kefauver was a controversial figure in his day, especially as a senator. Some of his enemies accused him of being an unprincipled demagogue, while some of his supporters were convinced he was a political saint—they put him in the same class as Franklin D. Roosevelt and Abraham Lincoln. Both views were extreme, but Kefauver did possess some of the personal magic of a Roosevelt, some of the integrity of a Lincoln.

Senator Clifford P. Case of New Jersey said Kefauver "was a loner. If there is such a thing as an 'establishment' in the Senate, I suppose he was perhaps the most unlikely one to be included in such a group."[14] His close personal friends in Congress were few, his bitter personal enemies even fewer. His colleagues generally were somewhat baffled by him, somewhat dubious of him, with estimates of his ability and integrity that ranged from grudging (and sometimes exasperated) respect to the sentiment expressed by another maverick who was his good friend, Senator William Langer of North Dakota:

"All in all, I want you to know that in the vast course of my political experience, which has run the entire gamut from the dizzy heights of success to the depths of lowest despair, I have met and seen many men in public life; and I just want you to know how very much I admire your courage, your facility of expression, your extreme courtesy to witnesses, and your all-around dignity as a United States Senator."[15]

Not all of his colleagues would have waxed so lavish, but a majority of them probably would have agreed with what the *Arkansas Gazette* said after his death: "Estes Kefauver was one of the really good ones."

12. Personal conversation, Jac Chambliss, Chattanooga, Spring 1955; Theodore H. White, "Kefauver Rides Again," *Collier's*, May 11, 1956; personal communication, Paul H. Douglas, Washington, July 20, 1970.

13. "Tennessean on a Hayride," *Newsweek*, Oct. 15, 1956.

14. *Carey Estes Kefauver, Late a Senator from Tennessee: Memorial Addresses Delivered in Congress* (Washington: Government Printing Office, 1964), 33.

15. Letter, William Langer to Estes Kefauver, Aug. 13, 1955; Kefauver Collection, Ser. 4-b, Box 5.

Chapter 2

A Sort of By-Himself Boy

When Carey Estes Kefauver was born in a back room of the two-story frame house on Cooke Street in Madisonville, Tennessee, July 26, 1903, the elderly family physician, Dr. Penland, called to the boy's father: "Come in here, Cooke. I want you to see the finest back I ever saw on a baby." And, said Cooke Kefauver years later when his boy was a United States senator running for President, "he seems to have had plenty of backbone from that day on."[1]

His elders in that day would have said the boy "came of good stock." His paternal great-great-grandfather, William H. Cooke, a descendant of settlers in 1645, had come to the southern part of East Tennessee about 1833 to settle on a 1,200-acre tract near territory occupied by Cherokee Indians. Cooke was a prominent banker and a senator in Tennessee's 1847 legislature. His son, Dr. Robert Fielding Cooke, established a farm and built a mansion with slave labor twenty miles northeastward, just south of the tiny community of Madisonville.

In the autumn of 1861, the Reverend Jacob Peter Kefauver brought the family name into Tennessee for the first time. A descendant of Huguenot brothers who settled in 1750 near Frederick, Maryland, he accepted a call as pastor of Chattanooga's First Baptist Church. A few months later, he met Dr. Cooke's daughter, Nancy, during a "protracted meeting" in Madisonville, and soon married her. When Dr. Cooke died in 1868, his daughter was his sole heir, and she and her husband moved from Chattanooga to Madisonville to operate the farm. Their four children were born there, and one of them, Robert Cooke Kefauver, became a hardware and farm implement merchant in Madisonville.

In 1897, Cooke Kefauver took as his bride Phredonia Bradford

---

1. Personal conversation, Cooke Kefauver, Madisonville, Tenn., Spring 1955.

Estes of Haywood County, in West Tennessee. Phredonia Estes was a descendant of the House of Este, oldest of the reigning houses of Italy, founded in the eleventh century by Alberto Azo II, marquis of Liguria. Azo's line itself was traced back to a Roman senator, Caius Actius, who lived around 410 A.D., during the reign of the Emperor Honorius.[2]

Members of the Estes family migrated, by way of France and England, to Virginia in 1770, and Phredonia Estes's great grandfather, Joel Estes, moved to West Tennessee with his wife and eight children in the autumn of 1824. His wife, Sarah Langhorne Bates, also was of an aristocratic line—the Carys, knights and nobles of England and a family that had been in America since 1640.[3]

Joel Estes built a sprawling, two-storied mansion, "Estes Hall," in a flat woodlot of maple and sweetgum trees, and prospered in the rich, hot land. He ran for Congress unsuccessfully against David Crockett in 1828, and Estes died in 1833, about the time William H. Cooke settled in a different part of the state, His grandson, Albert Cary Estes, fought for the South in the Civil War and afterward became one of the leading attorneys in Brownsville, county seat of Haywood County. He married Leonora Perry Mann, one of the town's most beautiful women, and Phredonia Estes was their daughter.

When she married Cooke Kefauver and went back to Madisonville with him, he built the house in which their children were born. Estes was their second son; his brother, Robert, was two years older, and both of their sisters who survived, Nancy and Leonora, were younger.

The countryside in which Estes Kefauver was born and spent his boyhood was by no means the "hillbilly" environment often attributed to all of mountainous East Tennessee. There are mountains in Monroe County—the Unicoi Mountains of the Unaka range—but

2. May Folk Webb and Patrick Mann Estes, *Cary-Estes Genealogy* (Rutland, Vt.: Tuttle Publishing, 1939), 83. This book, researched and written by two of Estes Kefauver's cousins, is one of the primary sources for the outline of Kefauver's ancestry. Other primary sources were conversations in the spring of 1955 with Estes Kefauver in Washington, and Cooke Kefauver and Mrs. Charlotte Johns in Madisonville, Tenn. Some interesting supplementary material is provided by Louise Davis, "The Lady of the Many-Storied House," *Nashville Tennessean Magazine*, Oct. 29, 1961, pp. 13, 19.

3. Ibid, 117.

they are in its eastern half. On a clear day, they can be seen, rising far and blue, over against North Carolina.

Madisonville and the county's other fair-sized town, Sweetwater, are in rolling foothills, rich with grassy valleys, offering good farmland. Some of the best of that farmland is just south of town where Dr. Cooke, Estes Kefauver's great-grandfather, had built a three-story mansion of brick in 1849, in a grove of magnolia, holly, cedar, oak, and hard maple trees. At the turn of the century, Estes' uncle, Paul Kefauver, lived in the mansion and ran what remained of Dr. Cooke's plantation.

Estes' earliest memory was not of the hills of home but of the Mississippi Valley bottomland, when he visited his mother's family in Brownsville at the age of three. The trip to West Tennessee could be made by train, via Knoxville and Nashville, with three changes. Brownsville then was "a sleepy town, a very aristocratic town," according to one of Estes' West Tennessee cousins, Allen E. Cox Jr.[4] Estes Hall was about two blocks west of the old brick courthouse in the town's center, surrounded by homes of other prominent citizens, on spacious grounds. The homes were built almost up to the court square, where a bank, a pharmacy, a general store, and other small-town business houses baked in the hot summer sun. Mules, flicking ears and switching tails against the flies, plodded into town pulling wagons, and occasionally a spanking trotter drawing a phaeton would raise the dust of the dirt streets.

While the Kefauver boys and their mother were there, they accompanied the Estes family on one of their frequent trips twenty miles westward to the extensive cotton plantation of Estes' great-uncle, Joel Estes, at Orysa in adjoining Lauderdale County. Young Estes Kefauver, resplendent in his first pair of knickerbockers, made by his mother from an old woolen skirt, was entranced at the sight of the white cotton fields and the experience of playing in a cotton gin instead of a hay loft, as at home.

It was appropriate that young Kefauver should remember one of his rare trips to West Tennessee first, for his mother's Haywood County background permeated the atmostphere of the Kefauver house in Madisonville. Phredonia Kefauver was what was known in

4. Telephone conversation, Allen E. Cox Jr., Memphis, Summer 1970.

that day as "a Southern lady": gentle but dignified, with a firmness beneath her gentleness that was founded in the consciousness of her heritage which would have put her perfectly at home directing the slaves in their chores on her grandfather's plantation.

Her father, a courteous gentleman with a Nathan Bedford Forrest beard, was fond of stately phraseology and sonorous admonitions and wrote shortly before his death in 1887: "My children, God bless you and make you noble men and women. The Estes blood and name is honorable, true and brave. Prove yourselves worthy members of this ancient family." From the cotton country, at the age of twenty-three, she brought to Madisonville a copy of the Estes coat-of-arms and a concept of family worth colored by the fact that one of her first cousins was governor of Missouri, another was Tennessee's state treasurer, and the family roster was studded with judges and prominent attorneys.

Cooke Kefauver, for his part, expected less of his two sons that they achieve professional prominence in later life than that they possess the virtues of honesty, courage, and self-respect. He was a tall, spare man, his Baptist conscience laced with a salty-tongued sense of humor—both acquired from his own father, the Reverend J.P. Kefauver, a big man with a full brown beard who enjoyed hearing himself talk.

Dr. Robert C. Kimbrough, a kinsman on the Cooke side of the family, once remarked that Estes Kefauver had "the Cooke gentleness in him," the Kefauvers being sharper-tongued.[5] Much the same could have been said of Cooke Kefauver. In his early thirties when his sons were born, he was tolerant and companionable with them during their boyhood. They called him affectionately "Popsy," an appellation Estes applied to him for the rest of his life.

Young Estes grew swiftly, and in a few years stood shoulder to shoulder with his older brother, Robert: the two freckle-faced, blue-eyed, mop-haired lads might have been twins. But Robert was the heir, and Estes lived somewhat in the shadow of the first-born, for Robert was considered the brighter, "the smartest child that ever lived" and "the one the family pinned their hopes on," ac-

5. Personal conversation, Dr. Robert C. Kimbrough, Madisonville, Spring 1955.

Estes (left), about eight, sits in the buggy with his older brother, Robert, his sister, Nancy, and their Aunt Nora Welch while Uncle Carey Welch holds the reins, in front of the Kefauver home in Madisonville.

cording to their Aunt Lottie, while Estes was "just the sweetest child in the world."[6] A neighbor said that Estes and Robert "was always together," roaming the Monroe County hills, swimming in Cherokee Lake, playing Indian or sandlot baseball with their schoolmates, or damming the nearby creek.

Dreams of the Old South and its lost courtliness permeated Estes' home and Uncle Paul's farm (his wife had been Lucy Cornelia Estes, a first cousin of Phredonia Kefauver). But to walk barefoot up the dusty street to the courthouse was to emerge from that antique enchantment into a world of buildings and buggies and hill-country people—the world of his father and his friends.

Like Brownsville and most other county seats in Tennessee, Madisonville was centered on the courthouse and its square, but its resemblance to Brownsville ended there. The two-story brick courthouse, surmounted by a four-sided clock tower, rose tall on the brow of a steep rise that sloped away sharply toward the eastern mountains. In the building were records dating back to 1819, when the land that became Monroe County was acquired from the Cherokee Indians.

The square was "town," surrounded by most of Madisonville's business firms and offices. Estes could step up from the street onto the board sidewalks across from the courthouse and walk past Doc Head's pharmacy, Tom Cole's poolroom and bowling alley, Captain Whiting's jewelry store, the law offices of Morris Harrison and Taylor Hunt, the Bank of Madisonville, and the dingy plant of the *Monroe County Democrat*, one of Tennessee's oldest newspapers, published weekly on an old flat-bed press by Judge Orrie Hicks and Ely Duncan. If he were with his mother, a dignified lady in ankle-length dress and broad-brimmed hat crowned in feathers, they might stop at the Toomey & Hicks grocery store, where she could buy sugar for a nickel a pound, new potatoes for $1.75 the 90-pound bag, butter for 14¢ a pound or ham for 10¢ a pound. Or

6. Personal conversation, Mrs. Charlotte Johns, Madisonville, Spring 1955. The picture of Kefauver's childhood was put together through conversations with Mrs. Johns, Cooke Kefauver, and neighbors of the Kefauvers in Madisonville in the spring of 1955. In the spring of 1971 I returned to Madisonville to fill out the picture of the town during Kefauver's early life and his activities there through personal and telephone conversations with older residents. Prices of goods and materials were obtained by reference to advertisements in newspapers of the period.

they might stop at the dry goods store run by Beeler Brakebill and Fletcher Sheets, where she would pay 10¢ to 18¢ a yard for domestic, colored lawns, ginghams, or percale.

The largely self-sufficient farms of antebellum days were no more, but the economy was still home-centered here, far from any city. Phredonia Kefauver might buy rather lavishly at the dry goods store, for she sewed almost all of the clothing for a growing family, as well as curtains, sheets, and domestic linens. But the grocery was mostly for staples like coffee, sugar, and salt. Most families had at least a small garden and perhaps a cow, and the Kefauvers were wont to obtain meat, vegetables, and dairy products from Uncle Paul's farm.

The school Estes and Robert attended was almost next door to them, on land that once had been part of the Cooke farm. It was a three-room building, with three grades in each room. In his early grades, Estes got the three R's, plus some basic American history, geography, and literature. His academic performance was about average, except in history, which interested him and brought him somewhat better grades than other subjects. He was a quiet, conscientious boy, and rarely experienced the school's normal disciplinary methods: "wearing a dunce cap or having to stay at the blackboard with your nose in a circle," he remembered years later.[7]

After school, the boys might drop by Tucker Meek's blacksmith shop to watch him strike sparks from hot iron on the anvil or grip a horse's leg with one brawny arm while he nailed on the shoe. They might wander to the cream-and-brown weatherboarded railroad depot to watch the Louisville & Nashville's afternoon train come in from Cartersville, Georgia, en route to Knoxville. Or they might linger by the skating rink their father owned, across the street from the big Tallent House, the only hotel in town until Cooke Kefauver built another in the century's second decade. The rink was a red plank building near the square, boasting a big red pipe organ, and its wooden floor was kept smooth for the roller-skaters by a pony that pulled a huge grindstone across it daily.

Or the boys might go to the square to play in their father's hardware store. While Cooke Kefauver measured out a half pound of car-

7. Personal conversation, Estes Kefauver, Washington, Spring 1955. One of Kefauver's elementary school report cards is in a scrapbook he kept, in Kefauver Collection, Ser. 9, Box 3.

At the age of four, Estes Kefauver (left) plays with his brother, Robert, in rocky terrain near their native Madisonville, Tennessee.

Estes with his sisters, Nora (left) and Nancy in Madisonville not long after the death of their brother, Robert, in 1914.

pet tacks for Mrs. McCroskey or helped Alf Tallent choose a ladder or perhaps talked crops with Uncle Paul or one of the other farmers, the two boys would mangle a board or two with saw and hammer or climb about in the back room on the cultivators and harrows.

When the boys were at home during the day, the mother's usual task of the time—maintaining the necessary discipline for her children—fell to Phredonia Kefauver, who preferred to do so by admonition rather than scolding. Both boys had bicycles (their father had owned the first one in Monroe County), and one day, while wheeling along a country lane not far from town, they raided a peach orchard atop a steep hill. But the owner appeared at the height of their adventure, and they fled on their cycles, their blouses stuffed with ripe fruit.

As they raced downhill, Estes lost control of his bike and collided with a buggy. Appalled at his multiple transgression—peach-stealing, wrecking his bicycle, and staining his shirt front with crushed peaches—Estes persuaded Robert to divert their mother's attention while he walked the crippled vehicle around to the back of the house, hid it in a shed, and disposed of the telltale shirt.

But discovery was inevitable, for his mother must notice eventually that he was no longer riding his beloved bike. Estes moped about the house for three days, and his preoccupation was apparent to Phredonia Kefauver. At last she inveigled him into a confession. When he had finished his woebegone story, she smiled and said: "Those things happen to boys. Now, if you had told the truth about it at first, you wouldn't have had to worry about it for three days."[8]

The Kefauvers were far from wealthy. Except for the farm, Dr. Cooke's substantial affluence had dissipated with the Civil War, and, as for his own enterprises, Cooke Kefauver commented once, "Well, I lost some and made some, and I reckon I did as well as a man could under the circumstances."[9] But, because of their background and the extensive farm with its brick mansion, they were considered "the aristocrats of this part of the country," according to Dr. Joseph Stickley, a Madisonville druggist. Cooke Kefauver was liked and respected enough to be elected mayor for five four-year terms at different times, the last one in the early 1930s.

8. Personal conversation, Estes Kefauver, Washington, Spring 1955.
9. Personal conversation, Cooke Kefauver, Madisonville, Spring 1955.

The Kefauvers were not an exceptionally devout family, just good church-going Baptists. Phredonia Kefauver gave her children Bibles, and in the front of Estes' copy she pasted a poem by Ella Wheeler Wilcox that admonished tempering ambition with common kindness.

For young Estes, who had just tucked the fourth grade under his belt, the summer of 1912 was a highpoint of his boyhood. It was the year he and Robert campaigned with their father for Woodrow Wilson. Cooke Kefauver had always been a Democrat in predominantly Republican territory. He was an enthusiastic supporter of William Jennings Bryan, the Democratic candidate for President in 1896, 1900, and 1908. Bryan was popular as a Chautauqua orator, and Madisonville was one of his Chautauqua stops during Estes' boyhood. Cooke Kefauver took his sons to hear "the Great Commoner," and Estes was deeply impressed by Bryan.[10]

Governor Woodrow Wilson of New Jersey, selected as the Democrats' 1912 presidential nominee after forty-six ballots, was an eloquent advocate of progressive policies, and Bryan supported him at the convention. Cooke Kefauver was ready to do more than his usual part for his party in the campaign that summer, for it was his idea that Theodore Roosevelt had "split the Republicans all to flinders" by bolting the GOP and running as a third party candidate.

The two boys campaigned with their father in the family's 1909 Ford touring car (Cooke Kefauver, a man who put his progressivism into practice, owned the first automobile in Monroe County). The vehicle, its overhanging canopy and folding windshield tied by struts to its flat fenders, its "oogah" horn curving down from a pressure bulb beside the high front seat, jounced along the dirt roads, frightening horses and rattling by to the imprecations of their drivers. "Mr. Cooke" sat behind the steering wheel, tall and gaunt, wearing a Panama hat and a four-in-hand. Beside him in the front seat sat the boys, nine and eleven, dressed for "visiting" in their round hats and flowing bow ties. From Cokercreek to Rockville they bounced and rattled, from Gudger to Vonore.

10. In an undated letter to Thomas N. Schroth of the *Brooklyn Eagle*, preserved in the Kefauver Collection, Kefauver wrote: "The experience I best remember at Madisonville when I was in Grammar and High School were [*sic*] once when William Jennings Bryan came with the Chautauqua. After that I studied all of his books and speeches."

They would approach a crossroads, featuring a general store, a blacksmith shop, and a house or two under the leafy oaks. As the "gasoline buggy" shivered to a stop, with a couple of expiring explosions from its exhaust, perhaps a half dozen or so men would converge on it. Its driver would unfold himself from beneath the steering wheel and climb down, shake hands with a couple of farm implement customers he recognized, then mount the store's wooden porch to clear his throat and begin: "I think most of you know me. I'm Cooke Kefauver, from over at Madisonville."

As he spoke, the boys diffidently handed out campaign literature and tacked posters to the nearby oak boles. Soft drinks would be drunk around (with maybe a mite of something stronger, like home-made peach brandy, for Mr. Cooke), and the campaigning Kefauvers would be off down the dirt road again.[11] Wilson's victory was a personal triumph for Cooke Kefauver and, of course, for his sons, too. Wilson carried Republican Monroe County by 1,133 votes to 727 for President William Howard Taft and 477 for Roosevelt.

As far as young Estes was concerned, the 1912 campaign did more than initiate him into the excitement of "politicking," with the taste of victory as a bonus. One of the advantages of campaigning informally at the amateur level was that Cooke Kefauver was dealing with shrewd hill-country farmers, most of them with Republican leanings, who were unimpressed with slogans and generalizations and wanted to know in so many words just why he thought Wilson would make a better President. The little speeches on store porches were almost always supplemented with individual discussions and arguments, in which Mr. Cooke would match his concept of Wilson's "New Freedom" of opportunity for free enterprise under government regulation against some local spokesman's argument for Taft's "let business alone" philosophy, while their small audience—including Estes and Robert—listened and weighed their respective points.

From the time they were old enough for such excursions, Cooke Kefauver often took his two sons picnicking and camping in the wooded country bordering the Little Tennessee River, about twelve

11. Kefauver's participation in the 1912 campaign with his father was described in the spring of 1955 in personal conversations with Estes Kefauver in Washington and Cooke Kefauver in Madisonville.

miles northeast of Madisonville at its nearest point, and its tributary, the Tellico River, which flows behind a ridge of hills a few miles east of Madisonville. They would hunt and fish, roaming the river banks, but the boys were warned against trying to swim the swift waters. Perhaps, by the summer of 1914, the prohibition against swimming the Tellico had been lifted. Estes had just returned from a trip to his great-uncle Paul Estes's farm in West Tennessee when he and Robert went with a group of their schoolmates for a swim in the Tellico. Estes was a good swimmer: once he had saved the granddaughter of Tucker Meek, the blacksmith and tanner, from drowning in the Little Tennessee, pulling her ashore by her long hair. He was the strongest swimmer in his group this day and had stroked his way to the farther bank, alone, when he heard his friends shouting frantically. Robert had vanished suddenly beneath the waters.

By the time Estes swam back across the river, the other boys had gotten hold of his brother and pulled him to the bank, unconscious. They administered artificial respiration and rolled Robert on a barrel to get the water from his stomach, but they had to carry him home still unconscious. Robert regained his senses at last and seemed to be all right, but he lapsed into a coma again after insisting on eating a second helping of peach ice cream for supper. He died in convulsions August 9, 1914.[12]

The shock of his brother's death had a profound effect on Estes, just turned eleven years old, and two of the people who knew him best—his Aunt Lottie and Judge Charles G. Neese, many years later his first administrative assistant in the U.S. Senate—believed the effect to have been a permanent one. They suggested that Estes felt somehow responsible for Robert's death because he had swum ahead and was not at his brother's side to help him. Knowing how bright had been his parents' hopes for Robert's future, Estes determined he would fulfil Robert's promise for them in his own life.[13]

12. Personal conversations, Estes Kefauver, Washington, and Mrs. Charlotte Johns, Madisonville, Spring 1955. It was Kefauver's recollection that his brother never did regain consciousness, but Mrs. Johns recalled the incident of the peach ice cream.

13. Personal conversations, Mrs. Charlotte Johns, Madisonville, and Charles G. Neese, Paris, Tenn., Spring 1955.

Whether or not Estes ever formulated such a resolve consciously, the folk of Madisonville saw a change in him after the tragedy. He trudged along the dirt streets, a lonely figure now for one who had rarely been alone before, the expression on his no-longer-freckled face grave and withdrawn. He became, in Dr. Kimbrough's words, "a sort of by-himself boy." Kefauver turned more to his books at home and became quieter and more studious in school.

Because Madisonville had no public library, his mother bought him a great many books, and few were of a light nature. The books he remembered from his boyhood were Thomas Dixon's stories of the Civil War; biographies of Robert E. Lee, Abraham Lincoln, and Andrew Jackson; Shakespeare's works; Campbell's *Tennessee History*; Green's *The American Commonwealth*; and Edward Gibbon's *The Decline and Fall of the Roman Empire*. Scores of other books lined the spacious shelves of the Kefauver home.

Cooke Kefauver bought Estes a pony, "Old Joe," and a little rubber-tired phaeton, and he was seen frequently, neatly dressed and quiet, driving it around Madisonville. Sometimes it was piled full of his friends, on their way to play under the big trees at the Kefauver farm or to swim in the pond. On occasion, his little sister, Nora, recalled, "he would ride me piggyback all over town, jogging like a horse." [14]

The year Estes finished the eighth grade, 1916, President Wilson ran for reelection. Again Cooke Kefauver took to the Monroe County countryside in behalf of the Democrats, this time with but one son to accompany him and hand out the campaign literature. Estes, older now and alone, bent himself seriously to the task of comprehending the historical background of the Democratic cause for which he worked, scanned the newspapers of the day, and listened attentively to the discussions of his elders.

Other political streams fed the boy's interest during this period, too. Joseph W. Folk, a first cousin of his mother, had won a name for himself by his prosecution of St. Louis grafters as a circuit attorney and sought with some success to extend his reforms to the state when he was governor of Missouri from 1905 to 1909. Folk was endorsed for President by his state's Democratic party organization in

14. Harold H. Martin, "The Mystery of Kefauver," *Saturday Evening Post*, June 2, 1956. A picture of the youthful Kefauver in the phaeton is in the Kefauver Collection.

1910 but withdrew before the 1912 convention in favor of House Speaker Champ Clark, also a Missourian.

Like Bryan, Folk was in demand as a Chautauqua orator, and Estes heard him speak under the big tent in Madisonville several times. Folk would stay with the Kefauver family—usually with Uncle Paul at the mansion—when he was in the area, and Estes was an interested listener when "Cousin Joe" got together with his father and Uncle Paul for serious discussions of national trends and problems amid drifting wreaths of cigar smoke.

Cousin Joe, a rather severe-looking, Roman-nosed man who wore bow ties and pince-nez, commanded Estes' interest for additional reasons at this time. Estes had decided to become a lawyer. Cooke Kefauver said once that his son's ambition to be a lawyer dated from the time Estes was five or six years old, but it seems to have come to focus right after Robert's death.

It was at this time that Cooke Kefauver built the Kefauver Hotel near the courthouse and gave up his hardware business to operate it. The hotel was a rambling building, with eighteen guest rooms and seven office rooms for rental, as well as a parlor, dining room, and kitchen, and at first it did rather a good business. But, according to Estes' sister, Nora, it became "something of a white elephant, because it was oversized for the town, and when the automobile came in, people would go on to bigger towns."[15] The Kefauver family lived in it for a year, when severe rheumatism began hampering Phredonia Kefauver at her domestic duties; then Cooke Kefauver sold Estes' birthplace and built a "town house" for the family a block from the hotel.

During the hotel's initial years of prosperity, the lawyers who converged on Madisonville from surrounding counties for periodic sessions of Circuit and Chancery Courts would stay at the Kefauver Hotel. When a court day ended, the lawyers would gather on the long porch to relax after their perspiring hours of argument and deference to the bench. As night fell over the quiet town, the boy would sit in the shadows and listen to the men talk over cases and clients and *corpora delicti* while the tips of their cigars and cheroots glowed in the darkness of the porch like resting fireflies and the

15. Personal conversation, Miss Nora Kefauver, Madisonville, Spring 1955. Some information on "Cousin Joe" Folk is contained in Webb and Estes, *Cary-Estes Genealogy*.

kerosene lamps inside cast long yellow rectangles on the wooden floor.[16]

"I remember," Estes Kefauver reminisced years later, "that I stayed out of school quite frequently to listen to the lawyers argue cases in the courtroom. In those days, lawyers spoke long and eloquently, and thus my determination was reached to be a lawyer." In the considerably less formal Monroe County magistrates' courts, which might be in brief session almost any day of the year, the gangling boy was welcome, and the justices of the peace would sometimes let Estes take a minor case when no lawyer was present to represent a client.[17]

The boy knew that Cousin Joe Folk, aside from politics, was one of the nation's most prominent attorneys, a law graduate of Vanderbilt University and holder of honorary law degrees from five other colleges. In the summer of 1917, right after American entry into World War I, Estes and his mother took the train to visit Cousin Joe in Washington, where he was chief counsel for the Interstate Commerce Commission.

It was Estes' first trip to a city larger than nearby Knoxville, a hilly and rather countrified place, and he was wide-eyed at the sights and at the lighted lavishness of the big Washington restaurant where Folk took his relatives to dinner. Estes concluded his meal by lifting to his lips the copper fingerbowl a waiter set before him; his mother stopped him before he had taken more than a few sips.

As they lingered at the white-damasked table, Folk asked the fourteen year old seriously about his plans for the future. Estes told Folk about his major interests in school—political science and history—and said he would like to become a lawyer.

"You could be a lawyer, indeed, Estes," replied Folk. "A mighty good lawyer."[18]

Another older cousin who visited frequently in the Kefauver home, Judge W.B. Swaney, was a prominent Chattanooga attorney

---

16. Letter, Estes Kefauver to Mrs. Clara Savage Littledale, editor of *Parent's* magazine, New York, Feb. 11, 1956, Kefauver Collection, Ser. 1, Box 74. Also, personal conversations, Estes Kefauver, Washington, and Cooke Kefauver, Madisonville, Spring 1955.

17. Personal conversation, Estes Kefauver, Washington, Spring 1955.

18. Ibid. Kefauver also related in this conversation the influence upon him of his cousin, Judge W.B. Swaney.

and a former president of the Tennessee Bar Association, and he willingly chatted with the boy about the ins and outs of the legal profession and the educational background necessary for it. Swaney, tall and spare like Cooke Kefauver, with snow-white hair and a goatee, was particularly well qualified as a mentor, for he had taught contracts and private corporation law for many years at the Chattanooga College of Law.

Swaney was a great admirer of Thomas Jefferson, whom he considered the single most influential contributor to the structure of American democracy. At law school, Swaney delivered many lectures on Jefferson's life and writings and urged his students to study the Declaration of Independence, the Statute for Religious Freedom of Virginia, and similar documents. Later he authored *Safeguards of Liberty*, a study of the Declaration and Virginia's Bill of Rights, with emphasis on Jefferson's contributions to them; and he communicated to his young cousin his own conservative brand of progressivism.

Another spur to Estes' legal ambitions lay in the availablility of reading matter to hand. Although one of Phredonia Kefauver's brothers, Albert Carey Estes Jr., was a lawyer in Brownsville, she acquired her father's extensive law library and added it to the books in the Kefauver home for Estes' benefit.

In high school, a former private academy down the eastern slope from the courthouse, Estes was characterized by his old schoolmaster, H.L. Callahan, as "a good average student" who nearly failed first-year Latin but made good grades in Caesar and Cicero. A big, strong boy, Estes reputedly could swing a 120-pound sack of wheat to his shoulder with one hand and bend a soft drink cap double between thumb and forefinger. He was center fielder on the school baseball team and as basketball center, at six feet three, he never faced an opposing center who had the reach on him.[19]

The school annual described him as "a jolly good fellow in body, soul and mind." In his senior year, he was secretary-treasurer of his class and editor of the annual. On the day of his graduation, he was approached by one of his classmates in the midst of the proud confusion and handed a "friendship book" with the request that he

19. Personal conversation, H.L. Callahan, Madisonville, Spring 1955; *Nashville Tennessean*, Dec. 13, 1951.

"write something in it for me." Estes took the pen the girl offered and scrawled tongue-in-cheek answers in the spaces provided; after "ambition," he wrote: *"To Be President."*[20]

One day that jesting entry would be true, but not then; it was in the same vein as his listing below it of his "favorite amusement" as *"Drinking"*—in bone-dry Madisonville, in bone-dry Tennessee. As he wrote *finis* to his boyhood with a jocular scribble on that sunny April day of 1920, his ambition was the more modest one of going on to college and ultimately realizing his determination "that some day I would become a lawyer."[21]

As a political campaigner, Kefauver often exhibited a country boy aspect that endeared him to many voters. He was a tall, big-boned man, with an awkwardness that was somehow appealing, and he would stumble over the words of a speech, fumble helplessly with a text, and at last perhaps lapse into some simple paraphrase of his theme that was obviously extemporaneous and betrayed his rural origin.

The favorable impression he achieved with such bumbling was the despair of his enemies, who sometimes tried to label him a mere bumpkin and sometimes claimed that the rustic flavor of the man was sheer pretense, for effect. Even close friends, those of them who knew him during the developing years of his young manhood, could not believe this part of him was genuine, for he was anything but loutish in college and as a Chattanooga lawyer.

It appears that the solution to this, one of the many contradictions in his personality, lies in the fact that he was so adaptable, even opportunistic, in superficial matters that the urbanization of Estes Kefauver was accomplished in a relatively short time, once he stepped forth into the larger world from his native Madisonville. To realize how swift was the process of sophistication, one would have had to be present at the very time of Kefauver's emergence from his rural cocoon, as was his second cousin, Thomas Jefferson Walker of Dyersburg, Tennessee.

Walker was standing on the platform of the Louisville & Nash-

20. Personal conversation, Mrs. Ed Hicks, Madisonville, Spring 1955. Reproductions of the page Kefauver inscribed in Mrs. Hicks's "friendship book" and other material from his high school days are preserved in the Kefauver Collection.
21. Personal conversation, Estes Kefauver, Washington, Spring 1955.

ville Railroad depot in Knoxville when the seventeen-year-old Kefauver climbed down from the train after the forty-four mile trip from Madisonville as the autumn of 1920 began to color the East Tennessee foliage. Walker, three years older than Kefauver and already a junior at the University of Tennessee, had agreed to meet his cousin and escort him to the campus; but Walker was mildly stunned at the spectacle that confronted him.

A cap, the small town fashion of the times, was perched atop Kefauver's head, and he carried a straw suitcase. But the item young Kefauver gloried in the most was his Sears Roebuck suit—"it was red when you looked at it one way, and green when you looked at it another way," Kefauver reminisced afterward—upon the breast of which were arrayed the buttons and ribbons he had won for perfect attendance at the Sunday school of the Madisonville Baptist Church.

Walker swallowed hard, but he accompanied the newcomer to a hack and they rode together to the Kappa Sigma fraternity house. Walker took Kefauver in by a side door, but they ran into a group of his fraternity brothers in the hall. When Walker introduced his cousin, the stares were something less than polite, and while Kefauver was diffidently explaining from whence he hailed, one of the group drew Walker aside to ask in too loud a whisper: "Gee, Tom, where did you find that rube?"

It was the beginning of a painful week for young Kefauver, who had invaded Knoxville equipped with a considerable ego, built on his star role as a basketball player, a class official, and a highly popular member of the in-group at Madisonville Central High School. When he spent his first weekend at home, he confided to his mother his wish that he not go back.

"I know how miserable you feel," she sympathized. "After all, you're only seventeen and haven't yet had much chance to learn one of the most important things of life. Estes, you must turn your stumbling blocks into stepping stones. Let hurt feelings be a prod to work just that much harder."[22] It was advice Kefauver was to remember for the rest of his life. For the time, it encouraged him to return to Knoxville, determined to "make good."

Walker said he "had an awful time getting my fraternity broth-

22. Estes Kefauver, "The Best Advice I Ever Had," *Reader's Digest*, Aug. 1954; repeated in paraphrase in "Tennessean on a Hayride," *Newsweek*, Oct. 15, 1956.

ers to accept Estes" in Kappa Sigma. Kefauver's amiable personality posed no problem; it was his clothing. Kefauver recalled years later that his new fraternity brothers would "swipe" his odd attire, piece by piece, and when he was poking around in puzzlement at its disappearance, one of them would always be on hand to give advice on more fashionable replacement.[23]

No longer the sartorial outcast of Kappa Sigma, young Kefauver began to adapt to the campus environment and found some of his best friends of later years in the fraternity house in which he lived. The fraternity so far forgave him his inauspicious start as to name him "Man of the Year" more than thirty years later for his work as chairman of the Senate Crime Investigating Committee.[24]

His roommate, Rom Wright of Hartsville, Tennessee, remembered him as a "hard worker, a square shooter," who "got everything he went after."[25] He began to acquire a polish, too: his University of Tennessee football captain, Roy B. (Pap) Striegel, described him as "popular with the girls," adding: "He may have been a country boy when he got there, but he was smooth as anybody when he left."[26] The student newspaper, the *Orange and White*, said of him after he had been at the university awhile: "He possesses the qualities of leadership and the ability to mix with and gain the admiration and good opinion of his associates."[27]

By his junior year he was a member of the Student Council, on the staff of the *Orange and White*, and on both the football and track teams. His Aunt Lottie, wife of an Episcopal minister in Vicksburg, Mississippi, and a well-traveled and urbane woman, approved the change in his appearance and demeanor when she saw him at Christmas vacation that year but wanted to know rather sharply how he could "do all these outside things" and keep his grades at a high level.

23. Ibid. Kefauver told me more in detail about his arrival at the University of Tennessee, including the whimsical description of the red-and-green Sears Roebuck suit, in a personal conversation in Washington in the spring of 1955. Further detail was supplied in a telephone conversation with Thomas J. Walker, Dyersburg, Tenn., in Autumn 1970.

24. *Nashville Tennessean*, Dec. 15, 1951.

25. Personal conversation, Rom Wright, Hartsville, Spring 1955.

26. Telephone conversation, Roy B. Striegel, Knoxville, Spring 1955.

27. Clippings and other records of Kefauver's days at the University are contained in the Kefauver scrapbook, Kefauver Collection, Ser. 9, Box 3.

"Well, Aunt Lottie, I'm able to concentrate," he replied. "I can sit down and study an hour every day, and while I'm studying I can shut out all distractions. That way, I can get my studies done in a hurry and have the rest of my time free for other things."[28]

Kefauver made considerable use of his "time for other things." He won his post on the Student Council by a margin of fifty votes in a four-way campaign. In his sophomore year, he received the Scarrabean Medal, awarded by an exclusive senior society, and was chosen for membership in the Scarrabean Society in his senior year. He was the first president of the Blue Pencil Club (college editors) and was at first associate athletic editor and later athletic editor of the *Orange and White*. He was a member of the YMCA Council, the Pan-Hellenic Council, the T Club (an athletic club), and the Athletic Council. In his junior year he was class president.

Kefauver acquired his first real nickname, too. In high school he had been listed in the annual as being nicknamed "Big Bill," but that was apparently because a nickname had to be listed for everybody; his sister Nora said nobody ever called him that.[29] At the University of Tennessee, though, some of his friends called him "Big Stuff," often shortened to "Stuff." Later, his schoolmates at Yale called him "Kef" (pronounced "Keef," but Kefauver himself always spelled if with one "e").[30]

The University of Tennessee was, then and thereafter, a strongly sports-oriented school. Kefauver had never seen a football game when he arrived there, but he had added a few pounds to the 170 he carried as a high school basketball player, and he was anxious to test his height and weight on the gridiron. E.H. (Hal) Blair of Nashville, who became captain of the football team in 1921, remembered the Madisonville seventeen year old as "overgrown, awkward, and gawky" when he appeared for practice in the fall of 1920. In fact, Estes' only obvious accomplishment as a freshman member of the scrub team was to break his nose in his earnest effort

28. Personal conversation, Mrs. Charlotte Johns, Madisonville, Spring 1955.

29. Personal conversation, Miss Nora Kefauver, Madisonville, Spring 1971. The annual page containing this nickname is in the Kefauver scrapbook, Kefauver Collection, Ser. 9, Box 3.

30. Personal communication, Allen E. Cox Jr., Memphis, Oct. 9, 1970. The pronunciation was given me in personal conversation by John H. Doughty, Knoxville, Summer 1970.

to "make the grade." His stubborn, perspiring concentration at the daily grind on the athletic field, however, gradually brought forth fruit and he was sent into a few games as a substitute in 1921.[31]

The 1921 team was loaded with veterans, but that year Coach M.B. Banks decided to try pulling guards out of the line to run interference for end plays, and for that he needed speed and power as much as weight. Striegel, then the team captain, had seen Kefauver perform on the track team and work out with the discus, and, after testing Kefauver with a hard workout, he persuaded Banks to put Kefauver in the line as a guard. In this position during his last two years at the University, Kefauver was hardly the phenomenon he was made out in later years (some publicist incorrectly dubbed him a former All-American), but he was a solid lineman with a solid local reputation. As Striegel's playing mate at guard, he was called "a stone wall in the path of Kentucky backs" by the *Knoxville News-Sentinel* for his performance in the 1922 game between Tennessee and the University of Kentucky, and in 1923, Art Fowler, sports writer for the *Knoxville Journal*, pinned the nickname "Old Ironsides" on him because he was never knocked down (Kefauver suggested later that might be "merely indicative of my ability in staying out of the way").[32]

Despite the football prominence attributed to him later in his political years, Kefauver actually did better at track. Costarring with Floyd Kay, the team captain, he broke the Southern discus record of 132.3 feet three times in a week and won the discus throw and numerous places in the shot put in virtually every dual meet in which Tennessee participated. In one trial he threw the discus 134.3 feet, but when he repeated the feat in the Southern Intercollegiate Track and Field Meet, a Mississippi A&M hurler topped him with 136 feet. At the end of that year, his junior year, he defeated

31. Personal conversation, E.H. Blair, Nashville, Spring 1955.
32. Anderson and Blumenthal, *The Kefauver Story*, 33-34. The source of this information was in part a conversation with Roy B. Striegel in Knoxville in the spring of 1955 and in part newspaper clippings preserved in Kefauver's office in Washington, many of them now to be found in the Kefauver scrapbook, Kefauver Collection, Ser. 9, Box 3. The remark about "my ability in staying out of the way," in slightly differing forms, is made in a letter from Estes Kefauver to Julius Hoffman, Philadelphia, March 8, 1957, Kefauver Collection, Ser. 1, Box 77, and in a note prepared for *Quick* magazine, in the Kefauver Collection, Ser. 1, Box 73, but omitted from Kefauver's quote as published in *Quick*, April 7, 1952.

Kefauver (second from right) practices as left tackle with the University of Tennessee football team in 1922.

Kay for captain but the same year was defeated for captain of the football team.

In his senior year Kefauver was in bed for three weeks with malarial fever, and his doctor told him, "You can play football if you'll take it easy. You're not to play more than fifteen minutes in any game." But Kefauver was one of only three seasoned linemen on the team and he exhibited a disregard for his health that was to reappear in later years; the big No. 3 on his jersey flashed on the field throughout every game of the season. Fortunately, the fever did not recur.[33]

Also in his senior year Kefauver became editor-in-chief of the *Orange and White*, and he was the state's first student to become president of the Southern Federation of College Students. That year was also his first year of law, and he became a member of Phi Delta Phi legal fraternity. An illuminating sidelight of his college life is that, as president of the All-Students Club, he led a drive to clean up college dances of drinking and "immorality"; by that time, he had tasted alcoholic beverages and approved the savour thereof, but he was not long enough out of Madisonville to condone its public consumption.

It was Kefauver's original intention to continue his legal studies at the university, but when he carried his Bachelor of Arts degree back to Madisonville in the spring of 1924, he found his mother's inflammatory rheumatism causing her a great deal of pain. He, too, was still feeling the effects of his bout with malaria the year before. After a family conference, Cooke Kefauver rented a house in Hot Springs, Arkansas, and Estes took his mother and sisters there for a summer at the healing spa.

One of the vices Kefauver had picked up at the University of Tennessee was golf; he escaped addiction to it, however, and never was very good at it—"just a dub" was the verdict of his friend Jere Tipton, who was often his partner on the links in Knoxville and later in Chattanooga. Golf was one of his amusements at Hot Springs and, through it, he met local sports lovers who, learning of his gridiron record at the University, arranged that he should be offered the then-princely salary of $150 a month to teach mathematics and coach football at the Hot Springs high school. He thought about it

33. Anderson and Blumenthal, *The Kefauver Story*, 34.

Kefauver with his mother (center) and friends at Hot Springs, Arkansas, in 1924.

Kefauver as a Yale University law student, about 1927.

for a long time, against his desire to finish his law studies, but decided at last to take the job for one season.

He was resoundingly successful. "He didn't storm at the players like many coaches do," recalled one of his fellow teachers, Mrs. Lucille Burns Bigbee. "They thought he was a tin god on wheels."[34] At the end of the school year, on the family's return to Madisonville, he received a letter from the Hot Springs school system offering him $2,500 a year and expenses to return to the job there that fall. It was a tempting offer. Something more than $200 a month was a better income than some three-quarters of American families could command at that time, and Cooke Kefauver had not shared in the Coolidge prosperity of the day. The increase of automobiles and the corresponding decline in railroad passenger traffic had cut down the patronage of the Kefauver Hotel so severely that its owner had to abandon its operation as a hostelry and turn his hand to real estate (eventually to become Madisonville's principal real estate owner).[35]

Besides, young Kefauver had changed his mind about returning to the University of Tennessee: he wanted to study law at Yale University and that would cost him a good deal more. One of his acquaintances at the University of Tennessee, John H. Doughty of Greeneville, Tennessee, had finished there while Kefauver was coaching in Hot Springs, and Doughty planned to go on to Yale; and Kefauver's cousin, Allen Cox of Helena, Arkansas, had just completed his first year at Yale and would be going back that fall. But the principal influence on Kefauver in favor of Yale seems to have been an older cousin, Mathesia Folk Webb of New York, a sister of "Cousin Joe" Folk of Missouri, who was convinced that the Yale law school was the best there was.

Mrs. Webb, wife of James A. Webb, a prominent attorney and author of a number of law books, was a pleasant-faced, dark-eyed lady of fifty-two whose consuming interest was the extensive Cary-Estes family and the accomplishments of its members; she had been working since 1907 on a family genealogy that was published eventually in 1939. She had persuaded Cox to go to Yale and obtained a scholarship for him, and she persuaded Kefauver too,

34. AP story, *Nashville Tennessean*, Jan. 25, 1955. Further details on Kefauver's teaching and coaching period at Hot Springs are contained in an article by Mary D. Hudgins in the *Arkansas Democrat*, Oct. 21, 1956.

35. Personal conversation, Miss Nora Kefauver, Madisonville, Spring 1955.

36

when he and his mother and sisters visited West Tennessee relatives while she was there.[36] Kefauver went to his father with his problem. "Boy, you'll have to decide on that for yourself," answered Cooke Kefauver. "But I'd sleep on it, if I were you."

Estes did, and the next morning announced his decision: "Popsy, if I go back to Hot Springs and teach, I'll wind up at forty as a football coach and be kicked out. I've always wanted to be a lawyer, and I've decided to go to Yale and be one."[37] He got in touch with Jack Doughty in Greeneville and made arrangements to travel to Yale with him and two fellow Tennessee graduates, Floyd Ambrister and Fred Thackston. Kefauver, endowed with $100 for a start from his father (what happened to his Hot Springs earnings is not recorded), joined the trio in Knoxville.

Concluding that it would be foolish to spend any of their limited funds on train fare and arrive at Yale without proper transportation for the academic life, the four young men invested in a decrepit Ford and tinkered with it until they got it running. The car performed creditably until they reached Bristol, on the edge of Virginia, but there it stopped. They were able to get it fixed that time, but a few miles up the road, at Lexington, Virginia, the old car gave up permanently, forcing the budding barristers to buy train tickets after all. They treated themselves to a consolation prize: an overnight stop in New York, where they not only acquired the voluminous gray flannel "Oxford bags" that were the latest style in men's trousers, but made the rounds of the city's nightclubs.

Doughty was a rather short, slight individual, with a squarish cast to his face and a skeptic's dry humor, a natural foil for the towering, energetic, earnest Kefauver. The two complemented each other so well that their two years together at Yale served as the foundation for a lifelong friendship.

On arrival in New Haven, the two procured a room together on the second floor of a high-roofed rooming house at 352 Orange Street, ten blocks from the heart of the Yale campus. Their lodgings were directly over the room of a schoolmate and his bride, Robert and Betty Criswell from Ohio, and Kefauver and Doughty soon found reason to make the Criswells their dearest friends—the Cris-

36. Telephone conversation, Allen E. Cox Jr., Memphis, Summer 1970.
37. Personal conversation, Cooke Kefauver, Madisonville, Spring 1955.

wells owned an automobile. They established contact with the Criswells habitually by pounding on a steam pipe that ran vertically through both rooms.[38]

Kefauver financed his way through Yale with a scholarship of "less than $250," a $2,500 loan from the college's scholarship fund and a series of odd jobs. The first of these supplementary jobs was firing furnaces and washing dishes, recourses that startled Cooke Kefauver when he learned of it because $100 went rather far in those days. He wrote his son to "give up those jobs and I'll send you some money"—"you can't get to be a lawyer that way." But Estes replied: "You've spent enough on me. You still have to educate Nancy and Nora." The result was that the elder Kefauver let Estes write checks on his account, but he said, "I don't think he wrote more than two or three checks, for $15 or $20, the two years at Yale."[39]

Doughty's opinion was that Kefauver's stay at Yale was financed primarily by his Aunt Lottie and that she even bought him the raccoon-skin coat, a college fad of the times, that caused such a sensation when he walked down the streets of Madisonville in it during the 1926 Christmas holidays. But Kefauver did work while there and sought the assistance of Dr. H.A. Morgan, president of the University of Tennessee, in finding jobs. Morgan gave him a note of recommendation, and said in a personal note to Kefauver: "The fact that you have to earn some of your expenses will be good for you. Lawyers after graduation have to live the simple life, and it is a pretty good idea to prepare yourself for this during college." Kefauver waited on tables, with Doughty, at the York Street Restaurant for a while and worked in the college bookstore.[40]

38. The description of the trip to Yale and Kefauver's activities there was furnished by John H. Doughty in a personal conversation in Knoxville, Summer 1970.

39. Personal conversation, Cooke Kefauver, Madisonville, Spring 1955. Estes Kefauver himself was the source of the story that he fired furnaces and washed dishes at Yale, a story that appeared in numerous newspaper and magazine articles during his presidential races in 1952 and 1956, though Doughty expressed doubt to me that he "ever fired a single furnace."

40. Personal conversation, John H. Doughty, Knoxville, Summer 1970. The recommendation from Morgan to Dean T.M. Swann, Yale Univ., dated Sept. 30, 1925, is in the Kefauver scrapbook, Kefauver Collection, Ser. 9, Box 3, while the accompanying letter to Kefauver, of the same date, is in the Kefauver Collection, Ser. 11, Box 4. Years later, Estes proved to his wife, Nancy, that he actually had

Kefauver found another, more interesting means of augmenting his income, one that might have been expected to interfere considerably with his academic standing but did not. "Let's put it this way," explained Doughty: "Kef was a very fine poker player." Sometimes he would stay with the cards far into the night and awaken Doughty with his bedtime ablutions as dawn was already changing the sky outside the windows. "Mr. Jack," he would say, "I hope you'll take plenty of notes this morning." Kefauver would cut class to sleep the morning away, and, said Doughty, "he'd take my notes and make better grades than I did." Kefauver's poker winnings financed many a weekend "beer bust" for the two of them, the Criswells, and another schoolmate, Roger Dann of New York.[41]

Kefauver and Doughty were roommates for their first six months at Yale, then Doughty left the rooming house for a living-in job as "sort of a house father" at nearby Milford Preparatory School. Kefauver moved into Corby Court, the Phi Delta Phi fraternity house just behind the Law School building, where Cox was his roommate for the rest of the year.

Despite his relative poverty, it was at Yale, that Kefauver perfected the urbanity that made him, in Doughty's words, "a favorite of the Four Hundred"—and of the feminine sex. There were rough spots in it when he went there; Mrs. Bigbee, his fellow teacher at Hot Springs, remembered him as a timid young man who "would blush when a woman spoke to him, and didn't know what to do with his big hands and feet." But by the time he had finished his first year at Yale, he had overcome that shyness to the point of being known as "the Kissin' Cousin" among those of his own generation in his extended family.[42]

With his odd jobs (and his socializing) to occupy his spare time, Kefauver went out for no sports and was involved in no student or-

waited on tables by slipping into a restaurant they were passing on a street and sliding a stack of plates onto his arm (personal communication, Carol Harford, Washington, Oct. 10, 1970).

41. Personal conversation, John H. Doughty, Knoxville, Summer 1970. Kefauver's habit as a young man of addressing close friends by their first names with a "mister" appended may have stemmed from the fact that people around Madisonville usually called his father "Mr. Cooke." Kefauver dropped the practice when he grew older.

42. Personal conversation, Wayne Murphy, a second cousin of Kefauver, Nashville, Spring 1971.

ganizations at Yale. He applied himself so assiduously to his law studies (and Doughty's notes, when the occasion demanded) that he, along with Doughty, passed his bar examination and was admitted to practice at the Tennessee bar in 1926, before returning for the final year at Yale. Kefauver graduated from Yale with his LL.B. degree, *cum laude,* in 1927. Among his fellow graduates were two men whose political paths would cross his own in years to come: Brien McMahon, who became senator from Connecticut, and Herbert Brownell Jr., who became U.S. attorney general during the Eisenhower administration.

For their return home from Yale, Kefauver and Doughty took a coastal steamer and disembarked after several days at Norfolk, Virginia, where Kefauver's parents awaited them. The group traveled the rest of the way back to Tennessee by train.[43]

The Estes Kefauver who ambled around the square in Madisonville in 1927, chatting with oldsters and greeting old schoolmates, was, in more than mode, a different creature from the quaintly dressed lad who had climbed aboard the train to Knoxville nearly seven years earlier. He had learned more than the law: like an eager sponge, his mind had absorbed the content of cosmopolitan currents that drifted past him in Knoxville, in Hot Springs and New Haven. College had rubbed smooth his homespun edges and bestowed upon him a social charm that, if sometimes puppyish, was nonetheless relaxed and convincing.

43. Personal conversation, John H. Doughty, Knoxville, Summer 1970.

Chapter 3

He Could Be Very Persuasive

Programmed by example and precept to think first in terms of family connections, Kefauver had entertained visions of going into law practice with "Cousin Joe" Folk, who had encouraged him so strongly in his ambition to become a lawyer, but Folk died during Kefauver's third year at the University of Tennessee.[1] College loosened the ties of family orientation too, and after their graduation from Yale, Kefauver and Jack Doughty scouted the relatively familiar terrain in Knoxville for opportunity.

The response they met among established attorneys was typified by that of Ray H. Jenkins, a young lawyer who told them that he was not making enough money to support himself and certainly needed no partner.[2] Doughty opened a Knoxville law office with another beginner, but Kefauver, his mind reverting naturally to the value of family ties, announced that he would try his luck in Chattanooga, where he might hope to join the law firm of his cousin, Judge W.B. Swaney.

Kefauver had been in Chattanooga only once before in his life, but he decided to scout the terrain there on a stopover between trains while en route to Decatur, Alabama, to attend a former classmate's house party. From the big stone railway station he strolled downtown, a matter of about a dozen blocks, for a visit in the law offices of Cooke, Swaney & Cooke. The three partners in the law firm were cousins, but the one whom Kefauver knew well, Judge Swaney, was not there at the moment. The only one present was the senior member of the firm, Colonel R.B. Cooke, and he was preparing to leave.

"I'd like to talk with you, Cousin Estes," he said, "but I have to

1. Personal conversation, Estes Kefauver, Washington, Spring 1955.
2. Personal conversation, John H. Doughty, Knoxville, Summer 1970. Jenkins later achieved considerable prominence in Tennessee Republican politics and in

go to Chancery Court to present a motion." With nothing better to do and a rather long wait between trains, Kefauver accompanied Cooke up the hill to the Hamilton County courthouse. It was Saturday afternoon and the courtroom was packed with fifty or sixty lawyers. When he had presented his motion, Cooke said to the judge: "By the way, Your Honor, I want to present a young kinsman of mine, Estes Kefauver. He's going to practice law with us." As Kefauver told it, the courtroom announcement took him completely by surprise, but, since that was what he wanted anyhow, after his Decatur house party he settled in Chattanooga without returning to Madisonville; then he wrote his family what had happened.[3]

When Kefauver, just turned twenty-four, reported for work at the Cooke, Swaney & Cooke law offices, he was assigned a little, battered desk in a corner and given the task of researching supportive legal precedent for cases handled in court by his seniors. All three of his cousins were veteran lawyers who enjoyed reminiscing about past legal frays, and when business was slack, he was apt to be regaled with expositions of Judge Swaney's Jeffersonian philosophy or poetic excerpts from Colonel Cooke's favorite, Robert Burns.

After a time the impatient young man was assigned his first case, that of prosecuting to collect a long-overdue $18 grocery bill, and one of his seniors advised him to fight the case "as if you were trying to collect $18,000 for United States Steel." Taking the advice to heart, Kefauver fortified himself thoroughly with legal precedent, but when the elderly, shabbily dressed defendant appeared at the magistrate's court and began sobbing quietly as Kefauver started presenting his case, the young lawyer was so touched that he obtained a recess and gained an agreement between the two parties that the grocer would drop his case if the woman would pay a little at a time on her bill, as she could.[4]

His first criminal case went no better. As he told the story, the

---

1954 was mentioned as a possible candidate against Kefauver for the U.S. Senate, but Jenkins did not make the race.

3. Personal conversation, Estes Kefauver, Washington, Spring 1955. John H. Doughty, in a personal conversation in Knoxville, Summer 1970, expressed the opinion that Kefauver was not as surprised by Col. Cooke's announcement as he said he was but, in fact, probably had indicated to Cooke his hope of joining the law firm on their way to court.

4. Bill Holder, "The Gentleman from Tennessee," *Nashville Tennessean Magazine*, Jan. 16, 1949.

defendant, a black man charged with burglary, had been wearing a pair of stolen pants when arrested but claimed he had bought them at a pawn shop for two dollars. Kefauver related the story:

"That was the case that was proved before the jury. No evidence was adduced about the defendant entering the man's house. I felt I had won my case, and was pretty cocky about it.

"Just before the case was ended, the state called the policeman back on the stand to prove some little point. I thought I had done so well that I would cinch my case absolutely. So I asked the policeman one final question: 'You found this man with these particular pants on, and that is all you know about the case?' The policeman answered, 'I testified about the pants, but I was not asked about anything else. I don't know anything more about the case except that the defendant confessed very fully to me that he had entered the man's house and stolen the pants.'

"I just asked one too many questions!" (His client went to jail.[5])

It was not long, though, before Kefauver built up a rather extensive law practice in one particular area. A young black woman came to the offices of Cooke, Swaney & Cooke, seeking a lawyer to handle her divorce case, and Colonel Cooke turned this comparatively minor matter over to the firm's new member. Kefauver went to work with the vigor of the novitiate and obtained the divorce for her expeditiously, charging her $35 for it. She was pleased with his handling of the case and his courteous treatment of her and recommended him to her friends, who, in turn, passed the word along to *their* friends. In a comparatively short time he built up a substantial clientele among Chattanooga's populous black element, not only in divorce cases but in other small legal disputes.[6]

At a time when segregation was still the accepted way of life in the South, Kefauver, in dealing with his black clients, most of them poor and not very well educated, treated them much the same way he had once helped his schoolmates with their lessons, as described by his old schoolmaster, H.L. Callahan: "with no assumption in voice or manner of superior wisdom and intelligence . . . always calm, kindly, courteous, genial and affable."[7]

5. Estes Kefauver, U.S. Senate speech, Sept. 23, 1950. *Congressional Record*, vol. 96, pt. 2, p. 15699.

6. Anderson and Blumenthal, *The Kefauver Story*, 43–44.

7. Personal conversation, H.L. Callahan, Madisonville, Tenn., Spring 1955.

His interest in his clients' welfare often went beyond the demands of the professional relationship. One exemplary case was that of an elderly black woman who consulted him because she was in serious financial straits. Her son, a habitual drunkard, wasted everything she made from taking in washing and scrubbing floors. Questioning her, Kefauver learned that her husband had been killed in an industrial accident, but she never had received any compensation for his death. Kefauver took the matter to court and obtained a $1,250 judgment against her deceased husband's employer. But he did not stop there. When she received her check, he escorted her to the bank, opened a $1,000 account for her, and showed her how to withdraw the money.

"But, Auntie," he advised her, "before you take any of this money out of the bank, I want you to talk it over with me, so your son won't get hold of it. And I want you to come up to my office once a month and tell me how you're getting along."[8]

During his first year in law practice, Kefauver learned from experience what Dr. Morgan had meant when he said beginning lawyers "have to live the simple life." His fees were small and to supplement them he began teaching a night class at the Chattanooga College of Law; he kept it up for several years. He also taught a public speaking class for three years in a vocational school, as well as an American Institute of Banking course. His first year as a lawyer, though, despite "moonlighting," brought him a total income of only $800, less than a third of the amount he had been offered for teaching and coaching at Hot Springs three years earlier.[9]

An old University of Tennessee friend, W. Corry Smith, was just beginning law practice in Chattanooga too, and in the absence of anything that might be defined as assets the two young men pooled their poverty. They found a room together in a boarding house and for transportation purchased a dilapidated automobile, the first of no less than six they owned jointly before either could afford one by himself. To their meager budget, Kefauver contributed $100 from the sale of his Yale coonskin coat but kept a derby hat he had worn at Yale on the theory it added dignity to his new professional status.[10]

Kefauver's apprenticeship among the minor legal squabbles of

8. Anderson and Blumenthal, *The Kefauver Story*, 44.
9. Bill Holder, "The Gentleman from Tennessee."
10. Personal conversation, W. Corry Smith, Chattanooga, Spring 1955.

the black community lasted only the one year. About that time, W.W. Welch, a fraternity brother of his, was asked by another brother who had stopped practicing law to collect a four-dollar bill for him. Welch was general counsel for the Mergenthaler Linotype Company and did not want to bother even dictating the correspondence in such a minor case, so he asked Kefauver if he would take care of it for him.

Not insulted at all, Kefauver collected the money and sent three dollars to Welch for his client, retaining one dollar for his fee. Welch felt he owed Kefauver a debt of gratitude and said a few words in the right places. About three months later, a representative of the company approached Kefauver with the request that he file a receivership for a printing plant. Kefauver handled the matter so expeditiously that shortly thereafter he was retained as Mergenthaler's representative throughout East Tennessee.[11]

A more important break for him stemmed from Kefauver's poring over the musty law books of Cooke, Swaney & Cooke in search of legal precedent. He became interested in a subject obscure even to those in the legal profession: ultra-vires, the no-man's-land beyond the legal and constitutional powers of persons, courts, or corporations. In his spare time, he wrote a fifteen-page paper tracing the development of the law on corporation practices, emphasizing judicial determination of those acts for which corporations have no chartered authority, and buttressed by seventy-two legal references. It was published in the *Tennessee Law Review* in December 1927—a rare recognition for such a young lawyer (it was the first of three Kefauver articles the *Review* published in a two-year period, however).[12]

One of those impressed by the article was A.W. Chambliss, former mayor of Chattanooga and an associate justice (later chief justice) of the Tennessee Supreme Court. The firm Chambliss had founded and headed until his appointment to the state court in 1923 was Sizer, Chambliss & Sizer; it dealt primarily in corporation law. Like Cooke, Swaney & Cooke, it consisted entirely of relatives, and the partners had been discussing the advisability of bringing in an outsider.

After reading Kefauver's article, Chambliss suggested to his son,

11. Anderson and Blumenthal, *The Kefauver Story*, 44–45.
12. Personal conversation, John Chambliss, Chattanooga, Spring 1955.

John A. Chambliss: "Estes is a diligent young lawyer, who looks like he would be substantial and stable, and would work. You would do well to consider him."[13]

The partners opened negotiations with Kefauver, who at the time was representing another widow in an effort to collect compensation from a steel company for her husband's death. He set forth her claim to the company—and was dismayed to receive a cold, business-like reply signed by J.B. Sizer, senior partner in the firm of Sizer, Chambliss & Sizer. Kefauver saw his hopes for advancement go glimmering, but there was nothing to do but to settle down to work and take his case to court.

During the argument on the case, the stern-faced Sizer hardly looked at Kefauver, and when the judge announced a verdict in the widow's favor, Sizer strode off without a word. But the next morning the unhappily victorious young lawyer was called to Sizer's office. "Estes, I liked the way you handled that case," said Sizer; and he hired the astonished Kefauver on the spot.[14]

"When Estes first came into the firm, I thought he was just a big, awkward guy who needed some experience," said John Chambliss. "So I did with him as I do the other new men: I gave him a case that couldn't possibly be won. I just wanted to see how he would respond to failure. But I never got to carry through my experiment. You know, he went to work and won the darned thing!"[15]

The firm represented a number of automobile liability insurance companies and handled quite a few compensation insurance cases. Kefauver had had some experience with Cooke, Swaney & Cooke with minor compensation cases, and at first he worked as an investigator and adjuster with Sizer, Chambliss & Sizer. When he began to try some cases, he teamed up often with Burnett Sizer, the firm's junior member.

As time went on, he handled workmen's compensation and auto accident cases for the Firemen's Fund and cases for Central Franklin Process Company, Peerless Woolen Mills, and the Life & Casualty Insurance Company of Tennessee, for which a second cousin, Patrick M. Estes of Nashville, was general counsel. In the early 1930s, he

---

13. Ibid. Justice Chambliss often helped young lawyers in Tennessee and sometimes gave them money to help them get through law school.
14. "The Best Advice I Ever Had."
15. Howard Turtle, *Kansas City Star*, May 4, 1952.

was appointed attorney for Paul J. Kent, receiver for the First National Bank of Chattanooga, which subsequently became the Commercial National Bank in an unsuccessful reorganization attempt. "Estes was not what you would call a brilliant trial lawyer," said John Chambliss. "He had a grave, almost courtly manner but he could be very persuasive and he was dogged and tenacious. He had all the law at his fingertips—he was very thorough."[16]

Attorneys who practiced with Kefauver in those years remembered him as "a tough opponent" who specialized in trial practice but was capable in all fields. Jac Chambliss, John Chambliss's son, who joined the law firm in 1932 and later inherited Kefauver's office in the suite, said Kefauver's effectiveness in court was founded in two characteristics: thorough preparation of a case and lack of flamboyance in the courtroom. Chambliss recalled that Kefauver would spend hours with doctors for medical proof and study diagnoses and photographs carefully.

In court, "the case was the thing, not the lawyer, for Estes," he said. "He was clear, concise, always pleasant. I have never seen him lose his temper. He never adopted the attitude, 'This client is a lucky man to have me for a lawyer.' Instead, he always gave the impression of feeling, 'How fortunate I am to be on the right side of this case.'"[17]

Kefauver became a junior partner in the firm early in 1930, and its name was changed to Sizer, Chambliss & Kefauver. He was a director of the Chattanooga Bar Association from 1931 to 1933 and its secretary-treasurer in 1932–33. In 1933 he was elected East Tennessee vice president of the Tennessee Bar Association and in 1935 became a member of the State Council of the American Bar Association.[18]

The advantages—economic, professional, and social—accruing to Kefauver through his move from Cooke, Swaney & Cooke to Sizer, Chambliss & Sizer lay in Chattanooga's nature as a city. His cousins' firm was established, respected, and reasonably successful, but Judge Swaney and the Cookes were of an older generation and

16. Personal conversation, John Chambliss, Chattanooga, Spring 1955.
17. Personal conversation, Jac Chambliss, Chattanooga, Spring 1955.
18. Anderson and Blumenthal, *The Kefauver Story*, 46–47, are incorrect on one of the two dates they cite for steps in Kefauver's legal career during this period. Clippings referring to the events are in the Kefauver Collection.

PART I: *An Honest Man*

a day that was passing. The backbone of their practice consisted of the tradition-imbued survivors of the immediate post-Reconstruction period, some of whom were still in influential positions; and around that clustered an accretion of poorer clients, such as those with whom Kefauver dealt. The Sizers and John Chambliss, J.B. Sizer's son-in-law, were very much at the forefront of a dynamic "new" Chattanooga.

Chattanooga, as Jac Chambliss described it, was a city of well-defined class distinctions. On one side was a large number of comparatively wealthy families who had dominated the local economic and political scene for years. The other side of the tracks contained the laboring people, poor and poorly educated, most of them immigrants from the far-flung countryside—the hills and plains of Georgia, Alabama, and Tennessee; they were refugees from the slow decline of agriculture as a self-sufficient way of life. Between these two extremes existed a less important middle class than in other Tennessee cities, but there was a growing liberal element, nurtured by some of the younger business and professional men and the afternoon newspaper, *The Chattanooga News*.

Sizer, Chambliss & Sizer was one of the state's leading law firms. Its offices were in the twelve-story Provident Building on Market Street, in the heart of the downtown district. The firm confined itself almost exclusively to civil and corporation law and represented one side or the other in almost every important case tried in Hamilton County during the time Kefauver practiced with it. His connection with the firm in 1928 brought an immediate upturn in his reputation and his income.[19]

After Kefauver switched to Sizer, Chambliss & Sizer, he and his roommate, Corry Smith, whose professional fortunes also were improving, felt they were ready to dispense with boarding houses. They got together with several other young lawyers, doctors, and professional friends and jointly rented the first of several apartments and houses in which they lived during the next half dozen years. In each place they hired a cook and man-servant. Their first apartment was on Georgia Avenue, only a few blocks from Market Street, and was within walking distance of all of their offices.[20]

19. Personal conversation, Jac Chambliss, Chattanooga, Spring 1955.
20. Personal conversation, W. Corry Smith, Chattanooga, Spring 1955.

Still athletically inclined, Kefauver kept in shape physically by playing squash and volley ball at the YMCA. Although he was energetic in his application to these sports, one of his friends, Jere Tipton, characterized him as "awkward" at them.[21] Kefauver still liked golf enough to list it as one of his two hobbies (the other being football) in a volume entitled *Prominent Tennesseans* published in the 1930s, but he remained pretty much of a duffer. He played most often at the Highlands course in a foursome including Tipton, Smith, and Johnny Grant. Kefauver's powerful but erratic drives were sometimes perilous to bystanders.[22]

Smith—a fun-loving young fellow, blond, good-looking, with a ready sense of humor—and Kefauver teamed up as often for double dates as for squash and golf. Chattanooga offered dancing at several private clubs on Lookout and Signal mountains and at some public night spots in the valley. There were numerous parties to which eligible young bachelors were invited, and there were football and basketball games as well as occasional concerts and stage productions.

Tennessee law forbade alcoholic beverages, but this fact was no more than an inconvenience for those who really wanted to drink—as Kefauver and some of his friends often did. Bootleggers abounded, and law enforcement officers usually looked the other way—for a consideration—when liquor statutes were violated. Sometimes, however, circumstances dictated a crackdown. Kefauver and a group of friends got caught in one of these attacks of official conscience one night when they visited a permissive night club at Cleveland, Tennessee, thirty miles north of Chattanooga. The place was raided, and the Kefauver party was hauled away to the town jail. Kefauver, being financially strapped at the time, resorted to one of his rare checks on his father's bank account to bail them all out.[23]

Kefauver and Smith concluded at last that each was able to own his own automobile, instead of sharing one. Thereupon Kefauver indulged that streak of flamboyance that had instigated a Yale mustache and a raccoon-skin coat. He purchased a high-powered, low-slung Auburn, one of the really unusual automobiles of the

21. Personal conversation, Jere Tipton, Chattanooga, Spring 1955.
22. Ibid.
23. Personal conversation, W. Corry Smith, Chattanooga, Spring 1971.

period, of such a peculiar maroon hue that some of his friends remembered it as purple, while others insisted it was brown.

For a year Kefauver roared around the streets of Chattanooga in the thing, but it came to grief on a vacation trip to Sea Island, Georgia. Kefauver was romancing a young lady so intently in the car on a sandy beach that the incoming tide surrounded them unawares. He had to wade ashore, carrying his date, and both her dress and the car's engine were ruined by the salt water.[24]

Light romance occupied a respectable portion of Kefauver's time when he was a young lawyer. Handsome, of good family and on the way up, he was considered a "good catch" among Chattanooga debutantes, but they found him elusive. His affections did not become seriously involved for nearly a decade after his graduation from Yale, not, however, for the reason he circumspectly gave in later years: "because I was so badly in debt, and did not have anything saved up." He did have some college loans to pay off and very probably contributed something to the cost of his sisters' education, but his income was relatively substantial and getting better: Jere Tipton recalled that Kefauver often "loaned me money to live on."[25]

Kefauver probably would have said at the time (and possibly did on appropriate occasion) that he was not ready to settle down. Meanwhile, he immensely enjoyed practicing his college-acquired charm, to the devastation of numerous feminine hearts. Jac Chambliss described him as "one of the most popular bachelors in Chattanooga . . . good company, with a great zest for living and a great capacity for meeting and remembering people." Smith's verdict was: "Oh, he was no country boy! There was nothing shy or withdrawn about him in those days. He had a good time."[26]

Kefauver maintained a cautious affectional distance from Chattanooga socialites whose marital interest might prove embarrassing and focussed his major ardor more safely on a variety of out-of-town acquaintances. Some of these he met at Chattanooga parties or get-togethers after football games in other cities, others on occasional trips on legal business or civic matters. He built up a string of attachments that, at one point, had him corresponding in more or

24. Personal conversation, Estes Kefauver, Washington, Spring 1955.
25. Personal conversation, Jere Tipton, Chattanooga, Spring 1955.
26. Personal conversation, W. Corry Smith, Chattanooga, Spring 1971.

less affectionate terms with nine women scattered from Wisconsin to Georgia. They ranged from a moody, sentimental poetess to a red-headed political secretary who enjoyed a drinking, dancing good time. He met some of them for weekends in Chattanooga, some in their home cities, and some at intermediate points. For a time before his marriage, he maintained an apartment at the Read House for the private entertainment of visitors.[27]

Kefauver's multiple romances were made possible by an appeal for women that remained with him throughout life and that in later years—looking at Kefauver, the political figure, solemn, dedicated, almost horse-faced—was well-nigh incredible. But in those days he was handsome and rarely solemn in social company; moreover, then and always he possessed an aura of strong masculinity and was unvaryingly kind and thoughtful.

He had the appeal, too, of liking to be "babied" and petted: he was, without any implication of "sissiness," very much a mother's boy, and his close childhood relationship with Phredonia Kefauver remained unimpaired throughout the years of his adult absence from home. She wrote him long letters, always beginning "My darling," in which the depth of the affection between them lent a tender hue to the everyday news from home.

However his charm may have originated, it stirred women deeply. The Tennessee poetess wrote him, "You are my falcon lover"; and even the carefree redhead wrote, "Am still your Baby and no one else's whether you want me to be or not. Just can't help it, Honey." At one point, Kefauver received a plaintive plea from a nineteen-year-old friend of the redhead to "please write _____," so her spirits would improve.

Some of the women attracted to the young Kefauver attempted at times to analyze his individual brand of sex appeal. "Your clear

27. Letters from these women, covering a period from 1933 to 1935 and a second brief period in 1938, are in a special box labeled "Early Personal Correspondence" in the Kefauver Collection. The box also contains letters from Nancy to Estes in 1934, 1935, and 1938, as well as miscellaneous other personal letters to him during the same general period. The box of correspondence was discovered among Kefauver's effects in his office, and Mrs. Kefauver refused to permit their destruction; she instructed that they be preserved because they represented legitimate aspects of his life (personal conversation, Lucile Myers, Washington, May 14, 1970). W. Corry Smith told me about the Read House apartment in a personal conversation in Chattanooga in the spring of 1971.

eyes must have clear thinking behind them," wrote one. Another said: "Your voice . . . thrills me like your touch. . . . I like your eyes, your child would be beautiful. I adore the gray in your hair. . . . You are handsome. . . ." A quality of restlessness that characterized Kefauver also exerted strong appeal. "You say you have all the impulses of your discontented forefathers," one woman wrote, and chided him that discontent and ambition were not synonymous.

Unquestionably, there were important ego aspects to Kefauver's dalliances; during his young manhood, "making out" with women was one of the accepted, if implicit, measures of masculinity. What deeper emotional significance his multiple sexual relationships had for him, then and throughout his life, must remain speculative because his own letters to women are not available and his personal reticence about his true feelings has been noted.

Kefauver's image of a permanent mate, certainly influenced by his strong attachment to his mother, encompassed qualifications not often gathered together in a single personality: intelligence, sensitivity, good breeding, and—of considerable significance—a measure of Victorian propriety. Thus, he sidestepped any binding commitment until he was thirty-one years old.

In the summer of 1934, he became acquainted with a secretary in a Chicago firm whose compatibility was such that she might well have become Mrs. Estes Kefauver had he not met Nancy Paterson Pigott very soon afterward. He wrote, telephoned, and telegraphed his Chicago love—whom he called playfully "Funnyface"—often, and he sent her flowers and presents and made trips to Chicago by train with considerable regularity. Dark-haired, dark-eyed, and slender, and completely in love with him, she offered him a warm understanding. "Keef, my darling," she wrote him: "Time, to me, revolves around you. Do I love you? I adore you. . . . There can never be anyone else for me, dear—I shall love you forever."[28] Kefauver did not give up his other amours after meeting her, but the implication, at least, of prospective marriage appeared in their conversations when they were together.

Just about the time Kefauver met "Funnyface," however, Nancy Pigott left a job in London to travel with her sister, Eleanor, to

28. Letter, "Funnyface," Chicago, to Estes Kefauver, Chattanooga, June 22, 1935. "Early Personal Correspondence," Kefauver Collection.

Chattanooga for a visit with an aunt, Mrs. John Lafayette Hutcheson. Vivacious, black-haired Eleanor was considered the beauty among the four Scottish-born Pigott sisters; her older sister, Nancy, seven and a half years Kefauver's junior, was red-haired and green-eyed, but quiet and shy. Although they turned Chattanooga bachelorhood topsy-turvy during their visit, somehow they missed meeting that most formidable bachelor of all, Estes Kefauver, until near the end of their stay.

Then, one evening, the Pigotts had dates with Calvin Smith and Dr. Leo Record, two of the young men living with Kefauver and Corry Smith in a big house on Battery Place several blocks east of the courthouse, the latest of the group's "bachelor havens." While the two young ladies were dressing for the evening at Mrs. Hutcheson's home on Missionary Ridge, Record was telephoning frantically in search of a substitute for Calvin Smith, Eleanor's date, who had become ill suddenly. At such a late hour, he had no luck until, as he searched the directory for another number, Kefauver ambled in from a hard day at the law firm. Record pounced on Kefauver with strong entreaty. Kefauver resisted, mildly but firmly; he was bone-weary and faced the task of looking up some legal references, after which he looked forward to nothing more exciting than a hot bath and bed. Only the most desperate sort of plea on Record's part gained his reluctant assent.

When they picked up the two Pigott girls, Eleanor was quite taken with her blind date. Nancy, on the other hand, thought that he was too handsome and therefore must be conceited. But, as the two couples danced the evening away at Fairyland on Lookout Mountain, Record suddenly became aware that he was paired more and more with Kefauver's date, Eleanor. Kefauver was quietly appropriating Nancy himself.

Nancy's first cool appraisal of Kefauver was altered completely before the evening ended. Kefauver himself was giving silent thanks for Smith's fortuitous illness. As he and Record prepared to leave their dates at Mrs. Hutcheson's front door, Kefauver announced impulsively that he wanted to give a party for them the next night, to which they might invite any of their Chattanooga friends they wished.

He set out with characteristic industriousness to make up for the misfortune of having arrived late on the scene of the Pigott sisters'

Chattanooga summer. At the party the next night, he and one of his former University of Tennessee schoolmates, Porter Warner Jr., set up a date with the girls for the Alabama-Tennessee football game in Birmingham October 20. It was the first football game the Scottish misses had ever seen, and although they did not quite understand what it was all about, they enjoyed it politely anyhow. And the time with Nancy that Kefauver gained during the accompanying festivities and the train trip back and forth more than made up to him for Tennessee's losing the game, 13 to 6.[29]

"It did all happen so quickly that I was almost afraid to think quite what was happening," Nancy wrote him later.[30] He proposed marriage to her before she left Chattanooga, and she accepted with the sole reservation that she must discuss the matter with her parents on her return to Scotland.

The American tour of the Pigott sisters included a side trip to Chicago and almost a month in New York. Kefauver was among those who saw them off at the railroad station the Sunday night after the Birmingham football weekend. Returning to his law practice and his bachelor haven, he moped around thoughtfully and remarked to Warner several times, "You know, that Nancy is a perfectly lovely person."[31]

Nancy penned him a letter as the *Dixie Flyer* sped through Illinois the next day: "My darling. . . . We seem to have so many ideas in common. I love the way you think, the way you act, your personality—in fact, I must admit there is nothing about you I don't love. . . . What tremendous fun we have had together. I imagine it is about once in a lifetime one finds someone else with whom one's feelings and thoughts seem to merge and drift along like a peaceful little stream. . . . It seems too beautiful to be true. I love you, Estes."[32]

As the Pigott girls' month in New York neared its end late in No-

29. Nancy's visit to Chattanooga and Kefauver's initial courtship of her were related in personal conversations in the spring of 1955 with Estes and Nancy Kefauver in Washington, and Eleanor (Mrs. Paul) McQuiddy, Nancy's sister, and Porter Warner Jr. in Chattanooga.
30. Letter, Nancy Pigott, New York, to Estes Kefauver, Nov. 8, 1934. "Early Personal Correspondence," Kefauver Collection.
31. Personal conversation, Porter Warner Jr., Chattanooga, Spring 1955.
32. Letter, Nancy Pigott, to Estes Kefauver, Chattanooga, Oct. 20, 1934. "Early Personal Correspondence," Kefauver Collection.

vember, Kefauver took the train up, and Nancy met him at the station. They saw New York together (he apologized to her later for drinking too much on their last night), and he gave her a radio as a farewell present and sent roses to their stateroom for their sailing December 1.

Although his marital future was virtually assured, Kefauver did not choose to inform his coterie of lady friends about the change in his love-life. During the subsequent months of his engagement and his wedding trip to Scotland, several of them were still writing him ardently, plaintively soliciting replies and hoping for meetings. For Christmas, a few weeks after Nancy's departure, he sent "Funnyface" an elaborate gift, a nightgown of heavy white satin, trimmed with "gobs and gobs of lace," and in her grateful acknowledgment she said, "You have all my love, beloved. I'm thinking of you always, and always will be your [Funnyface]."[33] He even continued to visit her in Chicago before leaving for Scotland the next summer.

Kefauver's birds-in-the-hand, though, were just that—even "Funnyface." He directed his serious intentions diligently toward Miss Nancy Pigott, daughter of American expatriates in Glasgow. Nancy, born January 21, 1911, in Helensburgh, near Glasgow, was the second of five children: her brother, Stephen, was older; her sisters were Eleanor, Maureen, and Patricia. Their father, Stephen Pigott, was a native of New York, and their mother (Mrs. Hutcheson's sister) was the former Mary Lewis of Chattanooga. Pigott had gone to Scotland in 1908 to demonstrate the Curtis turbine engine and remained as resident managing director of John Brown & Company, Ltd., Clydebank shipbuilders. He designed the engines for the liners *Queen Mary* and *Queen Elizabeth* and was knighted for his accomplishments after he became a British subject in 1939.

Nancy was brought up strictly in the big town house at 24 Kensington Gate, Glasgow. The children were not allowed to eat at the table with their parents until they were seventeen. When they reached dating age, the girls could not go out with young men except in pairs. Nancy, an artist in temperament and talent, usually preferred her sketchbook and easel to the social life, but she was

33. Letter, "Funnyface," Chicago, to Estes Kefauver, Chattanooga, Dec. 27, 1934. Kefauver's subsequent visits to her are indicated clearly in her later letters to him. "Early Personal Correspondence," Kefauver Collection.

sometimes bribed by her sisters to accept a date so one of them would not have to stay at home. After preparatory education at Glasgow's Park School, she spent four years at the Glasgow College of Art, graduating second in her class with a D.A. degree, with distinction, and a diploma in design and mural decoration.

In the safe company of a Glasgow minister's daughter, Nancy took her talent to Paris for further development under the instruction of Andrew Lhote, one of the more individualistic and articulate members of the School of Paris. Under his tutelage, she developed an impressionistic style of painting, full of light and soft color, that remained with her throughout her life.

During her two years in Paris, Nancy fell in love with a young Turkish student name Sami. The romance lasted for a few months, until Sami returned to the Middle East, and was serious enough for them to discuss marriage. Sami, more than Nancy, decided against it, fearing she would not be happy in Turkey. She carried a torch to the extent of searching her heart thoroughly to be sure there would be no lingering regrets, before accepting Kefauver's proposal of marriage.[34]

After completing her art training, Nancy went to London at the nadir of the British depression. She found the going tough for an aspiring young artist; she worked for nearly a year at dress designing, book illustration, and interior decoration—activities her father disapproved, but, she said, "I wanted to eat." In her spare hours, she studied for an imperial teaching diploma in Greek and operatic and ballroom art. She left London to make her first visit to the United States with Eleanor.

Upon Nancy's return to Scotland, the interposition of an ocean

---

34. Most of the detail of Nancy's early life was described in personal conversation with Nancy Kefauver in Washington in the spring of 1955 and supplemented in personal conversation with her sister, Mrs. McQuiddy, in Chattanooga during the same period. Some of the details, including her relationship with Sami, were referred to in a letter from Nancy in Glasgow to Estes in Chattanooga, March 12, 1935, in "Early Personal Correspondence," Kefauver Collection, and described more fully in personal conversation with Carol Harford, Nancy's personal secretary for several years, in Washington, May 11, 1970, and in personal communications from her Aug. 9, 1970, and Oct. 17, 1970. Miss Harford said that Sami later became a senator in Turkey, and after Kefauver's death wrote Nancy that there would "always be a senator in your life." Nancy visited Sami and his wife in Ankara a year before his death in 1965.

between her and her newly-met suitor did not interfere noticeably with their romance. It may have accelerated it, for Kefauver was an impatient man and this time he was well smitten. Nancy received "very beautiful letters" from him, and she wrote touchingly beautiful letters in reply. "He must mean it," commented Miss Margaret McRae, Nancy's Scottish nurse, to whom she confided some of the tenderer passages. "He's a lawyer, and he puts it in ink."[35]

Nancy told him of her romance with Sami in Paris. Kefauver, in turn, confided to her at least some of his armorous escapades, for she wrote "my darlingest": "I do appreciate your telling me all about you in the past—because it belongs to you alone really—only I love you for letting me share it by knowing more about you then."[36]

Kefauver wanted to be married as soon as possible. The time was not the most auspicious for announcing it to Nancy's family, as the marriages of both Eleanor and Stephen were upcoming shortly, but at last Nancy gave her importunate suitor permission to write to her father, and he did so, frankly and directly, in March.

"Your subject was not altogether a surprise," replied the future Sir Stephen. "Nevertheless, it did greatly relieve my feelings of uncertainty. . . . I did . . . wish to make very certain that the strong desire is mutual, and that the union would be one for lasting time. . . . It is a straightforward, manly statement of conditions and rings very true. If you both hold to your ideals you will be very happy together."[37] The wedding date was set for August 8, 1935, two weeks after Kefauver's thirty-second birthday.

Kefauver filed a petition in Circuit Court, seeking leave of absence for the trip to Scotland. It was a tongue-in-cheek document quoting the sixth verse of the twenty-ninth chapter of Jeremiah: "Take ye wives." An aptitude for original humor not being one of Kefauver's strong points, his sprightly petition was drawn and filed for him by Jere Tipton; and Judge Oscar Yarnell, with a twinkle in his eye, replied in kind, quoting the twenty-fourth chapter, fifth verse, of Deuteronomy—"When a man hath taken a wife, neither shall he be charged with any business"—and, granting the peti-

35. Personal conversation, Nancy Kefauver, Washington, Spring 1955.

36. Letter, Nancy Pigott, Glasgow, to Estes Kefauver, Chattanooga, April 4, 1935. "Early Personal Correspondence," Kefauver Collection.

37. Letter, Stephen J. Pigott, Glasgow, to Estes Kefauver, Chattanooga, April 2, 1935. "Early Personal Correspondence," Kefauver Collection.

tion, concluded: "Cost of the court will be paid by the clerk."[38]

Kefauver's elation at his good fortune in meeting, wooing, and winning Nancy so expeditiously seemed to him to call for some expansive gesture, and the first one that occurred to him as appropriate was that he and the rather large company he planned originally to take along from Chattanooga should wear kilts on their arrival in Scotland, in honor of his bride's native land. After some correspondence with Nancy, the kilt idea was abandoned—possibly because she emphasized that Scottish tailors were finicky about having customers measured for kilts in person but possibly because of the expense, about six guineas each. As something of an alternative, Kefauver purchased as a gift for Nancy's family several cases of the best imported Scotch whiskey and had escorted it a considerable portion of the distance back to its place of origin when he learned that the duty on it would exceed its original cost; he dumped overboard what was left of it by the time he approached Liverpool.[39]

Kefauver's plan to invade Glasgow with an impressive entourage of young Chattanooga manhood fared no better, as friends like Jere Tipton and Porter Warner Jr. did not feel they could leave their business affairs for more than a month. Corry Smith went along as best man; others who went to Scotland for the event were Justice and Mrs. A.W. Chambliss and John L. Hutcheson Jr., Nancy's cousin, and his wife. Kefauver's sister, Nora, arranged her schedule on a European tour to be present.

Nancy had done her best to describe her American beau, but her mother had the surer eye for a "typical Southerner." When Corry Smith preceded the somewhat bemused Kefauver down the gangplank at Liverpool, Mrs. Pigott, awaiting them with the rest of the family at the dock, threw her arms around Smith's neck and cried happily, "I always hoped my daughter would marry someone just like you!"[40]

After the vows, solemnized by the Reverend Norman Boydscott, the newlyweds considered a honeymoon trip to the continent but decided it was too expensive. They took a train north, to historic Fort Augustus at the southwestern end of Loch Ness. Kefauver

38. Undated clipping, Kefauver scrapbook, Kafauver Collection, Ser. 9, Box 3.
39. Personal conversations, Nancy Kefauver, Washington, and W. Corry Smith, Chattanooga, Spring 1955.
40. Personal conversation, W. Corry Smith, Chattanooga, Spring 1955.

hoped to brighten this first night of their honeymoon with a bouquet for his bride, but the tiny Highland village had no florist's shop open; so he raided the hotel dining room, swept all the flowers from the vases on the tables and presented them to Nancy. She was charmed, until she learned the source of the gift; a little later, she stole downstairs and replaced the blooms.[41]

Kefauver's marriage meant more than that he was ready at last to "settle down": it marked the culmination of a fifteen-year period during which he developed—by imitation, emulation, and a certain amount of deliberate application—from a pensive, ingenuous hill-country lad into a young man at ease in any society. When, after two weeks among the heather-sweet braes of the Oich and the Tarff, followed by attendance at Stephen's wedding in Ireland, Scottish Nancy set foot aboard the *Berengaria* to sail to her new home in America, it was with a husband who already was beginning to pick up the threads of his childhood interest in matters public and political.

41. Personal conversation, Nancy Kefauver, Washington, Spring 1955.

Chapter 4

There Were a Lot of Raised Eyebrows

From Lookout Mountain at night, Chattanooga is a pendant of jeweled lights strung upon the shining loop of the Tennessee River. Upon this romantic eminence, scented with pine and rugged with ancient rocks, the newly-wed Estes Kefauvers established their home, at first in a rented house.

Kefauver had all the variegated junk he had collected in the "bachelor haven" transported up the steep slopes to the new home. Among these effects was a piano he had received as a fee in one of his lawsuits. Kefauver himself was not talented musically, but now he rejoiced that he had kept the instrument, for he had heard Nancy and Eleanor play some lively duets during that summer's tag-end of getting acquainted. Unfortunately, it developed that Nancy had just been playing the bass accompaniment: it was all she could play. They sold the piano.[1]

They shared the cottage with a cocker spaniel—market value about four dollars—which had cost Kefauver some sixty dollars to transport aboard the *Berengaria* and sundry trains from Glasgow to Chattanooga. "He was a retriever—a bedroom slipper retriever," Kefauver reminisced in later years. Nancy loved the curly-haired, soft-eyed spaniels, and this one was the first of a long line. The Kefauver home was never without a dog of some kind after their marriage; at one time, they had thirteen.

They moved out of the cottage after a while and into a larger (still rented) home at 619 Grandview Avenue, on the edge of one of Lookout Mountain's highest, steepest bluffs. The house featured a cantilevered balcony, jutting out over empty space, that made many of their friends quite nervous. The Kefauvers called their new home "Mooneen." The Kefauvers were "not particularly social per-

1. Holder, "The Gentleman from Tennessee."

sons," Jac Chambliss recalled, though Nancy and Mrs. Chambliss were active together in the Junior League. The Kefauvers did some visiting and entertaining on a purely social basis, and their evenings were occupied increasingly by the spillover of Kefauver's enlarging interests.

From the time Sizer, Chambliss & Sizer became Sizer, Chambliss & Kefauver in 1930, Kefauver had been wading deeper and deeper into the waters of civic activity. He became a member of the Rotary Club and the Junior Chamber of Commerce and in 1933 was chosen chairman of a committee drawn from Chattanooga'civic, industrial, commercial, and trade organizations to plan a civic advertising program with the objective of bringing new industries and businesses into the area and improving tourist trade. There is no indication that the booster program met with any marked success.[2]

In 1933, Congress established the Tennessee Valley Authority, initiating the extensive, long-range development of the Tennessee River and its tributaries for power production and flood control. At the time, John Chambliss, Kefauver's elder law partner, was chairman of Tennessee's first State Planning Commission and to him fell the task of drawing up legislation for submission to the next legislature, enabling Tennessee to participate in the TVA program. He enlisted Kefauver's help in preparing the bills, and the two spent long hours at the task and made a number of trips to Nashville together to work on the project.[3]

Late in 1935, Chambliss appointed Kefauver chairman of the seven-man Hamilton County Planning Board, a semi-governmental advisory group, for a three-year term, and Kefauver was plunged at once into a round of civic work, most of it closely related to TVA. Chattanooga civic and political leaders, welcoming TVA enthusiastically, had gone to work at once to get a second dam built near the city (the first was Hales Bar), not only for navigation and to alleviate flood damage estimated at $1¾ million annually, but to combat the unemployment that was still acute in Chattanooga as a conse-

2. *Chattanooga Times*, June 28, 1933. Other clippings dealing with the committee's activities are in the Kefauver scrapbook, Kefauver Collection, Ser. 9, Box 3.
3. Personal conversation, John Chambliss, Chattanooga, Spring 1955; undated clippings about Kefauver's activities on the Hamilton County Planning Board and a text of a talk on the subject to the Chattanooga Lion's Club, Jan. 8, 1936, are in the Kefauver Collection, Ser. 5-a, Box 1, and Ser. 9, Box 1.

quence of the Depression. They succeeded, through the powerful influence of Tennessee's Senator Kenneth D. McKellar, despite the opposition of Arthur E. Morgan, TVA chairman.[4]

Construction started immediately after Kefauver was named chairman of the Planning Board, and as the $34 million dam began to take shape on the northeastern outskirts of Chattanooga, it became apparent that the Planning Board would have to devote much of its attention to the shores of the new suburban lake the dam would create. "The people of this section wish to have a beautiful region around Chickamauga Lake, in order to make it attractive, sustain land values, and to keep ugly and insanitary [sic] buildings and conditions from arising." Kefauver said in a newspaper statement.[5] As horrible examples to be avoided, Kefauver chose Wilson Dam and very nearly the entire state of Florida, both of which had suffered the effects of a boom and bust in land speculation.

To avoid the evils of wildcat speculation around the Chickamauga lakeshore, the Planning Board under Kefauver's chairmanship prepared a permanent zoning ordinance for Hamilton County and set up standards of construction in county subdivisions, with specific regulations to ban "cheap drinking places" from the Chickamauga Dam area. Related to these accomplishments were the board's adoption of a major road development plan for the county and a program of cooperation with TVA in flood control.

During this period, Kefauver plunged assiduously into the maze of developing TVA social theory, largely through contact and conversation with the TVA people—engineers, lawyers, and surveyors among others—who swarmed into Chattanooga upon the authorization for the construction of Chickamauga Dam. He picked up a habit not uncommon among busy professional men, except that Kefauver was more expansive than most: he would telephone his young wife from his office to tell her, "Honey, I'm having a few people from TVA up to the house tonight." Often, she said, the "few people" turned out to be "about fifty."[6]

On one occasion she employed two men to help cook and serve dinner for a TVA group he had invited. When Kefauver got home,

4. *Chattanooga Times*, Dec. 22, 1935; also several undated clippings in the Kefauver scrapbook, Kefauver Collection, Ser. 9, Box 3.
5. Undated clipping, Kefauver Collection, Ser. 9, Box 1.
6. Personal conversation, Nancy Kefauver, Washington, Spring 1955.

The newly-wed Kefauvers and their cocker spaniel at their rented home on Lookout Mountain, 1935.

Kefauver and his close friend, Representative Henry Jackson, talk with a soldier at a weapons of war show in 1944.

he diverted the pair to the garden to string up lights for the party, then went upstairs himself to take a shower; Nancy, necessarily, took over the cooking. Kefauver was still in his bath when the doorbell began ringing, and Nancy had to hurry from the kitchen to welcome a group of people she had never seen before. "Estes has so much drive that sometimes he may not appear to be very considerate, but he is essentially a very kind person," she remarked of that incident.[7]

Nancy, at the time she met Kefauver on their 1934 double date, was in what her sister, Eleanor (Mrs. McQuiddy), called "a state of artistic inertia." Early pictures of her show a dreamy-eyed young woman whose shyness and reserve are apparent in her features and her posture.

"I give Estes all the credit for bringing her out of it," said her sister.[8] But adaptation presented some initial problems. "It was a challenging situation, and it wasn't easy to meet," Nancy remembered of the period right after their marriage. The "challenging situation" was not a matter of personality incompatibility, but rather one of cultural difference—such as between a man with an American appetite and a woman with a British vocabulary. For example, Nancy's substantial Scottish rearing and her experience at making her own way in London had prepared her for the prospect of cooking the family meals, once she set up housekeeping, but her concept was based upon British meal-planning methods. Kefauver's tastes ran to robust steaks with string beans, ending on a note of chocolate ice cream (he was inordinately fond of shrimp cocktail, too, all his life). Now he was faced each Sunday—invariably, without alteration—with a massive pot roast, which remained in diminishing measure as the menu's main feature until it succumbed as hash the next Saturday night. Kefauver waxed unhappy enough to purse his lips disapprovingly over his predictable plate each evening, but he did not want to hurt his bride's feelings, so he said nothing. At last a mutual friend, who had experienced some of those meals, tipped Nancy off, and they hired a cook, Adalee.

For her part, Nancy, with her strict rearing and private school education, found Kefauver's carelessness with the common lan-

7. Ibid.
8. Personal conversation, Mrs. Eleanor McQuiddy, Chattanooga, Spring 1955.

guage of their two countries most disconcerting. "How he ever got such a high mark in grammar, I can't understand!" she exclaimed upon being informed that he had made 95 in the subject once in school. Once again, their friends attempted to explain to her the leveling influence of the American public school system, but it remained on her mind enough for her to mention it in 1952, during the California presidential primary campaign, to Bill McKnight, an attorney from Cleveland, Ohio, who had been Kefauver's classmate at Yale. Replied McKnight wisely: "Mrs. Kefauver, it's 'them people' who vote for you—not 'those people.'"

Nancy's cultural background proved invaluable, however, in adapting her to her role as the wife of a rising young lawyer who was just entering upon a career as a public figure. She felt that "women often try to control their marriage too much. The type of training I received doesn't condone subservience, but it does emphasize that a woman should make every effort to share her husband's interests."[9]

Following this theory, she began poring over Kefauver's law books during the day, when he was at the office, to gain some understanding of his profession. She made it a point to remain in the background when he was talking; but when he would lapse into silence and retire into himself, as he was already beginning to do in those days, she would sparkle to the fore and was known among their acquaintances for her elfin sense of humor. She treasured funny incidents for future recounting and always remained the artist: she had no qualms about embellishing a minor point or two to improve a story.

Nancy did not give up all of her own interests, however. She set up her easel in one of the rooms of their home and, not wishing to concentrate exclusively upon still life, advertised for a model. She was pleased when a strikingly beautiful young woman, dark-haired and dark-eyed, answered the ad.

Her husband was impressed at this demonstration of the power of advertising, and he happened at that time to need a stenographer. He, too, advertised—and the same young woman turned up; it seems she was a crack legal stenographer but had been working at other off jobs as an adventure. "But, Estes, you can't take my

9. Personal conversation, Nancy Kefauver, Washington, Spring 1955; this conversation is the source for all of the description immediately above about the Kefauvers' early married life.

model!" cried Nancy—to whom it occurred also that the young woman was exceptionally attractive to be sitting around in her husband's office all day. Kefauver agreed to wait until she had finished her painting before hiring the girl himself; but Nancy was so painstaking, so lavish in her attention to detail in the portrait, that Kefauver at last got tired of waiting and found another secretary.[10]

It may have been a wise subterfuge; for Kefauver had somehow neglected to inform at least the most seriously interested of his feminine correspondents that he was no longer footloose. Some of them learned of his marriage only after the event, from newspaper accounts. Their reactions varied: one wrote him a long, sad poem and enclosed a crushed butterfly; another wrote, of his marital domicile on Lookout Mountain, "I am glad you are happy, Keef. That's where you belong—on a mountain top."[11]

Several of the women continued to correspond with him for at least a year at his office, but their letters were tinged with disappointment and disillusionment. "Funnyface" wrote, in reply to an invitation, that she did not want to meet Nancy and could not help hating the name; one of Kefauver's friends informed him two years later that she had passed through Chattanooga, without seeing or getting in touch with him.[12]

Anyone observing young Kefauver as he progressed steadily with Sizer, Chambliss & Kefauver about this time might have predicted confidently the social and philosophical direction he would take. Because of his family and professional connections, his early associations fell naturally among the wealthy, conservative element of the city's population. But they would have been wrong. There were a number of different influences that turned him gradually but firmly into a course that, in time, diverged considerably from the convictions of his early associates—even those of them who remained his friends. Some of them did not remain his friends: they never forgave him for his later liberal course in Congress.

Liberalism and labor were not synonymous in Chattanooga, al-

---

10. Holder, "The Gentleman from Tennessee"; also personal conversation, Nancy Kefauver, Washington, Spring 1955.

11. Letters to Estes Kefauver, dated June 29, 1935, and Oct. 19, 1935. "Early Personal Correspondence," Kefauver Collection.

12. Undated letter from Chicago, signed "Herb," "Early Personal Correspondence," Kefauver Collection.

though they were drawn together in the 1930s by a mutual interest in governmental reform. Kefauver was brought into the orbits of both by the *Chattanooga News*, the city's afternoon newspaper. Sizer, Chambliss & Kefauver handled the legal affairs of the *News*, and Kefauver was assigned the account. The *News* was an advocate of public power, revision of Tennessee's constitution, reforms in local government, and improvement in labor conditions. George Fort Milton, president and editor of the *News*, was known widely as a Southern liberal. A Kappa Sigma fraternity brother of Kefauver, he was married to the sister of Kefauver's close friend, Porter Warner Jr., but was nine years older than Kefauver and had started his newspaper career as a reporter for the *Washington Times* in 1916.

Balding and corpulent (he was only five feet, nine inches tall, and weighed about 225 pounds), Milton pursued his newspaper's projects with tremendous energy, often bringing together a dozen or more influential people simultaneously at parties at his home on Fort Wood Place, not far from Kefauver's last "bachelor haven." At Fort Wood Place, Kefauver met Cordell Hull when Hull was still a United States senator from Tennessee and also met David Lilienthal after the latter became a member of the TVA board. There, too, once or twice, Kefauver met George Norris, the Nebraskan called "the father of TVA" because of his Senate sponsorship of the TVA Act.[13]

Kefauver's work as attorney for the *News* plunged him ever more deeply into the active concerns of government, for the *News* was a crusading newspaper and often at odds with state and local governments. Reform of Tennessee's constitution, unchanged then since 1870, when Reconstruction problems were paramount, was a major *News* editorial project. J. Charles Poe, bespectacled, studious executive editor of the *News*, and Kefauver became good friends, and Poe asked Kefauver to study the constitution and write a series of articles recommending changes. Kefauver did so, and came up with ten specific recommendations for reform, three of which were accomplished by the state's next constitutional Convention, twenty years later.[14]

13. Telephone conversation, Stanton Smith, Washington, Spring 1971.
14. Telephone conversation, J. Charles Poe, Memphis, Spring 1955.

"It is ordinarily said that a government is good or bad according to its officials," Kefauver told the Rotary Club while he was working on the series in 1933. "This is only partially true. Good officials may be so hampered and restricted by law that their best efforts for reform are futile. The tool that carves is not the guiding hand."[15]

The next year, Poe and Roy C. Reynolds, a leader in Chattanooga's organized labor movement, formed an informal group to push for reform of the county government. Hamilton County's archaic county court system, fundamentally unchanged since 1834, still worked satisfactorily in smaller, rural counties, but in Hamilton County it had led to a system of "fee-grabbing shops" set up by squires from some of the county's rural districts. Allied constables and other law enforcement officers would sweep through the city and its environs to find minor law violators to feed the coffers of the magistrates' courts, and the urban voters most affected by this practice could not even vote against the offending squires for reelection because each was elected only by the voters of his own county district.

Poe and Reynolds interested a large number of Chattanooga's business and professional men in pushing for a manager-council form of government to replace the county court as the administrative-legislative body, and for establishment of general sessions courts to take over the squires' judicial duties. Poe urged Kefauver to join the group, but he declined at that time, saying he felt establishment of the general sessions court ought to await a preliminary legislative step to deprive the magistrates (county court members) of most of their jurisdiction.

Seeking action by the 1935 state legislature, the reform group ran into the opposition of County Judge Will Cummings. Cummings, a pleasant-faced, mild-mannered man of the same age as Kefauver's father, had been in and out of the seat of power in Hamilton County since 1912; he had served as a squire himself, and his power was consolidated through reciprocal alliances with the county court members. Unwilling to legislate his political friends out of office, Cummings successfully put forward a legislative delegation that gave the reform group's plan short shrift.[16]

15. *Chattanooga Times*, Jan. 6, 1933.
16. A rather complete narrative of Cummings' life and activities, from an unqualifiedly friendly viewpoint, is Fred Hixson's *The Age of Will Cummings*, published by the author in 1962. Other details about Cummings' opposition to the

Regrouping for an early start for the 1937 legislature, the reformers adopted a name, "The Volunteers," and decided to follow the course Kefauver had recommended, dropping the general sessions court plan temporarily. Kefauver, who had just brought his bride back to Lookout Mountain, accepted the invitation to join the group this time, and was made a member of the executive committee. His friend, Jere Tipton, was chosen president of The Volunteers, and Kefauver soon stepped up to the vice presidency.[17]

So a major part of Kefauver's leisure vanished with his bachelorhood, and his marriage started off in a bustle of extraprofessional activities that included, besides his work as planning board chairman, meetings of The Volunteers every Monday night. For these, Nancy would drive him downtown and sit in the car, reading, while he was at the meeting.[18]

At the beginning of 1936, Kefauver was elected president of the reformers and headed a Volunteer committee charged with preparation of bills to present to the county's 1937 legislative delegation. The bills the committee hammered out were three: to establish a council-manager form of county government, to adopt a budget control ordinance, and to provide for the popular election of the county board of education rather than having it appointed by the county seat.

There was no open opposition to the reform plan by the Cummings political organization during the election campaign, and it was with some optimism that Kefauver and other committee members journeyed to Nashville with the bills when the biennial legislature convened in January 1937. Thereupon, the reformers discovered that there was a difference between getting general pledges from candidates and getting the pledges translated into specific action by elected officials.

Two of the state representatives, John T. Mahoney and D.M. Coleman, agreed to support The Volunteers' bills, but the county's

---

activities of the reform group and its successor, "The Volunteers," were supplied in personal and telephone conversations with Jac Chambliss in Chattanooga, J. Charles Poe in Memphis, and Estes Kefauver in Washington, all in the spring of 1955, and in personal and telephone conversations with Stanton Smith in Nashville in the spring of 1955 and in Washington in the spring of 1971.

17. Personal conversation, Jere Tipton, Chattanooga, Spring 1955.

18. Personal conversation, Nancy Kefauver, Washington, Spring 1955.

other representative, J.B. Ragon Jr., and its senator, Fletcher R. Morgan, refused to consider the bills on the ground that the changes they proposed were too drastic. Such were the characteristics of legislative procedure in Tennessee at that time that such local bills (bills affecting only a single county) had no chance of passage unless supported unanimously by the local legislative delegation, and the Volunteers' bills did not even come to a vote. Kefauver had with him a petition favoring the bills, signed by several thousand Chattanoogans, but complained publicly that Morgan refused to see him or to accept the petition.

Kefauver and the other committee members returned to Chattanooga, to find that a substitute proposal had been prepared at the behest of Cummings and the county court by T. Pope Shepherd, the county attorney. Shepherd proposed a three-member county commission, one member to be the county judge and the other two to be chosen by the county court, with the court retaining power both to fix the county tax rate and select the school board. The Volunteers' proposed five-member commission would be elected by the people at large and would assume all county legislative functions.

Kefauver and Shepherd met repeatedly, and argued over their differing versions for about a month before Shepherd actually drew a bill to offer the legislature. Shepherd's contention was that "my experience is that you can't get good men to run for office, whereas the county court usually shows good judgment" in selecting county officials. Kefauver, expressing a philosophy that was to become increasingly characteristic of his political approach in later life, retorted that the whole point of the reform program was to get the power out of the hands of the magistrates, elected by districts, and put it in the hands of officials chosen by the people of the county as a whole.[19]

Shepherd came forth at last with a compromise proposal, suggested publicly by Cummings himself, who had stayed behind the

19. The legislative history of the reform bills and the Kefauver-Shepherd meetings are described in newspaper articles in the *Chattanooga Times* and the *Chattanooga News* of that period. Many of these articles, usually with the dates and name of the newspaper clipped off, are pasted in the Kefauver scrapbook (Ser. 9, Box 3) and filed elsewhere in the Kefauver Collection. The text of a talk Kefauver delivered on The Volunteers and county government reform to the Chattanooga Rotary Club, dated June 25, 1936, is in the Kefauver Collection, Ser. 5-a, Box 1.

scenes at first. Shepherd accepted the principle of a five-member county commission elected by the people, but elected only after the staggered terms of the first commission members expired. That first commission was to include Cummings as a member, the other members to be named by the county court. And the county court was to retain its tax rate and school board selection authority.

Shepherd's compromise proposal moved far enough toward the principles advocated by The Volunteers to cause a split in the organization. Most of the young business and professional men in the group were satisfied to achieve popular election of a county commission after a few years' delay, in effect leaving Cummings in the saddle until his term as county judge expired in 1942. But the labor members of The Volunteers opposed the compromise, contending that it sacrificed too much of the substance of the reform.

To the surprise of a good many on both sides, Kefauver sided with the labor element. Said Stanton Smith, then secretary-treasurer of Chattanooga's Central Labor Union: "There were a lot of raised eyebrows when Kefauver sided with us. He merely decided we were right, on the principle of the thing."[20] Kefauver's decision, however, to ally himself with organized labor, though it was important to his future career, was not as sudden as his stand at the time made it seem. Nothing in Kefauver's background gave him any predilection for the cause of labor as such. His family on both sides was at least semiaristocratic and wholly oriented to the "genteel" professions such as law and medicine. As a Chattanooga lawyer, his natural associates were among the wealthy and privileged, and the law firm in which he was a partner was concerned primarily with corporation practice.

Kefauver's ideological movement toward a substantially pro-labor viewpoint was strictly individualistic, and it did not show any signs of development during his first few years in Chattanooga. As late as the summer of 1934, a Constitution Day address he made before a Chattanooga Sons of the American Revolution meeting brought Kefauver to a public clash with organized labor.

The combination of low wages and poor working conditions that had built so many Chattanooga fortunes had brought about a stub-

20. Telephone conversation, Stanton Smith, Washington, Spring 1971; Anderson and Blumenthal, *The Kefauver Story*, 50–51.

born organized labor movement in the heavily industrialized city long before the New Deal, but the unions had a hard time. Management had a rurally-based legislature on its side, backed by conservative courts and small-town governors, and the national government, too, was dominated by business-oriented Republican administrations. With the election of Franklin D. Roosevelt and the beginning of his reforms, organized labor in Chattanooga, almost crushed by the Depression, reacted with an aggressive burst of organizing activity. By the time Kefauver came into direct contact with the labor movement there, the city had some fifty different unions with about 10,000 members. Labor was developing into a powerful political force in Chattanooga, and at every step it met the bitter resistance of entrenched management. In 1934 there were labor troubles at a Chattanooga textile mill as a consequence of union efforts to organize the employees.

Kefauver told the Sons of the American Revolution that "a small radical group has taken the law into its own hands. If a mill should desire to resume operations, the public would like to know whether the sheriff and police commissioner would protect it." Expressing the belief that local police were unable to cope with the situation, he added: "If this is true, they should be frank enough to admit it and ask for militia to assist them. In fact, it seems to me that it is about time for the governor to take some action."[21]

This kind of statement, naturally, intensified the reservations the city's organized labor leaders had held about Kefauver, despite his position as attorney for the pro-labor *Chattanooga News*. The next issue of the *Labor World*, weekly news organ of the Central Labor Union, the administrative body for all of the city's labor unions, responded with an editorial blast entitled "Estes Kickover," written by its editor, Tommy Cuthbert. The Central Labor Union itself adopted a resolution condemning Kefauver and charging that he "was allowed to drape the American flag about himself and picture the strikers as law breakers." A couple of days later, Cuthbert was at work in his cluttered little office at the *World*, in a small building on a back street near the Read House, when a visitor entered quietly.

21. Undated clippings, Kefauver Collection. The development of the labor movement in Chattanooga was described in personal conversations with Stanton Smith in Nashville and Jac Chambliss in Chattanooga in the spring of 1955.

Cuthbert looked up and almost upset his ancient swivel chair. The visitor was Kefauver.

"I read your editorial," said Kefauver. Cuthbert smiled, somewhat wickedly, and braced himself. But Kefauver went on: "I guess you're right. I don't know too much about the subject." The astonished Cuthbert murmured something polite about "everybody makes mistakes sometimes."

"Well, now," said Kefauver mildly, "I thought it might do me some good to meet some of you fellows in the labor movement and find out what the facts are."

"Why, sure," said Cuthbert. "I'll be glad to talk with you . . . and you ought to talk with Stanton Smith, too. Why don't I work out a meeting with Stanton and give you a call?"[22]

The conference was duly arranged, and led to others. Kefauver began learning something about "the other side" of Chattanooga society, which he had known before only through contacts with poorer clients as a lawyer. He gained some comprehension of the human, economic, and political problems that had instigated the organized labor movement. But he was still considered basically a "company man" by the union leaders until his stand with labor on the reform measures convinced them that he would not sacrifice principle for the sake of his business and social connections.[23]

The Pope Shepherd compromise was duly offered to the Hamilton County legislative delegation in Nashville, but without the full backing of The Volunteers. Morgan passed it in the Senate, but two of the representatives, Mahoney and Coleman, were allied with the labor interests and refused to go along with the substitute measures. Their opposition was as sure a guarantee of their defeat in the House as Ragon's objection to the original bills had been when the shoe was on the other foot.

Kefauver and Shepherd held many meetings in an effort to find a meeting ground for the opposing views, but the legislature—

22. The meeting with Cuthbert is dramatized from information provided in personal conversation with Stanton Smith in Nashville in the spring of 1955 and from an article by Irwin Ross in the *New York Post*, May 8, 1956.

23. Personal conversation, Stanton Smith, Nashville, Spring 1955. Clippings from Chattanooga daily newspapers and from the *Labor World* describing the Central Labor Union's reaction to Kefauver's Constitution Day address are in the Kefauver collection.

limited to seventy-five working days in Tennessee then—adjourned without their having reached an agreement. The Volunteers disbanded in an atmosphere of discouragement and defeat.

In mid-year, Kefauver was honored by the Chattanooga Junior Chamber of Commerce as the city's 1936 Young Man of the Year, for his work with The Volunteers and other civic activities,[24] but Kefauver remained keenly aware that all of his work had failed to achieve the desired governmental reforms. During the ensuing months, he decided on a more direct course of action.

A British newspaper once carried a biographical sketch of Kefauver, containing such delightful inaccuracies as that he first met his bride-to-be "in Chattanooga, Kentucky, where they were both students, and . . . Nancy persuaded him to drop law for politics." About as close as that journalistic gem gets to the truth is that Kefauver did discuss the possibility of entering politics with Nancy, even before they were married—but it was his idea. He mentioned it to her in a letter when she and Eleanor were still in New York in November 1934, and she replied: "Yes, dear, I think polotics [*sic*] would be marvellous for you. I imagine it will mean a lot of work and money—but very worthwhile. As for me, I should love to help you in any way—if I could."

Kefauver, recapturing his early interest in politics once he had finished college and entered professional life, began participating in it actively as soon as he was established in Chattanooga. Campaigning around the city in 1928 for Alfred E. Smith, the unsuccessful Democratic presidential nominee, had not quite the same flavor as touring Monroe County with his father in Wilson's behalf, but Kefauver did so, calling Smith "a fearless champion of the working masses." He became a member of the Chattanooga Young Democrats Club, and he and Corry Smith worked with Joe C. Carr of Nashville (later Tennessee secretary of state) in incorporating the club into the state organization in 1931.[25]

Alliance with the conservative (and dominant) Democratic element in Chattanooga would have been the surest path to political preferment for Kefauver, if political preferment had been his guid-

24. *Chattanooga Times*, May 23, 1937,
25. Personal conversations, W. Corry Smith, Chattanooga, Spring 1955, and Joe C. Carr, Nashville, Spring 1970.

ing interest. But it was not, at first, and his eventual entry into politics as a candidate developed from a partly fortuitous association with the party's embryonic liberal element.

After the 1937 General Assembly adjourned, Kefauver spent a lot of time with Poe, Reynolds, and other Volunteer leaders, analyzing the failure of the organization to get their county government reforms passed. The consensus was that they had, rather naïvely, overlooked the key to the situation by merely formulating a program and expecting that pledges from legislative candidates would guarantee its realization. The Cummings-county court organization would not willingly see its power stripped from it, and as long as the organization was able to gain election of friendly legislators, it would not be done.

There was some discussion of putting up a "reform ticket" of four candidates for all of the county's legislative seats, but such a project, for any hope of success against the Cummings combine, would have required an organization at least as active and integrated as The Volunteers had been. One thing the Shepherd compromise proposal had accomplished was to split the labor and business-professional elements of The Volunteers apart to the point that little interest could be stirred in reorganizing it.[26]

Although he had been reluctant to join the reform movement at first, Kefauver had become very much involved with it emotionally during his year and a half with The Volunteers. Disappointed that so many of his Volunteer colleagues should give up so easily, he decided to go it alone and, in June 1938, announced as a candidate for the 1939 state Senate. Just what he expected to accomplish if elected is not entirely clear, in view of the virtual certainty that the Cummings organization would elect at least one or two friendly representatives who could block passage of any reform measures. But he was at least pragmatic enough not to run on the local reform issue directly. Instead, he took a roundabout approach in his platform to the same general end: amendment of the state constitution, with which he was so familiar as a result of his research for the articles in the *News*. This route would succeed or fail on the sentiments of legislators from all over the state, instead of just the four from Hamilton County.

26. Personal conversation, Stanton Smith, Nashville, Spring 1955.

His major pledge was to try to get legislative approval of a call for the state's first constitutional convention in nearly seventy years, and he specified his support of several issues he would ask that the convention consider. The only way that major local governmental changes, such as abolition of the Hamilton County court system, could be made at that time was through passage of local bills in the legislature. Kefauver asked that the constitution be changed to allow citizens of a county to alter their local government by resort to local referenda.

The constitution prohibited income taxes, except on stocks and bonds, laying a heavy burden on property owners in those pre-sales tax days. Kefauver proposed to amend the constitution to permit levy of an income tax and, in addition, pledged to offer a bill establishing a $2,500 tax exemption on homes and farms. Kefauver also wanted to eliminate the constitutional requirement of payment of an annual poll tax as a prerequisite to voting.

In addition to his recommendations for constitutional change, Kefauver pledged to sponsor bills to make possible consolidation of two or more counties for administrative efficiency, to reduce the state gasoline tax by two cents per gallon, to set up a permanent registration system for voters, and to increase old age pensions from twenty-five to thirty dollars a month.[27]

It was a progressive platform for the time, but it was by no means radical. His most extreme planks were those calling for constitutional authorization of an income tax and elimination of the poll tax. Most of the comparatively wealthy people at Kefauver's social level (he himself was approaching the $25,000 a year bracket) had had enough of Cordell Hull's federal income tax to be opposed violently to one at the state level; and the poll tax was considered throughout the state to be such a reasonable suffrage requirement that Kefauver's opposition to it was stirred only by his labor friends, who objected that it had the effect of disfranchising many poorer working people. In preparing his platform, Kefauver not only consulted his friends on both the labor and business sides of the old Volunteers, but wrote and telegraphed the Tennessee Taxpayers Association, the Pennsylvania state game warden, and other

27. Undated clipping and text of platform announcement, Kefauver Collection, Ser. 5-a, Box 1.

people and agencies for ideas to incorporate in his own approach. Before announcing, Kefauver assured himself of some influential support. He gained the endorsement of organized labor and the city's two major newspapers, the *News* and the *Times*. The *Times* said of him editorially: "Mr. Kefauver has revealed an interest in government which extends far beyond the controversial issues of the present. A student of government as well as of the law, Mr. Kefauver is the type of man whom the people need in the public service."[28] Kefauver also gained the endorsement of the man he hoped to succeed, Senator Fletcher Morgan, who was not seeking reelection. But Morgan's retirement did not leave the field clear for Kefauver. Judge Cummings threw his organization's support behind Joe S. Bean, a young attorney and old ally who still entertained senatorial ambitions after being defeated for the post by Morgan two years earlier.

Bean was about Kefauver's age, but the resemblance ended with age and profession. Blond and slender, Bean was an affable young man knowledgeable in Chattanooga politics, whose easy, confident delivery in the courtroom and on the stump contrasted strongly with Kefauver's serious, pontifical manner. And Bean was an aggressive, tough fighter in the political arena. Bean promptly charged that Kefauver had stolen his platform plank on increasing old age pensions, noting that he himself had championed such a bill during a previous term in the Tennessee House of Representatives. Kefauver retorted that Bean's plan had not suggested any means of financing the increase, while his own platform did; and he remarked, somewhat plaintively, in a radio speech: "I have always had liberal tendencies."[29]

As his campaign manager, Kefauver selected Lee Allen, a plump, gentle attorney of near his own age who had been one of his public speaking students at vocational school several years earlier. Allen had been chosen chairman of the Hamilton County Democratic Executive Committee in 1936 and was reelected in 1938. Kefauver found him an easy, sympathetic friend with whom he could talk unreservedly about his ideals and ambitions; "Estes has a lot of

28. Anderson and Blumenthal, *The Kefauver Story*, 51–52.
29. Text of speech over radio station WAPO, Chattanooga, June 29, 1938. Kefauver Collection, Ser. 5-a, Box 1.

friends, but he loves Lee Allen," once said George McInturff, later Chattanooga's vice mayor.[30]

Kefauver and Allen, with the aid and advice of Kefauver's friends in both business and labor, went to work to organize his campaign thoroughly. They obtained voter lists, showing who had paid their poll taxes and thus were eligible to vote. They made notes and diagrams on the structure of the campaign organization. Kefauver was provided with memoranda on individuals, such as: "Against Mr. K. Silky Phillips, department head, Standard-Coosa-Thatcher, owns barber shop and restaurant on Watkins Street near mill. Operates gaming devices, tip boards and etc. Lends money to other employees in the mill and is against Mr. K."[31] Kefauver also wrote hundreds of letters to people all over Hamilton County—whose names had been suggested by friends and supporters—asking their votes and help.

The essential elements of Kefauver's unique and successful brand of political campaigning in later years emerged in this first campaign for the Tennessee Senate in 1938. Some of the ideas may have been his own, but Kefauver was never a man to originate schemes; rather, he would listen to the criss-crossing multiplicity of proposals advanced by all kinds of friends and judiciously select and adapt those most useful to him. The letter-writing, the voter lists, and the detailed campaign organization in his 1938 race reflected the experience of Roy Reynolds and Stanton Smith, an ex-school teacher who found Tennessee's growing labor movement a compatible field of activity. Chattanooga's labor leaders, accustomed to opposition from those in power, had learned the value of precinct-by-precinct work in efforts to elect candidates friendly to labor.

Handshaking was nothing new as a subsidiary tactic in Tennessee political campaigns, but the 1938 race became the first of Kefauver's famous handshaking sprees through a combination of circumstances: the labor leaders' concern that he become known to the less affluent voters, Lee Allen's natural friendliness and avoidance of factionalism (he was the first man ever elected unanimously—twice—chairman of the county's Democratic Executive Committee), and Kefauver's inclination, once mounted on a good horse, to ride it until

30. Personal conversation, George McInturff, Chattanooga, Spring 1955.
31. Undated memorandum. Kefauver Collection, Ser. 5-a, Box 1.

it dropped. With Allen as his sole companion, Kefauver blanketed Hamilton County, visiting factories and stores and dropping in on every civic and community gathering he could find, to woo voters.

At one such handshaking stop, Kefauver indulged in one of his characteristic whims and thereby acquired a lifelong friend. He and Allen stopped by Avondale Elementary School in eastern Chattanooga to canvass an "ice cream supper"—one of those carnival-like affairs designed to pick up additional money for school purposes. As they approached the school grounds, a blue-eyed, chubby-faced youngster wearing a school band uniform scurried up to sell them tickets, each good for a certain amount of merchandise at the booths. Something about the boy appealed to Kefauver and he made inquiry: the lad was twelve-year-old Harry Mansfield, son of Mrs. Ada Mansfield, a widow who was supporting Kefauver in his race.

"How would you like to go around with us and campaign, Harry?" he asked.

Harry was willing and, with his mother's consent, made the campaign entourage a trio. He trailed around with the two men, sometimes riding on Kefauver's shoulders when he tired from the pace. Perhaps (one never knew with Kefauver) the sight of Harry passing out literature and tacking up campaign posters brought Kefauver memories of the long-ago Wilson races, when another boy had performed the same chores for his father in Monroe County.[32]

The Cummings-Bean forces went to work early to undermine Kefauver's most substantial reservoir of organized strength, his labor support. Kefauver received a letter in June from J.C. Cox, president of Labor's Political Conference—the political action arm of the Central Labor Union—asking not only about his platform but about the 1934 speech that had brought Cuthbert's criticism.

Cox also asked: "Is it true that your firm is the father of the 'Yellow Dog' unions in Hamilton County? Have you assisted in the formation of or the operation of the L.D.U. organizations which are now attempting to operate in Hamilton County?" The L.D.U. (League of Democratic Unions) was organized by Jac Chambliss and was a league of fifteen or sixteen unions not affiliated with the Central

32. Kefauver's 1938 campaign was described primarily in conversations with Estes Kefauver in Washington and Lee Allen and Harry Mansfield in Chattanooga in the spring of 1955.

Labor Union (which called the L.D.U. groups "company unions"). Chambliss contended they were more "democratic" than the C.L.U. unions in the procedures by which their members elected officers and approved union activities.[33]

Cox enclosed a circular, naming two hod carriers and two clay workers unions as sponsors, calling for Bean's election. The leaflet, Cox said, "is not in any way official because it is unsigned," but was "purportedly prepared by members of four local unions." Entitled "Labor Racketeering: Can a Leopard Change Its Spots?" the circular quoted stories about Kefauver's 1934 speech from both Chattanooga newspapers, charged that Kefauver was "a big corporation lawyer" who had "denounced unions" and "advocated protecting scabs," and called him "labor's Public Enemy No. One, trying to give labor the Kiss of Judas."[34]

"I suppose that 'Yellow Dog' unions refer to the L.D.U.," Kefauver replied to Cox, ". . . the firm of which I am a member has had no part or connection with the formation or operation of the L.D.U. . . . I have not assisted in the formation or the operation of the L.D.U. organization. I was not even consulted about the matter. This is entirely a personal matter with Mr. Jac Chambliss."

As for his Constitution Day address, he said his information at the time "led me to believe that certain outside people were using tactics which were not in line with Labor's own policies and it was to them I intended to refer. The factors coming to me after I made the address indicate that the premises upon which I based it were not wholly correct." He said he never had participated personally in any of his firm's litigation involving strikes and could cite instances when he had been friendly to labor "when other courses would have been much easier."[35]

Kefauver began probing for the origin of the handbills, and came up with the information that they came from Bean's office and that Bean himself was delivering them. As an added fillip, he obtained a sworn statement from Gene Jacobs (years later a Nashville city councilman) that Bean's brother, Crawford, had offered

33. Personal conversation, Jac Chambliss, Chattanooga, Spring 1955.
34. Letter, J.C. Cox to Estes Kefauver, June 23, 1938, and note, T.J. May, to Estes Kefauver, June 25, 1938. Kefauver Collection, Ser. 5-a, Box 1.
35. Letter, Estes Kefauver to J.C. Cox, June 24, 1938. Kefauver Collection, Ser. 5-a, Box 1.

him twenty-five dollars to go "to the campaign office of Estes Kefauver and start a fight" by slapping another man.[36]

The Kefauver people were looking for things to use against Bean, too. One of them, Jack Wilson, poring through court dockets, found that Bean had handled 330 out of the total of 622 garnishment cases in them. It was a good issue: garnishment—legal attachment of a portion of one's salary for payments on a debt in arrears— was anathema to the laboring people who, exclusively, were affected by it. Kefauver made use of it; and he turned the tables on one of Bean's early charges against him by charging that Bean was stealing *his* platform, calling Bean "not Mr. Crawfish Bean, but Mr. Jelly Bean" (the phrase was George Fort Milton's, handed to Kefauver, during his speech, in a note by Milton's wife, Alice).[37]

Bean lambasted back from the stump and on the radio, bearing down heavily on the characterization of Kefauver as "a wealthy corporation lawyer." In a final radio speech the night before the Democratic primary election, Kefauver commented: "The only objection I have to my opponent calling me a wealthy person is that it gets my creditors excited. If we should have a little earthquake, it would shake my small house down to the third mortgage." This, of course, was sheer campaign talk; the house was rented.[38]

On election night Kefauver sat in the midst of campaign leaders and friends in a suite at the Read House in Chattanooga and watched the returns come in. Things looked good. He had made good use of his Monroe County background in his county handshaking tour, and the farm folk rallied to him. Precinct after precinct from the rural sections and the city suburbs—where his social and professional acquaintances lived—rolled up a substantial lead for him. But the count in the heavy city boxes was slow, and when they started coming in, Kefauver's lead began to evaporate. Organized labor's efforts—Kefauver's big hope inside the city—had failed to

36. Affidavit by Gene Jacobs, dated July 13, 1938. Kefauver Collection, Ser. 5-a, Box 1. Although the affidavit says $25, in a personal conversation in Nashville in spring 1971 Jacobs said that he was offered $50 and that he refused because he was supporting Kefauver and his sister, Maude Mitchell, was working in Kefauver's campaign.

37. Memorandum from Jack Wilson, dated June 14, 1938, and undated note signed by Alice N. Milton. Kefauver Collection, Ser. 5-a, Box 1.

38. Speech prepared for broadcast over radio stations WDOD and WAPO, dated Aug. 3, 1938. Kefauver Collection, Ser. 5-a, Box 1.

overcome the precinct-by-precinct organization of the Cummings combine.

By the time the last box was reported, in the morning's early hours, Bean had won by 307 votes out of a total of about 15,000. Kefauver's youngest "campaign official," Harry Mansfield, cried himself to sleep. Kefauver backers were loud in outraged accusations of election irregularities. In one case, they charged W. Earl Manning, the chairman of the Democratic Primary Board, had carried one of the ballot boxes around for several hours in an unlocked automobile before the votes were counted. Kefauver was urged to contest the election, but refused, on the ground that the Cummings organizations's control of the election machinery would make the gesture useless.[39]

Kefauver had dipped his toe at last directly into the political pool and had found it chillier than he had anticipated. But he had done well for an amateur playing against the house, and he had learned some hard lessons about politics. It was the first, and last, election he ever lost in Tennessee.

39. Personal conversation, Lee Allen, Chattanooga, Spring 1955.

Chapter 5

The Country Needs Good Public Officials

Estes Kefauver's big frame appeared in the doorway of his senior's office at the law firm of Sizer, Chambliss & Kefauver. He asked softly: "Are you busy, Mr. John?"

"Come on in, Estes," said John Chambliss heartily. "What's on your mind?"

"Well, it's like this," said Kefauver, entering and sitting down. "I've been asked to go to Nashville to be Finance and Taxation Commissioner, and I can't make up my mind. What do you think?"

"I think it's ridiculous," responded Chambliss promptly. "You've reached the point of making a good income here now, and you have a real future ahead of you. Estes, you're too good a lawyer to fool around with politics."

Kefauver sat silent for a few moments, his face expressionless, lips pursed thoughtfully, his big hands folded in his lap. Then he replied seriously: "Mr. John, the country needs good public officials. I think a person ought to be able to make a good career in public service. It seems to me that this is the time when I ought to test out my reaction to public life."[1]

It was January 1939, five months after Kefauver's defeat in the state Senate race: Kefauver was thirty-five years old, he had been practicing law in Chattanooga for eleven and a half years, and he had been married for three and a half years. He was a big, handsome young man, but still with a touch of his adolescent awkwardness in movement and boyhood diffidence in manner. The interest in politics that he had mentioned to Nancy during their courtship had crystallized through his work with The Volunteers and his Senate race. The opportunity offered him so soon after his defeat stemmed from the outcome of a factional Democratic party feud waged by

1. Howard Turtle, *Kansas City Star*, May 4, 1952.

fiery-tongued Edward Hull Crump, acknowledged political boss of Tennessee.

Crump had built his power over three and a half decades on patronage, on scrupulously repaying political favors, on ruthless persecution of political enemies and rebels in his own organization—and on the structure of that organization itself. His machine was reputed to have a file on every registered voter in Shelby County, and James Street wrote in *Collier's* magazine in 1938 that Crump could "lift the telephone and with one command send 60,000 sovereign Democrats to the secret polls to do his bidding."

Sixty thousand Shelby County votes could constitute the margin in a statewide election, coupled with Crump's alliances with several lesser local bosses across the state. When Gordon Browning was elected governor in 1936, he received 59,874 votes in Shelby County to only 878 for his opponent, Burgin Dossett; and Crump had not endorsed Browning until 10 days before the election. Acknowledging his debt to Crump, Browning chortled, "There are 60,000 reasons why I love Shelby County." But he was a hard-headed, independent man and broke with Crump halfway through his two-year term. Calling a special session of the legislature, Browning attempted to push through a "county unit vote bill" that would have pulled big Shelby's voting teeth. The measure, patterned on the national electoral college system and similar to the Georgia system, would have given each county a unit vote based on population, the entire county unit vote going to the candidate for governor who received the majority of the county's popular vote.

Crump's opposition to the bill won the support of many people elsewhere in the state who were not allied with him politically. A Shelbyville state senator, Prentice Cooper, organized and led the legislative fight against the bill, and among those who journeyed to Nashville to testify against it in public hearings were Estes Kefauver and another Chattanooga attorney, Phil Whitaker. Kefauver told the Senate, sitting as a committee of the whole: "It seems to me that a person must not look at the expedient thing, but whether it is just and fair. Any law that limits the expression of the lawful voter strikes at the very foundation of our American system."[2]

2. *Nashville Tennessean*, Oct. 16, 1937; undated statement, Kefauver Collection, Ser. 5-a, Box 1.

Browning got his bill passed, but three months later the state Supreme Court declared it unconstitutional. In the 1938 primary Browning lost the support of many normally anti-Crump elements because of his high-handed tactics, and he went down to defeat at the hands of the Shelbyville state senator, Prentice Cooper.

Cooper was a prim, straight-backed little man with an acid personality. In his public life—as governor of Tennessee for six years and U.S. Ambassador to Peru from 1946 to 1948—he almost always had a "bad press," to which he responded with a venomous tongue, and his underlings were in constant fear of his temper. But he was a man of unshakeable integrity, and a few people scattered throughout the state liked him genuinely.

One of these was Kefauver. When Cooper was a bachelor lawyer in Shelbyville, about eighty miles northwest of Chattanooga, he and the big, amiable Kefauver got along famously. They doubledated occasionally, before Kefauver's marriage, and Cooper once recalled the severe twinge of jealousy he experienced when the two had taken their dates to a dance at the Belle Meade Country Club in Nashville, and Cooper's lady friend could not keep her eyes off Kefauver. Cooper remarked on this at last—sharply, as was his wont —and the girl sighed: "But, Prentice, he has such nice-looking shoulders!"[3]

Kefauver declined Cooper's first request that he become finance and taxation commissioner in the new administration. Joe Bean, Hamilton County's new senator-elect, recommended Thomas S. Myers of Chattanooga for the post, but Cooper ignored this suggestion so completely that Myers's name never got into newspaper speculation. Cooper kept after Kefauver. He knew that Kefauver had studied tax matters thoroughly in the course of his corporation law practice. Kefauver had commented several years earlier, in a speech to the Chattanooga Rotary Club, that "a business run as loosely as our lawmaking body would soon be in bankruptcy. Loose tax provisions are discouraging the establishment of new industries in our state. They are encouraging notorious tax-dodging practices, because they do not intelligently assess levies on intangibles."[4]

3. Personal conversation, Prentice Cooper, Shelbyville, Tenn., Spring 1955.
4. Pamphlet, address of Estes Kefauver to Chattanooga Rotary Club, Jan. 5, 1933, Kefauver Collection, Ser. 5-a, Box 1; undated clipping, Kefauver scrapbook, Kefauver Collection, Ser. 9, Box 3.

Cooper said later, however, that his major reason for wanting Kefauver was that Kefauver was "an honest man, politically and personally. You know," he added, "people will say, 'It shouldn't be hard to find an honest man.' But a politically honest man is not only honest himself—he sees to it that everyone who works for him is honest."[5]

John Chambliss's negative reaction to Kefauver's prospect of taking the post was not unreasonable: Kefauver's salary as commissioner would be only $4,000 annually, about a fifth of his current income from his law practice. Nor was it the most convenient time, economically, for Kefauver to take such a cut in income. Though his personal campaign expenses in the Senate race were only $487, his campaigning time away from his office had cut into his earnings; and, at the time, he was helping his father with the support of his two sisters, Nancy and Nora.

There were always little dribbles of money departing from the Kefauver bank account, anyhow, for he was a soft-hearted man, and destitute former clients were not hesitant in calling on his generosity. For extended periods he would contribute small amounts— perhaps $10 or $15 a week—to two or three of these people at a time, until they could get on their feet again. One of his former girl friends, who had sought her fortune "up North" after his marriage, wrote to beg a $75 loan from him to finance a study course that would lead to a better job for her; he probably sent her the money.[6]

A substantial incursion on Kefauver's pocketbook late in 1938 was the expense of a trip to Scotland. Nancy had not seen her family since their marriage, and Kefauver needed a vacation after his Senate race. Another consideration was that the Kefauvers wanted children very much, and American specialists had been unable to determine why Nancy had failed to conceive in more than three years of marriage, so she wanted to consult some prominent British doctors.[7] Kefauver's desire for children was very strong. He and "Funnyface" had discussed their prospects for children in 1934 when it appeared they might marry, and another Chicago woman friend

5. Personal conversation, Prentice Cooper, Shelbyville, Spring 1955.
6. Undated letter, [name withheld] to Estes Kefauver, Chattanooga, "Early Personal Correspondence," Kefauver Collection.
7. Personal conversation, Nancy Kefauver, Washington, Spring 1955.

made a game of pretending that Kefauver was her husband and that there was a "Junior" who would grow up to be "as sweet as his daddy."[8] Kefauver and Nancy, too, had talked during their courtship about the possibility of progeny, and Nancy said repeatedly that she married partly to fulfil a desire for children.

Kefauver stayed in Scotland with his wife for a short time (her family accused her of having picked up more of a "Southern accent" than Kefauver had); then he made a side trip to Paris before returning home. Nancy witnessed her father's participation in christening ceremonies for the liner *Queen Elizabeth*, whose engines he had designed, and then fell ill on her return to Glasgow with her family, thus delaying her return to the United States until near year's end.

Kefauver, restless and still fretting over his defeat, probably was more susceptible than he would have been under other circumstances to Cooper's invitation to go to Nashville and take an important state job. He accepted the appointment at last, "temporarily . . . upon the distinct understanding that a permanent commissioner will be selected within the next two or three months. I regret that I cannot accept the position for a full term, but my professional business does not permit it."[9] Among those sworn into the cabinet with him was his friend, Charlie Poe, who took a two-year leave of absence as executive editor of the *Chattanooga News* to serve as conservation commissioner.

Cooper was as tight-pursed as he was tight-lipped and as governor often rode a city bus from the Capitol to the Executive Mansion on West End Avenue. Browning's retiring finance and taxation commissioner, Walter Stokes, estimated a $1,761,000 reduction in state revenues in the 1938–39 fiscal year from 1937–38, and Cooper's first economy move was to order his cabinet to reduce the state payroll $1,000 a day through dismissals, salary reductions, and elimination of dispensable government functions.[10] The order, naturally, spread panic among state employes, and when Kefauver's tall figure

8. Several letters of this nature, some of them containing pictures of babies and young children clipped from magazines as part of the pretense, from [name withheld], Chicago, to Estes Kefauver, Chattanooga, in 1934 and 1935 are in "Early Personal Correspondence," Kefauver Collection.

9. *Nashville Tennessean*, Jan. 15, 1939.

10. Ibid, Jan. 3 and 22, 1939.

appeared in mid-January in the Finance and Taxation Department offices in Nashville's War Memorial Building, he was greeted by a uniform array of glum, silent faces. He took one look at them and turned to Mrs. Maxine Syerson, the department secretary.

"Tell them to get back to work," he said. "I'm not going to fire everybody."[11] He did not fire everybody, but he did comply with the governor's directive and reduced the department's personnel 15 percent in his three months in office.

Cooper had promised in his campaign that he would levy no new taxes. In order to avoid a state deficit of from $500,000 to $1,200,000 for the biennium ending June 30, 1939, predicted by Henry Burke, the outgoing state budget director, the governor prepared a hold-the-line budget $1 million a year lower than the Browning budget, and asked Kefauver to reorganize the tax structure and improve tax collection methods. In preparing the budget, Cooper said later, he would call on Kefauver, who would walk across Charlotte Avenue and up the steep hill to the Capitol "with several books held tightly under his left arm, and would invariably furnish me with an absolutely accurate estimate of the various tax yields."[12]

Kefauver prepared a completely new tax program, primarily one of combining and reassessing taxes more efficiently and including a provision for reciprocal agreements with other states on taxation of interstate trucks; despite Cooper's campaign promise, it also contained a special 5 percent tax on lotteries, such as theater bank nights, and increase of the gross receipts tax on theaters from 3 to 4 percent.

The program ran into heavy opposition in the legislature. Representative J.B. Ragon, Cooper's House floor leader, bolted the administration to oppose the theater bank night tax. W.D. (Pete) Hudson, a member of the state Railroad and Public Utilities Commission, lobbied against reforms in taxes on the petroleum industry. It took Cooper more than two weeks, with the backing of the Crump forces, to muster the legislative strength for passage of the measure by bare majorities, and loaded with amendments. The amendments, however, did not alter the program's revenue benefits to the state materially. Kefauver estimated that the reform would

11. Personal conversation, Mrs. Maxine Syerson, Nashville, Spring 1955.
12. Personal conversation, Prentice Cooper, Shelbyville, Spring 1955.

increase state revenues by about $200,000 annually.[13] Cooper gave Kefauver's reorganization of the tax system much of the credit for the fact that his six-year administration, ending in 1945, saw payment of $50 million on the state debt and closed with a surplus of $27 million, despite some overall reduction in taxes.[14]

A major front on which Kefauver attacked the revenue problem was that of tax collections. Aware of widespread evasion of state taxes, he reorganized his department's collections division under a new and more aggressive director and tightened bookkeeping methods. When Kefauver took office as commissioner, collections had declined 1.49 percent over a year's time. For the three months he held the office, collections increased 16.84 percent over the previous quarter and were up 4 percent over the same three months of the previous year. When the fiscal year ended June 30, instead of the deficit Stokes had predicted, a $160,000 state surplus appeared on the books.[15]

Before the legislative session was half over, Cooper found his revenue problem compounded: the Tennessee Valley Authority completed negotiations to buy the properties of the Tennessee Electric Power Company and other private utilities in the state. Tennessee stood to lose about $1 million a year in taxes the utilities had paid.

"Cheap TVA power is an undoubted blessing to the people and businesses of the state," Kefauver said of the development, ". . . However, the state cannot stand the tax loss."[16]

The solution Cooper proposed was two-fold: refinancing of some $20 million in county bonds the state had been backing and the levy of a tax on local electric power distribution systems. Local officials opposed both strongly. On county bond refinancing, the state had to agree to a compromise that saved it nothing on the long haul. The local officials found a powerful ally against the power systems tax in E.H. Crump, and the legislature defeated it.

Succor in the revenue area came from an unexpected quarter: the Crump forces introduced a bill to legalize liquor in Tennessee, which had remained "dry" after the repeal of the 18th Amendment. Cooper was a teetotaler personally and politically, and he

13. *Nashville Tennessean*, Feb. 8, 1939.
14. Personal conversation, Prentice Cooper, Shelbyville, Spring 1955.
15. *Nashville Tennessean*, July 1, 1939.
16. Ibid., Feb. 7, 1939.

vowed he would veto any legalized liquor bill that did not include a provision for a statewide referendum—a provision the state attorney general said would be unconstitutional. The liquor bill as introduced in the General Assembly contained no such referendum; instead, provision was made for local option, whereby a county or municipality could legalize package liquor sales by a local referendum. Both houses of the legislature passed the bill, resoundingly. Cooper vetoed it. Both houses passed it over his veto, thereby making Crump happy and possibly saving Cooper from a demonstration of the old man's wrath.

Cooper accepted his defeat gracefully, asked Kefauver to set up the machinery for collecting the alcoholic beverage taxes, and supplemented the repealer with a bill to increase truck weights on Tennessee highways and levy higher truck license fees. The legislature approved it with little dissent, and the liquor and truck taxes together provided Cooper with the necessary tax funds to balance his budget.[17]

Kefauver took advantage of his official presence in Nashville to fulfil one of the campaign promises he had made in the state Senate race: enactment of a bill to make possible consolidation of two or more counties in Tennessee. Since Cooper favored the idea and it was only enabling legislation, it passed without difficulty, with Ragon as sponsor.

Because Kefauver was in Nashville on a temporary basis, he and his wife lived at the Memorial Apartments Hotel, directly across Seventh Avenue from his office. He put in long hours at his work; many of the daytime hours were spent in listening patiently to aspirants for department jobs, who stood in long lines outside his door. Between these interviews and his work on Cooper's legislation, sometimes he was not able to dictate letters and memoranda until after supper, and usually worked late into the night. Nancy frequently went to the office to go out to supper with him and then sat with him in the office, reading, until he finished his work. Despite the pressure on him, employes of the department at that time remembered him as never irritable, never angry; and Nancy became rather a department favorite.[18]

17. Undated statement, Kefauver Collection, Ser. 5-a, Box 1.
18. Personal conversation, Mrs. Maxine Syerson, Nashville, Spring 1955.

Since Cooper was allied with Crump, Kefauver received a certain amount of joshing from his friends about becoming "a Crump man" after all his talk in his 1938 race about the evils of "machine politics" in Hamilton County. "Crump had nothing to do with it," snapped Cooper indignantly, years later. "I made the appointment on my own hook."[19]

Kefauver met Crump once while he was commissioner. The Memphis boss was in the habit of entertaining legislators and state officials periodically by chartering a train to take them to a horse-racing holiday in Hot Springs, Arkansas. On one such "Crump Special" early in 1939, the Kefauvers were in the club car, playing bridge with Edward B. Smith, political writer for the *Knoxville News-Sentinel*, and Fred Hixson, political writer for the *Chattanooga Times*, when Crump came through, waving a fistful of bills he said he had won in a crap game on the train. He stopped to speak to the newsmen, and Hixson introduced him to the Kefauvers. Crump peered at Kefauver through his huge, horn-rimmed spectacles, exhibited his winnings and commented jovially: "I'd make a good finance commissioner. I know how to get the money."[20]

The legislature adjourned in mid-March. In mid-April, Cooper appointed George F. McCanless to succeed Kefauver as finance and taxation commissioner, and Kefauver returned to his law practice in Chattanooga. He was well satisfied with his first brief fling as a government officeholder. The loss of income it had cost him was counterbalanced by the recovery of whatever political prestige he had lost along with his state Senate race; and he had learned a great deal, of practical value, about both politics and government.

The July after Kefauver left his post as finance and taxation commissioner, U.S. Representative Sam D. McReynolds of Tennessee's Third District, which included Chattanooga and Hamilton County, died in Washington. McReynolds, first elected to Congress in 1922, had become so well-loved a figure in the district that repeated challenges to his reelection had fallen short badly. He had had a major part in bringing Chickamauga Dam to the Chattanooga area, and, at the time of his death, he was chairman of the House Foreign Affairs Committee.

19. Personal conversation, Prentice Cooper, Shelbyville, Spring 1955.
20. Edward B. Smith, column, "Tennessee Notebook," *Knoxville News-*

A scramble among aspirants to succeed him in a special election appeared in prospect. Although Kefauver had hardly gotten his affairs straightened out well at Sizer, Chambliss & Kefauver, the time seemed most opportune to him, and he wasted little indecision in making up his mind to enter the fray. He announced his intent to his father on a visit to Madisonville. Cooke Kefauver did not think much of the idea.

"You're doing well as a lawyer," he said, "Don't let this politics thing go to your head."

"I'm a young man, Popsy," replied thirty-six-year-old Estes. "I'm interested in public service. I won't be making as much as I would if I stuck to my law practice, but I have some money saved and I can afford it for one or two terms."[21]

Under the assumption that he would face the same combination of political opposition as in his state Senate race, Kefauver before entering the race for the United States Congress conferred with key friends on the best course to chart: George Fort Milton, editor of the *Chattanooga News*, Roy C. Reynolds and Tommy Cuthbert of the Central Labor Council, Lee Allen, who was still chairman of the Hamilton County Democratic Executive Committee, and L.J. Wilhoite, who had just been named head of the Chattanooga Electric Power Board. He also had talks, when they were in Chattanooga, with Stanton Smith of the Labor Council, David Lilienthal of the TVA board, and Charlie Poe; Smith at the time was on a national tour for the American Federation of Labor, Lilienthal was headquartered in Knoxville, and Poe of course was still in Nashville as state conservation commissioner.[22] Kefauver could count on the support of the *News* and organized labor, and, it turned out, the *Chattanooga Times*. A third Chattanooga newspaper, the *Free Press*, established three years earlier as an afternoon competitor to the *News*, was Republican and anti-TVA.

Because Kefauver could not match the political organization of the city-county governmental machinery, his advisers emphasized the importance of a strong, appealing platform to interest indepen-

---

Sentinel, Dec. 27, 1960; personal conversation, Fred Hixson, Chattanooga, Spring 1971.

21. Personal conversation, Cooke Kefauver, Madisonville, Tenn., Spring 1955.

22. Telephone conversation, Stanton Smith, Washington, Spring 1971.

dent voters in his cause. The general planks, probably suggested by Milton, were support for the policies of President Roosevelt and for TVA.

With only three of its dams (in addition to Wilson) completed, TVA was already supplying electricity to many rural areas that had not enjoyed it before. New industry was being drawn into the state by cheap electric power. So obvious were TVA's benefits to the region that opposition to it was melting to a severe minority centered on those who had profited from the previous private power regime.

Support and opposition to Roosevelt and the New Deal in Tennessee had followed a parallel pattern: Southern conservatism was still strong enough among Tennessee Democrats for many of them to shake their heads dubiously at Roosevelt's liberal philosophy, but the New Deal had brought Tennessee out of economic crisis. Kefauver did not pledge unequivocal support of all of Roosevelt's proposals but did promise general support of his program and praised the President's "noble ambitions, high ideals, great work and splendid leadership."

Beyond support for Roosevelt and TVA, Kefauver was advised to make his specifics few, and not complicate his position unduly at the start by a lengthy exposition of philosophical underpinning. He chose two other platform planks: TVA tax replacement and federal aid to education.[23]

City and county governments were concerned not only with the loss of taxable power distribution facilities as a consequence of TVA, but also the flooding of taxable land by the TVA dam-created lakes, and Milton was a member of a commission appointed by Governor Cooper to study the tax loss and the best means of replacing it. It was evident that tax replacement would be an issue in the congressional race, because five of the twelve counties in the Third District —Polk, Marion, White, Warren, and Bradley—stood to lose more than $330,000 in tax revenues as a result of TVA's purchase of private power company facilities.

Dr. John R. Neal, a brilliant but eccentric man who had run for either governor or U.S. senator in almost every election since 1920, was considering entering the Third District race and already had promised to initiate court action on behalf of the tax-deprived

23. Press release dated July 28, 1939, Kefauver Collection, Ser. 5-b, Box 2.

counties. Kefauver learned from Lilienthal and Wilhoite that TVA itself was anxious to improve its tax replacement formula because it was already in court on constitutional grounds. The Supreme Court had before it a case filed originally in 1936 by eighteen private power companies, alleging that TVA, under the false guise of navigation, flood control, and national defense, was entering into a vast program of power production unconstitutionally. One of the major arguments of the private utilities was that TVA was robbing local governments of the tax revenues they had received from the companies.

Kefauver formulated a platform plank calling for amendment of the TVA Act to establish satisfactory payments in lieu of taxes, the formula to be worked out in conferences by TVA with local officials. (Eventually Congress provided a 5 percent of gross revenue formula, plus in-lieu payments by cooperatives and municipal distributors of TVA power.)

During the 1939 legislature too, Kefauver, as finance commissioner, had been in the line of fire of the anguished pleas of Tennessee educators, who were given short rations by the budget-balancing Cooper. The idea of federal aid to education was advanced to Kefauver by officials of the teachers' union in Chattanooga, and his conviction, as he stated it, that "the inequalities of rural educational opportunity must be corrected, and this can best be done through federal aid" caused him to add it as the final plank of his platform.

"Irrespective of the place where a child is born, he is entitled to equal educational opportunities," Kefauver said. "Education is an investment in citizenship and is, as I see it, the surest guarantee that democracy will survive."[24]

The strongest prospective candidate against Kefauver was James B. Frazier Jr. (who later did succeed him as congressman), son of a former governor and U.S. senator who had practiced law in Chattanooga since 1914 and had been appointed U.S. attorney in Tennessee's Eastern Division in 1933. Frazier, however, announced early in August that he had decided against the race because, under provisions of the newly enacted Hatch Act, he would have to resign his federal post to run.[25]

24. Ibid.
25. Undated clipping, Kefauver Collection, Ser. 5-a, Box 1.

The major candidate who did announce as Kefauver's opponent was Leonidas D. Miller, a fifty-four-year-old judge of Hamilton County Circuit and Criminal Court since 1932, a Chattanooga lawyer since 1910, and a former state legislator. Miller had run a creditable race against McReynolds the year before and could count on substantial support in all of the district's dozen counties. A third candidate was Lester Doak, state senator from Warren County, but he was conceded little chance, as he was not well known in Hamilton County, source of nearly half of the district's normal voting strength.

Kefauver's first big test, however, was not before the voters. Governor Cooper set the special election for September 13, but the question of whether nominees would be chosen by convention or by primary election was a decision within the discretion of the respective political parties. Third District Democrats would choose which route to take by action of their various county conventions, and big Hamilton County's convention obviously would be decisive.

Miller, with his established connections in the party organization, favored a special district convention; failing that, he wanted a poll tax requirement for voting in the primary. Kefauver stood for a party primary without a poll tax requirement, not only on principle but because, practically, his hope to appeal to a large number of committed voters appeared the best counter to Miller's influence with the party organization and its controlled vote. The first problem was to win this point in the county convention, where professional politicians predominated and Lee Allen's chairmanship of the executive committee was the best card in Kefauver's hand. As the situation developed, however, a recent upheaval in the Hamilton County political structure inclined the situation unexpectedly in Kefauver's favor.

Since 1924, one of Judge Will Cummings' staunchest allies in the County Court had been Wilkes T. Thrasher, one of its influential squires until the court appointed him county register of deeds in 1936. But Thrasher aspired to McReynolds' seat in Congress and ran against him in 1934. Cummings remained loyal to McReynolds and Thrasher was defeated. The angered Thrasher began quietly building up an alliance with various political figures, including Kefauver's state Senate opponent, Joe Bean. Shortly after Bean defeated Kefauver in the Senate race, the opportunity for revenge presented itself, and an insurgent bloc of "Thrasher men" won a 6 to 4 control of the court over the Cummings faction. The "Big Six" elected a number of Thrasher candidates for county offices over Cummings candidates, all by the same 6 to 4 vote.

Reaching out to exploit their newly-won power, the Thrasher forces sought to sponsor Frazier as Kefauver's opponent in the Congress race and, when he declined, coalesced behind Miller. Cummings took the opportunity to strike back at the rebels by swinging his loyal forces behind Kefauver. The Cummings faction, operating solidly in support of Lee Allen, Kefauver's floor manager in the county Democratic convention, settled the dispute thoroughly in Kefauver's favor. Not only did he get his primary free of a poll tax prerequisite, but four of the five members of the new Democratic Primary Board named by the convention were friendly to Kefauver. The primary was set for August 31.

In fact, however, the Hamilton County convention settled the contest. Miller withdrew from the race, charging that the primary board was "stacked" in Kefauver's favor. Doak withdrew a little later with similar charges: that the primary boards throughout the district were espousing Kefauver's cause actively, instead of remaining neutral.

"Indeed it is something of a paradox that Mr. Kefauver, who is perhaps best known in this county as an enemy of machine politics, is the avowed candidate of most of the machines throughout the district," the *Chattanooga Times* commented editorially. "This does not mean that Mr. Kefauver has gone over to the machines. It means rather that the machine politicians are hoping that by supporting a new political personality they can regain some of the prestige and influence they have lost. By observing the amenities, making new friends and biding his time, Mr. Kefauver has taken advantage of his one political reverse and has grown in stature. . . . He knows how to compromise without yielding in principle and . . . his word can be depended on."[26]

When Casto Dodson of Sparta, in the northern part of the district, was chosen by the Republican convention and Neal announced as an independent in the general election, it appeared that Kefauver was "in," but he could take no chances. The district had not

26. Anderson and Blumenthal, *The Kefauver Story*, 71.

elected a Republican congressman since the 1920 Harding landslide, but it had had only one Democratic congressman since then—McReynolds; and, as popular as McReynolds was, he had come within just over 3,000 votes of being defeated by a Republican in 1928.

Kefauver therefore campaigned through the first eleven days of September. He left the campaigning in Hamilton County to his friends because he was known there, while he swung through the other eleven counties of the district, meeting county officials and shaking hands with voters. Nancy accompanied him after overcoming the doubts of the Democratic organization; at first she was "relegated to the roughest section of Chattanooga, and sent to talk with the merchants" because the Democratic officials in charge of the campaign feared her British accent would alienate the rural voters.[27]

On election day, Kefauver and Allen toured the polls in Hamilton County all day, shaking hands with voters as they stood in line to cast their ballots. They ended the day in North Chattanooga and drove back toward the heart of the city. The sun was setting behind Signal Mountain as they drove, and the western sky was red with promise. No returns had come in on their car radio, but both were confident of Kefauver's victory.

"Well, Big Stuff," said Allen, "the polls are closed, and you're a congressman now. How does it feel?"

Kefauver was silent for a moment, staring thoughtfully straight ahead through the windshield, hunched down in the front seat, his hands in his lap.

"Aw, Lee," he said then, "they're a dime a dozen. But it might just lead to something."

"Sure," agreed Allen amiably. "You'll be President or Vice President, or a Supreme Court justice, some day."[28]

Their confidence was justified. Dodson carried only one small

27. Personal communication, Carol Harford, Washington, Aug. 29, 1970.

28. Personal conversation, Lee Allen, Chattanooga, Spring 1955; Harvey Swados, *Standing Up for the People: the Life and Work of Estes Kefauver* (New York: Dutton, 1972), 20, attributes the "dime a dozen" quote to Jack Reddy in conversation with Kefauver in Washington while Kefauver was still considering whether to make the race; this may be true, as it was characteristic of Kefauver to pick up such quotes and repeat them as his own later on.

county, and Hamilton County returned a 7-to-2 margin for Kefauver. Kefauver won the election by 14,268 votes to Dodson's 5,355
district-wide; Neal drew only 363 votes. He was in "polotics" (as
Nancy spelled it) to stay, until his death.

Chapter 6

Estes Had the Zeal of the Born Reformer

A few minutes before the end of the day on which Kefauver was chosen Democratic nominee for Third District congressman, German armies poured across the border of Poland to launch World War II. The day Kefauver was elected to Congress, President Roosevelt called a special session of Congress for September 21, eight days later, to repeal key provisions of the Neutrality Act of 1935.

The coincidences were symbolic. Kefauver entered Congress at a turning point of the legislative body's relations with Roosevelt, which had deteriorated markedly since 1933, when the President took office with a sweeping mandate from the American people to do whatever was necessary to end the Depression. Kefauver, more liberal in outlook than any of his Tennessee colleagues, was to have his troubles with other Southerners in Congress as it was, but his general support for Roosevelt and his policies would have made things even more difficult for him had not the outbreak of war in Europe, with its increasing threat to the United States, put him on the side of a slowly rising tide of renewed support for Roosevelt as a national leader.

Kefauver had expected to have the last few months of 1939 to wind up his affairs at Sizer, Chambliss & Kefauver and move some of his effects from Mooneen to a satisfactory residence in Washington. But when the call came for the special session, he and Nancy packed in a hurry and took a train to the capital.

They checked into the Mayflower Hotel and, the morning the session began, took a cab to the House Office Building to inspect McReynolds' two-room suite, Room 435, where Kefauver would be working. Miss Lucille Schilling, McReynolds' secretary, was there to greet them, and the Congressman's widow had put a bouquet on his desk to welcome the newcomer.[1]

---

1. Telephone conversation, Mrs. William H. Duggan, Nashville, Spring 1955.

After lunch, the Kefauvers crossed Independence Avenue to the Capitol, pushed through the crowds jamming the corridors and stairways, and sought admission to the House Chamber . . . only to be barred by Capitol policeman James Beamer, who told them that "Congressman Kefauver has already passed through the lines."

"What kind of business is this?" Kefauver demanded, the back of his neck beginning to flush. "I'm Congressman Kefauver."

"Sorry, sir," said Beamer firmly, "but the name is already checked off my list. The gentleman has already entered the chamber."

"Well, now, look, there's been some mistake here," said Kefauver. "Just get Congressman Cooper from my state to come out here. He knows me."

Representative Jere Cooper of Tennessee's Eighth District, a fraternity brother of Kefauver, straightened out the error and duly presented Kefauver to the House. The identity of the man who pretended to be Kefauver was never learned.[2]

For more than a month after Roosevelt's address to Congress that day, Kefauver had nothing to do except answer his mail and learn his way about Washington. The House was idle, in a series of three-day adjournments, while the Senate fought over the Neutrality Act. Speaker William Bankhead assigned Kefauver to four minor committees that had nothing whatever to do during the special session. Kefauver took advantage of the lull to get some information and advice on his new job from old-timers on the Washington scene, among them Speaker Bankhead, father of actress Tallulah Bankhead. Kefauver admired the colorful Alabaman, whom he called "one of the greatest characters I have ever known; he would have been a greater actor than John Barrymore."[3]

Kefauver attributed to Bankhead the advice that caused him to become an inveterate letter writer as a congressman. Bankhead said to him: "Work on your mail, young man. When people write you, see that they get good answers, and promptly. Sign them yourself. Send them some literature."[4] Kefauver continued this practice of seeking advice from his elders during his first years in Congress. Senator George Norris of Nebraska remained in the Senate for four

2. *Washington Post*, Sept. 22, 1939; personal conversation, Nancy Kefauver, Washington, Spring 1955.
3. Personal conversation, Estes Kefauver, Washington, Spring 1955.
4. Ibid.

years after Kefauver entered Congress, and Kefauver spent as much time as he was permitted in conversation with the mild-mannered, string-tied old gentleman, who preferred a quiet evening of reading to the social round common for Washington politicians. Kefauver said later that those conversations determined him to "follow in Norris's footsteps."[5]

Kefauver also consulted a fellow-Tennessean, Cordell Hull, who had served in both House and Senate before Roosevelt appointed him secretary of state.

"When I came to the House," Hull reminisced once to Kefauver, "I decided to try to be a master of one subject. I read everything I could on it, and made about one speech a year. Events of the world have shown that I was right. Take a lot of time in deciding how you will stand on issues, and never let your constituents down."[6]

Hull's "one subject" was economics. As a member of the House, he authored the nation's income tax legislation and the Federal Inheritance Tax Act of 1916, and he was best known during his term as secretary of state for his Reciprocal Trade Agreements program. As usual, Kefauver listened to all of the advice and selected from it what suited him best.

"There are two extreme types of Congressman," once said John Blair, who met Kefauver in the midst of his House career and became his closest adviser on monopoly matters. "One type takes a stand on everything and speaks on everything but doesn't have the information at hand to stand up under questioning. The other, like Norris, is interested in one field only and studies it so thoroughly that he becomes an authority on it. Kefauver takes a middle course. He goes into comparatively few fields, and is an acknowledged expert in them."[7]

Kefauver's maiden speech in the House, about three minutes long during the special session, was in support of a proposal to extend Hull's Reciprocal Trade Agreements program.

When the Kefauvers returned to Washington at the beginning of 1940, they sought lodgings less expensive than the Mayflower. They went to the Hotel Washington, on Pennsylvania Avenue hard by

5. Ibid.
6. Ibid.
7. Personal conversation, John M. Blair, Washington, Spring 1955.

the White House and conveniently close to the Capitol, because that was where Representative Cooper lived. The desk clerk looked somewhat disdainfully at the travel-weary couple from Tennessee and informed the gentleman that a room would cost $8.00 a day. Rather steep in 1940, when rates at good hotels across the country ranged from $1.50 to $4.00. Kefauver hesitated, then wheedled mildly: "Well, now, I'm a brand new Congressman." The clerk looked the tall figure up and down deliberately, then replied with a chilly smile: "That's all right. We have no objection to your staying here."[8]

They did stay there, for two weeks, while Kefauver made inquiries in search of something less expensive. He found it through another freshman colleague, Representative Albert L. Vreeland of New Jersey: the Wardman Park Hotel, which was several miles from downtown Washington but offered them an apartment at only $150 a month.

There were several alternative courses open to Kefauver in Congress. He could align himself with the Southern conservatives, as had McReynolds and half of the other six Tennessee House Democrats. He could ally himself with Speaker Bankhead and Representative Sam Rayburn of Texas, the Democratic floor leader, like three of his Tennessee colleagues, consistently behind President Roosevelt. He could become a member of the ideologically allied and loosely cooperating "liberal bloc" that included Representative Emanuel Celler of New York, Representative Mary T. Norton of New Jersey and, on the extreme left, American Laborite Vito Marcantonio of New York. Or he could become one of the rare lone wolves of Congress.

His previous course in Chattanooga indicated, accurately, that he would not go along with the conservatives, and he was both still too much of a Southerner and too much of a pragmatist to join the liberal bloc, which rarely succeeded in accomplishing anything except with the full power of the administration behind it. At first and for the course of World War II, he remained, for the most part, a supporter of the Roosevelt and Truman administrations, but his tendency to follow a solitary course appeared during his first short term and developed increasingly during his nine years in the House.

8. Personal conversation, Nancy Kefauver, Washington, Spring 1955.

The "junk" committee assignments he had been given by Speaker Bankhead in 1939 were only temporary formalities. Democratic committee assignments were made by the Democratic members of the House Ways and Means Committee, sitting as a party Committee on Committees. Kefauver, as a congressman newly elected in the middle of the two-year term of Congress, might have gone almost anywhere, except that one of the fifteen Ways and Means Democrats just happened to be fellow-Tennessean Jere Cooper. Through Cooper's sponsorship, Kefauver was appointed to fill a vacancy left by the resignation of another Tennessean, Walter Chandler of Memphis, on the Judiciary Committee—one of the three or four most sought-after committee assignments in the House.

The chairman of the Judiciary Committee was the veteran "Judge" Hatton Sumners of Texas, a picture of the traditional Southern gentleman, with convictions to match. Sumners generally supported Roosevelt's program, but he was a strict constitutionalist and broke with the President over Roosevelt's Supreme Court "packing" plan. Kefauver learned much from him and was of such service to him in routine committee work that Sumners called the young Tennessean "my good right arm."[9]

In fact, Kefauver proved to be rather good at the often tedious routine work of the committee. Two representatives who joined it later were free in their praise of his committee work. Representative Michael J. Feighan of Ohio called him "a very hard worker, and recognized by the members of the committee as being a particularly bright legal mind," and Representative Joseph P. O'Hara of Minnesota found him "industrious and an able member. . . . He evidenced fine legal training and experience."[10]

One not unimportant subsidiary benefit accruing from his Judiciary Committee experience was Kefauver's friendship with Celler, second-ranking Democrat on the committee. Some help from "Mannie," fifteen years older than he, was to come in handy many years later in some of his crucial Senate fights.

For the other half of the Kefauver family, the first two years in Washington were like a second honeymoon. Nancy had been plunged into the hurly-burly of social, civic, and political life ever

9. Personal conversation, Rep. Wright Patman, Washington, Spring 1955.
10. Personal conversations, Rep. Michael J. Feighan and Rep. Joseph P. O'Hara, Washington, Spring 1955.

since she had returned to Chattanooga with her new husband in 1935. Now, suddenly, they were virtual non-entities in the national capital, and they were together again. Childless, they had no living responsibilities except a cocker spaniel (or two or three, sometimes).

They golfed and sailed together on the Potomac. Nancy drove her husband downtown to his office in the morning and sometimes would return home to do the housework before picking him up in the afternoon, but as often as not would spend the day in the Corcoran Art Gallery, poking around, studying techniques, perhaps sketching, enjoying herself thoroughly. She took a morning art course there for a time.[11]

For Nancy, to whom her art and her husband as a person meant more than the entire spectrum of American politics, it was a precious interlude, but a short one. The beginning of their family was but two years away when they first went to Washington, and it took only a few months for Kefauver to find himself in the complex web of congressional force and counterforce.

During his years in the House, Kefauver was known to his congressional colleagues as a usual supporter of the Roosevelt and Truman administrations and as a liberal, to a degree extremely distasteful to many of his fellow-Southerners. He was known to the people of his Tennessee district as an administration supporter and a stalwart friend of the Tennessee Valley Authority.

Outside of Congress and his own district, Kefauver was known hardly at all. Insofar as he was known, it was in economic circles as a Cassandra-voice against increasing monopolistic practices and in political science circles as a bright young advocate of congressional reform.

"Estes had the zeal of the born reformer," said his erstwhile law partner, Jac Chambliss. "He had no sooner gotten into Congress than he wanted to change things."[12]

The comment was a little misleading, as Kefauver's efforts at congressional reform were among the least successful of his interests in the House, and his reputation in this area rested primarily on his co-authorship of a book, *A Twentieth Century Congress*.[13]

11. Personal conversation, Nancy Kefauver, Washington, Spring 1955.
12. Personal conversation, Jac Chambliss, Chattanooga, Spring 1955.
13. Estes Kefauver and Dr. Jack Levin, *A Twentieth Century Congress* (New York: Duell, Sloan, 1947).

He did introduce several reform bills. The first, offered when he had been on Capitol Hill only five months, was designed to correct a flaw in the Twentieth Amendment dealing with presidential succession, which Norris had sponsored in 1932. It provided that, in a situation where there was neither a qualified President nor Vice President, the speaker of the house would be next in line of succession, followed by the president of the Senate. It is likely that Norris himself suggested the bill to Kefauver. Kefauver managed to obtain House approval of the bill once, but was unable to push it through both houses. With typical persistence, he dragged out the same old bill and reintroduced it, year after year, shepherding it along the committee route, buttonholing colleagues and lobbying with senators for it. Late in 1944, he wrote an article, "We Might Not Have a President," touting his bill. He submitted it simultaneously to at least a dozen magazines and newspapers, without success, and at last managed to get it printed in the *New Republic* as a letter to the editor. A year later, shortened and revised, it was published as an article in the periodical, *This Month*.[14]

Kefauver did not see his presidential succession bill passed until 1947, when he enlisted as co-sponsor Representative A.S. Mike Monroney of Oklahoma, who already had gained a reputation as a successful congressional reformer. Only one of Kefauver's other governmental reform proposals succeeded, a bill to set up a judicial system in federal district courts to adjudicate most private claims for damages against the government, relieving Congress of the mass of such bills that clogged legislative calendars. It was incorporated at last in the Legislative Reorganization Act of 1946. He put forth a number of other government reform proposals, such as one (in which he joined Sumners) to attempt to provide for ratification of treaties by a simple majority of both houses instead of a two-thirds majority of the Senate alone. Such efforts gained Kefauver more recognition from political scientists than from political colleagues. In 1947, he was elected vice president of the American Political Science Association. But his legislative successes lay in other fields.

In mid-century, Kenneth Douglas McKellar still wore frock coat

14. Copy of article and letter, Estes Kefauver, Washington, to Helen Fuller, the *New Republic*, Washington, Oct. 17, 1944; telegram, Kefauver to Ada Siegel, *This Month*, New York, Dec. 27, 1945. Kefauver Collection, Ser. 1, Box 74.

and pin-striped trousers, white-edged vest crossed by a massive gold watch chain, and black bow tie. His bailiwick was the United States Senate, and he was its dean. Seniority and Southern Democracy had made him more powerful than the Vice President, and after President Roosevelt died in 1945 and Harry Truman entered the White House, McKellar, as president *pro tem* of the Senate, *was* the Vice President in everything but name and the right of succession. He was more than the Vice President in that he still retained the rights of a senator. In May 1946, McKellar stepped up from the acting to actual chairmanship of the powerful Appropriations Committee. President Truman accorded him the unprecedented privilege of sitting in on Cabinet meetings. The irascible old gentleman was a contemporary and political ally of E.H. Crump, who said once that "no one can beat him" because McKellar always answered telephone calls promptly, answered telegrams within the hour, answered his mail every day, and was "courteous and polite to every man and woman who visits Washington from Tennessee." A lifelong bachelor, McKellar lived at the plush and expensive Mayflower Hotel while in Washington and at the rather rundown and inexpensive Gayoso Hotel while in Memphis.

McKellar, like most Southerners, was an internationalist and a supporter of such liberal Democratic Presidents as Wilson and Roosevelt on many major issues, but a conservative in domestic matters; he was a leader in filibusters against civil rights legislation. He also had a reputation as a spoilsman: he objected to putting postmasters under Civil Service, and he fought the LaFollette-Monroney congressional reorganization bill because of its provisions eliminating patronage. The best and the worst of the McKellar approach came out in his attitude toward the Tennessee Valley Authority. He was one of the original TVA Act's strongest supporters, consistently supporting appropriations for construction of dams and development of the Tennessee Valley. "I have given the best years of my life and the best thoughts of my brain to this cause," he said once,[15] and one of his bitterest disappointments was that Roosevelt chose Norris, instead of him, to sponsor the original TVA Act. On the other hand, he found it difficult to adapt himself to the idea that TVA was not subject to patronage considerations. He complained bitterly

15. *Congressional Record*, vol. 88, pt. 3, May 1, 1942, p. 3875.

that his recommendations for appointments to TVA positions were ignored, and his last decade in office was marked by a feud against the TVA management that threatened at times to wreck the agency. Late in 1941, a few months after David Lilienthal became TVA's board chairman, McKellar's irritation at the agency's independence could be contained no longer. Speaking for the Tennessee Farm Bureau Federation and a large cross-section of East Tennessee residents, McKellar opposed construction of Douglas Dam on the French Broad River, which Lilienthal favored with Roosevelt's backing, because it would take out of cultivation 30,000 acres of productive farm land. When the United States was drawn into World War II, McKellar abandoned his opposition to Douglas Dam because its power obviously was needed for the war effort, but he did not abandon his enmity toward Lilienthal.

"This infamous skunk, Lilienthal, has been using TVA as a political club, for one thing: to beat me in my own state!" was McKellar's warcry, and on the floor of the Senate he called Lilienthal "a modern Uriah Heep in the flesh."[16]

McKellar's first salvo, in March 1942, was an amendment to the appropriations bill to require TVA to return surplus proceeds to the Treasury each year, instead of retaining them for operational purposes, and to come back to Congress for more money annually. The transparent effect of such an amendment would be to make TVA more subject to political domination.

Kefauver had supported McKellar on the House floor in a dispute with Lilienthal two years earlier over scheduling some dam construction, but he refused to go along with the aging senator on this one. When Lilienthal went before the Senate Appropriations Committee to testify against the McKellar amendment, Kefauver accompanied him and added his testimony to Lilienthal's. McKellar, sitting as committee chairman in the absence of ailing Senator Carter Glass, reddened with wrath at the boldness of his East Tennessee House colleague in defying his power.

Despite McKellar's power to block Kefauver's legislation in the Senate and interfere with patronage in his own district, the young congressman followed through. When the McKellar amendment cleared the committee and reached the Senate floor, Kefauver sat

16. Ibid.

beside Lilienthal in the gallery as McKellar made a personal appeal for it to his colleagues on the ground that Lilienthal was out to "get" him politically. When the Senate adopted his amendment, Lilienthal turned to Kefauver and said, "Well, Estes, he licked us."

"Not yet, he didn't," retorted Kefauver.[17]

When the McKellar amendment reached the House floor late in May, Kefauver made a full-dress speech against it. He told the House he found it "difficult to understand why an agency that is doing a great war production job should be attacked at this time."[18] The House defeated the McKellar amendment, and it was stricken out in the conference committee on the appropriations bill.

McKellar's unsuccessful 1942 amendment was the opening gun in his long battle to bring TVA to heel. Every year for the next six years, he renewed his "spring offensive." To his repeated proposal to eliminate the TVA revolving fund, he added a measure to require Senate confirmation of TVA employes earning more than $4,500 a year and, in 1944, a proposal to move TVA headquarters from Knoxville to Washington.

Kefauver was in the forefront of the House fight to block the McKellar proposals—all of which passed the Senate in 1944, the agency's closest call since its inception. Kefauver was recognized as the leader of the House TVA bloc to the extent that he was chosen chairman of an unofficial group of congressmen who got together to plan strategy whenever TVA was in trouble. With him stood a solid phalanx of Tennessee Valley area congressmen—among them notably Albert Gore and J. Percy Priest from Tennessee, John Sparkman of Alabama, and John E. Rankin of Mississippi—supported by friends from other sections of the nation and backed by the Roosevelt and Truman administrations. It took that kind of a House coalition to curb the redoubtable McKellar, who could count on both influence and friendship to round up votes for his schemes in the Upper House.

Kefauver and the Valley bloc were also mobilized repeatedly to defend TVA against its ideological enemies, who were encouraged by McKellar's assaults on the agency. In these fights, however, Mc-

17. Anderson and Blumenthal, *The Kefauver Story*, 92.
18. *Congressional Record*, vol. 88, pt. 3, May 21, 1942, p. 4446.

Kellar almost always threw his immense power solidly behind the TVA bloc and on one occasion was able to save TVA from crippling legislation when the House coalition failed.

In matters affecting TVA, Kefauver was not the lone wolf he was in many of his other legislative stands. He was a member of a closely cooperating team, whose members submerged whatever differences divided them on other issues when TVA's welfare was at stake. Although some of them disliked Kefauver intensely for his generally liberal philosophy, they readily granted him leadership in TVA fights in recognition of his ability and his extensive knowledge of the subject.

The TVA, of course, was a sturdy political horse for a Tennessee congressman to ride on the road to repeated reelection, but Kefauver's support for TVA conformed to his basic philosophy of government. He said once, "we must develop and use our material resources everywhere for the good of all of the people. . . . Above all, TVA is today the world's outstanding example of democracy at work—of the cooperation of the people with their government for the benefit of all."

McKellar's hostility to Kefauver had little effect on Kefauver's political fortunes in his own district. Organized opposition to Kefauver there on the basis of his stand for TVA and public power—as well as his support of New Deal policies in general—centered around the *Chattanooga News-Free Press*, which had become the city's only afternoon newspaper.

The *News-Free Press* resulted from absorption of the liberal *News* by the conservative *Free Press* soon after Kefauver's entry into Congress. Republican and anti-TVA, the *News-Free Press* was one of Kefauver's bitterest and most consistent enemies for the rest of his life. Its sustained opinion of him was expressed in an editorial once, attacking him for his support of TVA, which called him "an irresponsible, dangerous, opportunistic radical."[19] The merger of the *News* and the *Free Press* was one of the factors that led Kefauver into his major legislative field: antitrust activity. While his wife was still visiting her parents in Scotland, he wrote her that the *News* was in

19. Anderson and Blumenthal, *The Kefauver Story*, 82; Swados, *Standing Up for the People*, 23.

financial trouble and could not survive much longer. As the paper's attorney, he had inside information: the *News* did not fold until mid-December, 1939.

Its collapse and absorption by its afternoon competitor, the *Free Press*, was partly a consequence of financial mismanagement by its editor, George Fort Milton, but it was partly a consequence of a kind of competition that was bound to set Kefauver thinking. Subsequent probes by the Tennessee Railroad and Public Utilities Commission and a congressional committee determined that the *Free Press* had been subsidized by a private utility, the Tennessee Electric Power Company, affiliated with Wendell Willkie's Commonwealth and Southern, which was fighting the advent of TVA, and that the *Free Press* had strangled the *News* by cut-rate advertising. Roy McDonald, publisher of the *Free Press*, called the probes a "purge and . . . New Deal persecution," but Tennessee Public Utilities Commissioner Leon Jourolman came to the conclusion that TEPCO was guilty of 917 counts of "undue preference and advantages" favoring the *Free Press* and Home Stores, a 42-store grocery chain owned by McDonald, and was subject to court fines of $917,000.[20]

About this time, Kefauver was visited in Washington by his mother's double first cousin, sixty-seven-year-old Patrick Mann Estes, a founder, general counsel, and part owner of the Life & Casualty Company of Tennessee, headquartered in Nashville. Over coffee in a little restaurant near the House Office Building, "Uncle Pat" voiced a concern that had been bothering him.

"A lot of our locally-owned corporations in Tennessee are being acquired by big trusts," he said. "The big corporations are absorbing them faster and faster. They're forcing little business out of the state."

"What's the main reason behind it, Uncle Pat?" asked Kefauver.

"The loophole in the Clayton Act," replied Patrick Estes. He went on to explain that Section 7 of the 1914 Clayton Anti-Trust Act attempted to halt the growth of monopolies by prohibiting corporation mergers through acquisition of stock, but it failed to prevent mergers through acquisition of assets.[21]

"At the time when Congress enacted the Clayton Act, most ac-

20. Anderson and Blumenthal, *The Kefauver Story*, 90.
21. Personal conversation, Estes Kefauver, Washington, Spring 1955.

quisitions took the form of stock purchases," Kefauver explained several years later, when he himself had investigated the loophole and its background. "By comparison, acquisitions of assets were almost unknown. . . . The plain fact of the matter is that Congress simply did not foresee—not could it reasonably be expected to foresee—the loophole implicit in the possibility of acquisitions of assets."[22]

It was several years after his talk with Patrick Estes before Kefauver began to dip actively into the anti-monopoly field, although he had a number of discussions during that period with Judge Ewing Davis, a fellow-Tennessean who was chairman of the Federal Trade Commission, about the background of monopoly activity and anti-monopoly legislation. But, in the long view, all of his other legislative activities were simply subsidiary, excepting only those concerned with the principle of individual liberty. He became one of the most effective congressional enemies of monopoly in the nation's history.

His fight against monopoly was peculiarly well-suited to bring into focus some of the essential aspects of his personality. Lacking eloquence and a ready fire of indignation, he yet possessed beneath his usually bland surface a good deal of the crusading zeal of his Baptist ministerial grandfather. Such zeal may square with a broadly humanistic view, but it needs an adversary to burn at its brightest; and, in attacking monopoly, Kefauver found an adversary rooted in the fundamental selfishness of human nature.

As he became acquainted with his congressional environment, Kefauver began to be aware of the truth of A.F. Bentley's judgment in 1908 that pressure groups, not the electorate, determine the course of the legislative process; expressed differently in 1912 by Woodrow Wilson that "the masters of the government of the United States are the combined capitalists and manufacturers of the United States."

His first steps in the field, during the war years, were tentative, on behalf of small farmers and small businessmen, but in 1945, at his own request, he was appointed a member of the nine-man Select Committee on Small Business, chaired by Representative Wright Patman, a twenty-year congressional veteran. Like Hatton

22. Text of speech by Estes Kefauver before the American Economic Association, Chicago, Dec. 30, 1942, Kefauver Collection, Ser. 1, Box 74.

Sumners, Patman was a Texan and, like Sumners, he was in many respects Kefauver's legislative mentor for several years.

Patman, a tall, rather stout, pink-cheeked man wearing metal-rimmed glasses and with an orotund speaking delivery, was chairman of the Texas delegation in Congress despite the much greater seniority of colleagues like Sumners and Sam Rayburn. He was a high-ranking member of the Banking and Currency Committee, and Kefauver's background in a corporation law firm, plus the high opinion Sumners expressed of Kefauver's work in the Judiciary Committee, caused Patman to welcome the Tennessean to the Small Business Committee. He found Kefauver "a valuable member of the committee. . . . He took great interest in it and made a great contribution. There is nothing petty or trifling about Estes. He is always genuine, and works in the public interest."[23]

Soon after becoming a member of the committee, Kefauver met Dr. John M. Blair during a hearing on retention of the Smaller War Plants Corporation. Blair, a morose, single-minded man whose somberness did not endear him to his associates, was a veteran staffer of the Federal Trade Commission with a profound knowledge of economics in general and monopoly in particular. He had written a book and a number of articles warning that the monopolistic trend in the United States, if continued, would lead to economic strangulation. During a hearing at which Blair testified, Kefauver questioned him closely on some of his points, and when the meeting ended he invited Blair to have lunch with him and continue the discussion.

"There was a quick recognition, I believe on both our parts," said Blair later, "that we were intellectually, ideologically and idealistically *simpatico.*"[24] From then on, Kefauver and Blair collaborated more and more closely on anti-monopoly matters. Blair, who recognized in the Tennessean a potentially effective "voice" for his own economic and philosophical views, gradually became Kefauver's chief *aide-de-camp* in monopoly matters, influencing Kefauver's thinking on economics, in the long run, at least as much as did Patman.

Patman appointed Kefauver chairman of a subcommittee to in-

---

23. Personal conversation, Rep. Wright Patman, Washington, Spring 1955.
24. Personal communication, John M. Blair, La Plata, Md., Sept. 14, 1970.

vestigate the concentration of economic power in the United States. The investigation gave Kefauver much of the background for his later anti-monopoly fights, and the report he wrote on it was so comprehensive that the Small Business Committee continued to receive requests for it for years after it was out of print. Entitled *United States Versus Economic Concentration and Power*, the report concluded: "The danger is not in big business as such, but in the concentration of economic power which can be used to stifle free enterprise. . . . Either we must believe in, and take the necessary steps to make possible a competitive-enterprise system, or we must give it up, bit by bit, year by year."[25]

Among the practices uncovered by his subcommittee, he said in an article submitted in 1946 to *Collier's* magazine, but not published, were a conspiracy that "delayed the introduction of fluorescent lamps and sought to prevent their use on any basis that would reduce the consumption of electricity," and collaboration between American and German firms, through control of patents, to maintain artifically high prices in this country for tungsten carbide and plexiglas.[26]

The House was a hard and disappointing training ground for Kefauver in anti-monopoly matters. In 1945 and 1947, his name appeared as a sponsor on bills to close the loophole in the Clayton Act, but both times the measure was pigeon-holed in the powerful Rules Committee, dominated by "Judge" Howard Smith of Virginia. One of his rare successes in this area was the defeat of a 1947 bill, opposed by the Truman administration, that was clearly designed, Kefauver charged on the House floor, "to throw the anti-trust laws out of the window." The measure was labeled innocuously as designed "to aid in the stabilization of commodity prices," but what it did was to permit "voluntary agreements" on prices among sellers.

"Monopoly interests and their Republican spokesmen in Congress have now seen fit to strip from the consumer the last shreds of protection which he possesses against the rapacity and greed of mo-

25. Coleman A. Harwell, "Estes Kefauver—Man of Courage," pamphlet distributed in the 1956 presidential campaign, 8. The pamphlet reproduced a series of articles that appeared in the *Nashville Tennessean* early in 1956.

26. Text of article, "Wanted—Action on the Monopoly Front," Kefauver Collection, Ser. 1, Box 74.

nopoly business," Kefauver charged on the floor of the House. "Now . . . the lamb has been made ready for a shearing he will long remember. . . . Monopolies always conspire to raise prices, and never to reduce them, except for the deliberate purpose of eliminating smaller competitors, after which prices are raised to new heights. . . . The incredible is becoming the fantastic, and the fantastic is becoming the law."[27]

The fantastic did not become the law that time because congressional adjournment was only a few days off and the House refused to suspend the rules to vote on the bill. Two weeks later, in less oratorical terms and therefore more convincingly for a man who managed to mumble the most dramatic phrases in a level monotone on the House floor, Kefauver told the American Economic Association in Chicago that he knew of only four long-range alternatives to adequate anti-trust laws: the *status quo*, socialization, regulation, and deficit financing.

"Allowing the *status quo* to continue merely means that we allow our economic destinies to be governed by the managers and directors of a few large corporations," he said. "Not only is the whole idea of socialization repugnant to the political convictions of the American people, but there is little, if any, tangible evidence to support the contention that socialism would be efficient or workable as an economic system. . . . If any attempt were made to impose long-range controls over prices, production, wages, etc., over many of the nation's industries, we know that it would not be tolerated. This would stifle the spirit of initiative which has made our country great. . . . This leaves as an alternative to anti-trust only government spending, which, I believe, boils down to deficit financing."

He went on to say that his "belief in anti-trust rests upon a fundamental political basis. Is there not some real merit in the argument that a great concentration of industry would inevitably lead to some type of collectivistic state, in which our democratic liberties and political rights would cease to exist?"[28] This was a reference to a theme on which he had enlarged earlier in the year when he was arguing for release of the Clayton Act amendment from the Rules Committee.

27. *Congressional Record*, vol. 93, pt. 9, Dec. 15, 1947, p. 11393.
28. Estes Kefauver, address before the American Economic Association, Chi-

"In every one of the other industrialized nations of the world," he said then, "the prelude to the advent of collectivism has been the renunciation of the anti-trust laws or their rough equivalent in the common law. . . . If we may learn anything from the history of other nations, it is that the time schedule reads: first, big business; second, big labor; third, big government; and, fourth, collectivism. It appears that we in this country have long since passed the first stage. We have recently entered the second, and now we are embarking on the third. Can anyone be so blind as not to see what the fourth step will inevitably be?"[29]

cago, Dec. 30, 1947: *Press-Scimitar*, Memphis, Dec. 30, 1947; undated text of speech in Kefauver Collection, Ser. 1, Box 74.

29. *Congressional Record*, vol. 93, pt. 7, July 16, 1947, p. 9112.

Chapter 7

I Am Only Doing and Saying
What I Think Is Right

White hair tousled, face red, sixty-year-old Representative John E. Rankin of Mississippi, perhaps the nation's most vocal white supremacist, levelled a finger at his tall young colleague from Tennessee on the floor of the House, and shouted:

"Shame on you, Es-tees Key-fowver!"

Rankin, a member of Congress since 1920 and a coauthor of the bill establishing the Tennessee Valley Authority, had been a member of that staunch band of mid-Southern congressmen who always rallied with Kefauver when the TVA was under attack. But this day, October 12, 1942, he had seen this young Tennessean stand on the floor and support a bill to abolish the poll tax as a prerequisite to voting, with the words, "A basic principle of democracy is the free exercise of the franchise. . . . Any restriction, such as the poll tax, that works or is employed to prevent voting strikes at the heart of democracy."

Rankin got to his feet and pointed out furiously that Kefauver's predecessor, Sam McReynolds, had always opposed such bills, and Rankin compared supporters of this one to Alcibiades, Catiline, Judas Iscariot, and Benedict Arnold.

"I am truly sorry for the gentleman from Tennessee," he cried. "Shades of Andrew Jackson! Shades of Ed Carmack! Shades of Sam McReynolds! Shades of all of the other great statesmen that proud state has produced! . . . *Shame* on you, Es-tees Key-fowver!"[1]

The next day, before casting his vote for the bill (it passed the House but died in the Senate), Kefauver defended himself in mild

---

1. Robert L. Riggs, "The Man from Tennessee," in the *Progressive*, March 1956. The sentence does not appear in the *Congressional Record*, vol. 88, pt. 6, Oct. 12, 1942, pp. 8068–70, which quotes Rankin as saying: "I am afraid the people of Tennessee will bow their heads in shame when they realize that today he has supported a measure that would undermine and destroy this, the greatest

tones: "In my case, voting for this bill is not politically expedient. I am only doing and saying what I think is right."[2]

His assessment was correct: his stand and the future course it implied were not politically expedient. His vote against the poll tax as his first full term in the House was drawing to a close marked the beginning of his alienation from most of his colleagues in his own section of the nation, the South. He was one with his Southern brethren on more issues than some of them later would give him credit for, and some of his disagreements with them could be forgiven, but his opposition to the poll tax struck a raw nerve.

Kefauver did not oppose the poll tax in the role of an integrationist, for he was not one until he—like many other Americans—was overruled by the Supreme Court decision banning school segregation. Before then, he expressed himself openly in favor of continued segregation and opposed such civil rights measures as a Fair Employment Practices Commission and a federal anti-lynching law. His immediate objection to the poll tax, as he stated, was its disfranchising effect.

Despite its continued serviceability as a prop for Southern economic privilege, the poll tax's primary role was as a prop for political privilege. Even those Southerners who fought economic monopoly, like Wright Patman, would not go along with Kefauver in trying to eliminate the poll tax. Publicly, they talked the Constitution and states' rights, but privately the more honest ones would have contended that the tax effectively limited political control to "the better and more responsible people" of Southern communities.

In his opposition to the poll tax, Kefauver was influenced partly by the liberal zeal of the *Chattanooga News* and its editor and the views of his friends in Chattanooga's organized labor movement, to whom the tax was a liability in getting their own people to the polls. But, also, he was familiar with the effect of the tax generally in Tennessee. Its simplest use was to keep the vote low when the situation was safe for those in power, by discouraging the poor and

---

republic the world has ever seen." But the *Record* is sometimes edited after a debate. When I telephoned Riggs in Louisville in the summer of 1970 about the discrepancy, Riggs stated that he was present in the House Chamber as correspondent for the *Louisville Courier-Journal* during the debate and heard Rankin make the statement.

2. *Congressional Record*, vol. 88, pt. 6, Oct. 13, 1942, p. 8127.

the forgetful from going to the polls. But it could also be utilized against some upstart challenger by paying up the poll taxes of blocs of voters and being sure they got to the polls to "vote right," at the rather reasonable rate of $200 per 100 votes.

The latter process was a favorite trick of local "machines," which were not above voting a few names from the tombstones of a nearby cemetery when the election officials were friendly, as they usually were. It was reputed to have been used on occasion in Ed Crump's Memphis, and this above all brought an organized campaign against the poll tax in Tennessee. From the time "Crump men" began occupying the governor's office with the election of Hill McAlister in 1932, a favorite plank in the platform of anti-Crump candidates was repeal of the poll tax, on the somewhat frail assumption that legislative repeal would be upheld by the courts.

Kefauver's decision to fight the poll tax in Congress was a consistent continuation of his campaign position when he ran for the state Senate in 1938. He expressed it even before the bill on which Rankin castigated him, when the House earlier that year considered a conference committee report on a measure to allow soldiers to vote in elections back home. Rankin led House opposition to a Senate amendment removing the poll tax, wherever it existed, as a prerequisite for soldier voting. Kefauver, instead of confining himself diplomatically to the issue of the soldier vote, addressed himself to the fundamental question of the tax itself.

"Someday the poll tax must be eliminated," he said. "The poll tax is repugnant to democracy. It should not be tolerated. If a state may charge a small amount as a poll tax, then by the same principle it could levy the payment of a poll tax in the amount of $1,000. . . . There is in principle no difference between the $1,000 poll tax and the $1 poll tax. Both are unreasonable, without foundation, and have nothing to do with the qualification of the voter."[3]

Twice after the outspoken Harry S Truman entered the White House, the House passed a poll tax repealer, and both times it died in the Senate under the threat of a Southern filibuster. Kefauver supported the repealer both times, being one of the signers of a discharge petition that brought the 1945 repealer out of the Judiciary Committee, which had bottled it up.

3. Ibid., vol. 88, pt. 5, Sept. 9, 1942, p. 7074.

Although Kefauver's own state eliminated the poll tax by constitutional amendment in 1953, it was not outlawed nationally until the year after his death. But his support of such bills set his foot upon a lonely path that he was to tread for all of his political life: too Southern for the liberals, too liberal for the Southerners.

Although the liberals might welcome his defection from the Southern ranks on the poll tax and some other issues, he was much too traditional for them in some of his other responses. As late as 1948, he expressed the view that the Truman civil rights program was a political bid by the Democratic party to woo votes in the key states of the Northeast. He reiterated his opposition to the FEPC, federal anti-lynching legislation (which he called "an unjustified encroachment on the rights of the states") and "any non-segregation provisions." Kefauver's statement on segregation at that time made somewhat paradoxical his reputation during the ensuing decade as a presidential hopeful too liberal for moderate party leaders to accept.

"There is no real demand for anti-segregation laws in the South," he said. "The Negroes of the South are not interested in this kind of legislation. They want schools, better economic opportunity, and houses."[4]

So it was not Kefauver's position on segregation that offended the Southerners. Their reason for disliking him, less tangible but more fundamental, was a pattern of attitude and activity that threatened the foundations of their political feudalism. The last thing the Southerners wanted to do was to activate the "little fellow" as an autonomous political force, and that appeared to be the very heresy against privilege that Kefauver was determined to commit.

A substantial facet of his "renegade" political pattern was his position as one of the few congressmen from the South friendly to organized labor. Throughout most of the South, there was violent opposition to the encroachment of labor unions, primarily because they threatened to disrupt the region's advantageous reservoir of cheap labor. Kefauver's support of labor's position in legislative matters, in fact, was by no means so consistent as labor's political support of him in his district. The national CIO Political Action Committee recorded him as having voted "right" only seven times in sixteen key votes during his nine years in the House.

4. Ibid., vol. 94, pt. 6, July 29, 1948, p. 9549.

Kefauver voted in 1943 for the Smith-Connally Act, requiring a thirty-day notice before a strike against a war contractor and authorizing the government to seize strike-bound plants. It was opposed bitterly by labor and passed over President Roosevelt's veto. Kefauver also voted in 1946 for the railroad strike emergency bill, which labor opposed, to give the government the right to draft striking railway workers into the armed services. (It passed both houses, but in different versions, and no agreement was ever reached on it.) Kefauver's vote for the Smith-Connally Act caused him some rough times back home. One Chattanooga labor union member recalled that "we just gave him hell" when Kefauver appeared at a special conference of the city's AFL unions to give an accounting. He defended his vote for the measure then, but a few months later appeared before the Central Labor Union to confess that he had changed his mind and decided he had been wrong in voting for the act.[5]

Over against Kefauver's votes for measures to limit labor's strike rights in crucial situations stood his votes in favor of wartime and postwar domestic programs that, while not directly "union" bills, were much favored by organized labor. He opposed the immediate elimination of wartime price controls, supported federally financed housing, and supported Patman's "full employment" bill in 1945 to provide for federal investments and expenditures to take up the slack in employment brought about by the release of 7.6 million men and women from the armed services, the layoff of 3.7 million war workers, and cancellation of more than 300,000 war contracts.

"The clincher for Kefauver, so far as labor was concerned, was the Taft-Hartley Act," said Stanton Smith in 1955, when he was president of the Tennessee Federation of Labor. "If he had voted for that, in spite of all his past performance, labor would have turned against him. Since he voted against it, labor is solidly for him now."[6]

Kefauver's labor friends could not be absolutely sure ahead of time that he would vote against Taft-Hartley. He had a great deal of respect for its Senate sponsor, Robert A. Taft of Ohio, with

5. Personal conversation, Stanton Smith, Nashville, Spring 1955.
6. Ibid.

whom he had joined the same year in sponsoring a bill for federal aid to education. Furthermore the bill included provisions that Kefauver himself thought reasonable, such as a definition of unfair labor practices on the part of unions as well as employers, prohibition of jurisdictional strikes and secondary boycotts, and a mandatory sixty-day moratorium before striking against an industry in interstate commerce.

But there were Taft-Hartley provisions that Kefauver could not accept: primarily, absolute prohibition of closed shop contracts, a requirement that unions make their financial affairs public (though industries were not required to do so), and a provision that unions might be sued for breach of contract. Most of all, Kefauver was repelled by the machinations surrounding the Taft-Hartley fight in the House, in contrast to Taft's straightforward and consistent battle for his Senate bill. The accusation was made repeatedly that the National Association of Manufacturers wrote the House version of the bill and that "manufacturers spent over $100 million to put over the Taft-Hartley bill."[7]

Taft himself fought successfully to soften the House version of the bill. It was passed by a coalition of Republicans and Southern Democrats over President Truman's veto. Kefauver was one of only twelve Southern Democrats, out of the 112 in the House, who voted against Taft-Hartley. Taft-Hartley came near the end of Kefauver's House service, during which his record on legislation in which labor was interested reflected much of that curious ambiguity that marked his early switch to the labor camp in Chattanooga. It aroused, too, something of the same unease among labor people.

Stanton Smith told of one exemplary incident when he was secretary-treasurer of the Central Labor Union: "When he had not been in Congress very long, the Chattanooga Central Labor Union asked him to be against a bill. He wrote back and said, 'I'm sorry, I can't agree, and here's why. But I have an open mind, and if you show me where I'm wrong, I'll change my stand.' No other political figure had ever done this."

Smith described Kefauver as "never subservient to labor" but voting "generally along the lines labor approved. He has always been

---

7. Karl Schriftgiesser, *The Lobbyists* (Boston: Little, Brown, 1951), 112.

honest and forthright, and willing to discuss issues on their merits."[8]

Kefauver's consistent support by labor in Chattanooga during his House years could be attributed in large part to his friendship with Smith, a pleasant-faced, rather boyish-looking ex-school teacher who was so far from being a hard-line extremist that his subsequent administration as state AFL-CIO president did much to improve the image of organized labor in the minds of Tennessee's businessmen and predominantly rural legislators. He knew Kefauver well enough to recognize that Kefauver's stands contrary to the labor viewpoint on some specific issues did not outweigh Kefauver's approach to broad issues from a philosophical standpoint ultimately beneficial to labor's objectives; and Smith's influence in the Chattanooga labor movement was considerable.

Smith's perceptiveness of the importance of Kefauver's basic philosophy was shared by some of Kefauver's more uncompromising Southern colleagues in Congress, but from the opposite point of view. To them, his general independence of that tacit Dixie brotherhood dedicated to a balance-of-power role between the two major political parties was unpardonable.

One of the most important and implacable enemies Kefauver made among the Southerners on the basis of general principles rather than any specific offense was round-faced, shrewd-eyed Senator James O. Eastland of Mississippi. Eastland, a year Kefauver's junior, supported McKellar's efforts to hamstring TVA, supported the Taft-Hartley bill, and opposed the LaFollette-Monroney congressional reorganization measure.

Eastland heartily detested Kefauver, and his version of total war against the Tennessean extended to guerrilla tactics that had nothing to do with the ideological differences between them. At one time, Kefauver sponsored a bill to provide $10,000 in compensation for the destitute mother of a boy who had been killed while riding in a Civilian Conservation Corps truck. Passed by the House, the bill was blocked three times in the Senate before being cut to $2,500. Kefauver's Republican colleague from Knoxville, Representative John Jennings Jr., who was a member of the conference committee seeking to reconcile the two versions, found Eastland adamant on the measure.

8. Personal conversation, Stanton Smith, Nashville, Spring 1955.

"That's Kefauver's bill," said the Mississippian. "I don't want to see it passed."

"It's not Kefauver's bill," replied Jennings, fudging a bit when he saw how the land lay. "It's my bill."

"Oh, in that case, we'll pass it," said Eastland; he even agreed to an increase to $3,500 in the amount of compensation. Later, Kefauver returned Jennings's favor by persuading President Truman to sign a Jennings claim bill that the President had planned to veto.[9] Eastland's hatred of Kefauver was not mitigated even by Kefauver's death. A majority of Southern senators, including such philosophical enemies of Kefauver as Strom Thurmond of South Carolina and Herman Talmadge of Georgia, paid tribute to the deceased Kefauver, but Eastland was not among them.

Kefauver entered the House of Representatives as a still slender young man of thirty-six. When he left it at the age of forty-five, he was verging on full-bodied middle age. His weight had pushed up above the 200-pound mark a bit, his face had filled out, and his college-athlete waist had expanded to the point that his legs, though big-boned and yet muscular, looked skinny when he stripped for a shower.

His personality, too, moderated during those nine years. Always mild and deliberate in his responses, he lost the last vestiges of his youthful, playful flair under the pressure of hard work and increasing responsibility. As his legislative path diverged from that customarily trodden by Southern congressmen, the soft-spoken courtesy of the Old South, as if in compensation, became more evident in his conversation. Yet, at the same time, his air became increasingly preoccupied, so that often someone talking with him could not be sure Kefauver heard a word that was said until, after a pause, he would come up with a completely appropriate response. His activities in the field of congressional reform and his stand on the poll tax brought him an honorable mention, along with twelve other representatives, in *Collier's* magazine's choices of the "best in the nation" senators and representatives in 1946.[10]

9. Personal conversation, Rep. John Jennings, Washington, Spring 1955.
10. Anderson and Blumenthal, *The Kefauver Story*, 87.

Kefauver generally supported the programs of Roosevelt and Truman. There is no evidence that Roosevelt was aware of his existence, except marginally, but Truman was—and Truman did not like him. Superficially this dislike appears curious because Kefauver often took the President's side on the issues against most of his fellow-Southerners, but Truman remained always an "organization man" in his political philosophy, and Kefauver's individualism made him obviously independent of both the administration organization and the Southern organization. Truman probably would have liked him better had Kefauver allied himself solidly with the Southerners, even though that would have cost the President Kefauver's vote in many instances.

Kefauver occasionally took note of the strained relations developing gradually, for no apparent major reason, between himself and the White House. Once, when Truman had been President only a few months, the White House turned Kefauver down, as "a matter of policy," on a request that the President have his picture made with a group of visiting students from Chattanooga's Baylor School, and Kefauver was startled later to see the picture on the front page of the *Chattanooga News-Free Press*—arranged through Tennessee's junior Senator, Tom Stewart, who was aligned with the Southern bloc and voted against Truman's program as often as not. Kefauver wrote angrily to presidential secretary Matthew Connally:

"Frankly, I think it is a very shoddy way to do anyone and to say that I am embarrassed is putting it mildly. . . . I do not feel very much encouraged about continuing to try to fight for the President's program up here on the Hill when someone else who has not been much help to him can get considerations which were definitely denied me."[11]

While he was in the House, Kefauver acquired the nucleus of that permanent staff that was to become known as one of the most loyal and efficient in Washington. When he entered Congress, he retained N.R. (Pat) Patterson and Lucille Schilling from McReynold's old staff, but Patterson entered the Navy in 1945 and Miss Schilling left him to get married. The new staff members Kefauver employed were to remain with him until his death: Mrs. Henrietta

11. Letter, Estes Kefauver to Matthew Connally, Nov. 7, 1945, Kefauver Collection, Ser. 5-c, Box 1.

O'Donaghue, a friendly, graying woman of Kefauver's own age who had been a bankruptcy court clerk in Chattanooga and a secretary with the Interstate Commerce Commission before Kefauver employed her as his personal secretary in 1942; Frank Brizzi, an energetic New Yorker who was studying veterans' affairs in Washington when he was employed to replace Patterson on Kefauver's staff; and Lucile Myers of Chattanooga, a highly competent and fanatically devoted young woman who joined him in 1947.

Mrs. O'Donaghue, a widow who became known affectionately to her colleagues as "Henri," handled Kefauver's personal correspondence. It was Brizzi's job to act as "case worker," taking care of all of the requests and problems of constituents. Miss Myers, as she put it, "did everything else."[12]

Kefauver commanded an incredible loyalty from this trio. They worked long, hard hours, including weekends and holidays. Kefauver almost always dropped into his office for a while on Saturdays and Sundays to dictate leftover correspondence or clean up a few matters and almost always found one or more members of his staff there to do things for him.

Kefauver's staff believed wholeheartedly in his personal and political greatness, but the kind of devotion that led them to sacrifice much of their own personal time for him was generated largely by his rare consideration of them as people. Once Mrs. O'Donaghue bought airplane tickets for Kefauver and then absent-mindedly went off to lunch with Miss Myers, the tickets still in her purse. When the two women returned to the office, Kefauver was pacing the floor, his lips pursed in irritation.

"Henri," he said sharply, "you almost made me miss my plane." But when he reached the airport, he found a telephone booth and called back to apologize to Mrs. O'Donaghue for the tone he had used.[13]

In another such incident that endeared him to his staff, Brizzi came under fire from William Franklin McWhorter, Kefauver's primary opponent in 1946, who charged that Kefauver "couldn't even get a good Tennessee boy for his office, so he got a slick-talking New York pink." Brizzi went to Kefauver in tears and offered to re-

12. Personal conversation, Lucile Myers, Washington, Spring 1955.
13. Personal conversation, Henrietta O'Donaghue, Washington, Spring 1955.

sign, but Kefauver made him sit down and gave him a fatherly thirty-minute talk to the effect that "some folks can be awfully mean in a political campaign."[14]

After Kefauver's reelection to a second full term in 1942, he offered to take Harry Mansfield, the sixteen-year-old "little buddy" of his 1938 state Senate race, to Washington with him as a page or in some similar capacity. Harry was all for it, but his mother's decision was that he should finish high school. Harry never did join the Washington office "family" but was a recognized member of it *in absentia.*

From the first, Kefauver relied heavily on correspondence to keep himself in the thoughts of his constituents, eventually gaining a reputation as the most prolific letter writer in the House except Clare Boothe Luce of Connecticut. His habit of writing a letter on almost any excuse inevitably backfired occasionally. Once he wrote a note to Judge Sue K. Hicks of Madisonville to tell him how many people "said what a fine judge you made," sitting as a special judge in Chattanooga; but Kefauver had made up the note on the basis of an advance newspaper article—which had the date wrong. Hicks, getting the note well in advance of the actual occasion, retorted drily: "Either those people lied or you're lying to me."[15]

Kefauver augmented his correspondence with frequent visits back to Chattanooga. One of his friends there said he "campaigned every time he came home to the district—shaking hands with everybody and explaining how he stood on issues."[16]

Shortly after his election to his first full term in 1940, the Kefauvers moved from the Wardman Park Hotel to an apartment at the Somerset House, 1801 Sixteenth Street, Northwest, where they remained for eight years. There they started their family. Married for more than five years and still childless, they began to think of adoption, when Nancy discovered she was pregnant. Their first daughter was born October 24, 1941, and christened Eleanor, after Nancy's sister.

Before the decade was over, however, Eleanor heard the currently

14. Personal conversation, Frank Brizzi, Washington, Spring 1955.
15. Anderson and Blumenthal, *The Kefauver Story,* 77; a clipping of the newspaper article and the exchange of correspondence between Kefauver and Hicks are in the Kefauver Collection.
16. Personal conversation, George McInturff, Chattanooga, Spring 1955.

popular song, *Linda*, and was so taken with it that she decided to adopt the name for herself. She refused to answer to "Eleanor" at all until at last everyone—family, friends, and newspapers—surrendered, and "Linda" she became. In later years she changed the spelling to "Lynda."

With Linda-*nee*-Eleanor came "Bobbie"—Mrs. Barbara Hill, a Negro woman who hailed originally from Charlotte, North Carolina. They employed her as a cook and boasted that she was the world's best, never dismayed by squads of unexpected visitors. She was much more than cook; it was her own boast that she raised the three oldest Kefauver children. With her presence and baby Eleanor's, to say nothing of a pair of cocker spaniels, the Somerset House apartment became slightly overpopulated, so Kefauver rented an adjoining apartment to expand their living space.

It appeared for a time that Eleanor would be an only child, and when she was four years old the Kefauvers adoped a blond, six-weeks-old boy from The Cradle in Evanston, Illinois, and named him David Estes. As so often happens in such cases, they had not had David very long before Nancy found she was to be a mother again, and the third of their eventually four children, Diane Carey, was born December 19, 1947.[17]

Early in Kefauver's career in the House, they gave up Mooneen, their rented, balconied home in Chattanooga, and on visits back home they would move in, bag and baggage, children and dogs (and sometimes Bobbie), with Mr. and Mrs. Porter Warner Jr. on Lookout Mountain. On such visits, the Kefauvers got the upstairs and the Warners—with three children of their own, a dog and a servant—retained the downstairs. The resultant coziness appalled Nancy's aunt, Mrs. John Hutcheson, who commented, "I don't think that many people and dogs can live in that small a house, decently."[18]

Kefauver kept his partnership in the Chattanooga law firm of Sizer, Chambliss & Kefauver for several years, then entered nominally into a Chattanooga law partnership with Ben Duggan.

In his races for reelection, Kefauver always had at least nominal opposition but was never in serious trouble. His opponents were

17. Personal conversations, Nancy Kefauver, Washington, Spring 1955, and Lucile Myers, Washington, May 14, 1970.
18. Personal conversation, Porter Warner Jr., Chattanooga, Spring 1955.

hard put to find a real issue against him. They could come up only with such things as his opposition to an extension of the Hatch Act to local government employes in 1940 and a charge that Kefauver had used non-union engravers for certificates of congratulation to high school graduates in the district. As the *Chattanooga Times* commented in response to a charge by an independent candidate, Walter Forstner, in 1944 that Kefauver had urged constituents to join the "One Thousand Club" sponsored by the Democratic National Committee: "The people of this district know a good congressman when they see one." [19]

There were changes in the organized political structure in Hamilton County during Kefauver's House tenure. Judge Will Cummings turned the tables on the rebellious Wilkes Thrasher in 1940 by embracing the county governmental reformers and defeated Thrasher's slate of legislative candidates with a quartet who put through the 1941 General Assembly the reforms for which Kefauver and The Volunteers had worked. Thrasher was legislated out of office, and Cummings became the first chairman of the new County Council.

Cummings had ousted Thrasher, however, through a temporary alliance with an old rival, Wiley Couch, a tobacco merchant who had served three terms as county trustee. Couch also was a member of the new County Council, and in 1942 through a slight shift in the political orientation of City Hall, Couch defeated Cummings for county judge. Cummings retained control of the Hamilton County election machinery, however, and Kefauver at first was in the happy position of commanding the support of both struggling factions because neither wanted to offend him and his strong labor and popular support. By 1946, however, with reelection time approaching, Couch had solidified his control, and Kefauver was drawn into a threatening situation. [20]

In the 1945 Tennessee legislature, Burch Biggs, political "boss" of Polk County, engineered legislation transferring McMinn and Monroe counties from the Second Congressional District into Kefauver's Third District. Kefauver did not instigate the transfer, but

19. *Nashville Tennessean*, Oct. 27, 1944; *Chattanooga Times*, Nov. 8, 1944.
20. Hixson, *The Age of Will Cummings*; personal and telephone conversations with George McInturff, Chattanooga, Spring 1955, and Stanton Smith, Nashville, Spring 1955, and Washington, Spring 1971.

he encouraged it because it would give the homefolks in Monroe County a chance to vote for him. Couch opposed the transfer because a coalition between Biggs and the tightly organized McMinn County political machine dominated by House Speaker George Woods would set up a counterforce against his Hamilton County organization. As he began to exhibit a marked coolness toward Kefauver, reports circulated that he might support Frank Darwin, a popular appeals court judge, against Kefauver in the 1946 primary.

The situation was so perilous that Phil Whitaker, one of Kefauver's long-time friends in Chattanooga, wrote him: "You are facing a situation, Estes, where you will be forced to make a choice between two factions in this district. There is now open rivalry between Biggs and Judge Couch. You are not going to be able to retain the support of both. . . . Your real friends are in the Couch organization. Biggs' first loyalty is to the McKellar-Crump organization."[21]

Instead of heeding Whitaker's warning, Kefauver involved himself in the 1946 U.S. Senate race. Senator Kenneth McKellar was opposed by Edward W. (Ned) Carmack of Murfreesboro, who represented an anti-Crump faction of the state's Democratic party. Kefauver openly supported Carmack, offending Biggs and further irritating Couch; as both, despite their mutual enmity, favored McKellar. Newspaper reports appeared to the effect that the Biggs-Crump-McKellar organization in the district and the Couch organization would combine in a "purge Kefauver" drive.[22] Three of Kefauver's friends—Lee Allen, who had become Couch's secretary and was state president of the Young Democratic Clubs, George McInturff, and Virgil Ferguson—went to Couch to ask him about the reports.

"I'm going to beat the hell out of him," said the cigar-chewing Couch. The three urged him to talk things over, but Couch replied testily: "I never can find him. He's always speaking in New York or Chicago or somewhere. I'll talk to him tomorrow afternoon at the Read House. He'll have to be there, though. I'm not going to wait for him."

McInturff put in a hurry call to Kefauver in Washington and with some difficulty persuaded him to fly down. Allen and McInturff

21. Letter, Phil Whitaker, Chattanooga, to Estes Kefauver, June 27, 1945, Kefauver Collection, Ser. 5-c, Box 1.
22. *Nashville Tennessean*, May 2, 5, and 8, 1946.

met Kefauver at the airport the next afternoon and rushed him to the hotel, arriving a few minutes before Ferguson got there with Couch. Kefauver unfolded himself from the lobby sofa and ambled over to meet Couch with a big smile, holding out his hand.

"Hi, Wiley," Kefauver greeted him. "How's Mabel [Couch's wife]?"

"You don't give a damn how Mabel is," retorted Couch. But they sat down and talked seriously together for an hour and a half, and left the hotel with their arms around each other's shoulders.[23]

The "purge Kefauver" talk did not die down right away. Judge Darwin did not run, but Couch got into a public argument with County Auditor R.G. Allison about Allison's denunciation of the campaign tactics of the man who did run, William F. (Pup) Mc-Whorter, a road machinery salesman, who charged Kefauver with being "tied to . . . the un-American Political Action Committee." Biggs's Polk County organization pledged support to Kefauver in mid-May, and Ed Crump endorsed Kefauver in an apparent maneuver to turn the district power struggle to the advantage of his ally, Biggs. Couch supported McKellar and remained coy to Kefauver.

Again Kefauver and Couch got together to patch things up, this time at the Home Plate Restaurant in downtown Chattanooga,[24] and the "purge Kefauver" rumor was laid to rest at last when Couch was among those signing Kefauver's qualifying petition.[25] Kefauver swamped McWhorter by nearly 7-to-1.

For several years Kefauver had been thinking about running for the U.S. Senate. He had built up some political ties elsewhere in the state, not only with his 1946 support of Carmack but two years earlier when he had no primary opposition. In the 1944 presidential election year, he spent much of his time going around the country helping the Democratic Party with state organization work and fund drives and making Jefferson-Jackson Day speeches. He was a delegate to the Democratic National Convention and made the nominating speech for his friend, Governor Prentice Cooper, whom the Tennessee delegation supported to the end for Vice President.

Against his loss of House seniority and his assurance of effective

23. Personal conversation, George McInturff, Chattanooga, Spring 1955.
24. Telephone conversation, Stanton Smith, Washington, Spring 1971.
25. *Nashville Tennessean*, May 19, 23, and 26, 1946.

support in his home district, the Senate would offer a stronger power base from which to work toward realization of his legislative objectives, and especially to counter McKellar's persistent attacks on TVA. There were strong personal considerations, too: he did not want his children to be reared in an apartment, but he was reluctant to buy a house when he had to face the risk of being retired from Congress every two years.[26]

He seriously considered running against the seventy-seven-year-old McKellar in 1946 and wrote a good many friends all over Tennessee, asking their assessment of his chances. Some were highly sanguine, among them Charles G. Neese of Paris, who would become his campaign manager in 1948. Neese wrote him letter after long letter picturing his potential strength in West Tennessee in glowing terms.

Most, however, were dubious. His Uncle Noah—N.H. Grady of Chattanooga—warned, "an old senator and his banker, old King Edcrump I, is a mighty strong combination, and if they beat you, it would put a mighty crimp in your political prospects for the future." His former secretary, Mrs. William H. Duggan of Nashville (Lucille Schilling), commented that he might stand a better chance against the other senator, Tom Stewart, since Stewart was from the eastern half of the state and people might object to having both senators from that section.[27]

Former Representative Herron Pearson of Jackson expressed the view that it was not "the time to make the race," and Silliman Evans, publisher of the *Nashville Tennessean* and one of the state's most astute political figures, wrote: "Reports and judgments continue to be very discouraging, so much so that I think I should tell you that I think it will be almost futile, and I do not think you would serve yourself properly if you decided to undertake the race."[28]

Kefauver deferred at last to Carmack, with the tacit understanding that Carmack would defer similarly to him if he decided to run against Stewart in 1948. His subsequent work for Carmack, so em-

26. Personal conversation, Estes Kefauver, Washington, Spring 1955.
27. Letters, Noah H. Grady, Chattanooga, to Estes Kefauver, Oct. 27, 1945, and Mrs. William Duggan, Nashville, to Estes Kefauver, Jan. 25, 1946. Kefauver Collection, Ser. 5-c, Box 1.
28. Letters, Herron C. Pearson, Jackson, Tenn., to Estes Kefauver, Jan. 29,

barrassing to him in his own district, improved his acquaintance with the network of Carmack supporters throughout Tennessee, the nearest thing in the state to a formal anti-Crump political organization.

Developments in Kefauver's district a few months after his 1946 reelection confirmed his decision to try for the Senate in 1948. Wiley Couch died in April 1947, and, honoring his deathbed request, the County Court elected Wilkes Thrasher his successor as county judge. Thrasher was not a personal enemy of Kefauver, and Kefauver had no reason to believe that he could not get along with Thrasher, but Will Cummings still commanded a good deal of influence; a struggle for power broke over the disintegrating fragments of the Couch organization. There was always a good chance that one faction or another might see some advantage in putting forth a candidate against Kefauver in 1948, or later.

Running against Stewart was not so formidable a prospect as running against McKellar, but it was challenging enough. Stewart, who had been the district attorney in the Scopes trial at Dayton during Kefauver's collegiate days, had been in the Senate since 1938. He followed McKellar's lead faithfully on most issues and thus was not looked on as a "strong" senator, but by the same token he was not a controversial figure and was well liked throughout the state. At the time Kefauver announced publicly for the Senate late in 1947, all indications were that Stewart would retain the support of Ed Crump and his allies, which he had had in previous races.

Kefauver began rounding up support for his campaign soon after beginning his 1947 House term and announced to his family on a visit to Madisonville that he had decided to run. His mother was placidly optimistic.

"Well, Estes," she said, "you've overcome many obstacles before. I think you can surmount this one, too."

But Cooke Kefauver was against it, as he had been against his son's first House race. His argument was that Kefauver was established solidly as a representative and could be reelected as long as he wished to stay in the House.

1946, and Silliman Evans, Nashville, to Estes Kefauver, Jan. 11, 1946. Kefauver Collection, Ser. 5-c, Box 1.

"Popsy, I've served long enough in the House," replied Kefauver. "I can't keep on living in an apartment and running for reelection every two years. My family deserves a normal life, in a home of their own. I'm going to the Senate, or I'm going back to practicing law." [29]

29. Personal conversation, Cooke Kefauver, Madisonville, Tenn., Spring 1955.

PART II

The Greatest Campaigner of Them All

—Lyndon B. Johnson, 1956

Chapter 8

I'm Not Mr. Crump's Pet Coon

The coterie that accompanied Estes and Nancy Kefauver into the big dining room of the Peabody Hotel in Memphis June 25, 1948, was rather solemn. Kefauver's first campaign invasion of the Mississippi River city meant a serious commitment for those supporters who greeted him publicly.

Edward Hull Crump, undisputed political boss of Memphis and for many years the dominant political figure in the entire state, was vituperatively opposed to Kefauver's candidacy for the U.S. Senate. And Mr. Crump had been known in the past to invoke severe political and economic sanctions against those who dared oppose his will in his own bailiwick.

The congressman and his auburn-haired wife were less somber as they entered the dining room, packed with hundreds of people defying Mr. Crump's stated preference with varying degrees of trepidation. Kefauver, towering over everyone and ambling along unhurriedly, had a V-shaped smile and a handshake for everyone he met on the way. Nancy was sparkling, with a mischievous twinkle to her eye under her wide-brimmed straw hat. In addition to her purse, she carried a paper sack that bulged and wrinkled with some soft, bulky content.

Curious eyes were on the Kefauvers as they took their seats at the speakers' table. This was the man who Crump had said, two weeks earlier, "reminds me of the pet coon that puts its foot in an open drawer in your room, but invariably turns its head while its foot is feeling around in the drawer. The coon hopes, through its cunning by turning its head, he will deceive any onlookers as to where his foot is and what it is into."

Edmund Orgill, square-faced former president of the Memphis Chamber of Commerce, who had taken the job of chairman of Kefauver's Shelby County campaign committee, introduced Kefauver. Kefauver pushed his chair back and arose. Tall, sober-faced now, he looked around slowly on his equally sober-faced audience. Silently, he leaned over to reach under the table, and Nancy, sitting next to him, handed him an item from the paper sack. Kefauver straightened and in the same movement put the furry thing atop his head.

It was a coonskin cap.

A multiple gasp broke from the audience, then a roar of laughter. Nancy was convulsed with mirth. A big smile spread over Kefauver's face. Without mentioning the Memphis boss's name, he had answered Crump in his own terms.[1]

The donning of the coonskin cap was the dramatic high point of a campaign that began with a minimum of public awareness or interest. Most of the state's experienced politicians either had ties with Crump or were interested primarily in helping Gordon Browning, the former governor, who was making another try for the governorship in 1948. Excitement over Browning's challenge to Crump, who was supporting the incumbent governor, Jim McCord, for reelection, far overshadowed Kefauver's modest emergence from southeastern Tennessee with senatorial ambitions.

For his state campaign manager, Kefauver chose Charles Neese, not an experienced politician but with a little practice at the game. Kefauver met Neese in 1938, when Neese was resident secretary in Jackson, Tennessee, for U.S. Representative Herron Pearson, and they exchanged occasional letters thereafter. Later Neese was secretary to Governor Prentice Cooper for a time before entering World War II military service.

When Neese returned from the wars Christmas Eve, 1945, one of the first things he saw was a story in the *Commercial Appeal*, the Memphis morning newspaper, speculating on a race between Kefauver and McKellar. He wrote Kefauver to offer his services, and followed the offer with a series of glowingly optimistic letters. According to Neese, however, the optimism of the letters was not un-

1. The description of the Memphis banquet and the donning of the coonskin cap is based primarily on a conversation with Nancy Kefauver in Washington in the spring of 1955. I also discussed the incident in a personal conversation with Estes Kefauver in Washington, a personal conversation with Charles G. Neese in Paris, Tenn., and a telephone conversation with Edmund Orgill in Memphis during the same period.

Estes Kefauver, wearing his famous coonskin cap, and his wife, Nancy, during the 1948 U.S. Senate campaign.

qualified. He said later he warned Kefauver against making the wrong race at the wrong time, and in an early 1946 meeting with Kefauver in Johnson City suggested that, if he could not be assured of the necessary support, Kefauver should wait and tackle the more vulnerable Senator Tom Stewart two years later.[2]

When Kefauver asked Neese to manage his campaign, Neese objected that Kefauver needed "a professional politician" for the job, but Kefauver had made up his mind. At last, Neese laughed and said, "Well, if you have no better sense than to walk away from a lifetime job in the House, I don't have any better sense than to manage your campaign." His "price" was that, if Kefauver lost, the pair of them would enter law practice together in Chattanooga.[3]

One of the most important political figures Kefauver got into his corner was Silliman Evans, publisher of the *Nashville Tennessean*. Evans, a short, dynamic Texan who had been a friend of Franklin D. Roosevelt, had made virtually a career of opposition to Crump since buying the bankrupt *Tennessean* in 1937, supporting candidates against both McKellar and Stewart as well as Crump's choices for governor. Evans met Kefauver through fellow-Texan Hatton Sumners, while Sumners was still chairman of the House Judiciary Committee, and marked the young congressman as a potential "comer." When Kefauver went to Evans in 1947, his decision to run for the Senate in his hand, Evans said: "The *Tennessean* will help you, on condition you make one promise. You aren't well known in the state. I want you to promise that you'll shake five hundred hands a day between now and election time."[4]

No admonition could have suited Kefauver's natural political propensities better. He promised, and the *Tennessean* was the first newspaper in the state to endorse him editorially. Kefauver assumed that Stewart would have Crump's support in his bid for reelection, as in the past. He did not know, when he announced, that Crump already had decided to drop Stewart.

Stewart had squeaked past a challenge from Carmack by less than 8 percent of the state's vote in 1942, but Crump also had more

2. Personal conversation, Charles G. Neese, Paris, Spring 1955.
3. Personal conversation, Charles G. Neese, Greeneville, Tenn., Spring 1970.
4. Personal conversation, Estes Kefauver, Washington, Spring 1955. Versions of this conversation are many; two of them are in Anderson and Blumenthal, *The Kefauver Story*, 103, and *Life*, May 28, 1956.

personal reasons for withdrawing his support. Stewart had made some undiplomatic fumbles, such as inserting an editorial by Edward J. Meeman, editor of the *Press-Scimitar* in Memphis, whom Crump cordially hated, into the *Congressional Record*, and making a West Point appointment from West Tennessee without consulting Crump. More serious, Stewart supported a bill that was interpreted as anti-Semitic by William Gerber, a hard-faced and hard-eyed Shelby County district attorney who was Crump's most trusted and feared lieutenant. Gerber persuaded Crump over a period of time that the easy-going junior senator could not win reelection.

Stewart's friends were unable to sway Crump. Governor Jim McCord even went to Memphis to try to persuade Crump to change his mind, taking with him Joe C. Carr, Tennessee secretary of state, and J. Frank Hobbs of Lawrenceburg, one of Crump's principal rural allies. All they could get from Crump was an order to find him another candidate he could suport. The reluctant trio at last came up with the name of Circuit Judge John A. Mitchell of Cookeville, even less known throughout the state than Kefauver but highly respected and a veteran of both World Wars. The Crump blessing descended upon Mitchell.[5]

It was assumed, naturally, that Stewart would accept Crump's dictum gracefully and bow out, but Stewart, after some hesitation, yielded to the urging of some of his friends and stood for reelection anyhow. Kefauver found himself in a three-way race, against a Crump-backed candidate and an incumbent who could count on the loyalties of many local politicians with only loose and fortuitous ties to Crump.

Kefauver realized he would have to do much more than conduct the customary summer stumping campaign of six weeks to two months. In the spring of 1948, he embarked on a preliminary tour to line up political support and make himself known to key people in every county of the state. Because Nancy still had the three-year-old family Chrysler in Washington, he borrowed his father's new Dodge and impressed twenty-two-year-old Harry Mansfield into service as his driver.

5. The circumstances surrounding Crump's decision to drop Stewart and his choice of Mitchell were disclosed to me in personal conversation in Nashville in the spring of 1970 by one of the participants in the Memphis conference, who asked to remain unidentified.

Kefauver and campaign officials, including Charlie Neese (left) and Harry Mansfield (second from left), compare "lucky horseshoe" campaign ties during the 1948 race for the U.S. Senate.

Kefauver plays checkers with Grover Ault at Crossville during his campaign for the U.S. Senate in 1948.

Harry had become a husky, curly-haired young man, whose deliberately cultivated deadpan expression concealed a mischievous irreverence. He called Kefauver simply "Chief" and frequently prodded at Kefauver's absent-minded imperturbability with some brash remark or other. Kefauver looked on Harry more as an adopted son than anything else and seemed unable to realize that Harry was now an adult.

For example, Kefauver, who dearly loved his Scotch, hedged against the "dry" climate of most of Tennessee by carrying a bottle in one of his suitcases. It never occurred to him that Harry might have acquired a taste for the stuff, and Harry was hard put to it to sneak a slug from Kefauver's bottle now and then. Kefauver was shocked and dismayed when Harry made up for his deprivation by getting tanked on beer while Kefauver was speaking in Crossville one evening, and when Harry was still heavy-headed at dawn the next morning, Kefauver seized him by the ankle and yanked him from bed, cover and all, onto the floor.

"If you can't take it, young man, leave it alone," Kefauver admonished sternly. "And while I'm about it, I want you to quit wearing those bow ties!"[6]

The pair criss-crossed the state for weeks, accompanied only by a single reporter, from the *Tennessean.* Kefauver talked with local leaders behind closed doors, shook hands up and down the streets, and occasionally made a speech before some local civic group. He carried a list of county officials and would check it carefully in the back seat between towns, so he could address them by their names. By the time Stewart and Mitchell were ready to begin their campaigns, Kefauver had already completed one informal statewide tour and was beginning to repeat it on a formal basis.

In the midst of this first tour, Phredonia Kefauver suffered a cerebral hemorrhage. Kefauver was telephoned by his sister, Nora, in Memphis, where he was conferring with Orgill, Meeman, and attorney Lucius E. Burch about setting up a campaign committee. He

---

6. Personal observation. I was the reporter from the *Nashville Tennessean*, the third member of the pre-campaign trio, and witnessed these events except Kefauver's yanking Harry from bed. He and Harry shared a room, and I had a different room at a motel in Jamestown, Tenn., that night. Harry related to me what happened the next morning, while Kefauver was making contacts among the local political leaders.

flew to Knoxville and was at his mother's bedside when she died April 30, at the age of seventy-four.

Neese, meanwhile, organized the state campaign headquarters in Nashville. An important adjunct of it was a woman's campaign division, an innovation in Tennessee politics, and Kefauver chose Mrs. Martha Ragland of Chattanooga to head it.

Martha Ragland was a quietly vivacious young woman of strongly liberal bent who had moved to Chattanooga with her husband, Tom, president of a mill, about the time Kefauver entered Congress. Impressed by his record, she was surprised to find that some of his friends considered him "just a country boy . . . not too smart," and when she met him later she offered to help him if he ever ran for the Senate. She had not expected her offer to be accepted in such extensive terms, but during the campaign she wrote a total of some 20,000 letters urging support for Kefauver.[7]

A public opinion poll Kefauver had taken in the state early in 1948—which showed Stewart far ahead with 37 percent to Mitchell's 21 percent and Kefauver's 13 percent—disclosed that world peace was the principal concern of the voters, with the Crump issue much less prominent than many of Kefauver's supporters believed.[8] Neese coined the campaign slogan: "Peace and TVA." In addition to the formal campaign organization, dominated by Neese, there was a semi-official, semi-independent group of people working in and out of the state headquarters. Some of these did not like Neese at all, and some of them worked behind the scenes for various reasons, bypassing state headquarters and maintaining direct contact with Kefauver. Some, for example, held federal jobs and could take no chances with the Hatch Act. Joe Bean, who had become a Kefauver admirer after defeating him for the state Senate, now lived in Winchester, in Stewart's home county, and had to work under cover for Kefauver lest he offend clients ardently loyal to the incumbent senator.

A great deal of informal campaigning and information-gathering was done by people at all economic and social levels whom Kefauver met on his first statewide swing—the "rag-tag, bobtail boys," as one of them, Henry Bullard of Livingston, called them. Kefauver

7. Personal conversation, Martha Ragland, Nashville, Spring 1970.
8. Kefauver, "The Best Advice I Ever Had."

opened his formal campaign Saturday, June 5, with a speech from the steps of the old brick courthouse in Madisonville. From beneath the tower clocks, he told a crowd gathered from all over his congressional district:

"My course of action as a friend of the common man has gained for me much abuse. Some have hinted that I am a Communist. . . . If to believe in the right of every man to the good life, to the utmost liberty and to the most complete happiness is to be a radical, then I expect the description fits most of us."[9]

Nancy drove the family Chrysler from Washington to attend the opening speech and to join the campaign entourage, leaving the children with her sister, Eleanor McQuiddy, in Chattanooga. The caravan subsequently also included Mansfield, Lucile Myers, and Henrietta O'Donaghue alternating as secretaries, a changing group of volunteer workers and always one or more newspaper reporters. Both the maroon Chrysler and the blue Dodge had been fitted out with loudspeakers, and Kefauver would speak over one car's amplifying system while the other automobile went ahead to the next scheduled stop to advertise his coming.

The campaign immediately provided one of those mix-ups that were to provide a growing grab-bag of amusing stories in Kefauver campaigns from then on. The tape recording of the opening speech, to be used for a statewide radio broadcast the next week, was no good, but Kefauver did not learn about this until two days later when he was campaigning in Tracy City, a coal mining town northwest of Chattanooga. He and his two companions in the Dodge interrupted the campaign tour to race into Chattanooga and rerecord the opening speech in the radio station studio, the three of them providing the applause at appropriate points.

Before Kefauver announced, Meeman had advised him not to attack the Crump political dictatorship, "but if Crump fights you, as I think he will, fight back."[10] Neese was in accord with this philosophy, largely because he thought Crump was more interested in turning back Gordon Browning's challenge in the governor's race and might let Kefauver alone if Kefauver did not bait him publicly. With a few minor lapses, Kefauver accepted this approach to the

9. *Nashville Tennessean*, June 6, 1948.
10. Swados, *Standing Up for the People*, 37.

Crump issue, but Neese also wanted Kefauver to ignore his two opponents, Stewart and Mitchell, and talk only on issues. This was a little too much for Kefauver, who had a strong instinct for taking a fight to his adversary.[11]

Neese would send Kefauver his major campaign speech for each day, and Kefauver would purse his lips and frown slightly as he looked over these speeches, to find them comprised totally of what Nancy called "sweetness and light." Kefauver got around this by accepting for incorporation a few paragraphs almost daily, written for him by one or more of the newsmen with the caravan. These usually involved verbal pot-shots at Stewart for supporting McKellar's feud with TVA and at Mitchell for his lack of political independence (that is, though unstated, for being a "Crump man"). Their appearance in the newspapers occasioned some dismay at state campaign headquarters but were more interesting "copy" to the readers than a steady diet of "peace and TVA."

This peculiar situation prevailed throughout the first two or three weeks, spent in southeastern and central Tennessee. Then, after a swing through Nashville, Kefauver kicked off an invasion of West Tennessee—considered strong Stewart territory—with an evening radio speech in Clarksville, home of W.D. (Pete) Hudson, Stewart's state campaign manager—the same Pete Hudson who had opposed Kefauver's tax program in the 1939 legislature as a member of the state Railroad and Public Utilities Commission.

Neese had been working on the speech in Nashville, and it still had not arrived when Kefauver got to Station WJCM about twenty minutes before going on the air. He got a newsman with him to type a few pages for him hurriedly—and every sentence lambasted Stewart thoroughly. Neese's text arrived just as Kefauver went on the air, but Kefauver used the improvised material first and then went into the Neese text—with just a moment's surprised pause, for Neese, too, had devoted the first half of his speech to an eloquent blast against Stewart. By the time "peace and TVA" came up in the speech, Kefauver's radio time was up. Kefauver leaned back in his chair, shuffled the pages of his hybrid speech with a thought-

11. Personal conversation, Charles G. Neese, Greeneville, Spring 1970; personal observation and conversations with Estes Kefauver during the early weeks of the 1948 campaign.

ful frown, then grinned happily and delivered his judgment: "We sure gave him hell that time, didn't we?"[12]

From that time on, Kefauver's speeches were hardly dull because Crump had entered the fight. The Memphis "Red Snapper's" open wrath was aroused by a hitherto unheard-of defection in his own political back yard. He learned that Kefauver was conspiring with Meeman to persuade a group of prominent Memphis citizens to announce public support for Kefauver. On the day the announcement was scheduled, June 10, a full-page advertisement, signed by E.H. Crump, appeared in every major newspaper in Tennessee, proclaiming in bold, black type: "ESTES KEFAUVER ASSUMES THE ROLE OF A PET COON." Crump charged that Kefauver had been "a darling of the Communists and Communist sympathizers" ever since his entry into Congress. He cited Kefauver votes against continuance of the House Un-American Activities Committee, called him a "warm supporter" of the Fair Employment Practices Commission, criticized Kefauver's opposition to the filibuster, and said Kefauver's slogan was "America Last."[13]

It was a familiar Crump tactic, and it very nearly worked. There was some hasty discussion and soul-searching among Kefauver's Memphis supporters, but they held their ground and followed Crump's ad on the same day with an announcement that they had formed a committee to help Kefauver, whom they called "a statesman of national stature."

Orgill, a hardware and implement wholesaler, was chairman of the committee. It also included Kefauver's old friend, Charles Poe; Lucius Burch; Dr. Henry B. Gotten, a physician; Ed Dalstrom, a wholesale paper executive; and William M. Barr, a paint specialties manufacturer. Unscarred by previous political activity, all were so prominent in Memphis that, united, they constituted a respectable counterforce to Crump's reputation.

Neese did some hurried research on Crump's past political opponents, and Kefauver responded promptly to the Crump blast: "I am not going to take orders from Mr. Crump or any other dictator, wherever he may be." He noted that, of forty-five political opponents of Crump in the past, "every one of them has been a Com-

12. Personal observation. I was in the studio with Kefauver at the time and wrote his improvised text before the arrival of the Neese text.
13. *Nashville Tennessean*, June 10, 1948.

munist, a Fascist, a blackguard or a thief, according to Mr. Crump. No one ever runs for office against him without being called at least one of these things." Kefauver also challenged Crump to a debate. This was a campaign tactic of considerable publicity value. He already had challenged his two opponents to debate, singly or together, without response.

The headquarters people pounced joyfully on the "coon" issue. They adopted the raccoon as a mascot, and Kefauver supporters sent half a dozen or more live coons to the headquarters. In Kefauver's speeches began to appear such phrases as "a coon has rings around its tail, but this is one coon that will never have a ring through its nose."

Then one day George Clarke, an official of Chattanooga's Pioneer Bank, sent in a coonskin cap, given him by a Mississippi River boatman. The cap was a trademark of the bank, next door to Kefauver's old law office. When Kefauver passed through Nashville shortly thereafter and saw the cap, he wanted to don it for campaigning at once. Most of his advisers were horrified: it would be too undignified. But Neese exacted a promise from Kefauver not to put the thing on until he gave the word.[14]

About a week later came the Memphis visit, the Peabody Hotel luncheon, and the mock-solemn donning of the coonskin cap. After that, Kefauver always—usually by request—donned the coonskin cap at some point during each campaign speech (he never could pronounce the words correctly, and invariably called it a "skoonskin cap"). The next week on the campaign trail, he had a new phrase in most of his speeches: "I may be a pet coon, but I'm not Mr. Crump's pet coon."[15]

The coon ad and the cap caught the public imagination and solved in a short time a problem that Kefauver had not been able to overcome with all his statewide touring, both formal and extracurricular: the disadvantage of being a virtual unknown outside his own congressional district.

Crump's candidate, Mitchell, was not doing too well. A tall, thin man, he was accustomed to the bench and was stilted and stiff in

14. Personal conversation, Charles G. Neese, Paris, Spring 1955.
15. Neese's recollection that these were Kefauver's first words after donning the coonskin cap in Memphis is cited by Joseph Bruce Gorman, *Kefauver: a Political Biography* (New York: Oxford Univ. Press, 1971), 52, from a Neese letter to

both speeches and personal contacts. Stewart was not a particularly good stump speaker, either, but he had an easy affability and was well-known. Crump believed at first that Kefauver and Stewart would split the anti-Crump vote, which he recognized to be strong, letting Mitchell slide in to victory between them. But, as time went on, rumors began to be heard that Crump would drop Mitchell and swing his support back to Stewart. Crump very nearly did. He quietly telephoned Frank Hobbs to ask him if he could persuade Mitchell to withdraw from the race. To this Hobbs replied, with considerable courage, "I think you ought to be the one to do that, Mr. Crump, if anyone does." Instead, Crump talked the campaign situation over with Mitchell in a friendly, well-publicized meeting in Memphis, and the rumors died down.[16]

Kefauver was concerned about the rumors, recognizing that Stewart was the stronger of his two opponents and probably could win with Crump backing if Mitchell dropped out. Stewart was refraining carefully from saying anything about Crump, perhaps in the hope that just something like that would happen, and Kefauver repeatedly attempted to egg him into a repudiation of Crump. Stewart used no amplifying equipment, confining himself to handshaking and informal talks with small groups, and once Kefauver offered to let Stewart use his loudspeaker facilities "whenever he wants to say anything against Mr. Crump."

A day or two afterward, Kefauver suggested publicly that Crump might be planning to switch to Stewart at the last minute. Crump snapped back that "Kefauver knows that we never switched, never deserted any political candidate in our political history." Kefauver promptly cited a case in which Crump had done just that, in the 1930 U.S. Senate race. Such exchanges had the effect of making it impossible for Crump to drop Mitchell without losing considerable face.

Kefauver made the most of his opponents' failure to respond to his invitations to debate, and on several occasions when his campaign trail crossed one of theirs, he tried to trap them into facing

---

Lucile Myers in 1969. Neese was not present at the Memphis dinner, however; although I was not either, I know the recollection to be inaccurate. I coined the phrase for Kefauver on the campaign trail in West Tennessee the following week.

16. Personal conversation, Nashville, Spring 1970, with the source cited in note 5, above.

him on the same platform. Stewart was very nearly caught at the Houston County courthouse in Erin once, when Kefauver raced down from nearby Dover to arrive just as Stewart finished a short talk, but Stewart managed to break free from Kefauver's engulfing handshake and half ran across the wide dirt street to his car to make his escape. Mitchell similarly was almost caught in Pulaski and, with the courage of inexperience and conviction, would have confronted Kefauver, but the "pros" who ran his campaign hustled him so far out into the rural areas that for a while the judge was campaigning inadvertently in Alabama.[17]

These well-publicized evasions climaxed in Kefauver's solo "debate" in Memphis early in July. The Memphis League of Women Voters invited all three candidates to debate the issues of the campaign, but Stewart and Mitchell failed to show. Kefauver "debated" two empty chairs.

The general pattern of Kefauver's road tour started him out in southeastern Tennessee, where he was known; carried him up through Middle Tennessee, where there was extensive anti-Crump sentiment; and concentrated the heaviest mid-campaign work in West Tennessee, which was strong Stewart country outside of Memphis and Shelby County. In West Tennessee particularly, Kefauver was just a name that most people had never heard before he announced. There he made his most exhaustive effort at personal contact with as many people as possible.

The daily schedule called for as many as twenty-two stops at the scattered towns and villages, with brief speeches at most of them, and he sometimes interspersed unscheduled speeches or handshaking swings at a country crossroads or two where a few live voters were visible, much as his father had campaigned Monroe County for Wilson. Consequently, he always ran farther and farther behind schedule as a day waned because he refused to hurry, and none of his campaign party could drag him away from a place as long as a hand remained unshaken. They often lunched on crackers and cheese, purchased at some roadside store, in the cars en route from town to town.

Nancy's presence on the tour was a considerable asset. Tennes-

17. Personal observation. I was covering Kefauver's campaign and drove him from Dover to Erin in a wild ride to catch Stewart, and I was covering Mitchell's campaign when their paths crossed in Pulaski.

seans were not accustomed to seeing candidates' wives participating in the grueling campaign grind, and the fact that she was with her husband brought many women out to hear him. Usually she just greeted people with him, but occasionally she addressed a women's group or attended a "coffee." There was a good deal of curiosity about the congressman's red-headed Scottish wife, and Nancy's natural charm turned her meetings with the voters to good account for him.

The campaign ended with a torchlight parade through downtown Nashville and a rally at the city's Public Square, followed by a similar rally at the Read House in Chattanooga the next night. On election day, the Kefauvers voted at Lookout Mountain and flew by chartered plane to Memphis, where he had made it known he had asked the FBI to keep an eye out for any balloting irregularities. The Kefauvers arrived in the city festooned with Mitchell and McCord campaign banners and posters and visited a dozen polling places, including Crump's home precinct, to shake hands with voters. Then they flew to Nashville to await election returns at state headquarters.

The general feeling among political wiseacres on election day was that Kefauver's industrious and aggressive campaigning, coupled with Browning's vigorous anti-Crump tactics in the governor's race, had killed Mitchell's chances effectively, but that Stewart probably would reap enough of the benefit to win renomination. Such a feeling was not entirely absent from the Kefauver camp: Harry Clifton, one of his headquarters aides, was startled to find a secretary running off mimeographed statements conceding the race, prepared by Neese, just in case. Clifton angrily halted the mimeographing.[18]

But the expected lead that Kefauver picked up in early-reporting East Tennessee (on Eastern Standard Time) was not wiped out when the Middle and West Tennessee returns came in. Kefauver went into Shelby County 17,000 votes ahead of Stewart, and there Crump's decision to back Mitchell wrote the result. Kefauver's bold invasions of Memphis and the work of his Memphis committee broke Crump's traditional "Shelby County bloc": Mitchell carried the county with 37,771 votes, but Kefauver got 27,621 there and Stewart only 2,733.

18. Personal conversation, Harry Clifton, Nashville, Spring 1970.

Kefauver was the Democratic nominee with about 42 percent of the statewide vote—171,791 votes to 129,873 for Stewart and 96,192 for Mitchell. At the same time, Browning swept to a substantial victory over McCord in the governor's race. The long dominance of E.H. Crump in Tennessee politics was shattered.

During most of the era of Crump dominance, there existed a gentlemen's agreement that kept the Republicans of upper East Tennessee out of serious participation in statewide races. *Time* magazine quoted Kefauver's description of the situation: "East Tennessee is predominantly Republican, but the Republican organization there, headed by former GOP chairman B. Carroll Reece, has long played 'footsie' with the Crump crowd. It was a neat trade: the Crump boys simply refrained from offering Democratic opposition in county races there, insuring the GOP local control. In return, Republicans voted in the Democratic primary for the Crump statewide slate."[19]

But in 1948 the Democratic nominees for governor and senator were anti-Crump men, and Kefauver, moreover, was a minority primary winner. The Republicans were encouraged to put forth a slate against them: Reece against Kefauver and hillbilly singer Roy Acuff against Browning. The Republican candidates campaigned intensively. Reece traveled in a long black Cadillac, and Acuff drew crowds to a preliminary songfest at each stop with his Smoky Mountain Boys. Acuff would speak a few simple words after the songs, but when Reece got up to follow him with his campaign talk, most of the crowd usually wandered away.

After a rest, Kefauver hit the campaign trail again, sans coonskin cap and Nancy. Nancy drove to Washington with the three children to enter Linda in the first grade, returning later to join her husband for the last weeks of campaigning.

Reece pitched his campaign on the earlier Crump theme, that Kefauver was "soft" on Communism. Kefauver charged that Reece, who had served in Congress for twenty-six years before becoming GOP national chairman, had opposed the TVA and supported a civil rights program. But the basic issue, Kefauver said, was: "I believe in a policy of government that places human values above material

19. Estes Kefauver, undated manuscript, "How I Beat the Crump Machine," Kefauver Collection, Ser. 1, Box 73.

values. . . . My opponent, on the other hand, has always been on the side of the big monopoly interests."[20]

Kefauver's Democratic House colleagues in the state, who had remained carefully neutral in the primary, and campaign managers of both Stewart and Mitchell backed him enthusiastically against Reece. During this campaign, Representative Albert Gore pulled a memorable switch on Shakespeare while addresing a small audience of Sumner County farmers and businessmen with the Kefauver entourage.

Gore, handsome and wavy-haired at forty, had wound up to a fine oratorical frenzy over slurs on Kefauver's Americanism. He rose to an eloquent peak: "He who steals my *good name* steals trash. . . ." Gore's wife, Pauline, lifted clasped hands in the front row, whispering fervently, "Oh no, Albert! That's not it, Albert!" But Gore finished relentlessly and obliviously: ". . . but he who steals my purse steals that which enriches him not, but makes me poor indeed!"[21]

It was the sort of thing Kefauver himself might do—and did. Once in a later campaign, he started off full of oratorical confidence, "As Shakespeare said . . ." and ended with a crippled quotation that even Kefauver recognized as totally wrong. He stopped and appealed to his audience with a self-deprecating smile: "Well . . . that's not exactly what Shakespeare said . . . but it's what he meant to say."[22]

If the Republicans expected Crump to help them quietly in the general election, they were disappointed. Kefauver was elected senator by 326,142 votes to Reece's 166,947, while Browning defeated Acuff by a 2-to-1 margin.

So ended the longest and most fatiguing campaign in Tennessee's recent history. Kefauver had criss-crossed the state from end to end several times by automobile and two or three more times by plane, making several speeches almost every day and shaking hundreds of

20. *Nashville Tennessean*, Oct. 10, 1948.
21. Personal observation. I was covering Kefauver's campaign and was present during Gore's talk. Estes and Nancy Kefauver noticed the error, Kefauver pursing his lips and Nancy struggling to control her mirth, but most of the audience, at the Sumner County Courthouse in Gallatin, Tenn., appeared unaware of the transposition.
22. Martin, "The Mystery of Kefauver."

hands. He came through the grind little the worse for wear—just ten or twelve pounds lighter—but Nancy was nearly exhausted, as were the aides who accompanied him. The old Chrysler was done in, too: at the end of the campaign, it caught fire from an overheated engine and burned to a hulk.

"I've got to find some time this week to get in some shopping," said Kefauver when he returned to Washington. "The campaign wore out every suit and pair of shoes I own."[23]

When Senator Kenneth McKellar was born, President Ulysses S. Grant had not taken office yet. Tennessee's senior senator was eighty-two years old, but age had not dulled his tongue late in 1951 when he and his junior colleague, Estes Kefauver, aired a slight disagreement on the Senate floor over the terms of a bill to give Tennessee a fourth federal judgeship. It was McKellar's bill, but the Judiciary Committee had recommended Kefauver's amendment to make it a "roving judgeship" between Middle and West Tennessee, instead of confining it to Middle Tennessee.

"What single person," demanded McKellar, shaking his full mane angrily, "ever wrote to the Senator in favor of having a roving judge for West Tennessee, until after . . . he had written quite a number of letters to people in West Tennessee, asking them to support him in his roving judge idea?"

"In the first place, I have not written any number of letters asking for such support," said Kefauver austerely, beginning to turn pink at the back of his neck.

Kefauver had the floor, but after a moment, McKellar broke in again: "I rise to say that the Bar Association of Memphis. . . ."

"Does the Senator from Tennessee yield for a question?" interrupted the presiding officer.

"I do not yield for a question," answered Kefauver shortly.

"The Bar Association of Memphis," went on McKellar, unheeding, "was appealed to by the Senator and it refused to endorse his project."

"Mr. President, I do not yield," protested Kefauver.

Senator William Langer of North Dakota got to his feet.

"I should like to know," he queried, "which Senator from Ten-

---

23. *Nashville Tennessean*, Nov. 9, 1948.

nessee represents the Hatfields and which one represents the Mc-Coys?"[24]

A surface truce was patched up for a time between McKellar and Kefauver when Kefauver entered the Senate. Kefauver voted for McKellar for president *pro tem* and, in turn, McKellar observed the amenities and escorted Kefauver to the rostrum to take the oath of office; Kefauver was the seventh junior colleague to walk up the aisle on McKellar's arm during the old man's long career.

But the McKellar-Kefauver feud did not end with Kefauver's advancement to the Senate. With Kefauver instead of Stewart to deal with, McKellar abandoned his long fight to bring TVA under his political domination, but he did not forgive Kefauver for having been a key figure in balking him in that fight. Their mutual hostility flared up often in other areas.

During Kefauver's very first month as a senator, he bested Mc-Kellar in a disagreement over appointment of a U.S. marshal for Middle Tennessee, charging that Reed Sharp, the incumbent and McKellar's choice, was a "Dixiecrat." McKellar wrote Kefauver a blistering letter demanding to know if Kefauver's idea of cooperation was "that you want to do all the 'operating' and leave the 'co' to me?"[25] Later, McKellar said, he "ran him [Kefauver] out of my office with a cane"—an act entirely in character for the irascible old man.[26]

McKellar fumed over Kefauver's lack of homage for the short remainder of his Senate career. He was the Senate's most powerful individual and a member of both the body's inner circle and the Southern conservative bloc. Charlie Neese, who went to Washington as Kefauver's administrative assistant, believed McKellar's hostility to be primarily responsible for Kefauver's progressive isolation as a "maverick" in the Senate to a much greater degree than in the House.

But there were more substantial reasons for his exile-in-residence. William S. White once called Kefauver the only Southern senator except Claude Pepper of Florida to be read out of the lodge by the Southern bloc, attributing it to his opposition to the filibuster and

24. Anderson and Blumenthal, *The Kefauver Story*, 124–26; *Congressional Record*, vol. 97, pt. 9, Oct. 1, 1951, p. 12400.
25. Anderson and Blumenthal, *The Kefauver Story*, 123–24.
26. *Nashville Banner*, July 1, 1954.

his crime investigation.[27] Kefauver's first floor speech in the Senate was against the filibuster. On that occasion he and Pepper were the only Southerners to vote against the filibuster principle.

Some other Southerners could oppose the filibuster occasionally without penalty, and Lyndon Johnson, who took the oath of office as a freshman senator at Kefauver's side, did so in such calculated fashion from the very first that President Truman wrote Kefauver in January 1949 how pleased he was that "you and Lyndon are not permanently lined up with that crowd" (the Southern bloc).[28]

"How does Lyndon do it?" Kefauver once wistfully asked a friend, A. Bradley Eben of Chicago, when the Democratic party that had slapped Kefauver repeatedly in the face had elevated Johnson to a commanding position.[29] Lyndon "did it" by wooing the good will of the senators as assiduously as Kefauver wooed that of the voters. Kefauver, always as wrapped in a mystique of abstract principle—the equality of men under the law, the equality of senators under the rules—as Johnson was devoted to pragmatism, never really adapted himself to the abstract principle underlying the very existence of the Senate, as a counterbalance to the popularly representative House and what the 1787 Constitutional Convention called "democratick babblers." The Senate is called proudly by its members "the most exclusive club in the world," but Kefauver offended repeatedly against that aristocratic concept because he remained at heart a Representative.

Kefauver was treated well on committee assignments at the beginning; fortunately, as tradition calls for reassignment of a senator to the same committees, Congress after Congress, as long as he desires them, and the Senate leadership was not inclined to honor Kefauver's committee preferences a few years later. He received two assignments he listed as preferences: Armed Services, and Interstate and Foreign Commerce. Late in 1949, he had no difficulty trading his membership on Interstate and Foreign Commerce for a seat on the top-rated Judiciary Committee when J. Howard McGrath of Rhode Island retired to become U.S. Attorney General.

Kefauver's new offices were in Suite 410 of the Senate Office

27. William S. White, *Citadel* (New York: Harper, 1956), 78–79.
28. Letter, Harry S Truman to Estes Kefauver, Jan. 21, 1949, Kefauver Collection, VIP File.
29. Personal conversation, A. Bradley Eben, Chicago, Sept. 3, 1970.

Building. He took all of his old House staff—Brizzi, Miss Myers, and Mrs. O'Donaghue—to the other side of Capitol Hill with him, and they remained on his staff until his death. Brizzi was Kefauver's legislative assistant, second in authority to Neese on the staff. Mrs. O'Donaghue remained the senator's personal secretary, and Miss Myers was senior secretary on the staff. There was some tension between the two women as to who held the more privileged position in Kefauver's eyes, but aside from that the entire staff worked well together.

"He has an exceptional ability to delegate authority," Brizzi said of Kefauver during this period. "When he has something to do, he delegates it and forgets about it. He relies completely on his staff, and he doesn't hound them about it. All he asks is that they get results."[30]

Neese, a crisp-worded man with a ready laugh, was an informal but energetic "working boss" for the staff. He signed himself "Simon Legree Neese" in one memorandum outlining office hours (generally 9 A.M. to 5:30 P.M.) and detailing how mail should be handled. The high points of the last item afford considerable insight into one of Kefauver's major voter-wooing techniques: "The best rule to follow is this: WRITE JUST AS IF ESTES WERE *TALKING* PERSONALLY TO THE ADDRESSEE. . . . It is well to check with Henri and Lucile on letters from folks you think Estes might know well; further, it's good to check with Frank to get Estes' stand rather than saying 'glad to know your views.' In short, we need to personalize these letters with warmth."[31]

One of the other members of his staff was Sarah Murrey of Lewisburg, Tennessee, who had been a member of Senator Stewart's staff. To Miss Murrey, an elderly lady, fell the task of sitting in an isolated corner of the suite, wearing a green eyeshade, and going through the Tennessee newspapers daily to clip items that might be of interest or seemed to merit Kefauver letters.[32]

30. Personal conversation, Frank Brizzi, Washington, Spring 1955.
31. Undated office memorandum, Kefauver Collection, Ser. 4-c, Box 3.
32. Charles A. Caldwell, Kefauver's third and last administrative assistant, told me in personal conversation in Washington May 12, 1970, how, when he joined Kefauver's staff, he found Miss Murrey clipping obituaries from Tennessee papers for Kefauver to write notes of condolence to the survivors. Caldwell protested, "But, Estes, this is ghoulish!" Kefauver replied, "I don't think so, Charlie.

Kefauver rarely drove a car any more, except with his family. When Nancy or a member of the staff did not drive him to and from the office, he usually caught a cab. He always had to finish his breakfast coffee en route, usually sipping it from a fruit jar, to the detriment of his suits and shirts.

He never allowed more than twelve minutes, usually at the height of traffic, for the drive to National Airport to catch a plane. Brizzi would drive frantically, tires screeching, while Kefauver sat calmly in the back seat, puffing a cigaret in a Roosevelt-style holder and commenting, "That's fine, Frank. You're doing fine. Keep going."[33]

Kefauver's staff loved him. They joked about his idiosyncrasies, but his preoccupied inattention to all practical detail made every one of them feel that he depended utterly upon them for the success of his every venture.

Neese was more detached in his assessment of Kefauver than the rest of the staff, and personal relations between the two were, as Neese put it once, "man-to-man, and not employer-and-employee." Neese became one of the very few close friends with whom Kefauver enjoyed sitting down over a bottle of Scotch and talking intimate man-talk—sometimes no more profound than speculation over the amorous accessibility of some attractive woman. The two men did not always agree on political matters: Neese considered himself more practical and less gullible than the tolerant senator and would have preferred that Kefauver hedge more on some thorny issues to avoid arousing antagonism.[34]

Neese's letter of resignation, when he decided to return to Tennessee and reenter law practice after two years, expressed a good deal of the feeling of the entire staff for Kefauver: "I could not have been better to myself than you have been to me. You have given me freedom of action, accompanied at all times with a sense of your full confidence. . . . You have been patient, thoughtful and understanding of all of us. . . . No man, working for another, has ever enjoyed a more satisfying relationship."[35]

I think this is a time when someone especially appreciates a note of sympathy from their United States senator."

33. Personal conversation, Frank Brizzi, Washington, Spring 1955.

34. Personal conversation, Charles G. Neese, Greeneville, Spring 1970.

35. Letter, Charles G. Neese to Estes Kefauver, May 8, 1951, Kefauver Collection, Ser. 4-c, Box 3.

Kefauver bought the house he had wanted for his family, the two-story white brick home of Senator Carl Hatch of New Mexico, who was retiring from the Senate, at 4848 Upton Street, Northwest. Kefauver hired out as a weekend lecturer to help pay off the mortgage, and Nancy furnished the new home with furniture bought at an apartment hotel auction. A good seamstress who made many of her own dresses, Nancy made new covers for the furniture and saved money by doing her own shopping at a neighborhood supermarket.

The house was spacious and pleasant, with an upstairs isolated enough for the children not to be disturbed when Kefauver had political friends over for the evening. The children loved it; there were lots of other children in the neighborhood, who acquired the habit of walking into the Kefauver house unannounced at all hours, like the little people in the *Blondie* comic strip.

When Kefauver was at home, he was in the midst of the children. According to Nancy, he was the most popular father in the neighborhood.[36] The place was overrun with pets, most of them cocker spaniels. Kefauver devoted considerable leisure time to converting the backyard doghouse into a doll house and building a new dog pen.

Bobbie, the cook, was well occupied with household duties and growing deaf, so the Kefauvers employed Nanette Criper, a trained governess from England, to supervise the children. Not long after Miss Criper was employed, she had a fourth charge: a third daughter, Gail Estes, was born to the Kefauvers October 7, 1950.

After the 1948 campaign expenses, the Kefauvers had to cut living costs in every way possible. Linda carried her lunch to nearby Horace Mann Elementary School and had a lofty answer for schoolmates who ate luncheon at a nearby drugstore and wanted to know why a senator's daughter had to bring her own lunch: "Oh, we're not rich. We're just important."[37]

Kefauver traded in the blackened shell of the Chrysler on a new Packard for himself and bought Nancy a Studebaker convertible. He declined all substantial gifts from constituents, once sending back a television set Nancy had accepted gratefully, but little gifts

36. Personal conversation, Nancy Kefauver, Washington, Spring 1955.
37. Ibid.

Kefauver and "Popsy"—his father, Cooke Kefauver—sit on the steps of the Lincoln Memorial during one of the elder Kefauver's visits to Washington.

The Kefauver family at home in Washington, early 1950s. Linda pours coffee for her father; David sits beside his mother. At right are the younger daughters, Diane and Gail.

that fattened the larder, such as country hams and fruit cakes, were accepted.

After Kefauver had been in the Senate awhile, he built a home on Lookout Mountain at Chattanooga, next to Mooneen. It was of modern Alpine style, with a jutting porch and ramps between floors instead of staircases, but the Kefauvers rarely stayed there. They usually spent their summer vacations relaxing at the country place of Cowan Oldham, a movie theater owner in McMinnville, Tennessee, who turned it over to them for as long as they wished to stay there. It was a pleasant house with a big yard stretching down to the banks of broad Hickory Creek, across which a swinging bridge from the McMinnville-Manchester highway provided the only access, except a narrow, circuitous dirt road running several miles through the woods. Kefauver worked in the garden, swam and fished in the creek, and the children took turns ringing the big outside dinner bell when Bobbie had a meal ready. Sometimes close friends like Harry Mansfield visited them there, to stay a night or two. They called the place "Shangri-la," and David, once when his mother had been expounding on the beauties of Heaven, said, "You make it sound awfully nice, but couldn't we just skip Heaven when we die and go to Tennessee?"[38]

Oldham was an inveterate practical joker and few prominent Mc-Minnville citizens escaped his pranks—including Kefauver. One summer, Oldham phoned Shangri-la after Kefauver had just left a dentist's office for examination of an aching front tooth, pretended to be the dentist, and said study of the X-rays showed the tooth had to come out. Kefauver sat up half the night with a Scotch bottle, brooding over the effect on his public image of a gap in his front teeth.[39]

Kefauver's first year in the Senate was pleasant and promising enough, both personally and politically. He did not yet feel the often invisible and unspoken disapproval of the Senate elders, except for McKellar's hostility, which was expected. The Senate is tolerant of its newcomers, assuming that they will learn proper manners in the course of time, and "the club" had not crystallized its judgment against him yet. Early in 1950, *Time* magazine, noting

38. Ibid.
39. Personal conversation, Cowan Oldham, McMinnville, Tenn., Spring 1970.

Estes and Nancy Kefauver walk the swinging bridge across Hickory Creek at their summer retreat, Shangri-la, near Mc-Minnville, Tennessee, in 1951.

Kefauver has an admiring audience of "little people"— Diane and David—as he hoes at the edge of the garden at Shangri-la in 1951.

Nashville Tennessean photos

his opposition to the filibuster, his book on congressional reform, and his interest in electoral reform, rated him one of the nation's ten best senators.[40]

Kefauver's major concern, perhaps without his being entirely aware of it, was that he had not found an adequate vehicle for his crusading tendencies. TVA was an emotional issue in Tennessee, primarily, and McKellar was no longer taking potshots at the agency. Kefauver was not in a committee position to pursue his interest in anti-trust legislation as effectively as in the House, and a new project he picked up in 1949, Atlantic Union, languished in a foreign relations subcommittee.

In 1950, however, Kefauver found his vehicle, one that was temporary but would take him swiftly along an unexpected road: the Senate crime investigation.

40. *Time*, April 3, 1950.

Chapter 9

Is That Legal?

Kefauver was accused in many quarters later of having engineered the Senate crime investigation with the conscious intention of parlaying the publicity it brought him into a presidential boom. Not all of those who suspected something of the sort were Kefauver-haters: one of his oldest and best friends, Jack Doughty of Knoxville, for example, considered the investigation "the most opportunistic thing Kef ever did."[1]

It is true that the possibility of Kefauver's being on the national Democratic ticket in 1952 arose in conversation with Philip Graham, publisher of the *Washington Post*, shortly before Kefauver began pushing for the crime probe. Graham had become interested in the extensive activities of nationwide crime syndicates and felt the *Post*'s findings in the matter deserved a full-scale senatorial investigation. Looking around for a senator of untarnished reputation, on the right committee, and from a state where such an investigation would not be embarrassing politically, he settled on Kefauver. Graham said later that Kefauver was not much interested when he was approached, and Graham asked him at last, "Estes, don't you want to be Vice President?" After thinking it over, Graham said, Kefauver agreed to sponsor the probe.[2]

Kefauver apparently neglected to mention to Graham at the time that the idea of a crime investigation was not new to him. More than a year earlier—after Kefauver won his Senate seat in 1948 but before he was sworn in—Silliman Evans had written A. Bradley Eben, a Chicago attorney who had practiced with the Justice Department and had become acquainted with Kefauver through his participation in an antitrust case, that such an investigation by Ke-

---

1. Personal conversation, John H. Doughty, Knoxville, Tenn., Spring 1970.
2. Irwin Ross, *New York Post*, May 9, 1956.

fauver was in the offing and had asked if Eben would be interested in serving as counsel for the investigating committee. Eben, to his subsequent regret, turned down the offer.[3]

Graham and Evans, being newspaper publishers, were not unaware of the publicity potential in such an investigation; nor was Kefauver. Kefauver had a keen sense of the dramatic and a rather accurate sense of what made news. But it is doubtful that Kefauver or any of his boosters—even Graham, despite his remark about the vice presidency—foresaw the impact of the crime investigation on the public. At most, Kefauver probably hoped that the probe would enhance the Democratic party's image and thereby his own palatability to party leaders, putting him in a position where the lightning just might strike in 1952.[4]

Aside from any such probable overtones of opportunism, the crime investigation was rooted in some very serious and essentially nonpolitical considerations, extending back to Kefauver's first days in Congress. He said it stemmed from his selection by Representative Hatton W. Sumners in the spring of 1940 to present the Judiciary Committee's view that federal courts have authority to remove a federal district judge from office in case of malfeasance. His presentation was applauded, and in 1945 Sumners appointed Kefauver chairman of a six-man subcommittee to probe charges of judicial corruption against Judge Albert W. Johnston of Pennsylvania. The probe brought Johnston's resignation the following year.

Kefauver said later that, beyond the immediate facts of the Johnston investigation, it gave him a glimpse of links between the judiciary and the underworld. He also maintained contact with the subcommittee's investigators, Max Goldschein and Boris Kostelanetz, and met with them frequently during the next five years to go over annual reports of state crime commissions in an effort to determine to what extent crime transcended state lines and became a federal problem.

When, during Kefauver's first year in the Senate, the American Municipal Association asked the Justice Department for aid against

3. Personal conversation, A. Bradley Eben, Chicago, Sept. 3, 1970.
4. *Chattanooga Times,* Jan. 22, 1950; William Howard Moore, *The Kefauver Committee and the Politics of Crime, 1950-1952* (Columbia: Univ. of Missouri Press, 1974), 45, suggests that Kefauver derived opportunistic ideas from the career of his cousin, Gov. Joseph W. Folk of Missouri.

organized crime as a "matter . . . too big to be handled by local officials alone," Kefauver began drafting a series of bills aimed at interstate crime. But he discovered it was not possible to draw effective bills because nobody knew just how criminal organizations operated nationally, and there was not enough public interest in the problem to get such measures through Congress.[5]

Thus, the resolution Kefauver introduced in January 1950 had a double thrust and set the pattern for his future Senate probes. It was aimed at finding out what the problem was and what was needed to correct it, through a congressional committee investigation, and at arousing the public to the need for correction, through publicity. It was aimed simply at gambling, which Kefauver had found in his studies with Goldschein and Kostelanetz to have the most obvious interstate ramifications.

He ran into an immediate roadblock in the Judiciary Committee, in its chairman, silver-haired Senator Pat McCarran, whose home state of Nevada was well known as a gambling haven. It languished in a subcommittee for a month, until Kefauver was able to engender enough newspaper publicity to force McCarran's hand; whereupon McCarran took Nevada off the hook by attaching an amendment to broaden the probe to all "racketeers and gangs who cross state lines in their operation."

It hit another snag in the Rules Committee, where it had to go because of a $100,000 appropriation for committee expenses: a competing Truman administration resolution sponsored by bulky, stubborn Senator Edwin C. Johnson of Colorado, chairman of the Interstate and Foreign Commerce Committee, and aimed primarily at gambling. Johnson proposed to put Senator Ernest W. McFarland of Arizona in charge of a subcommittee of his own committee to conduct the probe.

The jurisdictional dispute promptly took on strong political overtones. Influential Republicans—especially Senator Homer Ferguson of Michigan and Senator Forrest C. Donnell of Missouri, who were demanding that any probe look into alleged criminal connections with the Democratic organizations in St. Louis and Truman's own Kansas City—threw their weight behind Kefauver. So did Mc-

5. Personal conversation, Estes Kefauver, Washington, Spring 1955; *Congressional Record*, vol. 96, pt. 1, Jan. 5, 1950, pp. 67–68.

Carran, who wanted no Arizona neighbor investigating gambling, and he rushed back from Nevada to buck Johnson in the Rules Committee. He succeeded in getting Kefauver's plan out of the committee late in March but with an appropriation cut to $50,000 and a July 31 deadline.

There was still marked reluctance on the part of the Democratic leadership to let the resolution reach the floor. Under it the probe would be a Judiciary Committee affair, and because Ferguson and Donnell were members of that committee, it would be difficult to avoid having at least one of them on the investigating committee—which the administration wanted to avoid at all costs.

At this point, coincidence intervened in Kefauver's favor. Charles Binaggio, Democratic boss and gang overlord in Kansas City, and his chief lieutenant, Charles Gargotta, were shot to death April 6, two days after Kefauver had applied unsuccessfully for a hearing on his resolution before the Democratic Policy Committee. Republican Representative Dewey Short of Missouri charged that Binaggio was "bumped off" because his connections with the Democratic political organization in Kansas City would have been embarrassing in the upcoming Missouri senatorial primary. There was an immediate public outcry for an investigation into the slayings, and it was obvious that suppression of Kefauver's resolution in favor of Johnson's probe exclusively of gambling, at this point, would have all the earmarks of a Democratic whitewash.

Senator Scott Lucas of Illinois, Democratic majority leader, came up with a satisfactory compromise: turn the probe over to a special committee, composed of members of both the Judiciary and the Interstate and Foreign Commerce committees. With a larger group of senators to choose from, Ferguson and Donnell could be kept off the committee without things looking fishy, the probe could extend beyond gambling as McCarran wished, and Kefauver, as a Judiciary Committee member, would be eligible for the chairmanship. The committee's appropriation was increased to $150,000 and the deadline for its report extended to February 28, 1951.[6]

Republicans raised a howl at the joint committee plan and fought bitterly to keep the probe in the Judiciary Committee.[7] The Demo-

6. *Nashville Tennessean*, April 12, 1950.
7. United Press story, *Nashville Tennessean*, April 13, 1950.

cratic leadership was in no hurry about the matter, and it was not until early May that Kefauver's insistence on bringing it up on every occasion, like a dog worrying at a bone, brought its approval, with Vice President Alben Barkley breaking a 35 to 35 tie vote.[8]

The two other Democrats Barkley appointed to the committee were Senators Herbert R. O'Conor of Maryland and Lester C. Hunt of Wyoming. Its two Republican members were Charles W. Tobey of New Hampshire and Alexander Wiley of Wisconsin. As the committee's chief counsel, Kefauver chose Rudolph Halley, an incisive, thirty-six-year-old New Yorker who had served as chief counsel to the Truman Committee investigating war contracts from 1942 to 1944 and then to the Senate Committee on Oil and Fuel Shortages. Halley was assisted by a seven-member legal staff, plus special counsel in several major cities, including Kostelanetz and Goldschein. Harold Robinson, who had worked with Halley on the Truman Committee and had become chief investigator for the California Crime Commission, headed an investigative staff that eventually numbered twenty-eight.

Although Kefauver had said several times that one of the purposes of the crime investigation was to arouse the public to the problem of organized crime, the investigation did not start out with a great deal of fanfare, developing only slowly into the "road show" it eventually became. The committee's first hearings were held in Miami May 26–27, 1950, behind locked doors and without previous announcement, with Kefauver and Hunt the only committee members present. It was not until June 22 that the first public hearings were held, in Washington. Subsequently, the hearings gained more and more publicity and stirred more and more public interest as they moved during the next year into more than a dozen major cities: Miami, Tampa, St. Louis, Kansas City, Chicago, Las Vegas, Los Angeles, New York, Philadelphia, Cleveland, Detroit, San Francisco, and New Orleans.

The Kefauver Committee hearings were preceded by careful staff preparation. Halley and his staff probed thoroughly into old income tax returns, real estate transactions, previous state investiga-

8. Associated Press story, *Nashville Tennessean*, May 4, 1950; Moore, *The Kefauver Committee and the Politics of Crime*, 50–64; Anderson and Blumenthal, *The Kefauver Story*, 144; Estes Kefauver, *Crime in America* (Garden City, N.Y.: Doubleday, 1951), 5–6.

Kefauver confers with Chief Counsel Rudolph Halley during hearings of the Senate Crime Investigating Committee.

Kefauver studies his notes during testimony at one of the hearings of the Senate Crime Investigating Committee. Seated at Kefauver's left is Rudolph Halley.

tions, and criminal records before witnesses were called to the stand. For the most part, the committee members listened, with an occasional question or comment, while Halley elicited from the witnesses material that he already had checked out rather completely. Very little of what the committee brought to public light, in fact, was really new. Most of the information had been acquired by local law enforcement agencies or investigators for some branch of the federal government.

To the public, seeing Halley call just the right witness to the stand at just the right time and ask him just the right questions to bring out the spectacular extent of law violation, while the senators sat and listened as though this was largely what they had expected all along, it seemed as though the Kefauver Committee must be gifted with some miraculous second sight. But the committee was largely putting together in a single picture extant bits of information, some of them once known but forgotten.

Most picturesque among the committee members was seventy-year-old Charles Tobey, scion of an old New England family, whose Baptist indignation at some the committee's disclosures gave him the aura of an angry prophet. The old gentleman, a former governor of New Hampshire, occasionally burst forth with exclamations of righteous indignation: such as to Superintendent John A. Gaffney of the New York State Police, "You are no good in my judgment, you are below par, and you are a counterfeit of what a good law enforcement officer should be. Just look at a picture of yourself, just look at yourself and search your own conscience."[9]

Kefauver himself remained imperturbably quiet, usually polite, but unflaggingly persistent in his dealings with witnesses. He was described by Alan Barth as "an oversize owl, benign and bland and forever genial."[10] But his dry questions and comments could unnerve an evasive witness more severely than either Tobey's righteous declamations or Halley's solemn, assured insistence.

The committee had to piece together much scattered information, some of it given reluctantly, to gain a picture of the network of organized crime that tied many major cities together. Behind it

9. Kefauver, *Crime in America*, 277–78.
10. Alan Barth, *Government by Investigation* (New York: Viking, 1955), 68.

all, Kefauver said afterward, lurked the Mafia, the Sicilian "Black Hand" society. The information the committee gathered, largely from narcotics agents, was adequate for Kefauver to call the Mafia "a secret international government-within-a-government," believed to be headed by Charles (Lucky) Luciano, one of America's gang lords during the 1920s and early 1930s who had been deported to Italy a few years earlier.[11]

The Mafia had evolved a code of death to those who resisted its demands or cooperated with legal authorities against it, and those who had occasion to know of its existence were terrified of it. When Philip d'Andrea, a former bodyguard for bootlegging king Al Capone, was asked at a committee hearing in Chicago if the Mafia was "a subject that is discussed among Italian families," he cried: "Oh God, no! No, sir! It is not discussed out of the home!"[12]

The Kefauver Committee found the old Capone "syndicate" affiliated with the Mafia and still operating in Chicago and spreading tentacles across the nation via the racing wire network. Capone had been imprisoned on income tax evasion charges in 1931, but the Kefauver Committee called before it the four contemporary heads of the continuing "corporation." White-haired Paul (The Waiter) Ricca and Louis (Little New York) Campagna, former Capone lieutenants, talked rather freely, though sometimes inconsistently, but Jacob (Greasy Thumb) Guzik, Capone's old paymaster, pouch-eyed and grey-faced, and the neatly-dressed, gorilla-like Anthony J. (Joe Batters) Accardo refused to answer most questions, invoking the Fifth Amendment.[13]

During and after Capone's reign, the mobsters increasingly bought off legal interference by bribing officials and police and were able to get some of their own colleagues elected to the Illinois legislature. Kefauver said the committee determined that Chicago was headquarters for a crime network that extended into New York, Los Angeles, Kansas City, Cleveland, St. Louis, and other big cities and obtained "evidence of gangsters muscling into legitimate busi-

11. Kefauver, *Crime in America*, 19–34; Moore, *The Kefauver Committee and the Politics of Crime*, 1–24, 114–34.
12. Kefauver, *Crime in America*, 29.
13. Ibid., 36, 53–56, 74–76; Moore, *The Kefauver Committee and the Politics of Crime*, 26–29.

ness and of political ties between gangsters and politicians of both parties."[14]

After repeal of the Eighteenth Amendment, organized crime had turned from bootlegging to other sources of revenue, a major one being illegal gambling, which Kefauver said had become a $17 billion to $25 billion annual business. The principal facet of this field was illegal bookmaking on horse races, in which the bookies were supplied directly or indirectly with racing information by the monopolistic Continental Press Service, an organization that leased 23,000 miles of telegraph circuits from Western Union and grossed more than $2 million, by its own estimate, in 1949.

Kefauver called Continental Press "a tool of the Chicago-Capone Syndicate." It would get its news hot to the bookies by getting concessions at race tracks or even by such exotic methods as spying with high-powered binoculars and using semaphore signals. The whole setup funnelled funds so efficiently into mobsters' hands that Kefauver called the racing wire service "Public Enemy No. 1."[15]

The testimony from criminals, law enforcement officials, politicians, and affected citizens that enabled the committee to piece together the mosaic of organized crime in the United States was sometimes sensational, sometimes dull, often humorous. Some of the criminal witnesses were loud and arrogant, some hearty and good-natured, some sullen, some fearful.

The testimony of one law enforcement officer, Sheriff James A. (Smiling Jimmy) Sullivan of Dade County (Miami), opened the lid of a political Pandora's box in Florida. Sullivan tried to explain to the committee how his assets had jumped more than $65,000 during his five years in office, though his salary ranged from $7,500 to $12,000 a year. Testimony from some of his former deputies convinced the committee the sheriff's office had been accepting bribes for "protection" from gambling interests.[16]

Sullivan subsequently was indicted for neglect of duty, failure to enforce gambling laws, and permitting his deputies to accept bribes and was suspended by Governor Fuller Warren of Florida. But when the indictment was dismissed on a technicality, Warren

14. AP story, *Nashville Tennessean*, Aug. 19, 1950; UP story, ibid., Oct. 8, 1950.
15. Kefauver, *Crime in America*, 35ff.
16. Ibid., 100.

reinstated him, saying his study of the evidence "does not show the violation of any law of the state of Florida by Jimmy Sullivan." Violent criticism of Warren erupted in the Florida legislature, which had been considering action to make Sullivan's suspension permanent, and the *Miami Daily News* called Warren editorially "lousy, stinking—and obvious."[17]

The Kefauver Committee reported to the Senate that it "strongly condemns the reinstatement by Governor Fuller Warren of Florida of Sheriff James Sullivan without a full and public investigation."[18] Warren was angered, and was to be even more incensed by further committee disclosures.

The "big money" in Miami was made by the S&G Syndicate, which monopolized Miami bookmaking with a pool of about 200 bookies and grossed an estimated $30 million to $40 million annually. The lucrative operation of the S&G aroused the cupidity of Chicago and Eastern mobsters who wintered in Miami, and the Chicago-Capone Syndicate tried to buy into it. The five S&G founders did not care to have any more partners; whereupon Governor Warren's crime investigator, W.O. (Bing) Crosby, appeared in Miami and (he admitted to the committee) was fed information by Harry Russell, a Chicago gambler who had been trying to negotiate with S&G, on bookie joints he might like to raid. In addition to its immediate troubles with the law, S&G had its Chicago-controlled Continental Press Service cut off and was paralyzed. It took the S&G partners just ten days to come around and let the Chicago "boys" in for a one-sixth interest.

Crosby was a friend of William H. Johnston, a 250-pound operator of horse and dog tracks who was a protege of Edward J. O'Hare, an associate of Al Capone. Johnston and two other men jointly contributed $404,000 to Warren's 1948 campaign—more than half of his total campaign cost. The committee called all three as witnesses. Johnston claimed that his only reason for contributing $100,000 was that he had known Warren for fifteen years and found him "an able, competent and honest man." But after Warren's election, Johnston and his business associates received a major share of the state's contracts for road building materials. The Kefauver Com-

17. Ibid., 101.
18. Ibid.

mittee was less interested in this than in Johnston's "long career of close association with Chicago racketeers of the Capone gang," as it phrased it in a report to the Senate.[19]

Warren was furious that the committee should delve into such local matters as campaign contributions and was especially furious at its findings. He repeatedly attacked the committee collectively and Kefauver and O'Conor individually. He called Kefauver "that ambition-crazed Cæsar" and a "shyster politician who is running desperately and, I believe, futilely for the Vice Presidency of the United States."[20]

Four months after the hearings opened in Miami, a bitter attack by Warren on Kefauver was inserted in the *Congressional Record* under the name of Senator Spessard Holland of Florida, who was politically friendly to Warren. Holland was flooded at once with indignant letters and telephone calls, most of them from people in Tennessee. He squirmed a bit, denied inserting the statement in the *Record*, and had it expunged with an elaborate explanation of how it got there.[21]

Even while Smiling Jimmy Sullivan was trying to explain his income to the committee, pressure was mounting for it to go into Missouri, President Truman's home state. W.D. Kruce, Republican leader in the Missouri House of Representatives, wired Kefauver to ask a probe of 1948 campaign contributions to Democratic Governor Forrest Smith and to charge a "definite alliance between criminal elements in Missouri and certain political leaders." A committee investigator in Missouri called for help because he found the situation there "too big" to handle alone. Wiley, still suspicious that the committee intended to deal gently with Democrats, demanded that the Missouri investigators stop "running around after mice" and focus on such things as "the Kansas City murders and the theft of ballot boxes" in the state.[22]

With the demand by Kenneth Wherry, Nebraska Republican

19. Third Interim Report of the Kefauver Committee, May 1, 1951, pp. 33–34; Kefauver, *Crime in America*, 106–13; Moore, *The Kefauver Committee and the Politics of Crime*, 93–95.
20. AP story, *Nashville Tennessean*, Oct. 3, 1951.
21. Ibid., Sept. 16 and 18, 1951.
22. Ibid., June 24, 1950; Moore, *The Kefauver Committee and the Politics of Crime*, 139.

Kefauver is welcomed by a home-state crowd at the height of the Senate Crime Investigating Committee hearings. Behind him is Harry Mansfield and escorting him is State Trooper Wallace Mills.

and Senate minority leader, to know whether the crime probe was to be "an investigation or a cover-up," there was not much way for the committee to avoid going into Missouri. As a compromise between the Republican demands and Democratic concern over helping Donnell's chances of reelection in 1950, Kefauver at first held closed hearings in St. Louis July 18 and in Kansas City July 20–21. In St. Louis he was accompanied only by Halley and some investigators; in Kansas City he was joined by Tobey. His only immediate disclosure was that the committee had uncovered evidence in St. Louis that Western Union agents in Missouri handled bets on a 25 percent commission basis but that gambling operations in St. Louis were "nothing approaching the magnitude" of those in Florida. Tobey piqued public interest by revealing that he had called in James Pendergast, Democratic political leader and a friend of Truman, for "a few questions."[23]

Politically, things were beginning to get a little sticky. Plans were made to go back to Kansas City for open hearings late in September, but Thomas G. Hennings Jr., who was running against Donnell for the Senate that fall, told Kefauver, upon being asked, that he would be just as happy if the committee waited until after the election in November. Hennings was under the impression that he had Kefauver's assurance this would be done. He was painfully surprised, therefore, to find the committee showing up on schedule in Kansas City September 28. He telephoned Kefauver in some agitation, and Kefauver explained lugubriously that he was unable to control the other committee members, who felt the group had to go into the city to protect their reputation for integrity.[24]

The most sensitive aspect of the Kansas City hearings was the indirect reflection any disclosures there would cast on Truman, since the Kansas City political organization stood in direct line of descent from the old Pendergast machine, with which Truman had been affiliated. Kefauver's excuse to Hennings for going into Kansas City with open hearings just before the election was not adequate for Truman: Kefauver after all was the committee chairman and com-

---

23. AP story, *Nashville Tennessean*, July 21, 1950.
24. Riggs, "The Man from Tennessee"; Moore, *The Kefauver Committee and the Politics of Crime*, 147. Hennings won his election anyway, the only Democrat to oust an incumbent Republican senator that year, and became one of Kefauver's better friends in the Senate.

manded a Democratic majority on the committee. To the President, the decision appeared simply a matter of party disloyalty.

The committee's disclosures and its verdict on the situation in Kansas City made him no happier. Kefauver said his first impression was that Kansas City was "a place that was struggling out from under the rule of the law of the jungle. . . . The Kansas City mob, led by men who were high up in the Mafia, had milked the town." The "milking," according to a federal grand jury investigating Kansas City crime, amounted to more than $34 million a year.[25] The committee offended Truman and other Democratic politicians in the state further by developing testimony linking Governor Smith with the assassinated gangster Binaggio. Smith made a surprise appearance before the committee and denied knowing Binaggio nearly as well as other witnesses had implied he did. But the committee concluded, in its report to the Senate, that "Smith's assertions under oath that he did not discuss politics with Binaggio, or discuss Binaggio's expectations, are simply not credible."[26]

Although the committee's revelations of Democratic perfidy in Missouri did not prevent the voters from throwing Republican Senator Donnell out of office, the party of Kefauver and Truman, of Forrest Smith and Fuller Warren did not fare so fortunately in Chicago. As in Missouri, Kefauver had not planned for the committee to investigate Chicago until after the November election, but it went there directly from Kansas City as a consequence of the ambush and gangland-style slaying of a prospective committee informant and an attorney associated with him. The committee considered the killings a direct challenge by the Chicago underworld.[27]

The committee followed up its first three days of closed hearings in Chicago with questioning of three Chicago police captains about the sources of their rather unusual wealth. One of the three was Daniel A. Gilbert, whose eighteen years as chief investigator for state's attorney John S. Boyle had not resulted in the conviction of a single important mobster but who was a candidate for sheriff of Cook County (Chicago) on the Democratic ticket in the coming election. Gilbert testified that his net worth was approximately $360,000

25. Kefauver, *Crime in America*, 141–42.

26. Third Interim Report, 37–43; Kefauver, *Crime in America*, 148–59; Moore, *The Kefauver Committee and the Politics of Crime*, 97–98.

27. AP stories, *Nashville Tennessean*, Sept. 27 and 28, 1950.

which seemed to the committee members to be doing rather well for a police captain—Chicago newspapers referred to him as "the richest cop in the world." Gilbert's explanation was that, though he had engaged in a little "honest gambling," most of his good fortune came from investments in stocks and bonds on tips from friends. He conceded, however, under questioning that his "honest gambling" included winnings of $10,000 to $12,000 in election bets in a single year, plus betting on football games and prize fights. When he gave details of his football bets, revealing the name and address of the betting commissioner with whom he placed them, Kefauver asked Gilbert gently: "Is that legal?"

"Well," answered Gilbert, "I would say it was legal if a fellow wants to make a bet on an election. There is nothing illegal about it. No violation of the law."[28]

Legal or not, Gilbert lost his November election gamble with the voters of Chicago, who learned about his sporting habits at once but through no fault of the committee. His testimony taken in secret session was not to have been made public until the committee reported to the Senate the following year. But Ray Brennan, a reporter for the *Chicago Sun-Times* who posed as a committee employee, obtained a transcript of Gilbert's testimony, and large chunks of it were published in question-and-answer form a few days before the election.[29]

Gilbert's bid for election as sheriff was repudiated solidly at the polls, and normally Democratic voters were so aroused that the en-

28. Kefauver, *Crime in America*, 60.
29. International News Service story, *Nashville Tennessean*, Nov. 2, 1950; Riggs, "The Man from Tennessee"; Anderson and Blumenthal, *The Kefauver Story*, 167; Moore, *The Kefauver Committee and the Politics of Crime*, 155–56. In mid-1976 reporters Seymour Hersh and Jeff Gerth wrote in the *New York Times* that attorney Sidney Korshak apparently succeeded in "blackmailing" Kefauver to delay public hearings in Chicago, by confronting him with a photograph taken of him in a compromising position with a call girl in his hotel room. Hersh's single source for the story was identified as "a highly respected Chicago business executive" by Arthur Hayes Sulzberger, publisher of the *Times*, in a letter to Lucile Myers, Oct. 20, 1976. The allegations were denied categorically by Downey Rice, who had been associate counsel for the Crime Committee, and George H. Martin, who had been a staff investigator, in a letter to the *Times* Aug. 16, 1976. William Howard Moore, Univ. of Wyoming historian and author of *The Kefauver Committee and the Politics of Crime*, said that, on the basis of his research, he concluded Hersh "jumped to conclusions" and "if the alleged incident with the

tire Democratic ticket went down to defeat—at least that was the interpretation placed on the election results by Scott Lucas, whose shortage of Cook County votes made the difference that retired him from the Senate in favor of that future Demosthenes of the Republican party, Everett McKinley Dirksen.[30]

Kefauver was distressed at the defeat of Lucas, with whom his relations had been cordial, but on a television program the following Sunday he said he thought Lucas' interpretation of the results was wrong because Lucas "had supported our committee all of the way through. Nobody connected him with any of the matters brought out." A few days later, he went by Lucas' office in Washington to express his regret at the election results and explain what had caused Gilbert's testimony to be made public.

"I don't want to talk about it," snapped Lucas, flushing angrily and turning his back on Kefauver.

Kefauver, rebuffed and hurt, hesitated a moment, then said, "All right, Scott," and left. Later, Lucas walked out of a Stork Club party in honor of the Duke and Duchess of Windsor when he found he was seated at the same table as Kefauver.[31]

Like Fuller Warren, Lucas held a grudge; and so did Jacob Arvey, who resigned as Cook County Democratic chairman after the 1950 election debacle. Thus, though the crime investigation brought Kefauver the public recognition that made him a serious presidential contender in 1952, it made powerful enemies for him at key points along the road to nomination.

Truman's reaction, although not based on such personal reasons, was still political. As was obvious to the President, to the Republican leadership and to virtually any experienced politician an urban-focussed crime probe was bound to hurt the urban-centered Democratic party more than it did the more rural Republicans, unless handled very discreetly. The very nonpartisanship that stirred public admiration for the investigation gave Truman reason to doubt

---

call girl actually took place and if an attempt at blackmail was made, it apparently did not work." Copies of the correspondence about the Hersh stories were sent to me by Lucile Myers in a letter of Dec. 1, 1977.

30. Kefauver, *Crime in America*, 58.

31. Drew Pearson, *Washington Post*, June 4, 1951; Moore, *The Kefauver Committee and the Politics of Crime*, 149–50, 157–59.

Kefauver's political judgment, if not his actual party loyalty.[32]

Much of the public recognition Kefauver gained from the probe stemmed from an unforeseen and, in fact, unpredictable factor: television. As in previous congressional committee hearings, television coverage of the Kefauver Committee's activity was confined to short takes for use on regularly scheduled news programs until the committee, late in January 1951, went to New Orleans, where Mayor DeLesseps Morrison testified that New York gambler Frank Costello got his start in organized gambling in New Orleans in 1936. Station WNOE gained permission from Kefauver to telecast the entire proceedings, shelving its scheduled commercial programs for the purpose. Public response to the innovation was so laudatory that television stations in other cities were encouraged to try the same thing.[33]

After the investigation, and especially during his presidential race, Kefauver was accused of having invited television coverage deliberately for the sake of personal publicity. The television stations, however, initiated the coverage, and Kefauver and the other committee members found it had its drawbacks.

Aware of a large audience watching them, they had to be more careful of their language, and they could not help being conscious that audience demand called for "moving along" with the testimony and not getting bogged down in tortuous details. The tension told on the senators to such an extent that—after a day of televised hearings in New Orleans and two days each in St. Louis and Los Angeles—Kefauver was determined to ban television cameras when the committee went to San Francisco. He relented when he was told commitments already had been made to the stations.[34]

From California the committee returned to Washington for a few days, then opened its first public hearings in New York March 12 (an earlier New York hearing had been behind closed doors).

32. Moore, *The Kefauver Committee and the Politics of Crime*, 145–49.

33. This was Kefauver's version of the way television coverage of the hearings began, in *Crime in America*, 313; described in greater detail by Moore, *The Kefauver Committee and the Politics of Crime*, 168–69. Blair Moody, "The United States Senate," *Holiday*, Feb. 1954, p. 90, says that Allen J. Nieber, a Detroit reporter, flew to Cleveland to get Kefauver's consent to televise the hearings on his paper's station; the Cleveland hearings immediately preceded the New Orleans hearings.

34. Cf. Harry W. Kirwin, *The Inevitable Success: Herbert R. O'Conor* (Westminster, Md.: Newman Press, 1962), 451.

Kefauver appears on the television screen during hearings of the Senate Crime Investigating Committee in 1951.

Vacationing in McMinnville after relinquishing the chairmanship of the Senate Crime Investigating Committee in mid-1951, Kefauver takes a telephone call from Washington.

fauver speaks in Nashville in the spring of 1951, during speculation that he will k the Democratic presidential nomination the next year. Behind him in the nt row are Silliman Evans, publisher of the *Nashville Tennessean*, Nancy, and vernor and Mrs. Gordon Browning.

There, *Time* magazine had arranged to sponsor television coverage of the hearings, and the investigation blossomed into a sensation overnight.

Housework was neglected and movie theaters and stores were nearly deserted as the number of home television sets turned on rose from the normal less-than-2 percent to more than 25 percent in the morning and from the normal less-than-12 percent to more than 30 percent in the afternoon. Consolidated Edison, New York's electric power supplier, had to add a generator to take care of the increased demand.[35] The New York television presentation was so successful that *Time* extended its sponsorship to the subsequent hearings in Washington. In addition, national networks picked up some of the hearing programs.

All together, Kefauver estimated later in his book, *Crime in America*, 20 million to 30 million viewers watched some or all of the televised proceedings. They included the Kefauver children, who smudged the screen patting the face of "that man on television" and pestered their mother periodically to tell them which ones were "the good men" and "the bad men" in the hearings.[36]

What the audience saw was a panel of dignified senators— Kefauver quiet and soft-spoken, O'Conor alert and keenly legalistic, Tobey righteously censorious—sitting in judgment while the bespectacled, self-assured Halley patiently and persistently drew damaging admissions from evasive and reluctant witnesses.[37]

Costello, described in testimony before the committee as "the most influential underworld leader in America," was the star of the entire investigation. The sixty-year-old native of Italy was or had been a bootlegger, a slot-machine operator in New York and New Orleans, a partner in New Orleans and Saratoga gambling casinos, and an investor in many legitimate businesses, ranging from television sets to kewpie dolls, as well as an influential participant in Tammany Hall political affairs.

He appeared before the committee impeccably and conservatively dressed, looking much like an absorbed and worried business exec-

35. Moore, *The Kefauver Committee and the Politics of Crime*, 184–85.
36. Personal conversation, Nancy Kefauver, Washington, Spring 1955.
37. The fame that accrued to Halley as a result of the crime investigation was given considerable credit for his election to the presidency of the New York City Council in 1951: Thomas L. Stokes column, *Nashville Tennessean*, Nov. 9, 1951.

utive, his name embroidered in red on his white breast-pocket handkerchief. He claimed to be suffering from a sore throat, but his evasiveness and reluctance to answer questions kept him before the committee for seven days. He threatened twice to walk out of the hearings, and did, but returned meekly later to answer questions. At one point, the committee ordered television cameras kept off his face, so he would not have an excuse to walk out; only his nervously writhing hands were shown on the screens.

Halley elicited from him admissions of associations with Tammany Hall leaders and favors from them. The committee determined that "Frank Costello has exercised a major influence upon the New York County Democratic organization, Tammany Hall . . . (and) had relationships with some Republican political leaders."[38]

William O'Dwyer, then ambassador to Mexico, took the stand in New York at his own request to answer committee questions about his failure as a district attorney to prosecute Albert Anastasia for his connection with the infamous Murder, Inc. O'Dwyer also was quizzed about a visit he made to Costello's apartment in 1942. O'Dwyer clashed with Tobey, accusing Tobey of sending "for money to help you in your primaries and your election, and you got it, and you don't know where it came from."

"That is not true!" Tobey burst out. "I will take the oath right now, if you will give it, Mr. Chairman! I hate a four-flusher!"[39]

O'Dwyer apologized the next day, saying he had referred to an unsolicited contribution made through the National Committee for an Effective Congress. After many hours of testimony from different witnesses, the committee concluded that neither O'Dwyer, when he was mayor of New York, nor any of his appointees "took any effective action against the top echelons of the gambling, narcotics, waterfront, murder or bookmaking rackets. In fact, his actions impeded promising investigations of such rackets."[40]

Televising of the hearings was criticized on other grounds than the boost it gave Kefauver for his presidential race. It was contended both in and out of the Senate that it violated the rights of witnesses by holding them up to public censure.[41]

38. Kefauver, *Crime in America*, 305.
39. Ibid., 289.
40. Ibid., 284.
41. Moore, *The Kefauver Committee and the Politics of Crime*, 225–30.

James Joseph Carroll, sixty-four-year-old St. Louis bookmaker, was the first witness to decline to testify before television, saying "the whole proceeding outrages my sense of propriety." Carroll subsequently traveled to Washington at his own expense to testify and said of television (which was kept off his face there), "You have injected the fright factor into this proceeding."

"The what?" asked John Burling, associate committee counsel.

"Fright—F-R-I-G-H-T—factor," said Carroll. "The phenomenon of light fright and mike fright, and that is what I am subject to . . . and I am speechless."[42]

Kefauver told the Senate later that the committee agreed "that if any witness did not want to be televised when he was testifying, we would respect his wishes." Despite this statement, several days after Carroll's Washington appearance the committee cited Morris Kleinman and Louis Rothkopf for contempt of Congress for refusing to testify before television cameras. Kefauver said the committee was citing them for contempt to make a legal test of the part television could play in congressional hearings.

The Senate upheld the committee's citations by a 38 to 12 vote, but a federal court dismissed the complaint against Kleinman and Rothkopf fifteen months later, ruling that the atmosphere of the hearing was improper.[43]

In fact, of the forty-six citations for contempt issued by the committee, there were only three court convictions. The remainder resulted in acquittals, dismissals, or reversals on appeal. The question went deeper than television: whether the witnesses could be required to answer committee questions when their answers might subject them to subsequent prosecution. As Judge David Bazelon of the Circuit Court of Appeals said in overturning a conviction of Charles E. Nelson, a District of Columbia gambler: "The committee threatened prosecution for contempt if he refused to answer, for perjury if he lied, and for gambling activities if he told the truth."[44]

Exacerbating the moral and legal issue was the fact that Kefauver intended that the committee hearings arouse the public. He believed Congress would not pass needed legislation, even if the facts

42. UP story, *Nashville Tennessean*, Feb. 25, 1951; Kefauver, *Crime in America*, 163; Moore, *The Kefauver Committee and the Politics of Crime*, 170.
43. Moore, *The Kefauver Committee and the Politics of Crime*, 228–29.
44. Barth, *Government by Investigation*, 78.

of organized crime were known, in the absence of aroused public sentiment. There was no way to arouse the public except by inciting public censure of the individuals against whose activities the desired legislation was to be aimed, and this resulted inevitably in a "trial by publicity" of witnesses.

As committee chairman, Kefauver succeeded in threading his way through the labyrinth of conflict between the purpose of the investigation and the constitutional rights of the witnesses well enough to win the praise of Herbert M. Levy, counsel for the American Civil Liberties Union. Levy said that "in contrast to other investigating committees" the Kefauver committee had taken precautions to preserve the rights of witnesses and "to prevent disclosure of names of persons who might be unjustly prejudiced."[45]

Kefauver also received the praise of his committee colleagues when he stepped down as chairman in May 1951. *Pageant* magazine chose him second best senator in the nation, and he received the Americanism Trophy of the National Military Order of the Purple Heart and a number of other honors.

The Senate continued the committee's life until September under O'Conor's chairmanship. When it concluded its fifteen months of existence, the Kefauver Committee had spent $315,000, heard nearly 800 witnesses, and submitted four reports to the effect that nationwide organized crime syndicates existed and that their existence depended on the support or tolerance of public officials.

Kefauver in his year as chairman traveled more than 52,000 miles from coast to coast. He had his hat stolen in San Francisco, his telephone tapped in a Chicago hotel, and received telephone threats on his life and the lives of members of his family. The white house on Upton Street was under police guard for a time, but the only threat Kefauver took seriously was a warning from the FBI that it had learned from gambler Frank Erickson's wife about a plot to kill him. None of the threatened actions materialized.

Kefauver was almost constantly on the road, sometimes arriving home from some distant city at night and unexpectedly. Since he did not carry a house key, he would plough through the shrubbery and call plaintively up at the darkened window: "Mom-meee . . .!" Nancy would go downstairs and let him in.[46]

45. W. McNeil Lowry, *Progressive*, June 1951.
46. Martin, "The Mystery of Kefauver."

Kefauver managed to sandwich in time to edit and approve a second book under his nominal authorship, *Crime in America*, written by his friend, Sidney Shalett, which attained the *New York Times* best seller list for twelve weeks in the second half of 1951 and made Kefauver several thousand dollars. Shalett also wrote under Kefauver's byline a series of four articles on the hearings for the *Saturday Evening Post*, which brought some criticism of Kefauver because the articles appeared before the committee report was released.[47]

Congressional interest in the crime hearings proved as ephemeral as the television programs. Congress failed to approve any of the nineteen bills growing directly out of the investigation, and the same fate befell virtually all of the scores of similar bills offered in subsequent years.[48] But the committee's work was responsible for the Treasury Department's setting up a special rackets squad to check on criminal fraud in income tax cases. Also, a decade later, Congress approved a number of bills, supported by President John Kennedy, that were a direct result of Kefauver's probe.[49]

In Kefauver's view, one of the major accomplishments of the investigation was the encouragement it provided to local law enforcement supporters to correct conditions in their communities. More than seventy local crime commissions were established, and the committee's disclosures about legalized gambling in Nevada were credited with influencing voters in California, Arizona, Montana, and Massachusetts to disapprove legalized gambling in those states in 1950.[50]

And, of course, one major result of the probe was that it plummeted Kefauver into the 1952 presidential race.

47. Personal communication, Anita (Mrs. Sidney) Shalett, Washington, Aug. 7, 1970; Moore, *The Kefauver Committee and the Politics of Crime*, 223.

48. Robert S. Allen, "How Congress Scuttled Kefauver," *U.S. Crime*, Dec. 7, 1951, blames Senators Edwin Johnson of Colorado, Walter George of Georgia, and Pat McCarran of Nevada for blocking anti-crime legislation.

49. Moore, *The Kefauver Committee and the Politics of Crime*, 231–34.

50. *Christian Science Monitor*, Nov. 22, 1950.

Chapter 10

The Boy Has Struck a Wave of Popularity

In 1952, Kefauver treated the entire nation to a more elaborate version of his 1948 campaign "road show," coonskin cap and all, in a direct appeal to the people to force the Democratic National Convention to accept him as the party's presidential nominee.

The first big question facing any Democrat with presidential ambitions that year was whether or not President Truman would seek reelection. Truman's popularity was not at its height, from surface indications anyhow, and after nearly seven years in office he exhibited some symptoms of a readiness to step down. But under sharp attack from Republicans over the country's entanglement in the Korean War, there was always the good chance that Truman would get his temper up and attempt to repeat the upset of 1948.

The prospects were increasing that the Republicans would nominate Dwight D. Eisenhower, over the strenuous resistance of the party's conservative wing. In this event, if Truman retired, Kefauver seemed the best match for Eisenhower's glamor among Democratic possibilities, thanks to the crime investigation and television. At least, this was the view, biased though it may have been, of Kefauver's friends and admirers.

There were some signs that the view was shared to a degree by the less pro-Kefauver hierarchy of the Democratic party itself. Kefauver was tabbed by the party stalwarts as the most effective Democrat to answer the citicism by another Republican "glamor boy," General Douglas MacArthur, of the Korean situation. When Truman recalled MacArthur from the Korean command in April 1951 and MacArthur appeared before the Senate, Kefauver was one of his questioners; and Kefauver was chosen by the Democratic leadership the following December to answer MacArthur's denunciation of the Truman administration the previous month.[1]

1. *Nashville Tennessean*, Dec. 5, 1951; *New Republic*, Dec. 17, 1951.

That assignment was one factor in his decision to enter the presidential lists. Scattered talk of Kefauver-for-President, popping up in occasional newspaper speculation, coalesced into a real boom after the New York crime investigation hearings on television. Porter Warner, George McInturff, and other Chattanooga friends formed a Kefauver-for-President club in his home city,[2] and Washington newspaper columnists found an increasing amount of copy in speculation on a Kefauver spot on the 1952 Democratic ticket.

Throughout most of the year, Kefauver held "the matter in abeyance, to see the drift of things," in the words of his father. But by the latter part of the year, Cooke Kefauver, visiting his son in Washington, said in reply to newsmen's questions about Estes's intentions that "it looks like his friends are running him."[3] The old gentleman may have derived that line of thought from a luncheon conversation he had with Senator Herbert O'Conor.

"The boy has struck a wave of popularity from Maine to California," O'Conor told the elder Kefauver. "Those people have put their money and their efforts into getting him boosted for the Presidency, and he can't do anything but ride with the wave. If he doesn't, they'll call him a quitter."[4]

Kefauver gave a quiet go-ahead to his friends to form a Kefauver-for-President club statewide in Tennessee, with headquarters in Nashville and McInturff as its president. En route to Seattle for the MacArthur speech, he agreed to permit his name to go on the California presidential primary ballot the next June. On the last day of 1951, Kefauver supporters in Washington opened a national headquarters in the Willard Hotel, Charlie Neese traveling up from Tennessee to take charge. Kefauver-for-President clubs sprang up all over the country, until by mid-January there were such clubs in 47 of the 48 states (the holdout was Delaware).

But until Truman announced his own intentions, there was always the chance that an announcement by someone else would be taken by him as a personal challenge. Kefauver's relations with the President had not been unfriendly, generally. He had supported Truman's program for the most part and had visited the President

2. *Nashville Tennessean*, April 22, 1951.
3. UP story, *Nashville Tennessean*, Jan. 14, 1952.
4. Personal conversation, Cooke Kefauver, Madisonville, Tenn., Spring 1955.

at the White House on occasion. But he was well aware that Truman was irritated at his failure to "protect" the party in the crime investigation. At one time during the probe the President had referred to him as "Senator Cow-fever."[5]

But Kefauver needed to capitalize on the mass of popular sentiment for him by wooing party support in the various states. Especially did he need to enter the most important of the seventeen presidential primaries in the nation to prove to the party leaders his vote-getting ability against all comers. He talked the matter over with a good friend in Congress, Ohio's forthright young Representative Wayne L. Hays, who was something of a fire-eater. Hays was a liberal in good standing with the party's high command and he was all for Kefauver.

Hays visited Truman on Kefauver's behalf January 6 and laid down a virtual ultimatum: either announce his own intentions by February 6—deadline for entering the May Ohio presidential primary—or see Ohio delegates commit themselves to Kefauver. Truman remained noncommittal, but three days later the Democratic organization in Ohio announced it would pledge a slate of primary candidates to former Senator Robert J. Bulkley as a "favorite son" to hold the delegation for Truman if he wanted it. Hays countered promptly with an announcement that a delegate slate pledged to Kefauver also would be entered.[6]

Hays urged Kefauver to talk to Truman himself and so did Silliman Evans, a personal friend of Truman, whose *Nashville Tennessean* had been one of only four major newspapers in the nation to support Truman in 1948. Kefauver sought a meeting with Truman and was given 30 minutes with him January 15.

Kefauver told the President he was thinking of running but would not if Truman planned to seek reelection. Truman said he could not give a definite answer because he had not made up his mind. In that event, said Kefauver, he hoped the President would not take his candidacy as an affront; he would try to run as a "good Democrat." Truman responded in a friendly tone with words that

5. Robert Coughlan, "How Stumping Kefauver Stumps the Pros," *Life*, May 28, 1956.
6. Glenn Everett, *Nashville Tennessean*, Dec. 30, 1951; Lois Laycook, ibid., Jan. 3 and 8, 1952.

the hopeful Kefauver took as a virtual green light. He said he knew Kefauver would conduct himself in the best interest of the party and the nation, should he decide to run. He said he felt it was time that "young Democrats" begin to build themselves up for national office. And he suggested: "Play up your victory over the Crump machine. The people will like that."[7]

So, at a press conference in the Hotel Statler January 23, Kefauver announced: "I am a candidate for President of the United States." He emphasized a foreign policy of "strength . . . economic, political, moral, as well as military strength . . . clean government. . . . we in the federal government must first clean our own house," and he promised a balanced budget.[8]

The general news media reaction to Kefauver's announcement was that it would not sit well with Truman and the party leadership. *Newsweek* magazine commented that "politicians live by a very special standard of morality, and by this standard Kefauver committed an immoral act. He embarrassed the party to which he belonged, and he injured his friends."[9] The *New York Herald Tribune* even detected "signs that the Administration will use its full power to destroy the Tennessean's bid."[10]

Although Kefauver had been trying to get a national campaign organization put together for more than a month before he announced, it was still a skeletal sort of thing and never did get to the point of working with professional effectiveness. Right up through the convention, the Kefauver campaign was essentially a one-man show, with the correspondence, fund-raising, and detail work being done mostly by Tennesseans in Washington and Nashville and with nobody but Kefauver himself working actively to round up the all-important delegate support for the convention.

Kefauver had to wheedle for several weeks to persuade Neese to leave his Tennessee law practice, which was just getting reestablished, to return to Washington to take temporary charge. "He put the heat on—he was very good at that," said Neese later, "and I fi-

7. Anderson and Blumenthal, *The Kefauver Story*, 169.
8. *Nashville Tennessean*, Jan. 24, 1952.
9. Ibid., Feb. 3, 1952.
10. Dorothy Schiff wrote in the *New York Post*, Oct. 30, 1955, that "Truman at that time seemed to have only one aim in life. That was to stop Kefauver at any cost."

nally agreed to come back for six weeks." The "six weeks" stretched to virtually the entire campaign.[11]

The first top campaign official to be brought into the Kefauver organization was Nathan Straus, owner of Radio Station WMCA in New York, as treasurer. Straus had served as U.S. housing administrator for five years during the Roosevelt administration, and it was as such that Kefauver met him during his first full term in the House. Straus was under attack from building-and-loan and real estate interests at the time, and Kefauver—saying "I don't know if it's the sensible thing for me to do, but it's the right thing to do"[12] —came to his support with some floor speeches in the House.

Straus's job was not an easy one. Generally, those people with substantial funds to dispense for political campaigns could find few people they would less like to see become President than a man with Kefauver's record of support for antitrust legislation and various New Deal and Fair Deal programs. A report in the *Pittsburgh Post-Gazette* that approximately 250 Tennessee businessmen pledged $1,000 each to Kefauver's campaign was simply untrue. McInturff said no such pledges were made to Kefauver in Tennessee, and as for actual contributors in the state the only major ones were a few wealthy men like Alfred Starr of Nashville and M.M. Bullard of Newport.[13]

Straus extracted some money from well-heeled liberals, mostly in the Northeast, but the most liberal of the liberals were not inclined to approve of Kefauver's spotty civil rights record. They preferred Averell Harriman of New York. Before the campaign was two months old, the Kefauver headquarters moved from the Willard to the nearby Raleigh Hotel to cut down on expenses. When it was all over, Kefauver's effort had cost around a half million dollars, and the Kefauver organization was still in debt nearly $40,000.[14]

Talking it over late in 1951 at Neese's vacation cabin on Ken-

11. Personal conversation, Charles G. Neese, Greeneville, Tenn., Spring 1971.

12. Irwin Ross, *New York Post*, May 11, 1956.

13. *Pittsburgh Post-Gazette*, May 3, 1952; personal conversation, George McInturff, Chattanooga, Spring 1971.

14. Kefauver reported that money disbursed by his national headquarters, which he said represented the bulk of his expenditures, totaled $356,387, of which the largest single item was $85,572 for salaries. Alexander Heard, *The Costs of Democracy* (Chapel Hill: Univ. of North Carolina Press, 1960), 334, 340.

tucky Lake near Paris, Tennessee, Kefauver, Neese, and Harry Mansfield decided that the campaign should have two directors: one a "front man" with a well-known name to lend prestige and charm delegates, and the other a "working boss" to "do the stuff" —such as direct organizational efforts, scheduling, correspondence.[15]

John T. O'Brien, forty-three-year-old director of information for the Office of Rent Stabilization, was appointed "working boss"— theoretically to succeed Neese, though Neese remained very much on hand, very active and influential. O'Brien was good at publicizing Kefauver and his philosophy and activities but less effective at detailed organization work.

A number of people—including Adlai Stevenson—were discussed as a possible "prestige" campaign director, but the man finally chosen was handsome Gael E. Sullivan, one of the glamor boys of the Democratic party. Sullivan, executive director of the Theater Owners of America and a former vice chairman of the Democratic National Committee who had worked very effectively in Truman's 1948 campaign, was acquired for Kefauver through the good offices of Starr, a theater owner.

Selection of Sullivan, Neese said later, was "the biggest mistake since the South lost the Civil War."[16] Sullivan did not take over until mid-campaign, and until then the organization, under the direction of Neese and O'Brien, did little except encourage the organization of Kefauver-for-President clubs, handle voluminous correspondence, work out campaign schedules, and try to raise funds. Virtually no attempt was made to woo convention delegates and local party organizations, except for what Kefauver himself did.

It was anticipated that Sullivan, with his extensive party contacts, would devote much of his time to doing that. But Neese termed Sullivan a grandstander, "an egotist who never did get to the hard realities,"[17] and the two men were almost constantly at odds.

One of Kefauver's reasons for announcing on January 23 was the date's significance as the twentieth anniversary of Franklin D. Roosevelt's first announcement as a candidate for President. Silliman Evans, who had been a key figure in Roosevelt's nomination by the 1932 Democratic National Convention and who exerted a marked

15. Personal conversation, Charles G. Neese, Greeneville, Spring 1971.
16. Ibid.
17. Ibid.

impact on Kefauver's thinking about the presidential race, saw numerous parallels between the Democratic situations in 1952 and 1932. It was Evans' view that Kefauver's campaign should follow the same basic course as that of Roosevelt in 1932. He should announce early and build up such a showing of popular support that he would go into the convention in the role of the popular choice for the nomination.[18]

Kefauver entered New Hampshire's first-in-the-nation primary against the advice of Neese, who predicted accurately that his entry would offend the President. But in 1932 Roosevelt had gotten off to a running start by defeating Alfred E. Smith, titular head of the party, in the New Hampshire primary. New Hampshire's convention delegates were elected separately from the presidential preference primary, but at the same time. Since the first of the year, Kefauver's New Hampshire state chairman, former Keene postmaster Hugh Waling, had been trying to put together a slate of delegates, but he had a hard time of it. Emmett J. Kelley, the state's national committeeman, had received word early in December from the national committee to file a slate of delegate candidates favorable to Truman, and by the time Kefauver announced, all of the well-known and influential organization Democrats were committed to Truman. Waling was able to field a full slate of Kefauver delegate candidates but only a partial slate of candidates for alternates; on the other hand, in most cases there were two pro-Truman candidates vying for each spot on the delegate ticket.

Kelley prevailed on James D. McPhail, a Manchester lumber dealer and a virtual unknown in party circles, to enter Truman's name in the preference primary because none of the state's party leaders was willing to accept personal responsibility for the action. They had waited in vain for Truman to give some indication of his desire in the matter, and his name was entered just before the deadline on the assumption that, since the national committee wanted a slate of Truman delegates, Truman would want his name on the preference ballot too.

Truman apparently did not. He reacted with the comment that primaries were "eyewash," and he could have the nomination if he wanted it, without having to run in any primary. For good mea-

18. See *Nashville Tennessean*, May 20 and June 15, 1952.

sure, he added that he would have his name removed from the ballot.[19] New Hampshire Democrats reacted critically. The state's party leaders became alarmed that they might lose the delegate contest and possibly control of the party organization. Republicans were delighted, among them Senator George D. Aiken of adjacent Vermont, who commented that the President was withdrawing "because Senator Kefauver would have beaten the tar out of him." Kefauver himself made the somewhat incautious remark that he thought he could win the nomination even if Truman decided to seek reelection.[20]

Immediately afterward, Kefauver, finding himself seated on a plane beside Frank McKinney, Democratic national chairman, offered to withdraw from the primary if Truman would do so too, letting the primary contest revolve solely around the delegate slates. McKinney agreed to consider the proposal, but he finally chose to urge Truman to remain in the primary.[21] The President made it known six days later that he would let his name remain on the ballot.[22]

"Estes," said Neese when the issue was joined, "you can't run for President like you did for the Senate."[23] But Kefauver did; and New Hampshire was ideally suited for a condensed version of his 1948 campaign—only 185 miles long and 80 miles wide, with about one-sixth of Tennessee's population. Kefauver flew into Concord from Chicago in mid-February to kick off his race with a press conference and a sandwich-and-coffee gathering with about a hundred people at the Eagle Hotel. Nancy joined him there from Washington, and he began a leisurely swing through the winterbound state.

For the most part of three weeks, then, he plodded doggedly through the New Hampshire snow, soliciting individual votes like a country constable, while politically wise newsmen from Washington and New York muttered into their portable typewriters. This "Don Quixote from Tennessee," as Theodore H. White called

19. Lois Laycook, *Nashville Tennessean*, Feb. 1, 1952.
20. AP story, ibid., Feb. 4, 1952.
21. Anderson and Blumenthal, *The Kefauver Story*, 171–72.
22. AP story, *Nashville Tennessean*, Feb. 8, 1952.
23. Personal conversation, Charles G. Neese, Paris, Tenn., Spring 1955.

194

him once,[24] seemed to think simple handshaking could overcome the prestige and power of a President still in office. Kefauver would read the reporters' slighting estimates of his chances, perhaps while sipping a milkshake or munching a cheese sandwich, and ponder them silently, with pursed lips. Then he would toss the newspapers aside, unfold his long legs, and amble out into the snowy streets again. He would intercept a surprised pedestrian, who might or might not recognize the long, sober face and the owl-like spectacles. Thrusting out a huge hand, Kefauver would say: "My name is Estes Kefauver. I'm running for President of the United States. I'd sure appreciate it if you'll help me." At his side, red-haired Nancy, chic and charming, would flash a pixie smile and jot down the name and address of the prospective voter for a follow-up letter as Kefauver chatted with him a minute or two and then moved on.

Kefauver tossed a snowball at an ice sculpture of a Republican elephant on Plymouth Common; he got his hand struck in a movie theater ticket window when he thrust his hand in to shake hands with the cashier. Nancy drove a racing jalopy around frozen Lake Winnipesaukee at Laconia and made a radio talk in French at Berlin, on the Canadian border.[25]

On the other side of the picture, the Democratic organization poured on the coal for Truman. Most labor leaders worked actively for the President, following up an endorsement with broadcasts and 65,000 leaflets distributed at union factories. But Truman, vacationing at Key West, stayed out of it personally, and efforts to get such out-of-state notables as Senator Brien McMahon of Connecticut and Representative John W. McCormack of Massachusetts to campaign in New Hampshire for him fell through; Scott Lucas did travel from Illinois to make two speeches for the President and comment that the Kefauver crime investigation had been a "televised road show."

Kefauver did not campaign against Truman personally. But his divergence from the President in many of his views was apparent, and the general newspaper viewpoint that he offered an alternative

24. *Collier's*, May 11, 1956.
25. *Nashville Tennessean*, Feb. 18, 1952; *Young Democrat*, April 1954.

Kefauver gets out to lend a hand in pushing the stuck campaign car, as Nancy smiles out the window at him, during his 1952 presidential primary campaign in New Hampshire.

Kefauver and Senator Richard Russell argue over Kefauver's congressional record during a joint television appearance the night before the 1952 Florida presidential primary.

and a corrective approach to some Truman policies was not inaccurate. Besides public differences on Korea, expressed before he was called on to defend the administration against MacArthur, he had stated before his announcement that he thought corruption in government would be an issue in the 1952 campaign and had implied strongly that the Truman administration ought to "clean up conditions."

Although, by campaign's end, Kefauver won the endorsement of some prominent Democrats, his defeat in a head-on contest with the President was taken for granted. An Associated Press poll of newspaper editors gave Truman a 3 to 1 margin, though some Democratic leaders conceded the President might do no better than 3 to 2.[26] Kefauver disagreed with them: ending his campaign in Manchester on March 10, he predicted he would beat Truman by a margin that would "surprise many people on the morrow."[27]

Many people, indeed, were surprised on the morrow: the results of the New Hampshire primary sent a shock wave through both political parties all across the country. In the preference contest, Kefauver defeated Truman overwhelmingly, 19,800 to 15,927, winning eight of the state's ten counties. All of the Kefauver delegates won, the Kefauver at-large slate outpolling both full Truman slates combined, and one Kefauver district delegate ousted Kelley, the national committeeman.

The parallel with Roosevelt was still holding up nicely. Kefauver's 55 percent share of the vote was not quite up to the 62 percent Roosevelt had gained in defeating Smith in New Hampshire in 1932, but Roosevelt had had the support of the state party organization. Kefauver had taken the party away from its national leadership in New Hampshire.

Kefauver buttons appeared at once in the lapels of some Washington newspaper correspondents and coonskin caps sold well all over the nation—so well that Kefauver issued an appeal to people not to wipe out the raccoon species, until it turned out that many caps were being made from old raccoon coats rescued from attics. All at once, Kefauver was the front-runner for the Democratic nomination, no matter what Truman decided to do; and he be-

26. *Time*, Feb. 25, 1952.
27. AP story, *Nashville Tennessean*, March 11, 1952.

came even more recognizably so before the end of the month, when Truman said he would not seek reelection.

Kefauver's strategy was to enter as many primaries as possible where he could win favorable delegates, but he kept his name out of the next primary on the list, Minnesota on March 18, because of an agreement with Senator Hubert H. Humphrey, the forty-one-year-old civil rights firebrand of the 1948 convention, who was entered as a favorite son. Kefauver and Humphrey were good friends, and there were reports—which Humphrey denied—that Humphrey had committed his support to Kefauver in the event that Truman did not run. In fact, Humphrey did announce his support for Kefauver after Truman said he would not run again.

Kefauver entered two primaries occurring on the same day, two weeks after Minnesota—Wisconsin and Nebraska—and campaigned actively in both states. In Wisconsin, where he was opposed by two Truman stand-ins, he was expected to win even before Truman withdrew his name from consideration. When Truman withdrew two days before the primary, one of the stand-ins, Charles E. Broughton, said he was running as a "draft Truman" candidate" and the other, Jerome F. Fox, remained on the ballot as head of an "uninstructed" delegation.

Kefauver repeated his ambling New Hampshire handshaking tour in this different state, touching up a few different issues such as farm and dairying problems and taking a slap at the Communist-hunting tactics of Wisconsin's Republican Senator Joseph Mc-Carthy. Truman's withdrawal dealt the final blow to any outside chance of Kefauver's losing Wisconsin's pledged 28 delegate votes. His ticket was elected by 207,520 to 18,322 for Fox and 15,683 for Broughton.

In Nebraska, Kefauver's image as a winning campaigner was at stake again. There he had active opposition by a serious contender of recognized stature for the first time: Senator Robert S. Kerr of nearby Oklahoma, who qualified his candidacy originally by saying that he would support Truman if Truman sought reelection, emerging as a serious contender for the nomination in his own right when Truman withdrew.

The Kefauver-Kerr contest emphasized a preexisting split in the state's Democratic organization. The "regular" faction, headed by national committeeman James Quigley, supported Kerr, and a dissident element, the "New Lifers," in which the Americans for Democratic Action was influential, supported Kefauver. Before Kefauver could do anything about organizing his Nebraska campaign, he found himself provided with a self-proclaimed manager, Frank Morrison, a McCook attorney opposed to the Quigley faction.

It was a sharp campaign, in which Kerr countered Nancy's presence with Kefauver by bringing in his own honey-haired wife to help him. Kerr slapped at Kefauver's internationalism and Kefauver retorted that this was the same sort of "smear campaign" as that levelled against him in Tennessee in 1948. When Kerr called Kefauver a "moral uplifter" whose supporters were spending large sums to win for him, Kefauver responded that Kerr represented "vested interests" in gas and oil, and the nation "can't afford to have a gas-and-oil President in the White House." Tennessee's Governor Gordon Browning went to Nebraska to campaign for Kefauver. Kefauver of distant Tennessee, the emulator of George Norris, stood much closer in spirit to the frugal Nebraskans, although the jocular, florid Kerr was from a nearby Democratic state. Kerr's denial that he was either a Truman stand-in or an instrument of a party "stop-Kefauver" movement was not convincing in view of the party organization's commitment to him. Kefauver's margin over Kerr in the preference primary was 64,531 to 42,467.

The delegate contest was a different story. Despite newspaper efforts to determine presidential preferences among delegate candidates, who were unpledged, voters could be sure only that Morrison would support Kefauver and Bernard Boyle, Kerr's state manager, would support Kerr. Both were elected, and the delegate count broke down eventually to five for Kefauver, four for Kerr, two for Adlai Stevenson, and one for Georgia's Senator Richard Russell.

Before Kefauver's next two major primaries, in Florida and Ohio, there were five primaries in which, as in Nebraska, expressions of popular preference for the presidential nominee were not binding on the delegates elected at the same time. The first of these, Illinois, turned the spotlight on Adlai Stevenson, who had been a political unknown in 1947 but in the intervening five years had become one of the nation's most respected governors.

Since the beginning of the year, Stevenson had been reported widely as Truman's choice for his successor, though at one point the *Chicago Sun-Times* reported that Stevenson had "firmly declined" the President's suggestion that he become the administration candidate. Stevenson himself did not absolutely close the door on the nomination but said in March that he was interested only in running for reelection as governor of Illinois.[28]

Leaders in the dominant Chicago Democratic organization, who felt they had been damaged by the crime investigation, were anxious for Stevenson to get into the fight, but they could not persuade him to permit his name on the ballot except as a candidate for governor. Eventually, Kefauver's name was the only one on the presidential preference ballot, and he won the primary with 526,301 votes to 54,336 write-in votes for Stevenson. But an effort by Kefauver supporters to file a full slate of fifty district delegate candidates was abandoned because there was no way to list their preference for Kefauver on the ballot, and a slate of uncommitted delegates supported by the Democratic organization was elected.

Shortly after the primary, Stevenson said he "could not" accept the presidential nomination because of his "prior commitment to run for governor."[29] After that statement, Illinois Senator Paul Douglas, a former economics professor and Marine Corps hero who had been chosen the No. 1 senator in the nation at the same time Kefauver was named No. 2, announced his active support of Kefauver.

"Some of the politicians, bureaucrats and king-makers may not like you because they know they can't control you, but the people are for you," said Douglas. Kefauver was moved to respond: "Paul, bless your heart!"[30]

Douglas, nine years older than Kefauver and almost as big and as tall, was more consistently liberal than Kefauver. He and Kefauver were usually on the same side of an issue in the Senate, but by no means always. They were not intimate friends—Douglas said he didn't believe anyone was really an intimate friend of Kefauver[31]—but they respected and liked each other. The importance of his endorsement to Kefauver rested not only in the nationwide respect ac-

28. Paul T. David, Malcolm Moos, and Ralph M. Goldman, *Presidential Nominating Politics in 1952* (Baltimore: Johns Hopkins Univ. Press, 1954), vol. I, "The National Story," 40.
29. Jack Bell, AP story, *Nashville Tennessean*, April 17, 1952.
30. *Nashville Banner*, April 17, 1952.
31. Personal communication, Paul H. Douglas, July 20, 1970.

corded Douglas as a senator, but in the fact that Douglas was from Stevenson's home state and had been elected in 1948 on the same ticket with Stevenson.

In four other states—New Jersey, Pennsylvania, Massachusetts, and Maryland—Kefauver won preference primaries with little or no opposition but gained few delegate commitments. Only in Maryland, the state's party convention chose the delegates and instructed them to support Kefauver on the basis of the preference vote. Despite this weakness in pledged delegates, when Kefauver faced the primary voters of Florida and Ohio at about the midpoint of the preconvention campaign, he was the recognized front-runner for the nomination and had demonstrated his principal claim to the nomination: "the people" wanted him. In nine preference primaries, he had received 1,253,578 votes, against a total of about 327,000 for all other candidates combined—including two Republicans, Dwight Eisenhower and Robert Taft, who won write-in votes in some Democratic primaries.

Yet, during the period of these primaries, nine other states and four territories chose national convention delegates by state committee or state convention action, and New York and Alabama by primaries without any preference provision. Thanks largely to the inactivity of Kefauver's national organization in the practical work of wooing local support, Kefauver gained nothing significant in the way of delegate strength from any of these except Alabama, where he had active local support, and Alaska, where he was befriended by Governor Ernest Gruening.

The ineffectiveness of Kefauver's national campaign organization in dealing with political realities was reflected in the total convention delegate strength he had won from all his hard campaigning and all his popular votes. Of the 554 convention delegates chosen during that period, only 54—from New Hampshire, Wisconsin, and Maryland—actually were pledged to Kefauver, and he ultimately received only 119 on the first convention ballot.

The Florida primary was a perilous venture for Kefauver, because Governor Fuller Warren controlled the state's Democratic machinery, and Warren was still as bitter as Scott Lucas about the disclosures of the crime investigation. O'Brien and McInturff advised Kefauver strongly against entering Florida because they said the odds were stacked against him too heavily.

"I've got to go to Florida," Kefauver told them. "I've got some mighty good friends down there, and Fuller Warren would crucify them if I don't. He's been saying all these bad things about me, and he'd say I was afraid to go into Florida. He'd make it impossible for them to live there."[32]

In Florida, Kefauver was pitted against his most formidable opponent since Truman in New Hampshire—Richard Russell of Georgia, who had become the focus for Southern conservative sentiment immediately upon his announcement at the end of February. Russell, who had polled more than 263 delegate votes against Truman in the 1948 convention, limited his presidential primary effort to Florida as a one-shot proposition. Russell hoped to win by a large majority to support his argument that, because Florida resembled the metropolitan East more than any other Southern state, he could do well in the nation at large if nominated. Kefauver, on the other hand, with no Democratic organization support in the South outside of Tennessee, hoped to defeat Russell to prove that the people of the South were for him, even if the professional politicians were not. Russell had the support of the Warren administration and Florida's entire delegation in Congress, all of whom campaigned actively for him. Governor Herman E. Talmadge of Georgia also campaigned for him in northern Florida, much of whose population consisted of immigrants from Georgia.

Kefauver, on the other hand, was backed essentially by the liberal wing of the Florida Democratic party, headed by former U.S. Senator Claude Pepper, who endorsed Kefauver and campaigned for him during the final days of the race. His campaign was headed by W. Raleigh Petteway, the state attorney general and the only well-known Florida public official to endorse him. Paul Douglas visited Florida briefly to speak in Kefauver's behalf.

Warren, whose personal support embarrassed Russell (Russell eventually disavowed it), greeted Kefauver's arrival in the state by announcing that he had a list of "21 questions" challenging Kefauver's fitness to be President. Warren demanded that Kefauver debate the questions with him. Kefauver was willing, but the two men could not agree on the length of the debate. Kefauver said he

32. Personal conversation, George McInturff, Chattanooga, Spring 1955.

could answer the questions in thirty minutes and could spare no more time from his campaign. Warren insisted on an unlimited debate, saying it would take him nearly two hours to discuss only four of the items.[33]

Thereupon Kefauver set out to track Warren down and meet him face to face. He almost did. When Warren refused to debate in Jacksonville, Kefauver headed for Tallahassee. He walked into the state capitol and moved down the corridor toward the governor's office, shaking hands with state employees as he went. But just as he entered Warren's office, the governor hastened out the back door—"to keep an appointment," his secretary said. The secretary handed Kefauver a copy of Warren's "21 questions." Followed by a coterie of reporters who had trailed him into the building, Kefauver retired to the capitol steps.

"Ask me anything you want to," Kefauver told the newsmen.

One of them picked up the list of "21 questions," scanned it, shook his head, and handed it back.

"They're too loaded for me, Senator," he said.[34]

Russell, however, had no qualms about meeting his colleague. He sought Kefauver out when the two were campaigning simultaneously in Jacksonville, the two Senators shook hands and exchanged pleasantries, and when Kefauver jokingly referred to Russell's relatively well-financed campaign and asked to borrow a dime, Russell gravely gave him half a dollar.[35]

Russell debated Kefauver the night before the primary, and the two candidates were not so kind in their words to each other. They slashed at each other with bitter sarcasm, often almost shouting, and ignored others who were supposed to be participating in the panel discussion. Taking note of Russell's statement that he would not accept a compulsory FEPC plank in the Democratic platform, Kefauver commented that he was "not going to pick up my marbles and run out" if the platform was not to his liking.

"If you mean that I'm going to leave the party," retorted Russell hotly, "oh, no! I'm not going to leave the party!"[36]

33. UP story, *Nashville Tennessean*, May 5, 1952.
34. Anderson and Blumenthal, *The Kefauver Story*, 176–77.
35. AP story, *Nashville Tennessean*, May 3, 1952.
36. Don Whitehead, AP story, *Nashville Tennessean*, May 6, 1952.

When the returns from Florida's May 6 primary were in, Russell had defeated Kefauver 367,980 to 285,358. Kefauver piled up a heavy majority in the urban areas, particularly Miami, but carried only eight counties. The Florida rural areas went strongly for Russell. Neither candidate had gotten what he needed in Florida. Russell's poor showing in the urban areas did not support his claim to possess non-regional appeal as a candidate. Kefauver's legend of invincibility at the polls had been broken, and his severe defeat in the rural areas indicated rejection by any genuinely Southern constituency. The preference primary that injured both men's chances for the nomination had no effect whatever on Florida's delegation to the national convention. Delegates were elected in a separate primary three weeks later. Kefauver-pledged delegates won five of the twenty-four seats on the delegation, the rest going to Russell-pledged delegates.

Kefauver's campaign in Florida was complicated by the necessity of devoting some attention simultaneously to Ohio, which held its primary on the same day. Ohio was important, not only because of its fifty-four convention votes, but because delegates ran pledged to a candidate. Kefauver's Ohio leaders—Hays, Cincinnati attorney Timothy Hogan, and Herbert S. Duffy, a former state attorney general—had their troubles with the Democratic organization, which was pushing Bulkley as a favorite son. The Kefauver people initially were unable to find out how many delegates-at-large would be authorized, until it was too late to field more than half a slate. Then efforts were made to disqualify Kefauver delegates. A state Supreme Court decision blocked a move to disqualify them *en bloc*, but a dozen Kefauver delegates were disqualified individually. The situation was complicated by a feud between supporters and opponents of Governor Frank Lausche.

Late in April, while Nancy, whom Russell called "Kefauver's most dangerous secret weapon," was campaigning with her husband in an open convertible under the pleasant Florida sun, Kefauver received an urgent telegram telling him he was needed to shore up fences in Ohio. He did not feel he could leave Florida at the moment, but within an hour Nancy was on a plane to Columbus. She campaigned in the state for several days, and at last was joined by Kefauver, delayed a day en route when his plane's radio went bad near the West Virginia mountains. The couple had to split up immediately, Kefauver speaking in Marion and Nancy speaking for him at Bucyrus, because of a tight time schedule.[37]

Porter Warner commented once that Nancy had adapted herself so well to her husband's way of life that "now she's a better politician than Estes is,"[38] and she was able to fill in effectively for these emergency speeches. She knew Kefauver's stands on public issues well and explained them clearly—and could embellish them with a touch of genuine humor Kefauver could not match. In any event, Kefauver won every county in which she spoke, by a comfortable margin.

In Ohio, Kefauver scored one of his major victories of the campaign, smashing the Democratic organization and capturing precisely half of the state's 54-vote delegation. Only 35 Kefauver candidates were on the ballot, and 31 of them were elected. The total vote for Kefauver delegates-at-large was 2,209,212, against 1,285,863 for the winning Bulkley delegates-at-large, who were unopposed. Defeated by relatively unknown Kefauver delegates were such party stalwarts as Albert A. Horstman, the state's national committeeman, and Philip P. Hannah and Jack Kroll, leaders of the Ohio Federation of Labor and CIO.

After the early struggles, the remaining 1952 primaries—West Virginia, Oregon, California, South Dakota and the District of Columbia—were anticlimactic, although the two far Western ones were important to him for their delegate strength and prestige. He lost the District of Columbia to Harriman, who was campaigning actively for the nomination, and won Oregon over Stevenson, who was still saying he was not a candidate. In California, a treasure chest of sixty-eight delegate votes, he was supported by James Roosevelt, son of the late President and leader of a rebel Democratic faction, and defeated Edmund G. (Pat) Brown, the state attorney general and a favorite son candidate.

Kefauver said he waged his campaigns "on pennies" in both California and South Dakota—about $2,000 in California and only $644.42 in South Dakota—which had primaries on the same day.

37. Glenn Everett, *Nashville Tennessean*, April 27, 1952.
38. Personal conversation, Porter Warner Jr., Chattanooga, Spring 1955.

In fact, Kefauver finances were so tight that Sullivan fired a third of the national campaign staff in Washington for lack of funds in mid-May.[39]

Kefauver retired from the primary lists ten pounds lighter, and confident of victory. In retrospect, he said he would have changed his campaign tactics some, if he had it to do over again: "I would not have spread my efforts so thin in several states in which I spent a great deal of time . . . where by virtue of the political machinery I did not have much of a chance of getting delegates in the first place. Then, too, it would have been better to have made a definite break with President Truman. As it was, I criticized the shortcomings of the administration, told of the necessity of cleaning up, getting out racketeers, but still tried to avoid a final and conclusive break with him. My campaign would have been stronger and I would have lost nothing if I had taken another course."[40]

In fact, however, these faults barely touched upon the deeper and more serious flaws in his preconvention campaign. Adoption of the general strategy of Roosevelt's 1932 campaign had succeeded well insofar as it was followed. Kefauver had been dramatized to the point that he was the Democratic candidate whose popularity and vote-getting ability were most likely to compete with Eisenhower's charisma in the November election. A poll listed him among the ten most admired living Americans.[41]

Neither of his two primary losses was so serious as Roosevelt's loss of Massachusetts to Smith and California to John Nance Garner in 1932. A Roper poll in June showed that Democrats questioned preferred Kefauver by 33 percent to 10 percent for Vice President Barkley, 9 percent for Stevenson, 8 percent for Russell, and 5 percent for Harriman.

On the surface, Kefauver's chances looked better against the context of the potential field than had Roosevelt's twenty years earlier. The only real barrier he faced was the distaste of the professional politicians. But the failure of Kefauver's campaign organization to translate his popular support into practical political strength

39. AP story, *Nashville Banner*, May 17, 1952.
40. Letter, Estes Kefauver to Paul A. Theis, Washington, March 23, 1954, Kefauver Collection, Ser. 5-f, Box 5, and Ser. 1, Box 73.
41. Elmo Roper, *You and Your Leaders* (New York: William Morrow, 1957), 241.

is indicated by the fact that only 227 ½ of the primary states' 482 convention delegate votes went for him on the convention's first ballot. Even had he not spent so much time campaigning in the primaries, Kefauver alone had not the time to do spadework in the many states where delegates were chosen by state convention or state committed action. Yet the Democratic leaders in many of those states, particularly in the Middle and Far West, were not tied so closely to the national party nor so enthusiastic about other potential nominees that they could not have been won to the Kefauver cause by organized and intelligent effort.

But Kefauver's national headquarters people did virtually no such work, confining themselves to encouraging volunteer Kefauver clubs and sponsoring various public relations projects.[42] The Kefauver-Roosevelt parallel broke down precisely where Kefauver had to depend on his aides instead of doing things for himself. In 1932, Louis McHenry Howe kept his ear constantly to the ground for Roosevelt, to take advantage of every tremor, and genial Jim Farley toured the country, making friends with local political leaders and gathering delegate commitments to Roosevelt. But Gael Sullivan was far from being a Jim Farley, nor was Neese a Louis McHenry Howe.

Kefauver did not seem aware of these fundamental weaknesses when he returned triumphant from California and South Dakota and had a forty-minute chat with Truman, in which the President was so cordial that Kefauver thought he had received the hoped-for assurance that Truman would not stand between him and the nomination.

"I'm going down to Tennessee," Kefauver said, "and after a few meals of black-eyed peas and Tennessee country ham, I expect to pick up all the weight I've lost."[43]

42. Personal conversation, A. Bradley Eben, Chicago, Sept. 3, 1970; David, Moos, and Goldman, *Presidential Nominating Politics in 1952*, vol. I, 64.
43. Lois Laycook, *Nashville Tennessean*, June 6, 1952.

Chapter 11

Not Realizing That They Had Already Cut His Throat

With a month intervening between the last 1952 primary and the opening of the Democratic National Convention in Chicago, Kefauver's concern for keeping the voters "involved" in his struggle for the nomination may have been behind his consent, a few days after the primaries ended, to a dubious grandstand tactic aimed at mobilizing public indignation in his favor. This was a television program from Chicago, on which Kefauver appeared with Gael Sullivan and charged that "ambitious would-be bosses" had seized "political monopoly" of the Democratic party, with the warning: "In that way lies certain defeat for our party." Sullivan was more specific. He said: "The backers of Governor Stevenson and Sen. Richard Russell of Georgia have been in conference . . . and have entered into a conspiracy calculated to deadlock the convention. . . . They will have Governor Stevenson throw his support to Harriman at the outset. They will have Senator Russell stay in the race with his delegates. The bosses expect that this will result in a stand-off for the three candidates, each with a bloc of delegates—Senator Kefauver, Mr. Harriman and Senator Russell. . . . Then Stevenson will magnanimously allow himself to be drafted."[1]

This declaration of war on virtually the entire Democratic party leadership seems to have been Sullivan's idea originally, but it was approved, after discussion, by the entire Kefauver campaign staff.[2] It was responsible, undoubtedly, for Truman's statement the same day denying that he was trying to get the nomination for anyone. In fact, all of the evidence at that time indicated that Truman was still accepting Stevenson's insistence that he would not run and was scouting about for a candidate on whom to bestow his blessing.

1. AP story, *Nashville Tennessean*, June 22, 1952.
2. Personal conversation, Charles G. Neese, Greeneville, Tenn., Spring 1971.

Sullivan's prediction was quite accurate, in part, as to the surface course of convention events, his major error being that Stevenson's backers never did support Harriman. But there was no indication that any prearrangement or conspiracy had anything to do with the way things developed. In any event, the cry of "ganging up" could only crystallize resentment among the party regulars who influenced those very uncommitted delegates Kefauver needed for a winning combination at the convention.

Kefauver paid a final call on Truman but, not too surprisingly, found him less cordial this time. He expressed the hope that Truman would "not interfere at the convention," to which Truman replied, as he ushered Kefauver to the door, "We'll just have to see what happens."[3]

Columnist Victor Riesel asked Kefauver why the President and the party regulars were so bitterly hostile to him, when he caught the senator relaxing in Cleveland after a handshaking session among CIO Communications Workers.

"Well," replied Kefauver, "I guess it's because I announced before the President made his position known. Also, there'll be lots of changes made in the organization if I'm President. A political party should belong to the people. I'd bring in young people and not just operate for the personal and political aggrandizement of professional politicians. And, I guess, some of those opposed to me can't forget what the Senate Crime Committee dug up, showing some links with political circles. That's about it."[4]

The problem Truman and the party regulars faced was finding a satisfactory alternative. In an Associated Press poll in mid-July, only Senator Richard Russell's 161½ delegate votes and W. Averell Harriman's 112½ provided any respectable comparison to Kefauver's 257½. Russell, with his Southern label and Dixiecrat support, was as unacceptable to the party hierarchy. Harriman, though not persona non grata with the President and party leadership, was in much the same position for opposite reasons: the party leaders calculated that, because of his strong liberal views, he would be unpalatable to Southern voters and might even cause a party split, as in 1948.

3. Anderson and Blumenthal, *The Kefauver Story*, 181.
4. Victor Riesel, *Nashville Tennessean*, July 10, 1952.

With Adlai Stevenson remaining coy (and showing only 41½ delegate votes in the AP poll), the party leaders put on the pressure for a time for Vice President Alben Barkley, but his boom collapsed upon his arrival in Chicago for the convention. Jack Kroll, director of the CIO Political Action Committee, said "we're not able to support him because of his age" and George Harrison of the American Federation of Labor said "we just don't think we can win with him."[5]

Kefauver, on his arrival in Chicago just before the convention, charged that Jacob Arvey, the Illinois national committeeman, was "conniving and scheming for a synthetic draft" of Stevenson. But Arvey, in fact, had almost given up on Stevenson and was involved in the short-lived Barkley boom. A committee of Volunteers for Stevenson did get to work wooing delegates, however, headed by Leo Lerner of the Independent Voters of Illinois and Professor Walter Johnson of the University of Chicago, and a twenty-member "draft Stevenson" committee was formed from eight Eastern and Midwestern states.[6]

Stevenson, at the convention both as governor of Illinois and as a delegate, received a ten-minute ovation when he welcomed the delegates at the opening convention session. He maintained his position of not seeking the nomination until the very last, but before his name was placed before the convention he had agreed privately not to decline the nomination.[7]

Having traveled 115,000 miles in his campaign, Kefauver made a final bid for delegates in Syracuse, New York, and flew with Nancy to Chicago July 16. He was met by a delegation of several hundred people, and Arvey, who was welcoming all delegates officially, rode with the Kefauvers in a red Cadillac convertible at the head of a mile-long motorcade to Kefauver's headquarters at the Conrad Hilton Hotel.[8] With combination living and working quarters in a penthouse atop the Sherman Hotel, Kefauver kept up the same blistering pace in search of delegates in Chicago that he had main-

5. *Time*, July 28, 1952; David, Moos, and Goldman, *Presidential Nominating Politics in 1952*, vol. I, 117.

6. AP story, *Nashville Tennessean*, July 20, 1952.

7. David, Moos, and Goldman, *Presidential Nominating Politics in 1952*, vol. IV, "The Middle West," 121.

8. Lois Laycook, *Nashville Tennessean*, July 17, 1952.

Kefauver pins a campaign button on one of his young supporters, John Greene of Nashville, during the Democratic National Convention in 1952. With them are Nancy, Bob Youngerman of Nashville (background), and Coleman Lowry of Jackson, Mississippi.

Kefauver (center) lines up with his opponents for the 1952 presidential nomination at the Democratic National Convention, prior to a *Meet the Press* program. With him, from left, are W. Averell Harriman, Robert S. Kerr, Richard B. Russell, and Vice President Alben W. Barkley.

tained during the primaries, with breakfasts, luncheons, conferences, interviews, and television appearances. In one day, he talked to eight state delegations.

Kefauver took his seat as a Tennessee delegate-at-large in the convention hall at the Chicago Stockyards on the convention's first day, July 21, and, by unwritten tradition, that should have marked his last appearance before the convention as long as he remained a candidate for the nomination. But he violated this tradition on the convention's third afternoon by entering the amphitheater with his father, eighty-one-year-old Cooke Kefauver.

As they made their way slowly to a mezzanine box, people in nearby seats rushed to shake Kefauver's hand, causing a small commotion. On the floor, Kefauver's "man in charge of setting up things," forty-four-year-old Chicago attorney A. Bradley Eben, recognized an unexpected opportunity. He hastened out and returned in a few minutes with boxes of red-and-yellow Kefauver whistles and other noise-makers, and a twenty-five-minute Kefauver demonstration overrode the gaveling of Governor Paul Dever of Massachusetts, temporary chairman.[9] Kefauver smiled and waved, raised his father's hand in a victory salute, and left the hall at last in the midst of the demonstration, shaking hands as he went. He answered subsequent criticism of his appearance by saying that he merely wanted to be sure his father was seated and then slip out quietly, and "the demonstration was . . . unexpected."[10]

Kefauver went into the convention as representative of a broader spectrum of political philosophy than any other announced candidate. His biggest bloc of more than 150 delegate votes, from the West Coast and the Middle Western farm states, plus New Hampshire, was moderately liberal in outlook. He had a conservative element of 59 delegates from his own Tennessee and other former Confederate states and more than 100 votes (including secondary support) from the North and East on the liberal end of the stick.[11]

The movement of the Kefauver candidacy to an extreme liberal position during the convention, which was not Kefauver's intention,

9. Personal conversation, A. Bradley Eben, Chicago, Sept. 3, 1970.

10. Lois Laycook, *Nashville Tennessean*, July 24, 1952.

11. This analysis is based on the first convention vote on the nomination, in David, Moos, and Goldman, *Presidential Nominating Politics in 1952*, vol. I, 152.

stemmed partly from the dominant role late-coalescing Michigan and Pennsylvania support assumed in his campaign organization, and partly from his alliance with the Harriman forces. The movement to the Harriman alliance came about more or less by chance. The first steps were taken when Kefauver and some of his campaign aides ran into some of the Harriman people at a Democratic dinner in New Orleans several weeks before the convention and started chatting about possible cooperation.[12] It was a logical course, however. With the party regulars in the center holding firmly to an anti-Kefauver position, Kefauver had to raid either the extremely liberal Harriman camp or the extremely conservative Russell camp for secondary support. The Harriman strength was not enough to put Kefauver over, while the Russell strength was, but so many Southerners disliked Kefauver so heartily and the Harriman viewpoint was so much more palatable to most top Kefauver campaign people than Russell's that the Harriman bloc offered the best prospect for starting a Kefauver bandwagon.

The alliance was formed, in actuality, a few days before the convention, with the objective of seating "loyalist" delegations from Texas and Mississippi. There were competing delegations from both states, one delegation from each state controlled by the state party machinery and sympathetic to the conservative "Dixiecrat" element that had bolted the Democratic party in 1948, the other pledged essentially to support the national party position. There were no Kefauver-pledged delegations from either state. But the loyalist delegation from Texas was known to favor his candidacy, and the "regular" delegations from both states were supporting Russell. Moreover, an open fight on the issue could put the convention leadership and the Stevenson forces in the public position of supporting ultra-conservative elements that had bolted the party in 1948. Kefauver joined Harriman's campaign manager, Representative Franklin D. Roosevelt Jr. of New York, in a statement that they would fight to the end against seating the Mississippi "States Righters" and the Texas "Shivercrats" (so named because the delegation was headed by Governor Alan Shivers of Texas).

The Kefauver-Harriman coalition was formed in a series of meetings beginning Wednesday, July 16, five days before the conven-

12. Personal conversation, A. Bradley Eben, Chicago, Sept. 3, 1970.

tion opened.[13] Kefauver himself envisioned the Texas-Mississippi contests as a straight credentials fight, based on the regular delegations' refusal to agree to support the national convention's actions. Hubert Humphrey, who joined the talks on Friday, agreed in this respect with Kefauver, but the two campaign managers, Roosevelt and Sullivan, were determined to confront the convention with a sharp liberal-conservative controversy. Their attitude was that fractionization of the convention along these lines was the best means of forcing the Stevenson boosters out of their advantageous middle-of-the-road position to one side or the other. Humphrey was interested primarily in maintaining a liberal bloc, so he went along with the decision that was reached finally—advocacy of a "loyalty oath," a proposal that originated with the Harriman camp. Sullivan's determination to go along with the Harriman group and other Northern state delegations differed sharply from Kefauver's understanding of the strategy that was planned. He said later that "our original plan was to support a loyalty pledge only for states where a contest was involved, which in that case would have been Texas and Mississippi."[14]

It came as no surprise to anyone that the National Committee's credentials subcommittee voted to seat the regular (States Rights) delegations, provisionally, from both Texas and Mississippi. While awaiting the opportunity to reverse that decision on the convention floor, Kefauver demonstrated that he was not averse to hedging his bets. The fifty-two-vote delegation from Texas was under the unit rule, and if the Kefauver-Harriman bloc was successful in seating the loyalist delegation, Kefauver was likely to get those votes. But if the regular delegation was seated. Kefauver would have to deal with Shivers, and Shivers and Tennessee's Governor Gordon Browning were good personal friends. Thus it is probable that Browning not only served as an intermediary between the two but persuaded Kefauver to approach Shivers in the first place.

In any event, on the evening of the credentials subcommittee's decision, Kefauver paid a secret call on Shivers in a suite at the Palmer House.[15] Apparently the question of delegation seating did

13. Alvin Spivak, INS story, *Nashville Tennessean*, July 19, 1952; David, Moos, and Goldman, *Presidential Nominating Politics in 1952*, vol, IV, 187.
14. Letter, Estes Kefauver to Paul A. Theis, Washington, March 23, 1954, Kefauver Collection, Ser. 5-f, Box 5, and Ser. 1, Box 73.
15. Lois Laycook, *Nashville Tennessean*, July 19, 1952.

Kefauver confers with Silliman Evans, publisher of the *Nashville Tennessean,* during the 1952 Democratic National Convention.

Kefauver and his campaign manager, Gael Sullivan, pose with Mrs. Eleanor Roosevelt and her son, Franklin Jr., during the 1952 Democratic National Convention.

not come up, but Shivers told Kefauver he did not like Stevenson and was rather inclined toward Kefauver. There was only one major point of disagreement between them. Texas was very much interested in passage of the tidelands oil bill, which would give coastal states title to submerged oil resources along their shores, but Kefauver had always stood for federal ownership and use of the revenue for the nation at large. If Kefauver were elected President, Shivers wanted to know, would he let Congress decide the issue and promise not to veto such a bill? The offer was tempting. Aside from Texas' own votes, Shivers was an influential Russell man, and his switch of support to Kefauver conceivably could swing enough Southern votes to start a bandwagon.

Kefauver had faced the issue before, when he had been urged by advisers in the California primary to accept or "at least, soft-pedal" state ownership of tidelands oil. He had refused then, and he refused Shivers now. As President, he said, he would have to veto a tidelands bill. Well, suggested Shivers, would Kefauver compromise by agreeing to give the states title to tidelands oil within a three-mile limit from the coasts? No, said Kefauver again. He felt Texas had a stronger historical claim than any other state to offshore oil, but he was for federal ownership. It was too bad they could not agree, said Shivers. Texas would have to stay with Russell. And he spoke critically of Kefauver in an address to his delegation two nights later.[16]

When the National Committee approved the seating recommendations of the credentials subcommittee the next day, the motion for approval was made by Arvey—indicating that the nebulous forces supporting Stevenson had swung behind the pro-Russell Dixiecrat delegations. Kefauver proposed a new strategic move by the Kefauver-Harriman coalition. He suggested that the Democrats adopt a "fair play rule" similar to that adopted in the Republican convention two weeks earlier, taking away the voting rights of the contested delegations in Texas and Mississippi until they were seated permanently. Kefauver's proposal was adopted by leaders of the coalition, and Kefauver sent letters to Barkley, Harriman, Russell, and Senator Robert S. Kerr, the other major announced candidates, saying that "serious efforts" were being made to split the

16. Anderson and Blumenthal, *The Kefauver Story*, 185.

party over the civil rights issue and suggesting a "formal pledge" by each candidate to support the civil rights plank of the platform if nominated. His letter was generally ignored.[17]

After Stevenson's welcoming address to the convention, Kefauver took advantage of a long speech by Senator Paul Douglas to slip away from the Tennessee delegation for a conference with national chairman Frank McKinney and leaders of various convention factions in McKinney's office behind the rostrum, to seek a compromise in the Texas-Mississippi loyalty fight. Not much progress was made. Unfortunately, Kefauver missed a second meeting in McKinney's office at the Conrad Hilton after the convention recessed for the afternoon. The group agreed to the Kefauver "fair play" proposal in essence: the "regular" delegations would be seated temporarily from Texas and Mississippi, but would refrain voluntarily from voting unless and until seated permanently. No agreement was reached on any "loyalty pledge" as a condition for seating the contested delegations. Leaving the conference, Senator Walter George of Georgia said, "I have not agreed to anything, because I think it is wholly a mistake to undertake to bind your delegates here."[18] That was not the way Kefauver heard it later, though.

It was at this point that the course of Kefauver's candidacy at the convention began to move farther and farther from his own preference and to be colored by the assumption of his campaign's leadership by the liberal "newcomers" to it. These were, principally, Richardson Dilworth of Philadelphia, Humphrey, Senator Blair Moody of Michigan, and Michigan's Governor G. Mennen Williams. Their ascendance almost completely eclipsed the influence of such preconvention "old timers" as Douglas, Browning, James Roosevelt of California, Wayne Hays of Ohio, and Monroe Sweetland of Oregon. Philosophically, these "newcomers" were closer to Harriman and Franklin Roosevelt Jr. than to Kefauver.[19]

Late that afternoon, Americans for Democratic Action issued a draft of a proposed resolution including both the "fair play" proposal and a pledge that "every delegate assumes a moral obligation to support the nominees of this convention." Dilworth, Franklin

17. AP story, *Nashville Tennessean*, July 20, 1952.
18. David, Moos, and Goldman, *Presidential Nominating Politics in 1952*, vol. I, 122.
19. Personal conversation, Charles G. Neese, Greeneville, Spring 1971.

Roosevelt, and several others brought a copy of the proposal to Kefauver to seek his support for it. Kefauver was dubious. He objected to an all-encompassing loyalty pledge for the full convention and felt that the issue should be confined to the two states with contesting delegations. But the ADA leaflet stated that "most Southerners have agreed to the above plank," and both Roosevelt and Dilworth, who had worked hard for Kefauver in Pennsylvania, assured Kefauver that the South had agreed to the proposal.

"We'll look ridiculous if we don't go along," Dilworth said.

If the South did not object to such a pledge, Kefauver saw no reason to object to it himself. He agreed to go along with it and passed the word along to Browning, whose position as head of the Tennessee delegation made him one of the bellwethers for Kefauver forces on the floor.[20]

When the convention went back into session at 12:20 A.M., both Mississippi and Texas announced they would abide by the "fair play" rule. But when Moody offered a rules change to the effect that no delegate should be seated unless he assured the credentials committee "that he will exert every honorable means" to see that the nominees were put on the ballot, Southern delegates leaped to their feet to protest that many of them were bound by prior pledges back home not to make any such commitment.

The convention hall was in an uproar, and Kefauver, watching the proceedings on television from the Stock Yard Inn across the street, was appalled to realize that he had been misled about the South's agreement to the Moody resolution. But it was too late to change course: Browning was already on his feet, speaking in favor of the resolution. After "several of our delegates had made speeches for" the Moody resolution, "there was nothing left to do then but go along," said Kefauver later. "We were told that the Moody resolution had been agreed to, all the way around."[21]

Kefauver's failure to find out differently until it was too late exemplified what he called one of his "chief errors" at the convention: "not having an advisory staff in Chicago to decide upon policy matters . . . we had an awfully hard time with communication be-

20. Anderson and Blumenthal, *The Kefauver Story*, 187.
21. Letter, Estes Kefauver to Paul A. Theis, March 23, 1954.

tween our floor managers." This was putting it mildly. Kefauver's managers had not foreseen such an elementary necessity as that for constant liaison between his headquarters and the convention floor and had not even had a special telephone installed, though they could have arranged for one easily. Much of the time, during fast-breaking events on the floor, the Kefauver leaders were acting separately and at cross-purposes.[22]

The Moody resolution was adopted over the Southerners' bitter resistance. The following evening, as the convention settled down to listen to a speech by Mrs. Eleanor Roosevelt, Kefauver and Harriman got together with some of their top lieutenants for a secret "stop Stevenson" meeting. Kefauver went to the Blackstone Hotel and, to throw reporters off the track, rode the elevator up three floors, got off, and sprinted up a flight of back stairs to the suite of Paul A. Fitzpatrick, New York Democratic chairman. There gathered Kefauver, Harriman, Fitzpatrick, Franklin Roosevelt Jr., Sullivan, Representative Henry Jackson of Washington, and Representative John Carroll, chairman of the Colorado delegation and a political confidante of the White House, who was supporting Harriman. After dinner they talked for a long time, and Kefauver and Harriman laid their cards on the table. Kefauver could claim more than twice as many first-ballot delegate votes as Harriman.

"Well, Averell," said Kefauver, "what's our recipe?"

Harriman hesitated. The implication was heavy that he should pull out and throw his strength behind a Kefauver ticket, perhaps with Roosevelt as a running mate. But Truman had been virtually incommunicado in Walter Reed Hospital, and Harriman was still acting under the assumption that the President would tap him for the nomination. At last, Harriman said that, if it came to a choice, he preferred Kefauver to Stevenson. But the only agreement that was reached was that neither man would withdraw nor release his delegates without prior consultation with the other; an agreement that ultimately was not honored.[23]

When the convention met Wednesday it was decided after some discussion that Texas and Mississippi "regular" delegations had

22. Ibid.; David, Moos, and Goldman, *Presidential Nominating Politics in 1952*, vol. III, "The South," 181.
23. John L. Steele, UP story, *Nashville Banner*, July 23, 1952.

complied with the Moody resolution, but Virginia, South Carolina, and Louisiana had not. McKinney assured leaders of these three delegations privately that he would find a way to get them seated anyhow, and he kept his promise the next day with a maneuver carried through "with a precision that suggested pre-planning."[24]

As the roll of the states was being called on presidential nominations, after all of the major candidates had been nominated, many of the delegates had left the hall for dinner when at 6:55 P.M. Louisiana was called on the roll, even though it had not complied with the Moody resolution. Louisiana yielded at once to another holdout state, Virginia.

Everyone but those in on the plan—the convention management and the Southerners—was caught by surprise. Minnesota delegates, right under the rostrum, leaped to their feet and shouted for recognition, but tough, bald Sam Rayburn had taken over as the convention's permanent chairman, and he ignored them. He obtained a formal ruling from the chairman of the credentials committee that the three states had not complied with the Moody resolution, returned to the roll call of states, and then recognized Representative Lansdale G. Sasscer of Maryland for a motion Rayburn interpreted as an appeal from the ruling. Rayburn interrupted the nominating roll call for a roll call on the appeal.

The Kefauver-Harriman forces went against seating Virginia, and the draft-Stevenson forces, caught by surprise, were so confused that the Illinois delegation—with Arvey, Lucas, and its chairman, Joseph Gill, at supper—accepted Douglas' leadership and voted 45 to 15 against seating Virginia. When the roll call ended after an hour and a half, delegates who had kept a tally found that the vote had gone against seating Virginia by about 650 to 475½. But Rayburn, instead of announcing the count, stood stolidly waiting, until Arvey, Lucas, and Gill returned hastily to the convention hall, and Arvey pointed out to the Illinois delegation that Stevenson would get no Southern support for the nomination if his boosters voted against seating Virginia.

Then Illinois was recognized, and they announced a change of vote—52 to 8 in favor of seating Virginia. This was followed by a

24. David, Moos, and Goldman, *Presidential Nominating Politics in 1952*, vol, I, 141.

parade of vote changes by thirteen other states, led by the heaviest pro-Stevenson states, Indiana and Missouri. At the end of the count, Virginia was seated.

The Virginia vote was unquestionably one of the critical junctures of the convention, and the concerted swing of the Stevenson delegates away from the liberal position dealt a telling blow to the Kefauver-Harriman coalition. The defeat was so severe as possibly to justify the conclusion that, after it, Kefauver had no further chance for the nomination: "Kefauver had become isolated as the candidate of a bitter-end faction, oppposite in its point of view to the southern faction and angrily at outs with the convention management."[25]

Had Kefauver's personal wishes been followed, however, the Virginia vote would not have been a defeat for him but a resounding victory, leaving the Stevenson bloc and the convention management united with the Harriman forces as a severe minority. When the Virginia question was tossed into the midst of the nominating roll call, Kefauver, at the Stock Yard Inn, wrote out a message to Gael Sullivan, asking that his delegates vote *for* seating Virginia, and sent it across the street. The fate of that message remains a mystery. It was not transmitted to any of the key Kefauver people on the floor whose actions gave Kefauver delegates a cue at critical moments; neither Browning nor Douglas saw it, nor did Vincent M. Gaughan of New York, Kefauver's official floor manager.[26]

There was sharp disagreement among the Kefauver leadership as to the proper course to take, the "adoptive" Kefauver leadership from Pennsylvania and Michigan was committed to the loyalty oath fight, and Sullivan himself apparently was obsessed with the Harriman-originated strategy of dividing the convention. It is possible the message was conveniently "lost," and Kefauver's own wishes simply ignored.

In any event, Kefauver delegates all down the line (including

25. Ibid., 150.
26. Personal and telephone conversations: Charles G. Neese, Greeneville; Vincent Gaughan, New York; Richard Wallace, Washington; Gordon Browning, Huntingdon, Tenn.; George McInturff, Chattanooga; Jack Norman, Nashville; Martha Ragland, Nashville; and Frank Wilson, Chattanooga, Spring 1971; and personal communication, Paul Douglas, Washington, May 28, 1972. Neese confirmed the existence of the Kefauver message, which he had in his possession at one point, but refused to discuss it further.

Tennessee but not his other Southern delegates) voted almost solidly against seating Virginia, and Stevenson's backers were able to get the credit for serving as a moderate, unifying force. But, as for being "at outs" with the convention management, Kefauver had been in that position from the start. Rayburn's hostility to the Kefauver cause was one of several major factors in his ultimate loss of the nomination. Repeatedly, at key points in the proceedings, Rayburn's handling of the gavel meant the difference between success and failure for the strategy of the Kefauver forces.

When it became apparent to the Kefauver managers just to what extent the convention management was against them, they issued an appeal over national television to the people to wire their delegates, urging Kefauver's nomination. But when the convention ended, Eben discovered scores of bushel baskets of undelivered telegrams, responding to the appeal. Upon inquiry, he was told that the convention management had refused to permit their delivery lest they "disrupt the work of the delegates."[27]

Rayburn was unable to subdue the outburst from the delegates and the galleries when Kefauver was nominated, however, though he hammered with his gavel, scowling and muttering, for more than an hour before the demonstration died down. Kefauver, chain-smoking cigarets and letting a roast beef sandwich get cold at the Stock Yard Inn, growled at the television screen at one point: "Now, don't be in a hurry, Sam. . . .You're just as rough as you can be."[28]

In fact the galleries—as some newspapers speculated—were packed with Kefauver people for the demonstration. But, in order to pack them, the Kefauver leaders had to outwit the convention management. Requests for passes for Kefauver supporters were refused almost invariably by party leaders, so the Kefauver forces bribed the convention hall guards to admit their friends without passes.[29]

After the stormy session ended at 2 A.M., Kefauver, Harriman, Humphrey, Douglas, Williams, Franklin and James Roosevelt, Sullivan, and Walter Reuther, president of the CIO United Auto Workers union, gathered in the Harriman dugout at the amphitheater to

27. Personal conversation, A. Bradley Eben, Chicago, Sept. 3, 1970.
28. UP story, *Nashville Banner*, July 25, 1952.
29. Personal conversation, A. Bradley Eben, Chicago, Sept. 3, 1970.

assess their strategic disaster. Anger among the liberal delegates from Northern states was as high as it had been among Southern delegates earlier, and much of the anger was directed at the Stevenson bloc for siding with the South.

All of the ingredients were present for a bitter-end liberal revolt against the Stevenson candidacy. In fact, a "Stop Stevenson" rally was even then gathering at the Congress Hotel, with most of the Minnesota delegation prominent among the 400 delegates in attendance. But, at this point, Horatio stood at the bridge between the liberals and Stevenson: Hubert Horatio Humphrey.

Recognizing that a swing of the Russell support behind Stevenson would virtually assure his nomination and that such a shift was possible if the liberals exhibited extreme hostility to the Illinois governor, Humphrey reminded his allies that Stevenson was basically liberal himself. He warned the liberal leadership not to let the South get credit for nominating Stevenson. The group went from there to the Congress Hotel and conferred intensively on a possible ticket involving Kefauver with Harriman, James Roosevelt, or even Stevenson. But Harriman refused to take second place on a ticket, and no deal was reached.[30]

Kefauver left the meeting and went back to his hotel for a nap of only a few minutes before arising at 5 A.M. for breakfast and a drive to the convention hall with his father and campaign aides. Harriman had told Kefauver he preferred him to Stevenson as the nominee, but Harriman was a personal friend of Stevenson. In mid-morning, Harriman had breakfast with Stevenson in the apartment of Stevenson's sister, Mrs. Ernest L. Ives, and told Stevenson he would stay in the race as long as he thought he had a chance at the nomination, but when the chance seemed gone he would drop out in favor of Stevenson. Meanwhile, Humphrey got a telephone call from the White House urging him to accept the Stevenson nomination as in the best interest of the party, and, during the breakfast at Mrs. Ives's apartment, both Humphrey and Williams telephoned Stevenson to offer support whenever the time seemed right.[31]

Uninformed of these preparations by his key allies to abandon

---

30. Anderson and Blumenthal, *The Kefauver Story*, 188; David, Moos, and Goldman, *Presidential Nominating Politics in 1952*, vol. I, 150.

31. David, Moos, and Goldman, *Presidential Nominating Politics in 1952*, vol. I, 151; vol. IV, 189.

his ship, even before it had pulled away from the dock, Kefauver watched from the Stock Yard Inn as the first nominating ballot began as 12:21 P.M. on Friday. When the result of the first ballot was announced at 4:14 P.M., Kefauver had 340 votes to 273 for Stevenson, 268 for Russell, 123½ for Harriman, and 224½ spread among ten other candidates and favorite sons. The vote demonstrated how heavily Kefauver's strength lay in the West. He had more than half of the votes from the eleven far Western states and more than a third of those from the twelve Middle Western states, but only about a sixth of those from the Northeast and nothing from the South except Tennessee and thirteen votes from Florida and Alabama.

"I think I'm going to win," he said.[32]

But even before the first ballot ended, Harriman was in his office preparing a statement withdrawing in favor of Stevenson. In the absence of his office staff, Mrs. Harriman ran it off on the mimeograph machine. For the time, he held onto it.[33]

In the middle of the second ballot, the presidential plane came in from Washington and President Truman stepped down, chipper and confident, and went straight to a downtown hotel. From there he issued directives decisive in the convention's choice. "The Democratic President, whom Kefauver had humiliated in New Hampshire, joined with the city bosses, who had felt threatened by his senatorial investigations," to put Stevenson across, historian Arthur Schlesinger Jr. wrote sixteen years later.[34]

During the second ballot, one last chance came Kefauver's way. Russell obviously was near the peak of his delegate strength, and Shivers of Texas was not fond of Stevenson. He proposed a statement to Browning saying only that Kefauver's "mind was open" on the tidelands oil issue, without further commitment, implying strongly that its signature would bring Kefauver the fifty-two Texas votes and possibly those of two other states (reportedly Louisiana and Mississippi). With the possibility of a determinative Southern swing to Kefauver in the balance, Browning hastened across the street to the Stock Yard Inn with the statement. Nathan Straus,

32. John L. Steele, UP story, *Nashville Tennessean*, July 26, 1952; Anderson and Blumenthal, *The Kefauver Story*, 189.
33. David, Moos, and Goldman, *Presidential Nominating Politics in 1952*, vol. I, 154.
34. Arthur Schlesinger Jr., *New Republic*, May 4, 1968.

with Kefauver at the time, pointed out that the oil issue was very complex and the statement really committed him to nothing.

"But my mind isn't open. The whole thing is a steal," said Kefauver. Handing the statement back to Browning, he said, "I can't sign it, Gordon."[35]

All of the major candidates except Harriman gained slightly on the second ballot, as favorite sons fell out. Kefauver had 362½ votes, Stevenson 324½, Russell 294, and Harriman 121.

"I don't see any draft movement here. I think the Stevenson strength is about at its peak," said Kefauver.[36] Alfred Starr, a delegate from Tennessee who was with him then, recalled him "sitting there with a drink in his hand and a happy, bemused smile on his face, not even realizing that they had already cut his throat."

During a long dinner recess after the second ballot, Truman sent his aide, Charles Murphy, to Harriman, asking him to withdraw in favor of Stevenson. The obedient Harriman, without notifying Kefauver as per their agreement, sent his already-prepared statement to Paul Fitzpatrick, most of whose ninety-four New York votes constituted the bulk of the Harriman strength. The New York leaders held a hasty conference with Truman before the convention reconvened after dinner.

Just before the recess ended, Williams and Moody went by the New York headquarters in the convention hall and learned of Harriman's planned switch to Stevenson. They hastened across the street to the Stock Yard Inn and informed Kefauver, urging him to withdraw in Stevenson's favor and get credit for unifying the party.

Kefauver was dismayed. He realized that the swing to Stevenson was on, and the only way to stop him would be to join forces with Russell in a holding action that might deadlock the convention and

---

35. Both Kefauver and Browning later denied that any "direct proposition" was made. Browning said he approached Shivers, and Shivers only asked him what Kefauver's position on the issue was. Browning said he went to Kefauver to ask him. (Personal conversations, Estes Kefauver, Washington, and Gordon Browning, Huntingdon, Spring 1955; Lois Laycook, *Nashville Tennessean*, Oct. 27, 1955.) But two different reporters obtained essentially the same story of the incident from two different sources: Douglass Cater, "Estes Kefauver, Most Willing of the Willing," *Reporter*, Nov. 3, 1955, from William Roberts, Washington attorney and a prominent Kefauver supporter, and Irwin Ross, *New York Post*, May 11, 1956, from Nathan Straus.

36. John L. Steele, UP story, *Nashville Tennessean*, July 26, 1952.

Kefauver and Governor Gordon Browning talk over lunch during the 1952 Democratic presidential campaign.

Kefauver sits with Senator Paul Douglas on the platform at the Democratic National Convention in 1952, waiting to make a withdrawal statement. Behind them are members of the liberal coalition that supported Kefauver: (from left) Senator Blair Moody, Senator Hubert Humphrey, and Governor G. Mennen Williams.

could benefit none of them. But he insisted that, before he withdrew, he must find his loyal ally, Paul Douglas, who had laid his political future on the line for Kefauver and might suffer repercussions from opposing the governor of his own state.

Kefauver made his way to Douglas' room, to find the Illinois senator, exhausted and disconsolate, stretched on the bed, bathed in perspiration in the room's 100-degree temperature. He had heard the news too. Unhappily, Kefauver patted him on the shoulder.

"Paul," he said, "as far as I'm concerned, the only thing that matters now is what I can do to pull you out of this."

They agreed to go together to the convention hall, hopefully before the third ballot began, and Kefauver would arrange with Rayburn to be recognized and then turn the microphone over to Douglas. Douglas would urge all the Kefauver delegates to switch to Stevenson and thus would get some personal credit for helping Stevenson get the nomination. Walking across the street, they attempted to enter by the back door, so they could summon Rayburn and speak quietly with him. But it was locked, as were the side doors. Perforce, they went around to the hall's main entrance.[37]

The evening session already had begun and, by prearrangement, Rayburn recognized Franklin Roosevelt, who introduced Fitzpatrick. Fitzpatrick read Harriman's statement, and cheers rang through the auditorium, but beneath them there was an almost visible wave of shocked outrage among the Kefauver delegations. Dever withdrew immediately as a Massachussetts favorite son in Stevenson's favor before the third roll call began.

The first states stood firm behind Kefauver and Russell, except Arkansas, whose Governor Sid McMath had heard from Truman; it became the first state to switch to Stevenson. When California was called, there was a momentary delay, and there seemed to be some argument in the delegation. Then James Roosevelt, who had made one of the seconding speeches for Kefauver, grabbed the microphone and shouted: "California keeps faith with 1,200,000 people who voted for Estes Kefauver in the primary! California casts 68 votes for Estes Kefauver!"

When the five Harriman votes in the Colorado delegation were

37. Anderson and Blumenthal, *The Kefauver Story*, 191; personal communication, Paul H. Douglas, Washington, Aug. 24, 1970.

switched to Stevenson, a delegate demanded a poll of the delegation. As the long roster of individual names neared its end, there was a disturbance in the back of the hall. Heads turned and necks craned, then shouts arose, and coonskin caps began to wave.

Arm in arm with Douglas, Kefauver, sober-faced, strode down the aisle toward the rostrum. Behind them came twenty-six-year-old Harry Mansfield, his face unhappy, near tears. Moody, Williams, and Humphrey brought up the rear. Nancy, taken by surprise, hurried through the press to her husband to cry, "Estes, what are you doing?" He murmured something to her and moved on.

The faces of the convention leaders on the platform were a study in consternation. Hubbub broke out in the hall, and a chant began from the floor: "We want Kefauver!" Some of the Kefauver delegates evidently believed their candidate's appearance was a dramatic maneuver designed to halt the Stevenson swing and capture victory miraculously. Kefauver and Douglas were stopped at the steps to the rostrum, and Kefauver addressed Rayburn: "Mr. Speaker, I have a statement. . . ."

"Oh, my!" exclaimed Representative Clarence Cannon of Missouri, the convention parliamentarian, in horrified tones. "You can't break into a roll call with an earthquake!"

Kefauver was to point out later that Rayburn had permitted interruption of a roll call for the fight to seat Virginia. But he and Douglas took seats at the rear of the platform and sat through the long, bitter roll call, Kefauver's long face impassive.

They sat there for three hours as delegation after delegation demanded polls of individual members. To thousands who watched the spectacle on television, it appeared that the party management was deliberately humiliating the man who, with a few words, could have stopped his supporters' last-ditch fight and resolved the nomination in reasonable harmony. In the absence of those words, most of the Kefauver support held fast in state after state—New Hampshire, Ohio, Oregon, South Dakota. When Tennessee was called, Browning again besought Rayburn to let Kefauver make a brief statement, but the chairman was adamant. At that, Jack Norman, vice chairman of the delegation, seized the microphone and cried: "Tennessee proudly casts 28 votes for the man who bows to no dictator. . . . Estes Kefauver!"

It was Kefauver's liberal friends who did him in. Aside from

Michigan's 40 votes, half of the Minnesota delegation, and his 21 ½ Pennsylvania votes, Kefauver lost a net of only 8 ½ votes from the second roll call. And the liberals' fears of a Russell-Stevenson deal proved groundless. Most of Russell's support was firm too, and he lost but 33 votes in all.

If the convention leadership had hoped to humiliate Kefauver by winning with Stevenson without his withdrawal, they were disappointed. With the Harriman strength, the Kefauver defectors from the three states of some of his principal convention leaders and a scattering of Kerr, Barkley, and favorite son votes, Stevenson was still two and a half votes short of the nomination when the roll call ended.

Kefauver was recognized at last, and he stood up at the microphone, head tilted back, the television lights flashing from his glasses. He said, firmly and calmly, "Ladies and gentlemen, I have fought the hard fight. We have done the very best we could. . . ." He went on a little longer, complimenting Stevenson, calling for party unity. In the balcony, white-haired Cooke Kefauver bit his lip and Nancy was misty-eyed. Then Kefauver stepped back out of the spotlight, into the shadows behind the podium, and Nancy was waiting for him, smiling. She put her arm around him.

"You did well," she whispered. "I love you."

"Thanks, honey," he said. "I love you."[38]

With Cooke Kefauver, Estes and Nancy walked together out of the convention hall without looking back, before Utah switched its remaining four and a half votes to put Stevenson over the top.

As they left, the band struck up, and the delegates began singing, "Happy birthday, dear Estes, happy birthday to you. . . ." It was the morning of his forty-ninth birthday.

---

38. Norma Mohr, UP story, *Nashville Banner*, July 26, 1952; she quoted Nancy as saying, "You did good," but Carol Harford, in a personal communication from Washington Aug. 29, 1970, questioned the accuracy of the quotation, probably justifiably, in view of Nancy's almost impeccable English.

Chapter 12

I Refuse to Appeal to Prejudice

Although he never said so, Kefauver in the 1952 Democratic National Convention may have tried to continue the 1932 pattern of Franklin D. Roosevelt, which served so well in the primaries. Exposed to Roosevelt's charisma during most of his years in the House, Kefauver admired Roosevelt's political acumen and emulated him in a number of different modes and gestures, even affecting a long holder for his cigarets for a time.

The seating contests from Mississippi and Texas presented Kefauver with a parallel to the Roosevelt situation in 1932, when the Roosevelt forces scored their first victory of the convention with the seating of pro-Roosevelt delegations from Louisiana and Minnesota. The parallel extended even to the opposition to the pro-Roosevelt delegation from Louisiana by one of Kefauver's most active 1952 enemies, Scott Lucas of Illinois.

Kefauver's approach to Governor Alan Shivers also had overtones of 1932, when the key to Roosevelt's victory had been Texas: Jim Farley, Sam Rayburn, and Silliman Evans had worked out a deal behind the scenes whereby Texas led the way for a switch of John Nance Garner's Southwestern bloc of votes that put Roosevelt over the top. But the Roosevelt forces in 1932 were organized to make use of these convention opportunities, and the Kefauver forces in 1952 were not.

Most important, the Kefauver people were not in a position at all to try a maneuver that in Roosevelt's strategy was highly consequential: electing their own convention chairman. As Farley said in 1932, "It was a wise thing that we did, because anything could have happened in that convention if you had . . . a chairman who was unfriendly";[1] and Rayburn was obviously unfriendly to the Kefau-

1. Ralph G. Martin, *Ballots and Bandwagons* (Chicago: Rand McNally, 1964), 324.

ver cause. But, even with a majority of friendly delegates, the Roosevelt forces barely elected their chairman in 1932, and in 1952 Rayburn was such an institution that any challenge to his right to run the convention would have been bound to fail. Kefauver's efforts to copy the Roosevelt strategy, if such they were, were so insecurely based, relatively, that they only contributed to his disastrous alliance with the ultra-liberal element and his alienation from the middle-of-the-roaders.[2]

Stevenson had indicated to Hubert Humphrey and Mennen Williams his willingness to accept Kefauver as a vice presidential running mate,[3] and included Kefauver among four preferred prospects at a meeting with President Truman, Rayburn, and Frank McKinney after his own nomination. Truman, however, vetoed Kefauver, and the four men agreed on Senator John Sparkman of Alabama, a Russell supporter, as a gesture to conciliate the South.[4]

Kefauver had already said he would not accept the vice presidential nomination "under any circumstances," after talking it over with Nancy. Nancy and Cooke Kefauver were more outspoken. Nancy's reaction was, "Tell them to go to hell!" and Cooke Kefauver said of Stevenson, "Let him take the nomination and to hell with it. I don't want Estes's popularity to put this ticket over. . . . Eisenhower will be the next President."[5] The Sunday after the convention, the Kefauvers flew to McMinnville to join their children, who had been at Shangri-la since July 1 with Nanette and Bobbie. Kefauver arrived in Tennessee to find his political ally, Governor Browning, in serious trouble.

Browning was running for a third two-year term in the state's Democratic primary, less than two weeks off, and his major opponent was a personable young orator, Frank Goad Clement, who was running with the support of the surviving elements of the old E.H. Crump organization. There were several major issues against Browning, but the Clement forces picked up what they considered

2. Cater, "Estes Kefauver, Most Willing of the Willing;" Edward B. Smith, *Knoxville News-Sentinel*, Dec. 16, 1955.

3. David, Moos, and Goldman, *Presidential Nominating Politics in 1952*, vol. I, 151.

4. Ibid., 156; Anderson and Blumenthal, *The Kefauver Story*, 195–96.

5. John L. Steele, UP story, *Nashville Tennessean*, July 26, 1952; *Chicago Herald*, July 27, 1952; *Chattanooga Times*, July 27, 1952; personal communication, Carol Harford, Washington, June 7, 1970.

an extremely effective one in his casting Tennessee's convention vote against seating "our sister state," Virginia.

As early as the second week of June, Gael Sullivan sent Dick Wallace a memorandum to the effect that "on advice from Silliman Evans, George McInturff, and Alfred Starr, EK is advised NOT to make reference to the governorship contest."[6] Kefauver did stay aloof from the governor's race until the national convention altered the situation. Then on the basis of simple gratitude—for Browning's loyalty to the Kefauver cause sometimes had been in contradiction to Browning's own judgment and political philosophy— Kefauver made a telecast for Browning in Memphis, in which he took full responsibility for the decision to vote against Virginia. Browning, however, lost the election to Clement, badly.

On his return to Shangri-la, Kefauver's exhaustion and the reaction to his defeat caught up with him. He was unable to sleep at night or to relax in the daytime. He tried to tire himself out with swimming, fishing, and boating with the children, but his evenings were spent sitting in silent gloom and hitting the Scotch bottle heavily. A few of his friends visited him. Kefauver did not want to talk about the convention, but he always brought the conversation around to the subject.

"Should I have held out and tried to deadlock the convention?" he wanted to know. "Did I do right in going to the convention hall to withdraw? Should I have advised my friends to vote differently on some of the issues?" Nancy tried to console him, but, at last, one night she told him bluntly: "It may be one of the best things that ever happened to you. You're just not accustomed to defeat." But it was not only his own defeat that bothered Kefauver, but Browning's, for which he felt vaguely responsible. "I just can't understand what happened to poor old Gordon," he would say, over and over.[7]

Noble Caudill of Nashville, one of Kefauver's closest friends in later life, theorized that Kefauver's heavy drinking and extramari-

6. Memorandum, Gael Sullivan to Richard Wallace, Kefauver Collection.

7. Personal observation. I visited Estes and Nancy Kefauver and their family at Shangri-La in Aug. 1952 and attempted to comfort Kefauver about his convention defeat while he nursed his Scotch and Nancy enjoyed a case of her favorite, champagne. Kefauver also wrote of his reactions as guest columnist for Drew Pearson, *Nashville Tennessean*, Aug. 21, 1952.

tal interests in later years were an aftermath of his 1952 disappointment.[8] But Caudill did not know him before then, and Charlie Neese, who had known him very well for a long time, said Kefauver was always a hearty drinker with a speculative eye for the opposite sex. Kefauver could down a quart of Scotch whiskey in an evening when he was in the mood for it (though he usually nursed his drinks), rarely showing its effects except by a heightened sociability or a deeper moroseness, depending on how he felt. According to Neese, he could always do this: "He had just made up his mind that he was going to live his allotted 80 years in 60."[9] Ed Gardner, for many years treasurer of Vanderbilt University in Nashville, recalled that when Kefauver was Tennessee finance and taxation commissioner, the state being dry at the time, he would share the goodies he acquired from his bootlegger with Kefauver periodically; and when Kefauver left Nashville, he called Gardner to suggest that he needed "some whiskey on the way," and he died owing Gardner two pints of bootleg whiskey.[10]

Kefauver's disappointment in 1952 did not prevent his working hard for Stevenson's election. In mid-August, at Stevenson's invitation, he flew to Springfield, Illinois, for a four-hour conference and recommended strongly that Stevenson dissociate himself from the Truman administration. When Stevenson asked his opinion about an invitation he had received to go to Washington the next day for a White House briefing, Kefauver replied: "Well, I think I'd come down with an attack of appendicitis or something. I wouldn't go." Stevenson did not take the advice.[11]

After a two-week European trip with Nancy, Kefauver campaigned intensively for Stevenson during the last month of the presidential race. He wrote hundreds of letters to angry supporters, saying things like: "I do hope that your bitterness toward certain individuals will not tend to lead you out of the fold, but rather to work harder so that the Democratic Party may become stronger."[12]

8. Personal conversation, Noble C. Caudill, Hendersonville, Tenn., Spring 1970.

9. Personal conversation, Charles G. Neese, Greeneville, Tenn., Spring 1971.

10. Telephone conversation, Ed Gardner, Nashville, Sept. 25, 1978.

11. Personal conversation, Estes Kefauver, Aug. 1952.

12. Letter, Estes Kefauver to Mrs. Mildred W. Phillippi, St. Louis, *Nashville Tennessean*, Sept. 5, 1952.

Eisenhower's landslide victory over Stevenson seemed to vindicate Kefauver's preconvention warning that the political monopoly of "bosses" in the Democratic party presaged "certain defeat." It is technically accurate to say that, in killing off the nationally-popular Kefauver as their standard-bearer in favor of the little-known Stevenson, the Democratic leadership lost their only chance of defeating Eisenhower in 1952. This may have been done knowingly: when Kefauver was but a boy, Governor Ben Odell of New York said, "When it comes to deciding between losing an election and losing control of the party, lose the election."[13]

But it is likely that, as political analysts saw it in retrospect, "party managers almost certainly underestimated the importance of the Kefauver faction in numbers, in emotional fervor, and in the degree to which it had been outraged by the way in which the convention had been run. At the end of the convention, many Kefauverites were clearly in a mood to take a walk."[14]

This mood was expressed in hundreds of letters to newspapers, and to Kefauver himself, from Kefauver supporters all over the country. The Democratic leadership may have underestimated the fact that this convention was seen on nationwide television, and many Kefauver supporters expressed indignation at what they saw, vowing to vote for Eisenhower. The party professionals were accustomed to Rayburn's dictatorial tactics with the gavel, often necessary to keep order in an unruly House, but the viewing public saw only arbitrary tyranny, with no pretense at fairness. The party professionals were accustomed to the arrogant exercise of power that went with the highest office in the land, but the television viewers saw Truman as simply a vindictive little man who flew to Chicago to steal victory from a man who had shown up his unpopularity in the New Hampshire primary.

More than anything, Kefauver said repeatedly in his campaign, their televised ringside seat at the proceedings convinced thousands of voters that he was right in his contention that ruthless party bosses were "out to get him." A survey conducted in eleven Western states just before the 1952 election showed that only 46 percent of those who had listed Kefauver as their first choice for President

13. Martin, *Ballots and Bandwagons*, 107–108.
14. David, Moos, and Goldman, *Presidential Nominating Politics in 1952*, vol. I, 155.

would vote for Stevenson; 44 percent said they would vote for Eisenhower and 10 percent said they would not vote at all.[15]

A shift of only 851,000 votes in fourteen states that Eisenhower carried by a narrow margin would have given the Democratic ticket victory, and some of these were "Kefauver states"—Tennessee, Washington, Florida, Minnesota, and Maryland. But among them also were states no more likely to vote for Democrat Kefauver than for Democrat Stevenson, such as Texas, Oklahoma, Illinois, and New Mexico.[16]

Eisenhower was considered at the time to be the most popular single individual in the United States,[17] and there was a great deal of popular disenchantment with the Democratic administration. Probably the best that can be said for Kefauver's chances, if he had captured the nomination, is that he might have run a much better race against Eisenhower than Stevenson. But, as the party's titular leader, he then would have been in a strong position to capture the 1956 nomination, when the Eisenhower enthusiasm had been tempered by his first four years in office. Of course, this is simply speculation.

Kefauver was not above expressing private satisfaction at the electoral defeat of several of his convention enemies, like Governor Paul Dever of Massachusetts (while, by contrast, a goodly number of Kefauver supporters won, sometimes against heavy odds, that year and two years later),[18] but if he felt any vindictive pleasure at Stevenson's defeat, he did not show it. He wrote Stevenson immediately after the election that he had "only the greatest admiration for the wonderful campaign that you conducted. . . . I feel that you have done our country a great service. . . . It just wasn't our year."[19]

In fact, in that campaign, Kefauver and Stevenson formed a last-

15. Alfred de Grazia, *The Western Public, 1952 and Beyond* (Stanford, Calif.: Stanford Univ. Press, 1954), 34.

16. Charles A.H. Thomson and Frances M. Shattuck, *The 1956 Presidential Campaign* (Washington: Brookings Institution, 1960), 229.

17. Roper, *You and Your Leaders*, 241, reported that 22 percent of the Americans surveyed listed Eisenhower as their choice for the greatest American, while Kefauver was tied with several others at 6 percent.

18. Glenn Everett, *Nashville Tennessean*, Nov. 16, 1952.

19. Letter, Estes Kefauver, Washington, to Adlai Stevenson, Springfield, Ill., Nov. 6, 1952, Kefauver Collection, Ser. 1, Box 71.

ing friendship that survived the bitterness of their primary opposition four years later. That opposition was inevitable: whatever Kefauver thought about the effectiveness of Stevenson's campaigning methods or whether he himself might have done better, when he was asked soon after the 1952 convention if he had given up his hope of becoming President, he answered quickly, "Oh, no!"[20]

However popular and respected a senator may be nationally, he must always remain aware of the particular interests of his home state constituency if he wishes to hold his job. Every six years, he must excuse any gambling at national conventions, any excursions into internationalism or any activities oriented to the national viewpoint, in terms of the attitudes of those voters who elect him.

From the time he walked out of the 1952 Democratic National Convention in defeat, there was no doubt in the mind of anyone who knew Kefauver that he would try for the presidential nomination again in 1956. But, in the meantime, there was the matter of getting reelected to the Senate in 1954. Kefauver never felt entirely secure politically in his home state. His support spanned a diversity of political views and economic interests brought together into an effective coalition through his personal campaign technique: farmers, workers, urban intellectuals, and political idealists. On the other side, there was a hard core of ideological hostility to him, voiced largely through the *Chattanooga News-Free Press* and the *Nashville Banner*, that constantly sought to stir up some emotion-charged issue against him and never flagged in its criticism of him.

Kefauver's alliances at the 1952 national convention, in his quest for the nomination, were natural points of attack for this opposition. Browning's 1952 defeat was interpreted by many as resulting in part from his hobnobbing with Northern liberals at the convention in Kefauver's behalf and especially his consent to the stand against seating Virginia, "our sister state." After Browning's defeat, the *Banner* called Kefauver "a political phoney whose turn comes next."[21]

Contributing to the persistence of that opposition was the fact that Kefauver never had a friendly state administration in power

20. John L. Steele, UP story, *Nashville Tennessean*, July 26, 1952; *Chattanooga Times*, July 27, 1952.
21. Aug. 8, 1952.

from the time of his 1952 presidential race until his death. With Frank Clement's defeat of Browning, the old, well-organized Bourbon clique of Tennessee's Democratic party returned to power, although E.H. Crump was no longer its dominant figure. From then until well after Kefauver's death, the governor's chair was occupied alternately by Clement and his ally, Buford Ellington, and their political organization controlled the state legislature and the election machinery.

The Browning organization was not enthusiastically friendly to Kefauver, but the two were compatible enough to make common cause when the occasion demanded. The Clement-Ellington organization was frankly hostile to Kefauver. Clement's personal ambition exacerbated a fundamental political conflict that existed between the two men, though their political philosophies often appeared quite similar.

The strongest potential threat to Kefauver's reelection in 1954 was Clement himself, who was known to have his eye on the Senate (he tried twice, unsuccessfully, for Kefauver's seat after Kefauver's death). Clement, one of the youngest governors in Tennessee's history, freshened the staid governor's office with the eloquence of a youthful Demosthenes, and his charisma rivalled Kefauver's, though on different grounds: his oratory rang with a religious fervor that aroused his hearers' emotions, while Kefauver's stumbling simplicity convinced audiences of his sincerity. The possibility of a direct popularity contest between the two became a subject of speculation with Clement's first election. But in 1953 the state's first constitutional convention since 1870 lengthened the governor's term from two to four years. Clement, wary about challenging the formidable Kefauver anyhow, chose to become the state's first four-year governor. He defeated a comeback try by Browning in 1954, and his decision forced anti-Kefauver forces to seek some other champion.

The one who eventually entered the lists was tall, handsome Representative Pat Sutton, a much-decorated World War II hero who had been reelected twice in the Sixth District south of Nashville, though *Redbook* magazine called him one of the nation's worst congressmen in 1952. Sutton's candidacy was not a matter for great rejoicing by the anti-Kefauver camp, centered in a group of about thirty conservative businessmen who would have preferred a more substantial candidate. They tried without success to get former Governor Prentice Cooper and Kefauver's predecessor, Tom Stewart, to run, but ultimately swung behind Sutton for the sake of unity.[22] If Sutton's backers had hoped for any active help from the Clement administration, they were disappointed. Not only did Clement have his hands full beating back Browning's challenge, but a great many of Clement's influential supporters were also Kefauver supporters. Noble Caudill of Nashville, for example, served as the principal money-raiser for both Clement and Kefauver.[23]

Kenneth McKellar, whose long Senate tenure had been ended by Albert Gore in 1952, did endorse Sutton late in the campaign.[24] But Crump refused to endorse either candidate, flatly denying a Sutton claim that he had Crump support, and Crump's few pronouncements on the race were generally favorable to Kefauver, whom he complimented for his support of TVA and his conduct of the Senate crime investigation. Because Kefauver was as much a national as a state figure, some out-of-state participation on both sides could be expected. For Kefauver, this was largely in the form of small contributions from all over the country, inspired by columns by his friend, Drew Pearson, and stories on the Tennessee campaign in such publications as *Newsweek* and the *New Republic*.

Sutton's outside support was more substantial and more concentrated. Although Kefauver was never able to pin it down to the point of charging him publicly with it, Sutton assured his backers that he had been pledged $150,000 by H.L. Hunt, an ultraconservative Dallas oil millionaire.[25]

There were also hints that the underworld was interested in the race. An article in February 1954 in the San Francisco Italian language newspaper, *L'Italia*, headlined "*Si, vendetta, vendetta . . .!*" and read in part, translated: "It is rumored in Chicago, with considerable probability of accuracy, that large sums of money have been sent into the state of Tennessee for the purpose of defeating the election of Senator Kefauver." Rumors in the New York underworld, said the article, were "that Frank Costello is organizing a

22. Heard, *The Costs of Democracy*, 330.
23. Personal conversation, Noble C. Caudill, Hendersonville, Spring 1970.
24. *Nashville Tennessean*, July 1, 1954.
25. Clarence Streit, *Freedom and Union*, Sept. 1954.

blood feud against Senator Kefauver because the Senator is guilty of having made him lose prestige and business" through the crime investigation.[26]

Whatever the source of Sutton's funds, he had enough to wage a spectacular campaign, such as had never been seen in Tennessee before. He traveled in a helicopter, unique enough then to draw good-sized crowds in itself, and near the end of the campaign he resorted to the "talkathon," a non-stop television performance lasting over a period of hours, during which he interspersed comment and campaign pronouncements with answers to questions from viewers.

Kefauver stuck to the tried-and-true 1948 campaign technique, traveling by car and blanketing the state exhaustively, concentrating as much on handshaking and personal conversations as on formal speeches. Nancy traveled with him during part of the campaign, though not as constantly as in 1948, and filled in for him when he had to go back to Washington for important Senate business. The children were old enough to go along, too, by then, but after trying it once, at Woodbury, with all four of them, Nancy decided "it just wouldn't work."

"They were squabbling among themselves as to which one would pass out the buttons and which the stickers, and who had the most buttons," she said afterward.[27]

Charlie Neese managed Kefauver's campaign again and once more advised Kefauver to wage a "positive campaign," ignoring Sutton's charges against him. Kefauver went along with this at first, as in 1948, and, in fact, never did mention Sutton as other than "one of my opponents" (the other two opponents were minor candidates). But it was not easy to do. Sutton, bidding for Dixiecrat support that had emerged strongly in the state six years earlier, attempted to associate Kefauver with the newly-announced Supreme Court decision outlawing school segregation.

Kefauver's basic reply to this tactic, set forth in his opening speech, was: "I refuse to appeal to prejudice in connection with it. Men and women of good will, of both races, should be giving their

26. *L'Italia*, Jan. 28, 1954; trans. *Nashville Tennessean*, Feb. 7, 1954.
27. Personal conversation, Nancy Kefauver, Washington, Spring 1955.

best thoughts to these very knotty problems, with the end in view that nothing must be allowed to disrupt our fine public school system or destroy the good racial feeling that now exists."[28]

It was a difficult viewpoint to put across. In Trenton one afternoon, Kefauver had a long conversation with John Jetton, a former supporter who had turned away from him because of this issue, while about two dozen men gathered in Jetton's hot, muggy farm implement showroom to listen.

Kefauver asked Jetton at length about his racial views, but never did argue his own. Instead, at the end of the conversation, he said, "I'm sorry. I know that you're a big man, and I respect somebody with a different opinion."

Jetton watched the tall senator pass out through his front door and move slowly down the street. He was silent for a few moments. At last he said to those around him: "I disagree. But he's a deep man. He's the only really deep man the South has in the Senate." Soon afterward, Jetton was supporting Kefauver again.[29]

Sutton's major campaign pitch was that Kefauver was "soft on Communism." He blasted Kefauver for his House votes against continuance of the Un-American Activities Committee, stating that Kefauver "does not believe in our form of government or our Constitution."[30]

Sutton's Communism charges were developed well enough by the time Kefauver began his campaign for Kefauver to take note of them in his opening speech: "I have fought the Communists at home as well as abroad. . . . Let us remember that he who is an effective anti-Communist seeks to eliminate the conditions under which Communism breeds—poverty, ignorance and despair." Kefauver reminded the voters, too, that a good deal of the internationalism for which Sutton criticized him had been directed against Soviet strategy: support for the North Atlantic Treaty Organization, the Greek-Turkish loan, and the Point Four program.[31]

Later, in a Dyersburg radio address, Kefauver labeled as "slander" the "wild, reckless and irresponsible charges that I have 'coddled Communism.' " He was getting restless at being on the defen-

28. *Nashville Tennessean*, June 13, 1954.
29. Personal conversation, Nat Caldwell, Nashville, Spring 1972.
30. *Nashville Banner*, May 1, 1954.
31. *Nashville Tennessean*, June 30, 1954.

sive. In Shelbyville early in July, he snapped at "little Hitlers and little Stalins" who sought only "personal power."[32]

The next day, in McKenzie, Sutton came up with another issue: Kefauver had not served in the armed forces during World War II, though he was of draft age and physically fit. This seemed a good issue to someone with Sutton's war record, but Sutton did not stick to the facts. He said: "The records of the draft board in Chattanooga show why he did not go. . . . If he does not tell why by July 15, I will, for I know."[33] This statement avoided any definite charge against Kefauver, but the plain implication was that Kefauver had something to hide.

Kefauver did not answer the charge, but the *Nashville Tennessean* checked state Selective Service headquarters. It was found that Kefauver, the day after Pearl Harbor, had written President Roosevelt and the War Department, offering his services "in any capacity with the armed forces." He had refused to claim exemption with the Hamilton County draft board. His offer was declined because of his membership in Congress.[34]

Not long after the military service issue was laid to rest, Kefauver spent a night with Caudill at his home near Nashville. As they drove through the city from the airport, Kefauver commented, "I'm getting awfully tired of Pat saying all those things about me." Despite the mildness of the words, Caudill recalled, "he was really angry, as angry as I've ever seen him."[35]

At Kingston in mid-July, Kefauver opened up on Sutton. He charged that Sutton's telethons were being conducted by Bob Venn, an associate of Arthur B. (Mickey) McBride of the Continental Press gambling wire service and of "Al Polizzi, the Cleveland mobster." Sutton's helicopter, he said, was partly owned by Charles B. Murphy, former New Orleans accountant for Frank Costello, and reportedly was financed by Dallas Oil interests. Moving to West Tennessee, he called Sutton a "nihilist," charging that Sutton stood for "McCarthyism, Hamiltonian Republicanism and isolationism."[36]

32. Ibid., July 8, 1954.
33. Ibid., July 10, 1954; Lou Owen, *Nashville Tennessean*, July 9, 1954.
34. Charles L. Fontenay, *Nashville Tennessean*, July 10, 1954.
35. Personal conversation, Noble C. Caudill, Hendersonville, Spring 1970.
36. Wallace Westfeldt, *Nashville Tennessean*, July 15, 1954; Charles L. Fontenay, *Nashville Tennessean*, July 25, 1954.

Finally, Kefauver attacked Sutton for sponsorship of a 1953 House bill to remove the thirty-day time limit on criminal deportation proceedings, which he said would have given "every foreign criminal in this country . . . forever and a day to fight against deportation with money, political influence, threats, every means at his command."[37]

Sutton, meanwhile, became somewhat incautious. On a final, mammoth television talkathon at Nashville, he was challenged by one of his listeners to name one of the "known Communists" with whom he said Kefauver was friendly. He named Edward Lamb.[38]

Lamb, a prominent Ohio publisher who owned several television stations, had been a Stevenson contributor in 1952 and had refused time on his stations to Senator Joseph McCarthy for an attack on Stevenson because McCarthy failed to give him an advance copy of the script, as required by the Federal Communications Commission. Shortly after Eisenhower's election, two reputed "McCarthy men" were appointed to the FCC, and subsequently the FCC balked at renewing the permit for Lamb's Erie, Pennsylvania, station. FCC hearings on allegations that Lamb was a member of the Communist party or had been in some way associated with that party were still in progress when Sutton made his charge.

Kefauver and Lamb had been friends since 1952, and Kefauver testified in his behalf in 1955. But Sutton found out that he was on shaky ground in his charge against Lamb: the allegations that Lamb was a Communist were still no more than allegations. The next day Sutton retracted his statement and apologized. Lamb sued Sutton and two Nashville television stations for libel anyhow and eventually was awarded a $25,000 judgment against Sutton, after Lamb was cleared by the FCC.[39] Sutton had miscalculated the effectiveness of his charges against Kefauver, and of his dramatic and expensive campaign. Kefauver won the primary with nearly 70 percent of the vote.

Tennessee's Republicans had expected Sutton at least to make a good enough showing to weaken Kefauver in the primary. In the anticipation of a bitterly divided Democratic party in the state after Sutton's effort, they had chosen a serious challenger for Kefauver

37. Charles L. Fontenay, *Nashville Tennessean*, July 24, 1954.
38. *Nashville Tennessean*, July 13, 1954.
39. *Nashville Tennessean*, June 16, 1954; April 19, 1958.

in November: Ray Jenkins, the Knoxville attorney with whom Kefauver and Jack Doughty had sought a partnership after their graduation from Yale. Jenkins had skyrocketed to national prominence as special counsel for Senate subcommittee hearings into charges by the Army that McCarthy, the subcommittee chairman, had exerted pressure to obtain preferential treatment for a former subcommittee investigator. But, in the wake of Kefauver's overwhelming primary victory, Jenkins refused to make the race.[40] Kefauver defeated his replacement, Nashville attorney Tom Wall, over 2 to 1. His home base secure, Kefauver turned his attention at once to the 1956 presidential campaign.

40. *Nashville Banner*, Aug. 7, 1954.

Chapter 13

It's Just Not Worth It!

Adlai Stevenson, as the 1952 nominee, was considered the front-runner for the 1956 Democratic presidential nomination. Averell Harriman, who had won a hard race for governor of New York in 1954, was in an improved position to challenge him, but Kefauver was looked on as his principal likely competitor.

Kefauver had participated in fights against the Eisenhower administration that stood out as major partisan issues in 1956, such as a conflict-of-interest controversy that forced the resignation of Harold E. Talbott as secretary of the Air Force and efforts to restore high, rigid farm price supports instead of the administration-backed flexible supports. The party leadership was still as cool toward him as ever, but everyone knew that would not prevent him from making the race.

Early in 1955, Kefauver was in Chicago with Noble C. Caudill, treasurer of Genesco, the giant shoe manufacturing firm who had been his principal money-raiser in the recent Senate campaign. They were talking about prospects of Kefauver running for President again in 1956.

"I think I still have one more good race in me, and I think maybe I ought to make it now," Kefauver remarked thoughtfully. "But I don't have any money."

Caudill thereupon took Kefauver for an evening's visit to the home of a friend of his, Walter Stern, an international hide merchant. Stern and his entire family were so charmed with the soft-spoken Tennessee senator that he made out, on the spot, two $5,000 checks to get the presidential campaign rolling, one to Kefauver and the other to Nancy.[1]

---

1. Personal conversation, Noble C. Caudill, Hendersonville, Tenn., Spring 1970.

Kefauver's decision to try again in 1956 was not eminently popular with his family. Late in 1955, the Kefauvers bought a new home at 4929 Hillbrook Lane, Northwest, and when someone asked Nancy at a Democratic women's luncheon on Armistice Day if she were ready to hit the campaign trail again, she answered emphatically, "No, I'm not! We've just finished moving into our new house."[2] She was even more decisive in her comment to Charlie Neese, about the same time, as she chatted with him while painting in her studio.

"I'm not going to get into it this time, Charlie," she said. "I just refuse to do it. The children need me at home."[3]

Bitterest against the race was fourteen-year-old Linda. As the oldest daughter and for a long time the only child, she was very close to her father and deeply resented the political activities that kept them apart.

"I don't know why he wants it," said Nancy in a newspaper interview after Kefauver had already made the plunge and was away campaigning. "I try to figure it out myself. He just seems to be driven by this idea. He's not ambitious about anything else—money or material things. I think he's always been aiming at a goal a little higher."[4]

Neese had a more psychological explanation: "He was still trying to atone for his brother's death. He was still trying to prove himself to his mother, to prove that he could be what Robert might have been. And to be President was the top . . . you couldn't get any higher than that."[5]

Kefauver's own explanation, when he was asked: "There are many reasons why a man would want to be President, but they all come down eventually to a single fact. The future of free men—your and my children—depends on how wisely and charitably we *now* apply our knowledge of the past to the problems of the future. . . . I believe that the great experiment which our forefathers began has a potential for human good which even we can barely grasp. . . . I believe that in our preoccupation with the ways of the market place, we are in danger of . . . losing the contentment of our souls. . . .

"I have an abiding faith that free men can, as our forefathers be-

2. *Nashville Tennessean*, Nov. 12, 1955.
3. Personal conversation, Charles G. Neese, Greeneville, Tenn., Spring 1971.
4. Irwin Ross, *New York Post*, May 9, 1956.
5. Personal conversation, Charles G. Neese, Greeneville, Spring 1971.

lieved, guide their own actions wisely. . . . There are those who cynically contend that a politician cannot be true to himself and succeed—that compromise with principle is a necessary evil. I deny that this is the case, for I believe in the essential goodness and reasonableness of the human race. . . .

"I would like to become President for the same reason that any of you want to do something about the pressing problems of the present and future."[6]

Just before leaving in August 1955 for a round-the-world trip through Scandinavia and Russia, Kefauver called fifteen friends from all over the country together in Washington, to lay before them the proposal that he run for President again and ask their opinions. After speaking to them briefly, Kefauver left for his office, and the group discussed the matter for two days.

The first and most important question argued was whether Eisenhower would run for reelection. It was apparent that he would be an extremely difficult man to beat, if he did. But the group was optimistic that he would not, although this was a month before the President's heart attack sent a shock wave through both major political parties; Eisenhower was sixty-four and had made remarks about younger Republicans moving up to national leadership, and Mrs. Eisenhower was understood to be opposed to his running again.

The "preliminary planning committee" agreed that Kefauver had a good chance to win the nomination, if the ultimate power of decision in his campaign were delegated to a competent professional politician as campaign chairman. They hoped to avoid the divisiveness and disorganization that had hampered the 1952 campaign.

The committee chose Kefauver's 1952 Chicago organizer, A. Bradley Eben, as its chairman. Eben, five years younger than Kefauver, had served as a page boy to Jim Farley in the 1932 Democratic National Convention, and his stepmother had served in the White House continuously through both the Roosevelt and Truman administrations. He had met Kefauver through his participation in a big antitrust case, and had joined Kefauver's presidential campaign early in the 1952 race.

Charlie Neese was named secretary of the planning committee, and Caudill, treasurer. Others in the group included columnist

6. Undated statement, Kefauver Collection, Ser. 5-g, Box 52.

Robert S. Allen and Representative Andrew Jacobs of Indiana. Several other names were added during the meeting, including former Senator Millard Tydings of Maryland and J. Howard McGrath, former senator, attorney general and Democratic national chairman.[7]

Kefauver's campaign chest was in its usual state—empty. After the committee members contributed $100 each for initial expenses, Caudill, Nathan Straus, and Colonel William A. Roberts of Washington set out to raise money. Most of what they obtained was in small gifts—$5.00 to $100—from friends and admirers all over the country. Most of the large contributions ($5,000 was a large contribution for Kefauver) came from well-to-do Jewish supporters, who approved his position on civil liberties and his objection to "sending arms to Saudi Arabia while denying them to little Egypt . . . I mean, little Israel."[8]

The search for a "pro" as campaign manager started with Matthew McCloskey, treasurer of the Democratic National Committee, but he declined. Vincent Gaughan of Buffalo, who was to become Kefauver's most effective advance man in 1956, recommended his friend, Paul Fitzpatrick, New York Democratic chairman, whom he understood to be offended at Harriman's behavior toward him since being elected governor.

Fitzpatrick was willing. Unfortunately, by this time Kefauver was on his world tour, and Eben's efforts to reach him by telephone in the Far East for approval were unavailing. Harriman, meanwhile, apparently got wind of what was going on and hurriedly patched up his relationship with Fitzpatrick.[9]

The next "pro" sought was Michael V. Di Salle, former federal price administrator, who had been one of those Stevenson delegates in 1952 to feel the backlash in November: he had failed by 300,000 votes to turn out Senator John W. Bricker. He also agreed to serve but changed his mind as a result of a hot argument with one of the Kefauver committee members over when Kefauver should announce his candidacy.[10]

7. Personal conversations, A. Bradley Eben, Chicago, Sept. 3, 1970, and Charles G. Neese, Greeneville, Spring 1971.

8. Irwin Ross, *New York Post*, May 10, 1956.

9. Telephone conversation, Vincent Gaughan, New York, Autumn 1970; personal communication, A. Bradley Eben, Chicago, Oct. 14, 1970.

10. Personal conversation, A. Bradley Eben, Chicago, Sept. 3, 1970.

Eben sounded out McGrath, on the theory that a better professional politician could hardly be found, and McGrath, too, was willing. But somehow McGrath never understood that he had a definite offer of the top post and eventually became a vice chairman, while F. Joseph (Jiggs) Donohue, a Washington attorney and former commissioner of the District of Columbia, was chosen general chairman. It was an unfortunate upside-down situation. Although Donohue had close ties to former President Truman and, like Di Salle, had been one of four men considered for Democratic national chairman, McGrath was recognized as much the better "pro."

The campaign nucleus, established in Washington's new Pennsylvania Building, had 1952 charts on which to build: Kefauver "bibles" had been compiled for every state—black, leather-bound books containing thousands of names and addresses of friends and supporters. The familiar name by which each individual was to be called was underlined or parenthesized, and sometimes a pertinent comment was added after the name.

Kefauver announced his candidacy at a press conference December 16, 1955, tossed his coonskin cap into a ring four times for the benefit of photographers, and answered newsmen's questions. Then he called to Nancy, sitting to one side, "Come on up, honey." Cool-eyed, touched with Scottish dourness in contrast to her usual sparkle, Nancy forced a smile for the cameras and answered reporters' questions laconically.[11] Kefauver announced at once that he would enter the California primary, and before year's end he had added Wisconsin, New Hampshire, and Florida to the list. Neese was strongly against his entry in the primaries; he agreed with Di Salle, who reportedly told Kefauver that his own survey indicated that Kefauver would be ruined by an all-out fight with Stevenson.

"His appeal to the voting public was already established," Neese wrote later. "Governor Stevenson had the stigma of an earlier defeat by the Republican nominee against his record; and, the power of the White House was no longer in the Democratic picture in 1956. After four years as 'outs,' the Democratic delegates wanted victory and would, in my judgment, have compromised on Kefauver in the comparatively uncontrolled climate."[12]

11. Ruth Cowan, AP story, *New York Times*, Dec. 17, 1955.
12. Letter, Charles G. Neese to William B. Rudell, Princeton, N.J., 1960, Kefauver Collection.

But Kefauver did not feel that he could afford to avoid the primaries. Aside from questions of consistency, Stevenson was nominal head of the party, with the support of organized labor and the liberal intellectuals—including some of Kefauver's influential friends such as Paul Douglas and Hubert Humphrey. (Douglas told Kefauver that, however he might feel about the matter personally, he could not afford to oppose Stevenson, an announced candidate from his own home state.) Kefauver was the "outsider" still, and he felt his best chance for the nomination was a direct appeal to the voters.

Stevenson quit the New Hampshire primary because he said it interfered too much with his effort in Minnesota, where he had the support of Humphrey and the state party organization. Freshman Senator John F. Kennedy of neighboring Massachusetts offered to enter New Hampshire as a stalking horse for Stevenson, but Stevenson, perhaps wisely, declined the offer.[13] He did agree to a well-organized write-in campaign, on the theory that a good showing could be interpreted as demonstrating Kefauver's weakness when the people had the opportunity to vote for Stevenson.

The nation's newsmen had learned four years earlier not to underestimate Kefauver in primaries; only columnists Joseph and Stewart Alsop, reflecting the official Democratic party line, painted a picture of Kefauver's New Hampshire supporters deserting him so that he looked there "a little like a sinking ship," and the writers added that "a defeat in New Hampshire could well be fatal to Kefauver, since his whole strength is built on his 'grass roots' support." The "widespread desertions" the Alsops saw apparently were a single prominent defection, that of Henry Sullivan, who had become Democratic national committeeman on the basis of his 1952 support of Kefauver but who endorsed Stevenson in 1956 and urged him to challenge Kefauver in New Hampshire.

Kefauver did have some rebuilding to do in New Hampshire, however, as all of the prominent party regulars were pulling for Stevenson. In mid-January he began a three-day race across the state in a driving sleet storm, shaking new hands and renewing old contacts, and made a final swing through five towns the day before the state's March 13 primary. Although Nancy accompanied him only

13. Theodore C. Sorensen, *Kennedy* (New York: Harper, 1965), 80–81.

In a show of unity, presidential aspirants Kefauver, Averell Harriman (left), and Adlai Stevenson (second from right) clasp hands with former President Harry S Truman at a 1956 banquet.

on the second tour, and that somewhat reluctantly, his tactics were effective: as Theodore H. White put it, he "rewired the loyalties" of Dover in a visit of only 25 minutes there.[14]

But Kefauver abandoned the coonskin cap that had been his trademark since 1948. "Some people think it's too undignified," he explained to newsmen. There was a great deal of argument among his campaign advisers *pro* and *con* concerning the coonskin cap, but the one who persuaded Kefauver to abandon it was his ten-year-old son, David, who lectured his father that the cap was all right for youngsters during the "Davy Crockett" craze, but he considered Kefauver too old for such things.[15]

On New Hampshire primary day, Kefauver put in a full day of campaigning in Minnesota and then settled down with a group of supporters and a Scotch-and-soda to watch the returns come in. Sitting serenely amid his friends, he watched the Democratic organization in New Hampshire smashed by his hand for a second time. The Stevenson write-in effort proved pathetic: Kefauver beat him more than 5 to 1.

New Hampshire had been a necessity for him. Wisconsin was a shoo-in, where he had no opposition but campaigned anyhow. Minnesota was the coldest political plunge in the nation. The Democrat-Farmer-Labor state central committee had endorsed Stevenson, and Humphrey and Governor Orville Freeman, both highly popular, were working actively for him. Humphrey said he had told Kefauver "very frankly that I thought Adlai Stevenson was better qualified for the office of the Presidency."[16]

Kefauver and Eben had visited Freeman to consult him about the Minnesota primary, and Freeman urged Kefauver, for his own good, not to enter, promising to beat him badly if he did. After leaving Freeman, though, Kefauver and Eben stopped to visit the owner of a large printing firm in St. Paul. He said he thought Kefauver had a good chance and promised a substantial contribution if Kefauver ran in Minnesota.[17]

Donohue was strongly against taking the risk at Minnesota, but Kefauver was the recipient of solicitation by dissident elements of

14. "Kefauver Rides Again."
15. Personal conversation, David Kefauver, Knoxville, Spring 1970.
16. Lois Laycook, *Nashville Tennessean*, Jan. 28, 1956.
17. Personal conversation, A. Bradley Eben, Chicago, Sept. 3, 1970.

Kefauver dons snowshoes during his campaign swing through New Hampshire in 1956.

Estes and Nancy Kefauver at the 1956 Democratic National Convention. At right is A. Bradley Eben, Kefauver's floor manager, and at left is Jay Solomon of Chattanooga, many years later U.S. General Services Administrator.

the Minnesota party organization, including such factions as a St. Paul labor group "thoroughly disgusted with the high-handed manner being used by the Minnesota DFL state committee" and centered on Hjalmar Petersen, state railroad and warehouse commissioner and a former governor, and Representative Coya Knutson. This group sent a delegation headed by Petersen to intercept Kefauver in Wisconsin. Kefauver listened to their pleas for two hours in a LaCrosse hotel and then telephoned Washington. Donohue was still strongly opposed, and Charles Alldredge, a campaign aide accompanying Kefauver, begged him not to enter Minnesota.

"Well, I don't know," said Kefauver thoughtfully. "We might just win, and if we do we've changed the entire pattern of the campaign."[18]

Later that night, in Madison, he sat down in a hotel lobby and scribbled three sheets of note paper headed "J. Howard McGrath" to the effect that "Upon the urging of my Minn. friends I have finally determined to permit the use of my name by entering the D. Pres. Primary in Minn. . . . The machine has even gone to the extent of putting strong presure [*sic*] upon my friends and supporters in an effort to keep me out. . . ." He read the statement over the telephone to Donohue and told him to announce it to the press.[19]

Minnesota had been spared the Kefauver campaign technique in 1952, but now the state had a concentrated dose of it. In a four-day swing in late February, Kefauver moved from Pipestone to Luverne to Worthington to Mankato, and so on through the farm country—kicking off his alligator shoes in the car or the bus or the plane, dictating a few letters or some speech ideas to a secretary traveling with him, and sleeping en route, the light shut out by a black felt eyeshade with a silk stocking tucked around the edges. He carried his mail around in open-topped wooden office boxes, his suits on open hangers, and his size 17-36 shirts in paper bags.

On New Hampshire primary day, a week before the Minnesota primary, the Kefauver "glow wagon" showed up from New Hampshire and rolled into Marshall, Minnesota. It cruised around in the snow, waiting for its master: a converted truck, garish with neon

18. Richard Lewis, "Will the People Choose the People's Choice?" *New Republic*, Feb. 6, 1956; White, "Kefauver Rides Again."

19. Undated note in Kefauver's handwriting, Kefauver Collection, Ser. 5-g, Box 48.

and streamers, bearing a big sign—"*Kefauver, the Man who can Win.*" Kefauver arrived an hour later than scheduled and plunged into a final Minnesota campaign drive.

Stevenson, not really enthusiastic about the primaries but forced into them by Kefauver's challenge, had chosen Minnesota as a "safe" test, where, backed by the party organization and its popular leaders, he could demonstrate his strength in the farm belt. Now he found himself having to campaign strenuously, almost but not quite meeting Kefauver on his drive up and down the state. Humphrey and Freeman campaigned just as strenuously for him, criticizing Kefauver for being so forward as to enter the primary in the first place. Kefauver, for his part, waged his usual informal campaign, fielding touchy questions deftly and calling for graduated price supports for farmers and a food stamp plan.

A final statewide poll by the *Minneapolis Sunday Tribune* a few days before the primary showed Kefauver gaining but still well behind: Stevenson 52 percent, Kefauver 39 percent. Donohue predicted confidently that Kefauver would get "a good 35 percent of the vote." Stevenson said he would be satisfied with 60 percent, or even 55 percent.[20]

On primary day, Kefauver flew from Washington to Minneapolis to await the returns with Minnesota friends in a suite on the tenth floor of the Hotel Nicollet. By 10 P.M., the trend was clear, and Kefauver arose and went to his room to shave and take a telephone call from Nancy in Washington. "You know what that means," said Paul Swensson, managing editor of the *Tribune*, who was among those in the suite.[21] A press conference was set for 11:30 P.M. Shaved, Kefauver returned to the crowded suite to sit calmly, nursing a Scotch-and-soda, while well-wishers crowded around him, and Freeman appeared to concede and to congratulate him.[22]

Kefauver won approximately 57 percent of the vote and virtually a clean sweep of the Minnesota delegation to the national convention. So effective had been his campaign that Ken Allen, editor of the *Albert Lea Tribune*, wrote: "Kefauver spent only a few hours in

20. Douglas B. Cornell, AP story, *Nashville Tennessean*, March 18 and 20, 1956; Thomson and Shattuck, *The 1956 Presidential Campaign*, 39.
21. *Nashville Tennessean*, March 21, 1956.
22. Douglas B. Cornell, AP story, *Nashville Tennessean*, March 21, 1956.

this southern Minnesota town, and I'm certain we could elect him mayor tomorrow. And we are kind of particular who we pick for mayor."[23] Freeman and Humphrey, who had been counting on Stevenson's victory to get them delegate spots for the Democratic National Convention in Chicago, were reduced to accepting Kefauver's invitation to accept seats on his pledged Minnesota delegation in order to have any official voice in the convention.[24] The gesture of generosity on Kefauver's part proved fortunate for him later. On the floor of the Senate the next day, Senator Alexander Wiley asked rhetorically, "What happened in Minnesota yesterday?" Senator William Langer replied with evident relish, "The politicians met, and they were for Stevenson. The common people met yesterday, and they reversed the decision."[25]

The prospects had never looked better for Kefauver. When Wisconsin came in April 3, he had won 62 pledged delegates to Stevenson's four, with 598,251 popular votes to Stevenson's 190,529 in three primaries. Stevenson was so far from being the acknowledged front-runner any longer that Lyle C. Wilson of the *United Press* speculated that he "probably" had been knocked out of the race.[26] But Stevenson was not "out of it," by any means. He congratulated Kefauver on the Minnesota victory and set about to change the image of the cool, aloof intellectual that had cost him so dearly in Minnesota. He succeeded admirably.

Both men spent most of the rest of their campaigning time on two forthcoming "big primaries," Florida and California. In both states, Stevenson developed a consuming interest in shaking everyone's hand, with a quick smile and perhaps a joke. In his determined effort to out-Kefauver Kefauver, he even inadvertently shook the hand of a clothing store mannequin in Florida.[27]

Kefauver and Stevenson had been polite and generous in their references to each other, and their courtesy and good humor lingered for a time in Florida. When their paths crossed in Tampa,

23. Ken Allen, *Nashville Tennessean*, March 25, 1956.
24. Douglas B. Cornell, AP story, *Nashville Tennessean*, March 22, 1956.
25. *Congressional Record*, vol. 102, pt. 4, March 21, 1956, p. 5236.
26. *Nashville Banner*, March 21, 1956.
27. Peter Lisagor, *Nashville Banner*, May 22, 1956; Thomson and Shattuck, *The 1956 Presidential Campaign*, 53.

they traded quips over a couple of cigars and pinned campaign buttons on each other.[28] But Florida was a treacherous, touchy state, split between liberals in the urban areas and typical Southern conservatives in the rural areas and northern Florida. Its importance to their hopes put the pressure on both men.

The "new," aggressive Stevenson was smarting from his Minnesota disaster and disturbed by a mid-April Gallup poll showing that he had dropped to 39 percent against Kefauver's 33 percent among Democrats, compared to 51 percent against Kefauver's 17 percent at the beginning of the year. In Florida, Stevenson initiated the bitter, personal phase of the contest that was to cost Kefauver so dearly.

Stevenson launched an attack on Kefauver's absentee record, listing votes for which Kefauver had not been present in the Senate, and observed that "there may be such a thing as wanting to be President too badly. And that may be one of the reasons why none of Senator Kefauver's colleagues in the Senate have endorsed him, and so few of the party's leaders around the country."[29]

Kefauver, stung, retorted: "I had no ill word against him. . . . I'm sorry that Mr. Stevenson feels he now must engage in mud slinging. He's not in character doing it." He remembered that a number of the Senate absences with which Stevenson charged him had been at a time when he was not yet in the Senate.[30]

"I have many friends in the Senate," Kefauver said, and he set out to demonstrate it. But his colleagues were not inclined to leap to his defense. He was not even able to get an endorsement from his Tennessee colleague, Senator Albert Gore, who responded to his request by saying that he had "publicly pledged myself to remain aloof from a possible contest or controversy regarding the Tennessee delegation, saying I would be glad to support either you or Governor Clement for national preferment."

There were, in fact, substantial rumors that young, ambitious Frank Clement was trying to work a deal with the Stevenson forces to get the vice presidential nomination if he could hold Kefauver's home state away from him at the national convention. There was also speculation that if Clement failed to attain national office, he might run against Gore at the end of both their terms in 1958.

28. UP story, *Nashville Tennessean*, April 14, 1956.
29. AP story, *Nashville Banner*, April 6, 1956.
30. Ibid.; AP stories, *Nashville Tennessean*, April 7 and 8, 1956.

Stevenson had lured Kefauver into a dog-fight, which seemed to have been his major purpose, as he did not repeat his absenteeism charge. He simply called the mud-slinging accusation "nonsense" and challenged Kefauver to a debate. Kefauver agreed promptly, and set about to find issues for a counterattack. One that he found was that Stevenson, as governor of Illinois, had vetoed a 1951 bill to increase old age and blind pensions by 10 percent, and another was that Stevenson, while titular head of the Democratic party, had represented the Radio Corporation of America as an attorney in a defense against antitrust charges. He was able to back up the first charge, but he had been misinformed on the second through sloppy staff work in Washington: Stevenson had represented RCA only in a related civil suit.[31] Kefauver corrected the literal misstatement but still attacked Stevenson on the issue in California.

The issue capable of generating some real reaction in Florida at that time, however, was the Supreme Court's 1954 decision requiring desegregation of public schools. Six candidates for governor were making it the major thrust of their campaigns. Kefauver and Stevenson vied in efforts to appear "moderate" on the civil rights issue, without at the same time appearing so moderate as to damage their subsequent chances in more liberal California, while the backers of each man tried to pin an integrationist label on the other. The Stevenson people were the more blatant at that activity, though Kefauver supporters circulated material depicting Stevenson as a champion of Negro rights. The Stevenson campaign organization—virtually synonymous with the Florida Democratic organization—was joined in segregationist attacks on Kefauver by former Governor Herman Talmadge of Georgia and Sam Wilhite, political adviser to Senator James O. Eastland. At the same time, somewhat inconsistently, Humphrey was charging in Minnesota that it was not Eastland, new chairman of the Judiciary Committee, who was blocking civil rights legislation, but Kefauver, in failing to attend committee meetings and lend his vote to the cause.

In fact, the civil rights positions of Kefauver and Stevenson, especially with respect to the Supreme Court's integration decision, were almost identical. Both called for compliance with the ruling as

31. AP story, *Nashville Tennessean*, May 24, 1956; UP story, *Nashville Banner*, May 25, 1956; personal conversation, A. Bradley Eben, Chicago, Sept. 3, 1970.

"the law of the land," and both expressed a desire that it be implemented locally and without federal interference.

So similar were their positions that their May 24 television debate offered a good opportunity to emphasize the fact and take all the steam out of the charges by the Stevenson camp that Kefauver was more "integrationist" than Stevenson. With this in mind, one of Kefauver's supporters, Dr. Bernard L. Strehler, a Chicago political scientist, prepared a thorough briefing and program for Kefauver for the debate, inviting Stevenson to join Kefauver in a "manifesto" outlining their agreement in some major policy areas, including civil rights, the Taft-Hartley Act, and aid to Israel. If Stevenson agreed, Kefauver would have demonstrated the initiative in an important ideological area. If Stevenson refused, he would appear to be reluctant to commit himself to positions conforming closely to Democratic party philosophy. Unfortunately, Donohue temporized and never did approve Strehler's plan.[32] As a result, the nationally televised "debate" was dull enough to reflect no credit on either candidate. Both were tense and sparred warily, trying to outparry each other in cautious statements about issues against the Republicans.[33]

As soon as they went their separate ways, the infighting got nasty again. Former Governor Millard Caldwell of Florida, a Stevenson delegate candidate, quoted an editorial calling Kefauver an "integrationist" and "a sycophant for the Negro vote," and Stevenson, sitting just behind Caldwell, did not comment on the accusation.[34] Kefauver thereupon accused Stevenson of using a "smear and smile" technique. Stevenson, for his part, said he was "mad as the devil" about Kefauver's "fantastic and amazing" charges about his social security record in Illinois.[35]

As S.A. Para of Tennessee's Brotherhood of Railroad Trainmen, an unofficial Kefauver scout, wrote after a ten-day survey, "If Florida is as important as the political analysts claim, most certainly more concentrated resource and organization effort should have been ap-

32. Letters, A. Bradley Eben, Chicago, to Joseph Donohue, Washington, May 15, 1956, and Bernard L. Strehler, Chicago, to Richard Wallace, Washington, May 16, 1956, Kefauver Collection, Ser. 5-g, Box 48.
33. Peter Lisagor, *Nashville Banner*, May 22, 1956.
34. *New York Times*, May 23, 1956.
35. UP story, *Nashville Tennessean*, May 26, 1956.

plied."[36] Stevenson edged out Kefauver, 221,718 votes to 209,447.

Stevenson was running scared and was back in California to campaign before the Florida polls closed. The California primary, with sixty-eight delegate votes and the issue of comparative popular appeal at stake, was crucial to both men now, in view of Stevenson's loss of Minnesota and Kefauver's loss of Florida.

A week after the Minnesota primary, Stevenson had put the California primary race, too, on a basis of personal accusations. He said in Los Angeles that Kefauver's charges of "bossism" were "discrediting the leaders of the Democratic Party" and would "weaken and divide the party, and thereby help the Republicans." Kefauver, in turn, arriving in San Diego the day after the Florida primary, charged that "Stevenson made segregation the principal issue in Florida, and six of the state's seven Congressmen . . . felt he was more suited to maintain the *status quo* in the South."[37]

Kefauver would have done better to have adhered to his reaction at the time of Stevenson's Los Angeles accusation: "I do not intend to say anything disparaging about Mr. Stevenson." His attack at the close of the Florida campaign gave Stevenson the opportunity to reproach him for "personal abuse and deceit," and to remark, "There is such a thing as wanting to win too much."[38]

But Kefauver was so near exhaustion from his arduous effort in state after state that he could do little more than react. Some newsmen following the campaign noted that he went through the familiar routine of handshaking, greeting, speaking, like an automaton, his face slack and sleepy, and Mrs. Martha Ragland of Nashville, who traveled with him part of the time, said that once when he ended a day of touring three widely separated states, he appeared to be drunk, "but he wasn't—he was just dead on his feet."[39]

Day after day he would campaign from 7 A.M. until 10 or 11 P.M. and then meet privately in his hotel room with supporters in groups and individually until 3 A.M. His aides went with him in shifts; his

36. Letter, S.A. Para, Nashville, to Richard Wallace, Washington, May 23, 1956, Kefauver Collection, Ser. 5-g, Box 48.
37. *Nashville Tennessean*, May 31, 1956; AP story, *Nashville Banner*, May 31, 1956.
38. *Washington Post*, May 25, 1956.
39. Personal conversation, Martha Ragland, Nashville, Summer 1970.

pace exhausted them. After one such day in San Francisco, Kefauver and Eben had to catch a 7 A.M. plane to Los Angeles, and Eben showed up at Kefauver's room at 6 A.M. to find the big senator stumbling sleepily around the room, trying to match a shirt to a tie.

Kefauver was muttering something so indistinctly that Eben could not make out what he was saying. Even edged closer and caught a weary, dispirited mumble: "It's not worth it. . . . It's just not worth it!"[40]

"The Senator's time was overscheduled," Curran V. Shields of the University of California wrote to Eben in mid-campaign. "By the time the Senator left Tuesday nite, he was utterly exhausted. . . . Our campaign is not getting out to the voters the Senator's stand on the vital issues. . . . We have no adequate briefing materials for our Speaker's Bureau people and nothing printed about issues for general distribution. . . ."[41]

Kefauver was too bemused by weariness to think clearly about his course of action, and his campaign advisers were made desperate by a steady flow of bad news. Charlie Neese had warned him that if he defeated Stevenson in an early major primary, it would alarm the party organization in other states, and "they have the know-how to win primaries if they try hard enough." Kefauver won half a dozen primaries where he was unopposed, but wherever Stevenson was on the ballot, Kefauver lost, after Minnesota.

Under this pressure, his "brain trust" in Washington could come up with nothing more original than to push him to the limit of his physical powers and direct him to more intense personal attacks on Stevenson. Kefauver himself, turning away from his own proposals for a presidential program and criticism of the Eisenhower administration, went no farther than to charge Stevenson with "civil rights equivocation" in liberal California, but Donohue issued the flat statement that "a vote for Stevenson is a vote for Eastland, Talmadge, Ellender and other white supremacy boys."[42]

Such tactics proved Kefauver's worst enemy in California. He received many critical letters from the state after the primary. One from Palo Alto said his methods "reminded me of the type of cam-

40. Personal conversation, A. Bradley Eben, Chicago, Sept. 3, 1970.
41. Letter, Currin V. Shields, Berkeley, to A. Bradley Eben, Chicago, June 13, 1956, Kefauver Collection, Ser. 5-g, Box 36.
42. Frank van der Linden, *Nashville Banner*, June 4, 1956.

paign Nixon or McCarthy would conduct. I am sure many other Californians who were beginning to switch over to you during the last few weeks stopped short of doing so after seeing such tactics." Another wrote: "As one who has long admired your constructive liberal record in the Senate, I was terribly shocked by your campaigning," and a third said, "I wanted to vote for you but could not find it in my heart to do so. . . . In this campaign you seemed to have deserted your stand."[43]

Stevenson smashed Kefauver in California, nearly 2 to 1. Two weeks later, when Kefauver had rested and recovered his sense of proportion, he apologized for his attacks on Stevenson. "I got mad and lost my head," he said. "I did get somewhat out of character."[44]

The 1956 primary disasters in Florida and California, effectively destroying Kefauver's apparently excellent chances for the presidential nomination, emphasize not only the grave weaknesses in his campaign organization but an aspect to Kefauver's own personality that was rarely manifested: an aspect well expressed by Stevenson, whatever his motivation for saying it, in his statement that "there is such a thing as wanting to win too much." As Nancy remarked at Shangri-la after Kefauver's defeat at the 1952 convention, "Estes really doesn't like to lose."[45]

The qualities of Kefauver's character emphasized repeatedly by colleagues, friends, and admirers in recalling his political life and legislative career give overwhelming evidence that his refusal to compromise on principles, even under threat of high political cost, was a key factor in winning him such widespread support and such fanatic loyalty. Although fearful for his political life in both of his last two Tennessee Senate campaigns, he overcame the severe temptation to compromise on such explosive issues as civil rights and was rewarded with tremendous outpourings of voter confidence. In his stands on legislation in the halls of Congress, he wavered only a very few times, often knowing that not only would he be defeated but that the worst possible interpretation would be placed on his position by his enemies. But, exhausted by the demands of the 1956 primaries on his stamina, under pressure from some of his more "practical" advisers, he yielded to the desperate

43. Kefauver Collection, Ser. 5-g, Box 58.
44. AP story, *Nashville Tennessean*, June 18, 1956.
45. Personal conversation, Nancy Kefauver, McMinnville, Tenn., Aug. 1952.

fear that his prized ambition was slipping from his grasp and temporized badly and baldly in both Florida and California; and it is within the realm of possibility that this very desperation cost him what he sought.

Although he vowed to fight "harder than ever" after California,[46] it was clear that his cause was lost with the collapse of the legend that his voter appeal was almost invincible. For nearly two months, he sat tight, while his opponents and the newspapers speculated. His top campaign advisers disagreed vigorously as to whether he should withdraw or stay in the race. McGrath and Donohue set up appointments for him with about thirty top Democratic leaders to discuss his prospects, and their assessment caused him to reconsider his candidacy seriously. It was not just that Stevenson now was ahead of him in delegates and increasing his lead; Kefauver's position in the party was such that he was unlikely to be able to draw on substantial reserves after his first ballot showing—a matter of about 250 delegate votes.

Although Kefauver had said in Philadelphia before the primaries that he would not "accept an alternative" to the presidential nomination,[47] he began to think in terms of the vice presidential spot. Meeting Jacob Arvey, one of Stevenson's principal advisers, on a plane, Kefauver sounded him out about it. Arvey said he himself had no objections, but he did not know whom Stevenson wanted.[48] Before the campaign, Stevenson, in answer to a suggestion for a Stevenson-Kefauver ticket from Oscar Chapman, former secretary of the Interior, had threatened that if Kefauver entered the primaries against him, "I'll never take him on the ticket."[49] Now the Stevenson camp handed Kefauver a figurative but public slap in the face: Paul Butler, Democratic national chairman, named Kefauver's gadfly enemy, Governor Frank Clement of Tennessee, to deliver the keynote address at the national convention. At the same time, Stevenson was telling both his own and Kefauver's supporters that he was "going to make no deal with Estes or anybody else."[50]

46. AP story, *Nashville Tennessean*, June 11, 1956.
47. Ibid., Dec. 18, 1955.
48. Martin, *Ballots and Bandwagons*, 378–79.
49. Drew Pearson, column, *Nashville Tennessean*, June 6, 1956.
50. Ibid., July 29, 1956; Martin, *Ballots and Bandwagons*, 378.

After California, in fact, Stevenson acquired the somewhat Arcadian idea that he had the nomination sewed up, and he could not understand why his campaign manager, James A. Finnegan of Philadelphia, insisted on continuing to seek delegate support. When Finnegan told him, "Averell Harriman might beat you," Stevenson stared at him and replied, "Incredible!"

But there was nothing incredible about it. Harriman announced his candidacy four days after the California primary and began at once to build a delegate-seeking organization centered on an axis between New York and several Western states, with former President Truman and a number of his allies prominent in his camp. Truman, admitting that he had blocked Kefauver in 1952, had met both Kefauver and Harriman earlier in the year and had proclaimed his neutrality "this time," but after California the ex-President commented he was "inclined to anyone else besides Kefauver."[51]

Now Harriman had money, he had New York, he had the hard core liberals, he had an astute campaign manager—Tammany's Carmine deSapio—and he had Truman. He was in a much better position than in 1952 to force Stevenson's hand on the explosive civil rights issue and fractionize the convention, if he could work out the same sort of an alliance with the Kefauver forces. Key people in the Kefauver and Harriman organizations began discussing such an anti-Stevenson bloc. Harriman went personally to Kefauver's office to assure him that he was "very much embarrassed" by Truman's remarks and did not share his sentiments.[52] DeSapio talked with Kefauver about a possible coalition, and another Harriman lieutenant, Frank McKinney, approached Donohue.

Donohue was more receptive to the Harriman overtures than Kefauver himself. Donohue and George Backer, a Harriman representative, held a series of meetings to work out a joint Kefauver-Harriman statement condemning "strong forces of moderation" in the party. Backer was led to believe that Kefauver himself favored the agreement.[53] Recognizing that he no longer had any real chance for the nomination, Kefauver still hesitated to withdraw.

51. *Nashville Tennessean*, Feb. 3, 1956; Doris Fleeson, column, ibid., Aug. 7, 1956.
52. Lois Laycook, *Nashville Tennessean*, July 17, 1956.
53. *New York Times*, Aug. 2, 1956.

"My people went through hell for me," he said. "I can't withdraw. They went through hell for me."[54]

Again he called in key supporters from all over the country, told them the situation, and left them to talk it over. McGrath, Donohue, and Eben were spokesmen for three different courses of action. Eben urged that Kefauver fight to the bitter end. He and Strehler had evolved a strategy: stay in the race, explode the convention with fights over credentials, civil rights, any issue that could be seized, force Stevenson to commit himself on touchy issues, and hope to emerge the winner in a polarized convention. The majority at the meeting agreed with him.

"We have a great man, a great leader," said Gerald Flynn of Racine, Wisconsin. "It's an honor to go down fighting for him."

"A man is never defeated when he goes down fighting, and I came here to fight, not to bury Kefauver," said Joe da Silva of Los Angeles.

Donohue had an offer from the Harriman people. They would pick up the tab for Kefauver's $75,000 campaign debt if Kefauver would withdraw in Harriman's favor. But it was strictly a commercial proposition: the vice presidential nomination was not included. In fact, although he had not mentioned it to the group, just before the meeting Harriman had telephoned Kefauver personally and offered to pay both the campaign debt and Kefauver's hotel expenses in Chicago. Whether the vice presidential nomination figured in that conversation was never revealed.

McGrath, the old pro, had a professional type of offer. If Kefauver would withdraw in favor of Stevenson, Stevenson would not tap him for the vice presidential nomination, lest the Republicans make capital out of such an obvious "deal." But Finnegan and Mayor David Lawrence of Pittsburgh had assured McGrath absolutely that, in such a case, Stevenson would throw the vice presidential race open.

With his bloc of committed delegates and his ready-made organization, Kefauver would have a strong advantage in such a situation. In addition, Finnegan and Lawrence promised Kefauver most, if not all, of the big Pennsylvania delegation in a vice presi-

54. Martin, *Ballots and Bandwagons*, 383.

dential fight.[55] Kefauver, as usual, listened to the report of the discussion and made his own decision. On the last day of July he withdrew in favor of Stevenson—no strings attached.

"I've got a lot of respect for a man who gets into the primaries and fights it out, as Adlai did," Kefauver said. "I couldn't gang up to throw the nomination to someone who didn't get into the primaries and make the race according to the American tradition."[56]

With that, he returned to Tennessee for a fifty-third birthday celebration with his family at Shangri-la.

55. Lois Laycook, *Nashville Tennessean*, Aug. 1, 1956; Drew Pearson, column, *Nashville Tennessean*, Aug. 8, 1956; Robert S. Allen, undated column, Kefauver Collection, Ser. 5-g, Box 16; personal conversation, A. Bradley Eben, Chicago, Sept. 3, 1970.
56. Drew Pearson, column, *Nashville Tennessean*, Aug. 8, 1956.

Chapter 14

I've Just *GOT* to Have Those Delegates!

Kefauver's withdrawal from the 1956 presidential race upset several political apple carts. One of them, of course, was Averell Harriman's. Harriman had hoped for either a Stevenson-Kefauver fight to the finish, possibly deadlocking the convention and letting him come in as a compromise candidate, or a Kefauver withdrawal in his favor.

If reports were correct, another upset cart belonged to Tennessee's Governor Frank Clement. The Kefauver and Clement camps had agreed that the Tennessee delegation would support any Tennessean who "had an opportunity" for a place on the national ticket—which could mean either Kefauver or Clement, depending on the way the wind blew. Reportedly, Clement planned to vote the delegation for Kefauver on the first ballot, then "decide" that Kefauver no longer "had an opportunity," and swing the psychologically important vote to Stevenson in the hope of starting a bandwagon and capitalizing on Stevenson's resulting gratitude.[1]

A third belonged to Hubert Humphrey, who announced his vice presidential candidacy the day before Kefauver's withdrawal. As one of Stevenson's principal advisers, Humphrey had reason to hope that loyalty and liberalism would not go unrewarded if Stevenson won the nomination without owing anything to any other serious presidential contender. Kefauver's withdrawal in Steven-

---

1. John N. Popham, *New York Times*, June 16, 1956; Doris Fleeson, column, *Nashville Tennessean*, Aug. 7, 1956. Clement, of course, could not control the Tennessee delegation to the Democratic National Convention in 1956 arbitrarily and without qualification, any more than Browning could in 1952. But his personal wishes carried great weight, and, though the state convention contained many Kefauver supporters, it was predominantly made up of "Clement people" —those allied with the old Crump-McKellar Bourbon wing of the party. Among these was Herbert S. Walters of Morristown, state Democratic chairman, who, like Clement, wanted an uninstructed delegation and certainly not one pledged to Kefauver.

son's favor created a Stevenson debt to Kefauver, whether Stevenson wished to recognize it as such or not.[2]

Kefauver flew to Chicago with Nancy August 10, announced he would accept the vice presidential nomination if it were offered to him, checked in at the Sheraton-Blackstone Hotel, and paid a courtesy call on Stevenson. They discussed the best way to swing pro-Kefauver delegations to Stevenson, and then Kefauver asked Stevenson flatly for his support for the vice presidential nomination. Stevenson refused to commit himself.[3]

Kefauver supporters opened a "Kefauver for Vice President" headquarters in a rather large parlor of the Conrad Hilton Hotel. His close financial straits are indicated by a memorandum to him from Lucile Myers: "We can't afford to entertain them, but we could man such a spot with volunteers who know you and your friends." To quench the thirst of well-wishers who appeared on opening night, nothing more aristocratic was provided than three barrels of beer.

Kefauver took Stevenson to introduce him at a meeting of his delegates, and urged them to go along with Stevenson. When Truman announced publicly for Harriman, a Kefauver man was posted near the door of Truman's suite, posing as a newspaper reporter. Every delegate who visited Truman had a later visit from Kefauver, urging support of Stevenson. Many Kefauver delegates were saying they would not go over to Stevenson unless they were assured he would tap Kefauver as his running mate. Stevenson was warned by at least one Democratic leader that if he chose anyone else, the convention might override him. Walter Reuther, one of Stevenson's most influential supporters, was strong for Kefauver, and the California delegation voted in caucus 3 to 1 for a Stevenson-Kefauver ticket.[4]

On the other hand, the Harriman forces, angry at Kefauver's

---

2. Doris Fleeson, column, *Nashville Tennessean*, Aug. 7, 1956. Thomson and Shattuck, *The 1956 Presidential Campaign*, 149, say Kefauver had four advantages for the vice presidential nod: (1) a Stevenson-Kefauver ticket would promote Democratic unity in California, a key state; (2) support for Kefauver by Walter Reuther, head of the powerful United Auto Workers; (3) Kefauver's efforts to keep his delegates in line for Stevenson; and (4) Kefauver's strength among the nation's farmers and small town citizens.

3. Martin, *Ballots and Bandwagons*, 387.

4. Lois Laycook, *Nashville Tennessean*, Aug. 18, 1956.

switch to Stevenson, were opposed bitterly to Kefauver. So were most of the Southerners, and none more so than Sam Rayburn and Lyndon Johnson; Johnson had his own vice presidential hopes. The attitude of Kefauver's own Tennessee delegation was made known by Leslie T. Hart, columnist for the *Nashville Banner* and an unofficial spokesman for Clement: "If Stevenson gives the nod to Tennessee Sen. Estes Kefauver, it will be considered an insult to a majority of the Tennessee delegation and to Gov. Frank Clement in particular."[5]

The Tennessee delegation plan was to put Clement forth as a favorite son candidate and withhold the state's votes from Stevenson, thereby reflecting unfavorably on Kefauver.[6] But they never got the chance: by the time Pennsylvania was passed in the roll call, Stevenson had won the nomination.[7] He swamped Harriman in a first ballot avalanche.

The Stevenson management's commitment to Kefauver to throw the convention open was known to only a few people. In fact, when McGrath reported it at the Kefauver meeting in Washington, it had not been decided firmly, and Finnegan himself subsequently opposed it. But Lawrence was strong for it, and so was Arvey. Lawrence won over Wilson Wyatt, Stevenson's 1952 campaign manager, and between them they convinced Stevenson that such a move would be a dramatic contrast to Eisenhower's hand-picking of Vice President Nixon at the Republican convention. Finnegan did not resolve his doubts about it until after Stevenson's nomination. But, once the decision was made, he overrode the furious opposition of Rayburn and Johnson, who were convinced it would benefit Kefauver more than any other candidate. At last, as Stevenson and Finnegan remained adamant, Johnson said, "Mr. Sam, it's the governor's decision. After all, he has to live with it, not us."

"All right," said Rayburn to Stevenson, "if your mind's made up, give me your arm and I'll take you out there and introduce you to the convention."[8]

The announcement shattered Humphrey's hopes, but it suited John F. Kennedy just fine. Kennedy had been pushing his vice

5. Leslie T. Hart, *Nashville Banner*, Aug. 16, 1956.
6. Wayne Whitt, *Nashville Tennessean*, Aug. 19, 1956.
7. *Time*, Aug. 27, 1956; Thomson and Shattuck, *The 1956 Presidential Campaign*, 151–52.
8. Martin, *Ballots and Bandwagons*, 400–401.

presidential chances since June and already had hints of the "open convention" plan: right after Kefauver's withdrawal, Sargent Shriver, Kennedy's brother-in-law, had heard about it from Stevenson himself, at the end of a plane trip from California to Chicago.[9]

Many of the Kefauver people, unaware of the previous talks, thought Stevenson had thrown the contest open as an underhanded way of beating Kefauver because he was afraid of the reaction to his choosing anyone else. Their feeling was reflected very well in an article the next day by Jim Bishop: "The Proper Little Man from Illinois was not in by a good many miles. There was no Stevenson bandwagon. Kefauver put the wheels on Adlai's wagon and sent it rolling downhill to the nomination. . . . Kefauver had a moral right, on Thursday night, to expect Stevenson to tell the delegates . . . he would like to have Kefauver as his running mate. . . . Stevenson, I feel, chickened out."[10]

Kefauver himself was not sure of the thrust of Stevenson's gesture. Shortly before Stevenson's announcement, Eben came into McGrath's suite at the Sheraton-Blackstone to find Kefauver and Donohue debating tensely, Donohue contending it was all a trick to humiliate Kefauver and "I don't want to see you humiliated." Eben, who had been visiting Minnesota and other delegations for Kefauver, broke in.

"You're going to be humiliated if you don't get in and fight for it," he said. "I've been talking to these delegates, and they're going to put your name in nomination, whether you run or not."[11]

But Kefauver, remembering 1952, was still inclined to listen to Donohue. The sequence of events that afternoon and evening is not entirely clear, but at one point he was persuaded to write out, and sign, a statement withdrawing his name from consideration. Most of the voluble friends who surrounded him in his headquarters at the Conrad Hilton contended that the convention was loaded, and Kefauver was on the verge of sending the statement to the convention, packing immediately, and heading home to Tennessee.

A few friends, among them Representatives James Roosevelt and Wayne Hays, were urging him to remain and fight it out. His ad-

9. *Time,* Aug. 27, 1956.
10. *New York Journal-American,* Aug. 18, 1956.
11. Personal conversation, A. Bradley Eben, Chicago, Sept. 3, 1970, and personal communication, ibid., Oct. 14, 1970.

ministrative assistant, Dick Wallace, pleaded, "No, don't go home. Stay here. It's not true, It's not loaded."

At this point, Elmo Roper, the pollster, entered the room. He had just been across the street to congratulate Stevenson, and Wyatt had commented in Stevenson's presence that he wanted to work with Roper in lining up delegates for Kefauver.

"At least talk to Adlai before you leave town," urged Roper. "At least hear what he has to say."

Kefauver did not want to visit Stevenson "unless he at least asks me," and Stevenson was reluctant to invite him, lest it appear that a deal was brewing between them. At Stevenson's suggestion, Kefauver visited him as Roper's guest. Stevenson told Kefauver he really wanted an open vice presidential race but might have a preference nevertheless; he added that he would be happy for Wyatt to help line up delegates for Kefauver. Kefauver, still dubious, announced no decision right away. Late that night, after Stevenson threw the vice presidential race open, he discussed the situation with a group of his closest friends and advisers for about an hour.

"Well, let me talk with Nancy about it," he said at last.

He conferred privately with his wife for a short time in a bedroom and returned to the waiting group about midnight.

"All right," he said. "We'll go."

Cheers went up, and the Kefauver people plunged into the all-night task of tracking down delegates, running into supporters of other candidates doing the same thing. Eben ran into John Kennedy so often that the two men began sharing cabs, arguing against each other when they got where they were going.[12] Minnesota posed an ethical problem: Kefauver had won the delegates in the primary, but their senator, Humphrey, was running. Kefauver released them. But Roper went to Humphrey.

"I'm in it to win," said Humphrey. "If it turns out that it's deadlocked between Kefauver and Kennedy, I'll withdraw. If I have the wisdom to perceive the moment that I no longer have a chance to make it, I'll swing my support to Estes."[13]

Since Kefauver could not get even a seconding speech from the

12. Martin, *Ballots and Bandwagons*, 402–404; personal communications, A. Bradley Eben, Chicago, Oct. 14, 1970, and Lincoln M. Polan, Huntington, W. Va., Dec. 4, 1970.
13. Martin, *Ballots and Bandwagons*, 404–405.

Clement-controlled delegation of his home state, Mike Di Salle of Ohio was chosen to nominate him and Senator Richard L. Neuberger of Oregon and James Roosevelt of California for the seconding honors. Albert Gore complicated matters further by plunging into the race. Gore had talked with Stevenson and said later that he was convinced he was Stevenson's real choice.

"I got the impression that he didn't want Kennedy because of Kennedy's religion, and he didn't want Estes because of the bitterness between them in the primaries," said Gore. "I got the definite impression that he wanted me. After all, Estes had run for President, not Vice President, and the vice presidential race was wide open."[14]

The Tennessee delegation was streaked with Kefauver support from East Tennessee and Nashville but was predominantly anti-Kefauver. (When Kefauver got the nomination, Fleming Hodges, a state senator and delegate from Dyersburg in West Tennessee, groaned, "I'm sick!") But the delegation could not afford to join the coalition of Harriman people and Southerners forming behind Kennedy because of its agreement to support any Tennessee candidate as long as he had a chance. After a secret caucus, the delegation announced that, voting *en bloc* under the unit rule, it would push Clement for Vice President. Alfred Starr, a Kefauver delegate, remarked bitterly as he emerged from the meeting, "They are here but for one thing: to stab Estes Kefauver in the back." But any real hope Clement had had for the vice presidential spot had gone down the drain with his keynote address, at least insofar as Clement may have hoped that it would catapult him into the nomination as William Jennings Bryan's "Cross of Gold" speech had done many decades earlier. The talk was characterized by many as one of the worst in Clement's career; whether or not this was true, everyone agreed that it was too long, and further, according to various observers, Clement seemed to recognize this too and became rather tense and perhaps over-anxious in his delivery toward the end. At any rate he did not make the anticipated impression on the delegates: so, when Gore appeared with stars in his eyes, the Tennessee delegation switched to him at once. So did Texas, which had been ready to go with Clement.

14. Personal conversation, Albert Gore, Nashville, Autumn 1970.

So Kefauver saw his own state, which had backed him so loyally four years earlier, nominate his junior colleage as an opponent. But the first ballot made it clear that neither Gore nor Humphrey had a chance unless a Kefauver-Kennedy deadlock developed. Kefauver led with 483½ votes to Kennedy's 304, while Gore had only 178 and Humphrey 134½ , behind Mayor Robert Wagner of New York.

Kennedy could expect to pick up most of Gore's votes when the Gore candidacy collapsed, and his lieutenants turned their attention to other candidates. Governor Abraham Ribicoff of Connecticut rushed to Carmine De Sapio, boss of the New York delegation, with a Kennedy message: "Tell Carmine he can get out of this with something. He can make this one—if he'll go now." Kennedy had already paid De Sapio the compliment of being the only candidate to talk to him personally. Wagner pulled out, and most of his votes turned to Kennedy.[15]

Both Gore and Humphrey sat tight for the second ballot, but Humphrey released any of his Minnesota delegates who wanted to vote for Kefauver. Eight of them did. But both Gore and Humphrey were in for a surprise, from Texas. Gore's nucleus of strength was Oklahoma, whose Senator Mike Monroney was his chief strategist, but Texas represented nearly a third of his first ballot strength.

"I knew that Texas would never go for Estes," Gore said. "Neither Lyndon Johnson nor Sam Rayburn wanted him. Sam Rayburn was 'my man' in Texas. I expected Texas to stick with me, and I'd been promised some more strength from other states on the second ballot. I thought Estes and Kennedy would knock each other out and I would go in as a compromise candidate."[16]

Humphrey, too, was counting on Texas. He had been led to believe that Texas, after fulfilling its first ballot commitment to Gore, would switch to him on the second ballot, torpedoing Gore's hopes and putting Humphrey in the balance-of-power situation between Kefauver and Kennedy. But Texas caucaused between the first and second ballots. Theodore C. Sorensen credited Lyndon Johnson with beating down the anti-Catholic sentiment in the Texas delegation[17]; in any event, it was Johnson who announced Texas's 56-vote

15. *Time*, Aug. 27, 1956.
16. Personal conversation, Albert Gore, Nashville, Autumn 1970.
17. Sorensen, *Kennedy*, 89–90.

switch to Kennedy, already well in the lead after Wagner's withdrawal and New York's 96½-vote contribution.

At the Stock Yard Inn, Kennedy was in the bathtub when Representative Torbert Macdonald of Massachusetts shouted from the living room, "Sam Rayburn just swung Texas to you!"[18] Kennedy was dressing for a trip to the convention hall when someone came running in to say that Humphrey was en route to Kefauver's room.

Kennedy sent Sorensen to "intercept Hubert. Tell him I'd like to see him, too." But when Sorensen arrived at Kefauver's room, Mohammed had already gone to the mountain. Kefauver, trailed by Noble Caudill, had hurried across to find Humphrey.[19] Governor Mennen Williams of Michigan and Neil Stabler, the Michigan state Democratic chairman, were already in Humphrey's room, begging Humphrey to switch to Kefauver, when Governor Orville Freeman entered the room with the words, "It's all over." A moment later, Kefauver came running up the two flights of stairs and burst into the room, to find the disappointed Humphrey weeping. Kefauver threw his arms around his colleague and broke into tears himself.

"Hubert, I've just *GOT* to have those delegates!" he sobbed. "Hubert, you've just *got* to help me!"

They stood there, locked in mutual embrace, both of them weeping, exchanging incoherent commiseration. "Everybody was crying," said Caudill.[20]

"I'm for Kefauver!" cried Humphrey, and then he raced to the convention hall to get word to his supporters. Meanwhile, here came Sorenson, seeking Humphrey to suggest that he drop over for a chat with Kennedy. He encountered Representative Eugene McCarthy, who told him a little coldly that the Kennedy people had better forget about it.[21]

Entering the hall from beneath the speaker's platform, Humphrey was unable to push his way through the press, so he stood on

18. James Macgregor Burns, *John Kennedy* (New York: Harcourt, Brace, 1959), 189.

19. Sorensen, *Kennedy*, 89.

20. Lois Laycook, *Nashville Tennessean*, Aug. 18, 1956; Martin, *Ballots and Bandwagons*, 434–35; personal conversation, Noble C. Caudill, Hendersonville, Autumn 1970.

21. Martin, *Ballots and Bandwagons*, 434–35.

a chair to signal to the Minnesota delegation. But, after New York and Texas, there was danger that the bandwagon frenzy might put Kennedy over before the Humphrey support could switch.

In the Indiana delegation, which had gone 20 for Kefauver to 3½ for Kennedy, chairman Charles Skillen gave in to frantic delegate pleas and shouted into the microphone, "Mr. Chairman, Mr. Chairman, Indiana wants to change its vote to Senator Kennedy!" But his cry was unheard, and former Representative Andrew Jacobs stopped Skillen and forced a poll of the delegation, saying, "You're not switching *my* vote to Kennedy!"[22]

In the California delegation, which had gone 37½ for Kefauver, 25 for Kennedy, chairman Pat Brown waved the state standard, crying that the delegation was now unanimous for Kennedy. James Roosevelt retorted that he was still for Kefauver, and if Brown did not poll the delegation, "I'll break your leg."[23]

In the Tennessee delegation, the few Kefauver delegates frantically demanded a switch from Gore. Oklahoma, seated right behind Tennessee, was bound to Gore as long as he was in the race, and the Oklahoma delegates hounded the Tennesseans to switch. But Clement sat silent, looking stonily straight ahead. Delegates from other states swarmed to Tennessee's front row chairs to plead for Kefauver. Clement spread his hands and said, "There's nothing I can do. I'm bound by the delegation."[24]

Gore, though a teetotaler, sat in a small bar hard by the convention floor and watched on television as his support melted like butter and the second ballot ended on a note of 618 votes for Kennedy, 551½ for Kefauver. Kentucky switched from Gore to Kennedy, putting him up to 648 votes, only 38½ short of the nomination. During the hubbub, Mrs. Martha Ragland and Monroney found Gore there and urged him to release his delegates. No, said Gore, he was in the race to the finish.[25] There, too, Gore was found at last by Eben, sent on an urgent mission by Silliman Evans Jr., publisher of the *Nashville Tennessean* (the senior Evans died in 1955). Eben hastened back to Evans, standing in an aisle on the convention

22. Ibid., 444–45.
23. Ibid., 445.
24. Wayne Whitt, *Nashville Tennessean*, Aug. 18, 1956.
25. Martin, *Ballots and Bandwagons*, 438–39.

floor, and escorted him to Gore, followed by millionaire M.M. Bullard of Newport, Tennessee.

Young Evans seized Gore by both lapels and snapped furiously, "You son of a bitch, my father helped make you and I can help break you! If you don't get out of this race, you'll never get the *Tennessean*'s support for anything again, not even dogcatcher. The *Tennessean* will beat you if it takes a million years!"

"Yes," added Bullard, "and I'll raise a million dollars to beat you . . . a million and a half if I have to."[26]

Gore, glassy-eyed, said not a word but turned and went back into the convention hall, which was in bedlam, with state banners waving all over the place. When Gore reached the disgruntled Tennessee delegation and told Clement he would have to switch, Clement moaned, "Oh, no, not Estes!"[27] But he and Gore, right beneath the platform, jumped and waved their arms for recognition. Colonel William Roberts, informed that Gore was trying to withdraw in Kefauver's favor (and knowing Rayburn's sentiments), telephoned Kefauver delegates on the floor to get runners up to the platform to shout to Rayburn, "Tennessee is going for Kennedy!" Representative Clarence Cannon, the convention parliamentarian, caught the shouts and turned to Rayburn, saying, "Tennessee . . . Tennessee!"[28]

Rayburn seized the gavel from Senator Warren Magnuson of Washington, cast a cold eye down to the foot of the rostrum, and

26. Bullard denied making such a statement, and Gore insisted that "I talked with Silliman several times, but he was always courteous to me." However, not only is the statement in character for Evans, but both Eben and Vincent Gaughan, Kefauver's floor leader, were present at the exchange, and two other witnesses, Richard Wallace and Joe Hatcher, political columnist for the *Nashville Tennessean*, were close enough to hear a portion of it. I reconstructed the incident from conversations with all six—Bullard, Gore, Eben, Gaughan, Wallace, and Hatcher—either in person or by telephone in autumn 1970, from a conversation during the same period with Mrs. Martha Ragland in Nashville, and from a letter from Eben of Oct. 14, 1970. Also see Martin, *Ballots and Bandwagons*, 439. Lois Laycook, in the *Nashville Tennessean*, Aug. 18, 1956, says, on the other hand, that Kefauver left his headquarters near the end of the second ballot and called Gore to the convention hall corridor for a conference; Laycook, one of the reporters covering the convention for the *Tennessean*, speculated that Kefauver persuaded Gore to withdraw during that conference but was not able to confirm this from either man.

27. Martin, *Ballots and Bandwagons*, 440.
28. Ibid., 441.

Kefauver greets his some-time political enemy, Governor Frank G. Clement.

rasped, "Does Tennessee desire recognition?" Gore was granted the floor and withdrew "in favor of my colleague, Senator Estes Kefauver." Rayburn stood for a moment as though frozen; for once, his granite face showed his shock.[29]

Oklahoma gained recognition and switched its 28 votes to Kefauver. And now Humphrey's move began to be felt: Minnesota got the floor and switched its 30 votes to Humphrey's "good friend, Senator Estes Kefauver."

Missouri still held a 34½-vote bloc of Humphrey votes. John Bailey, Connecticut state Democratic chairman, buttonholed Senator Thomas C. Hennings Jr. of Missouri and shouted at him to switch to Kennedy. But Kennedy had voted in the Senate for sliding scale price supports, which were not popular in the farm states. "What about the farm vote?" growled Hennings, and turned away to find Representative John McCormack of Massachusetts and whisper to him.[30]

McCormack had seconded Kennedy's nomination but so reluctantly that reportedly he had to be pushed toward the platform. Kennedy had wrested control of the Massachusetts party from him in a bitter squabble that spring. Rayburn was standing on the podium, gavel raised, surveying the uproar, and trying to decide which state to recognize, when McCormack came pushing through the press of delegates, yelling, "Sam! Sam! Missouri, Sam!"[31]

The last time McCormack had shouted for recognition of a state, it had been South Carolina, and South Carolina had gone for Kennedy. Missouri, Truman's state, was generally believed to be strongly anti-Kefauver. Rayburn cracked his gavel and asked, "Does the state of Missouri desire recognition?"

"Mr. Chairman," shouted Hennings into the microphone, "the state of Missouri desires at this time to change its vote to 37 votes for Estes Kefauver."[32] It was not the nomination, but it was the decisive vote, putting Kefauver ahead of Kennedy. Appropriately, California put him over the top with an additional 12½ votes.[33]

29. Ibid., 442.
30. *Time*, Aug. 27, 1956.
31. Ibid.; Martin, *Ballots and Bandwagons*, 447; Burns, *John Kennedy*, 175–80, 190.
32. Martin, *Ballots and Bandwagons*, 447.
33. Thomson and Shattuck, *The 1956 Presidential Campaign*, 161. The *New*

After winning the Democratic vice presidential nomination at the 1956 National Convention, Kefauver (right) joins upraised hands with Averell Harriman behind Adlai Stevenson.

When Missouri switched, there was a sudden rush of reporters, photographers, and radio and television people from the Kennedy box down the gallery to the box where Nancy Kefauver was sitting alone. Kennedy strolled into the convention hall just in time to concede to Kefauver and move that he be nominated by acclamation.[34] Stevenson never did say what running mate he preferred. But when Kefauver went over the top, his remark reportedly was "printable—but a phrase not generally regarded as an expression of high joy."[35]

Nancy at his side, Kefauver appeared on the platform to accept— "half dead from his strenuous exertions," *Time* magazine reported, the back of his white shirt stained with perspiration. He took off his horn-rimmed glasses and smiled wearily.

"I don't know how you feel, but I feel tired," he said to the delegates. "I've been in a lot of races, but never one like this."[36]

In Madisonville, Tennessee, where Cooke Kefauver lay ill, Estes' sister, Nora, watched the convention on television at a neighbor's house, whooped and raced back to announce, "Estes has won, Daddy!"[37] "I knew he would beat that crowd," said Cooke Kefauver with satisfaction.[38]

When the shouting was over, Caudill found they were $85,000 in debt—just for Chicago, not including the primary campaign deficit. An entire hotel floor had been rented for the vice presidential drive, and the expense of rounding up and entertaining delegates had been enormous. Caudill started on his rounds late at night, seeking contributions. He had no trouble, for now Kefauver was the nominee, and people such as Harriman and Mrs. Eleanor Roosevelt were willing to pitch into the kitty. He had the necessary contributions in a few hours.[39]

Estes and Nancy Kefauver returned to Tennessee to a hero's wel-

---

York Times, Aug. 18, 1956, said Missouri put Kefauver over the top, while Martin, *Ballots and Bandwagons*, 448, said his winning margin came from Iowa, Montana, and the District of Columbia.

34. Martin, *Ballots and Bandwagons*, 450–51.
35. Ibid., 452.
36. Douglas B. Cornell, AP story, *Nashville Tennessean*, Aug. 18, 1956.
37. Huston Horn, *Nashville Tennessean*, Aug. 18, 1956.
38. AP story, *Nashville Banner*, Aug. 18, 1956.
39. Personal conversation, Noble C. Caudill, Hendersonville, Autumn 1970.

Kefauver relaxes with his children at Shangri-la after winning the vice presidential nomination in 1956.

come at the Nashville airport, and Kefauver had to spend more than an hour signing autographs and talking with friends before boarding a private plane for McMinnville. Two hours earlier, Clement had arrived, to be booed by early arrivals awaiting Kefauver. Even earlier, Gore had come in to find an almost empty airport lobby; only Representative J. Percy Priest of Tennessee, waiting for Kefauver, recognized him.[40]

After the excitement of the convention, the 1956 presidential campaign itself was something of an anticlimax. Kefauver traveled through 38 states and 210 cities and towns, covering 54,000 miles and making 450 speeches.

His principal role was as a foil to Vice President Richard Nixon, his Washington neighbor of a few doors down the street, who conformed thoroughly to the image of the Republican party as the Democrats liked to paint it, complete with innuendo about Communism and a record of economic favoritism. His major thrust was the Democratic party's greater interest in the individual and the contention that the Republicans care nothing for "Joe Smith . . . the average man."[41]

Kefauver's typical campaign methods, which he carried into this race too, matched the philsophy he advocated: poking along, shaking every hand in sight, speaking to every little group that would listen, falling farther and farther behind schedule. His leisurely style contrasted sharply with Stevenson's briskness and obviously exasperated the high-strung Stevenson on the few occasions they campaigned together. But the Democratic brain-trusters saw him as an effective balance for Stevenson's polished intellectualism. As Mike Di Salle put it, "they want Adlai to make the speeches, and Estes to tell the people what they mean."[42] Finnegan, who was now campaign director for the party, termed Kefauver "one of the most formidable campaigners to appear on the American scene in many decades," and added: "The American people believe in Senator Kefauver because they understand him. They feel instinctively that he understands them." And Lyndon Johnson, introducing him in Texas, called him "the greatest campaigner of them all."[43]

40. *Time*, Aug. 27, 1956.
41. Alvin Spivak, INS story, *Nashville Tennessean*, Sept. 30, 1956.
42. Drew Pearson, column, *Nashville Tennessean*, Sept. 6, 1956.
43. "Tennessean on a Hayride," *Newsweek*, Oct. 15, 1956.

Kefauver and Lyndon Johnson look over a 10-point buck Kefauver shot during a visit to Johnson's ranch at Stonewall, Texas, late in 1956.

The campaigning Kefauver waves to the crowd as he emerges from an automobile.

Kefauver was used by the party primarily in the Middle West and Far West, and there was a deluge of mail, some of it written in pencil, urging headquarters to send Kefauver to speak for the ticket. He was so popular in the Farm Belt that he was introduced inadvertently at Winterset, Iowa, as "the next President of the United States," and when he corrected the speaker, there were shouts of "We wish he was right!" and "Wait till next time!"[44]

Through these areas the refrain was reiterated, "We've got the ticket upside down."[45] A poll through six Midwestern farm states by *Wallace's Farmer and Iowa Homestead* forecast the ratio of the eventual Eisenhower-Stevenson popular vote almost on the nose— Eisenhower 49 percent to Stevenson's 37 percent—but showed Kefauver favored over Eisenhower 51 percent to 36 percent.[46]

Kefauver's role as Nixon's opposite number required some "dirty work" of a kind the presidential candidates were able to avoid. He termed Nixon "the darling of every reactionary in the Republican Party," who was "trying to get into the White House on false premises, a false front and a false face."[47] Nixon reacted angrily, charging Kefauver with "below the belt, low-road tactics."[48]

On election day in November, Kefauver worked at the polls in Miami for three hours and then flew to Washington to watch the Democrats carry only seven states—not including Tennessee. The Stevenson-Kefauver defeat may have been because the ticket was "upside down" as the Iowa farmers claimed; it may have been due to the Middle Eastern crisis that struck just before the election, as Kefauver and some political analysts thought; or it may have been just that Eisenhower was too popular to be beaten by anyone. In any event, Kefauver had his run for it, such as it was, and it was his last campaign for national office. After the election, Kefauver and Stevenson exchanged letters, written the same day and passing each other in the mail.

"In all matters," wrote Kefauver, "I found you to be a thought-

44. Joe Hall, AP story, *Nashville Tennessean*, Oct. 21, 1956.

45. Ruth Montgomery, INS story, *Nashville Tennessean*, Oct. 28, 1956.

46. *Wallace's Farmer and Iowa Homestead*, June 16, 1956; William H. Stringer, in the *Christian Science Monitor*, March 30, 1956, cited a *Minneapolis Tribune* poll showing Kefauver with 52 percent to 45 percent for Eisenhower, but Stevenson trailing Eisenhower.

47. B.L. Livingston, AP story, *Nashville Tennessean*, Oct. 16, 1956.

48. AP story, *Nashville Banner*, Sept. 21, 1956.

ful gentleman and a kind friend, and at all times honest and thoughtful in your approach to problems of the campaign and to issues. You have given our party good, intelligent leadership."[49]

"I want you to know," wrote Stevenson, "that I count myself fortunate to have had you in this contest with me. I suppose our politics has disclosed few more gallant figures than yours."[50]

49. Letter, Estes Kefauver, Washington, to Adlai Stevenson, Chicago, Nov. 9, 1956, Kefauver Collection, Ser. 1, Box 71.
50. Letter, Adlai Stevenson, Chicago, to Estes Kefauver, Washington, Nov. 9, 1956, Ser. 1, Box 71.

Chapter 15

We're Not Going to Operate That Way

Kefauver's last political campaign, for reelection to the Senate in 1960, involved the most pragmatic "deal" of his career. He traded his support of Lyndon Johnson's presidential ambition for Johnson's astute interference on his behalf in Tennessee.

The 1956 presidential primaries had eroded Kefauver's confidence in his direct appeal to the voters, and he took thought that in 1954 young Frank Clement had polled 40,000 more votes in the governor's race than he himself had gathered in defeating Pat Sutton. Clement's evangelistic oratorical style, so well suited to the Bible Belt, evoked in Tennessee voters a fanatical support that matched that of the Kefauver advocates—whom Hubert Humphrey described as "avid and livid. They were fighters. They'd scratch and bite."[1]

Ever since Clement's meteoric emergence upon the political scene, Tennessee political observers had been anticipating a race between him and Kefauver because both seemed invincible at the polls. It looked as though 1960 would be the time because Clement, constitutionally ineligible to succeed himself in 1958, had passed up the chance to run against Gore that year and had returned to private law practice to bide his time.

Kefauver could avoid such a clash by running for President again in 1960, and it was generally assumed for a long time that he would. As the 1956 vice presidential nominee and with Adlai Stevenson definitely out of it, Kefauver had a wide edge over all other potential Democratic candidates; and, with Eisenhower stepping down, he had an excellent chance of winning the election. His friends all over the country were eager for him to make the try, and when he first disclaimed his intention of doing so, Stevenson ex-

1. Martin, *Ballots and Bandwagons*, 418–19.

claimed, "He won't run again? Give me half an hour with him!"[2]

But with Tennessee dominated by an unfriendly state administration—that of Clement's successor and ally, Buford Ellington—Kefauver had to choose between national ambition and reelection. He had considered stepping down from the Senate to run for governor in 1958, in an effort to secure his home base, but decided against it. Had Mayor Edmund Orgill of Memphis, who had headed Kefauver's Memphis campaign effort in 1948, polled only about 10,000 more votes in that race, Kefauver could have pulled a Lyndon Johnson act: Johnson was renominated and re-elected to the Senate in Texas in 1960 at the same time he was nominated and elected Vice President. But Ellington had squeaked through to victory with barely over 31 percent of the vote in an eight-man race in the Democratic primary.

So, immediately after the 1958 election, Kefauver burned his presidential bridges behind him and turned his face resolutely toward reelection. He refused to enter the New Hampshire, Nebraska, and Oregon presidential primaries. He even abandoned his decade-long struggle for membership on the Senate Foreign Relations Committee. Instead, he went after a more practical political plum. Just before leaving for a NATO Parliament meeting in Paris in mid-November 1958, Kefauver wrote Johnson: "I have, as you probably know, a rough campaign coming up in 1960, and I need some real breaks to come through successfully. . . . in our talks some time back I understod you felt that I might get on either Appropriations or Foreign Relations this next term. I have thought it over a great deal, and I would like to apply for a place on the Appropriations Committee. I think I would enjoy the work, and it would help my situation down home."[3]

From that approach to the majority leader, Kefauver received an education in practical politics in answer to the question he had asked Bradley Eben once, plaintively: "How does Lyndon do it?" For Johnson had need of Kefauver, to whom he had written earlier, "it is men like you that have done so much to make our party popular

2. Frank van der Linden, *Nashville Banner*, Jan. 4, 1957.
3. Letter, Estes Kefauver to Lyndon Johnson, Nov. 14, 1958, Kefauver Collection, Ser. 1, Box 76.

in the hearts of the American people."[4] Johnson's presidential ambition ran head-on against that of John F. Kennedy, and in a battle against Kennedy, Johnson needed Kefauver's broad-based national support to supplement his Southern nucleus.

Kefauver got the Appropriations Committee spot, and more. To almost everyone's surprise, Clement was suddenly no longer a potential Senate candidate in 1960. He was content to wait until 1962 and run for governor again. Clement's unexpected restraint remained a public mystery, but what happened was that "the right people" pointed out to Clement quietly and diplomatically that he had a long future ahead of him, and Lyndon Johnson seemed quite interested in Kefauver's return to the Senate. He was reminded that, if he did succeed in defeating the redoubtable Kefauver, Johnson's power could guarantee him a very unrewarding role as a freshman senator.[5]

Instead, Kefauver's opponent was Judge Andrew T. (Tip) Taylor of Jackson, who had come within 9,000 votes of beating Ellington in 1958. Taylor, a man of long political experience and many friends in both the old Crump organization and the Browning faction, entered the race with the assurance of Ellington administration support. Taylor met twice with Ellington and state Adjutant General G. Hilton Butler and was told by the governor that he would send Butler and Secretary of State Joe C. Carr across the state to "beat the bushes" for Taylor. Ellington also promised to endorse Taylor publicly late in the campaign, if necessary to pull him through.[6] But Ellington and Lyndon Johnson were good friends. Also, if Tay-

4. Letter, Lyndon Johnson, Hye, Texas, to Estes Kefauver, Sept. 9, 1957, Kefauver Collection, ibid.

5. This information was from a close political friend of both Clement and Ellington, who asked not to be identified. Confirmatory evidence was contained in a personal communication from Lincoln M. Polan, Huntington, W. Va., Aug. 27, 1970, who wrote: "Estes' debt to the Johnson campaign had been paid by my efforts on Mr. Johnson's behalf [at the Democratic National Convention in Los Angeles]. That was the arrangement that had been made. Mr. Johnson caused Governor Clements [*sic*] to desist from announcing against Estes; he cut out two-thirds of Estes' opposition from the high political level in Tennessee; he appeared with Estes in Tennessee."

6. My informant here was the same political friend of Clement and Ellington cited in note 5, one of the three people present at these meetings, in a personal communication Sept. 13, 1970.

lor made a strong showing against Kefauver without quite winning, he might prove a formidable opponent for Clement in the 1962 governor's race. Clement expressed his support of Kefauver, and the Ellington administration did nothing for Taylor.

For his part, Kefauver did not participate—as he might have otherwise—in an unsucessful liberal revolt early in 1960 aimed at curtailing Johnson's authority as majority leader, led by Gore. And, five days before he made his own announcement for reelection in May, Kefauver said he would support Johnson for President. In mid-July, Kefauver sent Nancy, who was a great admirer of Johnson, and several of his political friends to the Democratic National Convention in Los Angeles to help Johnson's candidacy.[7] Kefauver wanted very much to attend the convention himself but did not quite dare to leave his Tennessee campaign.

Johnson wanted Kefauver at the convention too, to help personally. Johnson aide Bobby Baker reached Kefauver by telephone in mid-convention and begged him urgently to fly to Los Angeles to help. But Kefauver was advised against leaving Tennessee unless Ellington personally would guarantee him victory in his Senate race —which, of course, Ellington could not have done, even had Kefauver asked him.[8]

In Taylor, the anti-Kefauver forces felt they had found a champion to prove Tennessee's prdominant conservatism in a clear-cut, two-man battle. Added to the very real possibility that their optimism was justified, Kefauver was worried about the impact on his campaign of his first round of hearings in his massive investigation of the drug industry, which began in December 1959 and concluded in mid-1960. He was so concerned that he considered either delaying the probe or turning it over to some other senator who had no immediate reelection problems.

As chairman of the Senate Antitrust and Monopoly Subcommittee, he was being pressed by the subcommittee staff to go ahead

7. Ken Morrell, *Nashville Banner*, July 7, 1960.
8. Personal communication, Lincoln M. Polan, Huntington, W. Va., Aug. 27, 1970. Polan wrote that he interrupted Kefauver's conversation with Baker from another telephone to urge Kefauver "not to come to California, since it could appear that he was involving himself in national politics after he said he was not interested at that level and would run only in Tennessee. If he did have to come, that he should come only with a guarantee of victory from Governor Ellington, but that he should not come."

with the probe. But opposition to it had been expressed to him by some doctors and Chambers of Commerce in Tennessee, and the Tennessee Pharmaceutical Association, a nationally-affiliated organization of retail druggists, had warned him pointedly that it had at least one member in every town in the state. Paul Rand Dixon, counsel and staff director of the subcommittee, lived not far from Kefauver in Washington and usually drove him to and from the Senate Office Building.

"We had many discussions concerning the timing of these hearings," said Dixon. "Realizing the emotional impact of such hearings, it was not an easy decision for Estes to make. It was my opinion that if he conducted these hearings, the druggists and doctors of Tennessee would oppose his reelection [but] the people of Tennessee would support his reelection. . . . The decision was not mine, however, it was his. . . . It was an act of courage."[9]

"Is it right?" Kefauver would ask. "Is it in the public interest? Does it need to be done?" Dixon would always answer in the affirmative, and Kefauver said at last, "Well, then, we had better go ahead."[10]

Disclosures of excessive prices for ethical (prescription) drugs, concealment of adverse side effects of drugs, and conflict of interest in the Food and Drug Administration drew wide praise. But Kefauver was disturbed by reports that Tennessee doctors and druggists had sent out, along with their bills, 80,000 pieces of literature compiled by pharmaceutical interests, calling Kefauver a Socialist who was injuring the health of the American people. A public opinion poll in Tennessee in the spring of 1960 showed Kefauver trailing Taylor by a considerable margin.

"I never should have gotten mixed up in this drug thing, John," Kefauver said to his old friend, John Blair, economic consultant for the subcommittee, as Kefauver prepared to drive to the airport to embark on his Tennessee campaign. "Now I've got the drug people, the pharmacists and the doctors all stirred up. They're going to throw the book at me down there."[11]

There were repeated reports that big drug manufacturing firms

9. Personal communication, Paul Rand Dixon, Washington, Sept. 8, 1970.
10. Richard Harris, *The Real Voice* (New York: Macmillan, 1964), 41.
11. Ibid., 116–17; personal communication, John M. Blair, Washington, Sept. 14, 1970.

were contributing substantial financial support to Taylor's campaign. The reports were half-confirmed by Eugene Perrin, registered Michigan lobbyist for Dow Chemical Company, who paid a visit to Tennessee and said afterward that he would not be surprised if "the chemical and drug industry generally doesn't have a lot of money in the Tennessee campaign."[12]

At least one anonymous circular attacking Kefauver was distributed, and a pamphlet bearing the seal of Commonwealth Engineering Company referred to the senator as "Comrade Kefauver" six times and attacked his "mass misrepresentation of the pharmaceutical industry" under the heading, "Communism in Congress." But many individual druggists and doctors in the state rallied to Kefauver's support.[13]

More perilous to Kefauver were his votes in favor of the 1957 and 1960 civil rights bills, which provided Taylor his major issue. Tempers were inflamed throughout the state by Negro sit-in protests against discrimination in a number of different businesses in Tennessee, and Taylor charged that the bill "which Estes Kefauver voted for this year will allow federal referees or federal agents to come into Tennessee and tell us who can and who cannot vote."[14]

"I thought it was a fair and just bill," responded Kefauver, "and I could not clear it with my conscience to vote against the right to vote."[15]

Taylor called Kefauver a "lone wolf" among Southern congressmen and asked: "Are these 18 Southern Senators [who voted against the civil rights bill] out of step with what's right for our people, or is it by any chance that Mr. Kefauver is out of step?" He appealed to the people to retire Kefauver so Senator Olin D. Johnston of South Carolina, "a true Southern Democrat if there ever was one," could move up a seniority step in the Judiciary Committee.[16]

What happened thereafter appeared to bear what Kefauver would have called "the fine Indian hand" of Lyndon Johnson, who was

12. Nat Caldwell, *Nashville Tennessean*, July 31, 1960.
13. *Nashville Tennessean*, June 23, 26, 1960; Charles Bartlett, *Chattanooga Times*, March 24, 1960. Some of the propaganda against Kefauver is contained in the Kefauver Collection, Ser. 5-h, Box 13.
14. Neil Cunningham, *Nashville Banner*, July 15, 1960.
15. David Halberstam, *Nashville Tennessean*, July 12, 1960.
16. Ibid., July 3, 1960.

strongly influential among his fellow Southerners if Kefauver was not. The very Olin Johnston whom Taylor cited joined eight other Southern senators—Johnson himself, Herman Talmadge of Georgia, Lister Hill and John Sparkman of Alabama, Ralph Yarborough of Texas, George Smathers of Florida, Russell Long of Louisiana, and John Stennis of Mississippi—in writing laudatory letters to Kefauver, which he utilized in campaign advertisements late in the race.[17] Adlai Stevenson, too, sent him a telegram of endorsement, calling his reelection "absolutely imperative, both from the standpoint of the country and of the Democratic Party."[18]

Kefauver hit the civil rights issue directly when he invaded Taylor's home town of Jackson, in segregation-conscious West Tennessee, in mid-campaign. Before a crowd of about 200 people at the courthouse square, he outlined the provisions of the civil rights law, one by one, and said after each, "Well, I'm for that. I think it's right. Is there anyone in this audience who's against it?" He was applauded each time.[19]

As if to clinch matters, into Tennessee marched Lyndon Johnson, bearing the vice presidential nomination fresh from the national convention, for a Democratic rally at Nashville's Colemere Club. Kefauver, arriving an hour and a half before Johnson, was borne to the speaker's platform on the shoulders of supporters. Taylor was there too and was one of the first who hurried to greet Johnson when he arrived in a motorcade from the nearby airport.

Then Johnson spotted Kefauver. He strode over to Kefauver and enfolded him in a warm hug. In his speech, Johnson came very close to an outright endorsement: so close that *Newsweek* magazine had it that Johnson "appeared on behalf of" Kefauver.[20]

"Wherever I may go," said Johnson, departing from his prepared text, "I will never speak as a Southerner to Southerners, or as a Protestant to Protestants, or as a white to whites. I will speak only as an American to Americans." When Johnson left the rally, he embraced Kefauver again. Taylor had left early.[21]

17. *Nashville Tennessean*, July 31, 1960.
18. *Chattanooga Times*, Aug. 3, 1960.
19. David Halberstam, *Nashville Tennessean*, July 17, 1960.
20. Aug. 15, 1960.
21. Wayne Whitt, *Nashville Tennessean*, July 31, 1960; Mac Harris, ibid.; *Chattanooga Times*, July 31, 1960; Jack Setters, *Nashville Banner*, Aug. 1, 1960.

The returns on primary day brought Kefauver almost as overwhelming a victory as that against Sutton in 1954, with 64½ percent of the vote. His Republican opposition in November was minimal. "I want to thank the people of Tennessee for sending Estes back to us," said Senator Gale McGee of Wyoming as the returns coming into Washington showed his victory was secure. Senator Stephen M. Young of Ohio said, "I know every member of the United States Senate is delighted over his triumphant renomination," and Senator Joseph O'Mahoney said Kefauver's defeat would have been "a national tragedy."[22]

When Kefauver returned to the Senate floor, slipping in through a side door in the midst of a speech by Wayne Morse of Oregon, the Senate burst into applause and many of his fellow senators, among them John Kennedy, the new presidential nominee, went to his desk to congratulate him.[23] It was a rare tribute to any senator, and its award to this man who could not get even a simple testimonial of friendship from a single colleague in his own defense four years earlier says something about his anomalous position in that peculiarly ingrown body, the Senate. He was a lone wolf—Representative Samuel S. Stratton of New York remarked after his death that he was never "permitted to enter the so-called 'club' that allegedly runs the other body" (the Senate)[24]—but there were occasions when that same admiration that moved so many of the people at large animated his colleagues, too.

Kefauver's lack of orthodoxy in politics damaged him as much with the liberals as with the Southern conservatives and the party regulars in his presidential races. Columnist Stewart Alsop, writing in the *Oregonian* in 1956, called "the total lack of enthusiasm of the liberals and intellectuals—the old New Dealers, if you will" for Kefauver's presidential aspirations "one of the queerest phenomena" of the time. Kefauver's Minnesota victory over Stevenson, Alsop noted, "was wildly unpopular in liberal intellectual circles all over the country—this despite the fact that Stevenson is a very much more conservative man than Kefauver." Alsop speculated that Kefauver "lacks the elegance and eloquence liberals like in their heroes."

In the same vein, Michael Straight wrote about the same time in

22. Lois Laycook, *Nashville Tennessean*, Aug. 5, 1960.
23. Ibid., Aug. 11, 1960.
24. *Carey Estes Kefauver, Late a Senator from Tennessee*, 120.

the *New Republic* that liberals and intellectuals who were turning to Stevenson felt that "executive capacity, a sense of proprieties and the ability to summon outstanding men to public service are the further requirements of a President, and they sense that Kefauver lacks these qualities. They suspect further that Kefauver's intense interest in people and his warmth and his obvious honesty are not deep-seated traits of personality, but the outward features of a chosen political image."[25]

Kefauver was consistently too liberal for the conservatives and too conservative for the liberals, yet he never really came across as a middle-of-the-roader. His uniqueness stemmed in part from adjustment of personal liberal convictions to the realities of Southern politics, but part of it was true nonconformity. He told Oklahoma Jaycees in a 1954 speech that the nation "owes its birth and its genius to highly unorthodox ideas," and he observed in a letter two years later that "our forefathers were not conformists."[26] He espoused such novel causes as Atlantic Union, various proposals for congressional and electoral reform, and a food stamp program. Kefauver did not have the original, creative mind to initiate heresy, but he was a philosophical nonconformist who would co-opt a good heresy when it was offered him. And in nothing was he more heretical than in his exasperatingly successful campaign methods.

One of his fundamental unorthodoxies was that there never was a "Kefauver organization" in Tennessee, as there was a "Crump machine" and, to a lesser extent, a "McKellar organization," a "Browning organization," a "Clement organization," and so on. Right after Kefauver's election in 1948, Charlie Neese and George McInturff tried to persuade Kefauver to build a permanent political organization in the state, with one man in each county through whom any appointments and favors would clear. "No, that's the way other people operate in politics," Kefauver answered. "We're not going to operate that way."[27] Consequently, every race he ran in Tennessee had to be organized from scratch, although he had a solid core of devoted adherents on whom to build.

Kefauver was so determined not to become a political "boss"

25. Quoted in Riggs, "The Man from Tennessee."
26. Letter, Estes Kefauver to Russell Egmer, Minneapolis, Feb. 25, 1956, Kefauver Collection, Ser. 1, Box 77.
27. Personal conversation, George McInturff, Chattanooga, Spring 1955.

that he was very reluctant to endorse publicly any candidate in a Tennessee race, even a good friend. He abrogated the principle in 1952 for Browning because Browning's support of him at the national convention had cost Browning heavily in his own race. But he would not throw his influence into the 1958 governor's race behind Edmund Orgill, although it might have been enough to have given Orgill victory over Ellington and perhaps make a 1960 presidential bid possible for Kefauver.

Instead of the customary political organization, Kefauver relied on his personal approach, "a sort of built-in radar" as one newsman called it. He had an intuitive ability to project to someone he was meeting for the first time an impression of utterly sincere friendliness with his handshake—"like being wrapped in a warm blanket," his last administrative assistant, Charles Caldwell, called it. It worked magic in a congressional race and even in a statewide campaign, but his abhorrence of the organizational method was costly in his presidential efforts. Relatively few convention delegates were chosen directly by the voters and, even so, the nation was just too big for Kefauver to shake every hand in it.

The Kefauver glad-hand technique differed from that of other successful politicians only in its exceptional effectiveness. In him it was somewhat surprising because it failed to jibe with other aspects of the man: the judicious and dignified committee chairman, the student of government who read an average of a book a week and could bury an opponent on the Senate floor under a dull but deadly barrage of facts, and the disengaged individual who could withdraw completely into himself in the midst of a noisy crowd. This paradox caused some people, including some of his colleagues, to accuse Kefauver of insincerity in his folksy approach, while others were convinced that his studiousness was the pose of an essentially shallow person. Of the two sides of him, his handshaking affability was the less natural, but it was not insincere.

When he entered politics actively, Kefauver made a conscious effort to adapt his behavior to the conventional image of the politician. He adopted handshaking with all of the warmth and verve— and much of the overwhelming effect—of the bear hugs the young collegian had bestowed upon members of the opposite sex. He studied the details of campaign tactics—the use of first names, letters of solicitation and appreciation, ascertaining issues of particular interest to an individual or group—as assiduously as he had studied the law.

In the days when he was still working consciously to build up his technique, Kefauver even jotted down funny stories he heard and tried to use them as other politicians did—not very successfully except when he fumbled them, as he often did. He had a remarkable propensity for putting his foot in his mouth on the most serious issues, as when he contributed the obvious whopper during the 1956 presidential campaign that hydrogen bombs could "right now blow the earth off its axis by 16 degrees, which would affect the seasons."[28]

Kefauver was one of those rarities, an effective orator who had no talent whatsoever for oratory. After practicing law for a decade, winning five races for Congress and one for the Senate, and going through most of a highly effective presidential campaign, he was still so inept a public speaker that Charlie Neese took him in hand in Salt Lake City one night and told him, "Estes, your voice falls at the end of sentences so much that people sometimes can't understand what you're saying. Imagine there's a balcony up there, some distance away. You don't have to raise your voice, but keep it loud enough for the people on that balcony to hear every word." Kefauver took the advice and practiced it for some time but without spectacular results.[29]

Yet his non-oratory was effective—and in a home state whose people prized political oratory, whose most beloved political legend was the eloquent "War of the Roses" between Bob and Alf Taylor, where he was forced into comparison with such contemporaries as the evangelistic Clement, the orotund Browning, the fluent Gore. People in other states reacted just as contrary to form. Of Kefauver's 1952 appearance in a South Dakota town, Douglass Cater wrote in the *Reporter*: "It was a drab speech to a drab little audience. But afterward, they crowded around him with genuine enthusiasm. Something had happened. They got it. I didn't."[30]

In fact, Kefauver's very failure at playing the politician's role was a prime factor in his political success. To him, political activity basi-

28. *New York Times*, Oct. 17, 1956; B.L. Livingstone, AP story, *Nashville Tennessean*, Oct. 17, 1956; *Nashville Banner*, Oct. 25, 1956.
29. Personal conversation, Charles G. Neese, Greeneville, Tenn., Spring 1970.
30. Cater, "Estes Kefauver, Most Willing of the Willing."

cally was something that had to be performed to put him and keep him in a position to achieve desirable social objectives. In a way, it was not quite real and serious, but a kind of necessary play-acting. Although it was not apparent in the way he spoke his lines, Kefauver had a certain flair for the dramatic, and he had real fun "hamming it up" when the occasion called for it in a political campaign.

But the play-acting was not aimed at fooling his friends, the voters. They sensed accurately that Kefauver included them in on the act, which was played out for the benefit of that sober and somewhat pompous social structure that, in later years, would be dubbed "the Establishment." He was at his best when he stood in the midst of an informal audience of overalled farmers, perhaps in a tobacco-stained courtroom in the Upper Cumberland hill country, without any prepared speech, and talked undramatically and ponderously about the why and wherefore of developments in foreign and domestic policy, answering questions seriously and without ever "talking down" to his hearers. This tacit and intimate alliance with "the people" existed to an extent denied even to his own campaign workers. But he did share it, almost openly, with many of those indispensable cynics, the newspapermen, whose recognition of the "stage play" aspect of politics, sometimes coupled with a quixotic idealism about the issues that lay behind it, matched Kefauver's own.

Thus, in one Minnesota town in 1956, one newsman grabbed his sleeve and pointed out that Kefauver had never referred in his informal talk to his prepared text, on which some of the reporters had based their stories and were already in print. Kefauver turned and went back to the microphone.

"If you folks will just bear with me for a minute, I want to read something for the reporters," he said, and solemnly read several paragraphs from Dick Wallace's rumpled text.[31]

Only someone with Kefauver's sense of the farcical, underlying this very serious game of politics, could have gotten away with his solution to the lack of portable stairs when his plane landed in Rock Springs, Wyoming, where he was scheduled for a speech and a reception as the 1956 vice presidential nominee. He resorted to the baggage chute, "and, in a grand swoop, he slid down out of the plane

31. Unidentified clipping dated April 17, 1960, Kefauver Collection, Ser. 1, Box 77.

For Kefauver on one of his campaigns, the shortest route between inside and outside is through the window.

through the chute, and into the crowd."[32] Eisenhower or Stevenson or Nixon would have appeared ridiculous pulling such a stunt.

Kefauver's fumbling of words too, and especially his frequent bungling of people's names, would have been deadly in a conventional politician. In Cleveland in 1956, he tried three times without success to pronounce "Cuyahoga County" before deciding it was "as hard to pronounce as 'Kefauver.'"[33]

During the same campaign, introduced at a California rally by actress Shelley Winters, he thanked "my fine friend, the charming and lovely Miss Shelley Williams," and repeated the error twice before an aide's frantic coat-tugging and whispering got through to him. Kefauver stopped, looked around and smiled sheepishly.

"I've been calling Miss Winters 'Miss Williams,' when I know her name very well," he said. "You know, you get confused over names on a campaign like this, and I was thinking about another very old, very dear friend of mine, from my own state—Tennessee Ernie Williams."[34]

When, on a visit to Missouri in 1960, he referred to senatorial candidate Edward V. Long as "my very dear friend, Earl K. Long" (the recently deceased governor of Louisiana and an erratic member of that state's famed Long dynasty), the object of his remarks reacted with muffled merriment. But the speaker's platform was a flimsy construction of planks laid across sawhorses, and Long's suppressed mirth vibrated it so dangerously that the puzzled Kefauver was almost unable to go on with his talk.[35]

Kefauver's sympathetic identification with the anonymous and abstract "average voter" justified Nancy's statement once that "he's not an easy person to know. He's great with the mass of people, but not much interested in individuals."[36] Kefauver could be bafflingly impersonal, most of all with friends whom he did not need to woo with his campaign "face." But the sense of relationship he created with his supporters was a very personal and individual feeling.

32. Sen. Gale W. McGee in *Carey Estes Kefauver, Late a Senator from Tennessee,* 57.
33. John Chadwick, AP story, *Nashville Tennessean,* Oct. 7, 1956.
34. Personal conversation, Bernard Fensterwald, Washington, May 15, 1970.
35. Ibid.
36. Irwin Ross, *New York Post,* May 9, 1956.

Preoccupied inwardly with large and sometimes distant goals, Kefauver seemed unable ever to escape the nagging realization that they could be achieved only by maintaining a constant relationship with the ultimately all-powerful voters. Often when visiting his old college buddy, Jack Doughty, in Knoxville, he would kick off his shoes, relax with a drink in his hand, and remark to Doughty, "It's good just to get away from *people* for a little while."[37] But this was rare. Once when he and Nancy accompanied Mr. and Mrs. Porter Warner Jr. to Highlands, North Carolina, for a short vacation after a hard campaign and stopped in a small restaurant for supper, Warner suggested to the waitress that they be seated in a corner so Kefauver could rest. But Kefauver protested, "Why do you want to get way over there, Mr. Porter? Let's don't get *too* secluded!"[38]

Wrapped in his goals, Kefauver often forgot the little, practical requirements of everyday living. Once during the 1956 Florida campaign, he made a speech with his hands in his pockets to keep his pants up. Somehow, he had lost his belt.[39]

Facing a dinner engagement with tan shoes on during the crime investigation, he solved the problem by exchanging shoes with a Senate Office Building elevator boy who happened also to wear size 12.[40] Thereafter, Kefauver made sure there were always black shoes in his luggage: he packed them himself. Once, however, he packed both shoes for the right foot, with the result, according to Nancy, that "he looked like he was coming around a corner all the time."[41]

Aside from the fact that his campaigns kept the family finances frequently in a precarious state, Kefauver himself rarely carried as much as a dime in his pockets for a soft drink. He depended on his staff, campaign aides, and friends to handle little details such as paying bills.

Noble Caudill, a man of comfortable wealth, was the nearest to a personal financial angel Kefauver ever had. For some years, Caudill and Sam M. Fleming, president of Nashville's Third National Bank, underwrote Kefauver's personal incidental expenses to the

37. Personal conversation, John H. Doughty, Knoxville, Summer 1970.
38. Personal conversation, Porter Warner Jr., Chattanooga, Spring 1955.
39. Martin, "The Mystery of Kefauver."
40. Kefauver, *Crime in America*, xiv.
41. *Young Democrat*, April 1954; personal conversation, Nancy Kefauver, Washington, Spring 1955.

tune of $5,000 each annually.[42] Caudill reserved a private apartment for Kefauver's use in his home near Hendersonville, and sometimes the pair of them and Silliman Evans Jr., publisher of the *Nashville Tennessean*, would talk far into the night before the fire in the apartment's living room. Caudill traveled a great deal for his firm and was constantly running into the peripatetic Kefauver. Once he ran across Kefauver in Boston and offered to share his room in the Ritz-Carlton Hotel with the senator. Caudill had to leave early for Nashville but told Kefauver to sleep as late as he wished before checking out, and the hotel would bill him. A few days later, Caudill was astounded to get a $450 bill from the hotel for the single night. His indignant telephone call elicited the information that Kefauver, before checking out for Washington, had invited Mayor John Hynes and a whole coterie of Boston politicians up to the room for breakfast.[43] On another occasion, Caudill ran across Kefauver in Phoenix, Arizona, and they decided to fly back East together. First, though, Kefauver suggested, Caudill might just run downstairs and take care of the hotel bill, while he packed. It ran to some $650. Said Caudill, "I think everybody in Phoenix must have signed a chit on Estes' room."[44]

No Caudill was conveniently around when the Kefauvers found themselves unable to pay the hotel bill in Bakersfield, California, in 1956. They dallied in Bakersfield and campaigned, to the delight of supporters, while awaiting a response to a frantic plea for financial help from Washington. One of the hastily-scheduled events in their honor was a big reception for Kefauver in the hotel ballroom, and during it, Nancy was accosted by one of the town's wealthier citizens who slipped her an envelope containing a contribution of $1,500. When Kefauver got away from the reception and went up to their room, he found that Nancy had packed all their bags.

"Let's go," she said. "We're leaving."

"But honey, we can't," he protested. "What about the hotel bill?"

"It's paid," she said.

42. Personal conversations, Noble C. Caudill, Hendersonville, Autumn 1970; Dec. 1, 1978.
43. Ibid., Autumn 1970.
44. Ibid.

Later, telling of the incident, Nancy remarked, considerably piqued, "He never did ask me where I got the money."[45]

Although Nancy characterized him as "not much interested in individuals," Kefauver was very good at thoughtful gestures toward individuals, whether or not they could or would help him politically. Robert Kennedy remarked that the 55,000 Christmas cards Kefauver sent out annually in his later years had more to do with beating his brother at the 1956 convention than did the issues. When Kefauver's longtime political enemy, Representative B. Carroll Reece, died in 1961, his widow succeeded him briefly in Congress by appointment. Kefauver tried so hard to help her that she wrote him, "every day you show in a new and wonderful way your friendship."[46]

Shortly before his death, Kefauver met actress Dinah Shore for the first time at the annual Ramp Festival in Cosby, Tennessee, and it rained, hard. Miss Shore wrote Kefauver afterward: "Your thoughtfulness and consideration made some of the hardships easier for all of us, and I don't think that handsome suit of yours will ever recover from your having put that protecting raincoat around my drenched wardrobe instead of yours. . . . I knew you were wise and courageous—and a statesman, but I didn't know how much fun you were."[47]

After Kefauver's death, Senator Abraham Ribicoff of Connecticut said the people "knew him when he walked down the main streets of their cities and towns. They knew him as a friend. . . . He was of them, by choice, and for the common good of all."[48]

45. Personal communication, Carol V. Harford, Washington, June 7, 1970, and telephone conversation, June 9, 1970.

46. Kefauver took the lead in establishing a memorial fund for Reece at that time. Correspondence between him and Mrs. Reece is in the Kefauver Collection, Ser. 4-h, Box 3.

47. Kefauver Collection, 4-h, Box 12.

48. *Carey Estes Kefauver, Late a Senator from Tennessee*, 88.

PART III

A Senator of the People . . . of the Nation

—Abraham A. Ribicoff, 1963

Chapter 16

But He's So Damn Single-Minded

The swift disappearance of Estes Kefauver from the presidential arena after Eisenhower's overwhelming 1956 victory was primarily of his own doing. Kefauver's reputation for electoral magic was damaged little by the loss of a ticket on which he held second place. Had he yielded to the urging of enthusiastic adherents, he would have constituted a tremendous roadblock to the emerging aspirations of the new crop of presidential hopefuls—John F. Kennedy, Lyndon B. Johnson, and Hubert H. Humphrey.

Kefauver chose, mainly because of the conflict of his 1960 Senate race with a presidential election, to step down emphatically from pursuit of the presidency. He put it behind him in the fading past, never to be known again: the grueling pace of the presidential campaign, its twenty-one-hour days, its interminable handshaking and midnight conferences and long plane rides from state to state, its triumphs and disappointments the excitement of its conventions.

Perhaps, had he lived, it would have happened again, for he loved it, and he was not old, for a presidential contender. After Kennedy's election in 1960, he may even have weighed the tremendous odds of bucking a popular incumbent in 1964—for the tragedy of an assassin's bullet in Dallas could be foreseen no more than the tragedy of a ruptured artery in Washington. But, as it was, the final act of his life was played out, not on the campaign trail or in the convention hall, but on the Senate floor and behind the doors of committee rooms.

Senator Thomas Hennings said once that Kefauver "probably would be a good President. He knows how to put together a good staff. He has some very striking abilities. He has a good mind and a phlegmatic nature which would help him bear the White House burdens."[1]

---

1. Quoted anonymously in Riggs, "The Man from Tennessee"; identified in a personal communication from Riggs, Washington, Dec. 22, 1970.

But Kefauver's relinquishment of that possibility gave rein to those same talents in a very different context. The 1956 election divided his decade and a half of Senate tenure almost precisely in half. In its second half, once he had turned his face resolutely from the lure of the campaign trail, he was able to focus gradually all of his ability and experience upon the expression of his philosophy in the arena he had chosen with his entry into politics in 1938—the legislative halls.

In comparison to the period after 1956, Kefauver's first eight years in the Senate—though they had their high points—were almost a long interlude in his congressional career. During most of this period, his attention to legislative matters was always subject to something that might take him away from Washington: a crime hearing, a presidential primary campaign, perhaps a speech that might advance his political ambition.

This flitting back and forth, with only one eye on legislative work and the other on political activity, was responsible for his reputation among his colleagues as one who did not carry his share of the hard work of the Senate and could not be depended on in the pinch of a legislative battle. It was used against him in the 1956 primaries: the *New York Times* commented that Kefauver's opposition "has a common basis in a feeling that he does not pull his oar in the galley-work of regular committees, but goes sailing off on investigations to make the headlines."[2]

Hennings told Robert L. Riggs, Washington correspondent for the *Louisville Courier-Journal*: "Very few members actually dislike Estes. But he's so damn single-minded. He expects you to get interested in the things that interest him. But when you try to get him stirred up about something that interests you, he can barely hear you. You make a point to be on hand to vote with him on something that's important to him. And when you need his vote, he's quick to promise. He says, 'I'll be there at 3 o'clock when the roll is called.' But you know all the time he's making that 3 o'clock promise that he has a ticket in his pocket for a flight that leaves the airport at 1:50 o'clock."[3]

After Kefauver set aside his presidential ambition, this picture

2. March 25, 1956.
3. See Note 1.

changed. He did not flit away in the midst of legislative projects as he had before. The man Humphrey had accused in 1956 of not carrying his share of the load of commmittee work became the man so insistent on his committees getting on with their job that his colleagues sometimes complained he was demanding too much of their time.

He lost his reputation as "a headline grabber" (again, Hennings' characterization) though it was still used against him in some of his legislative fights. South Carolina's Senator Olin Johnston described Kefauver after his death as "the Senate's plodder, who insisted on completing a job, regardless of whether it was one which brought headlines and fame, or whether it was one of the menial tasks which sometimes brings on criticism and even bitter opposition."[4]

The end of the presidential period was welcomed by Kefauver's family, who for eight years had had to adjust to his leading a "traveling salesman" kind of life for long intervals and appearing at home only occasionally. During the crime investigation, his absence was taken so completely for granted that one morning, after he had returned home unexpectedly late the night before, five-year-old David raced downstairs and demanded excitedly, "Mother, what's Daddy doing home?"

Kefauver tried to make up for his absences during the crime probe by spending a great deal of time with the children when he was at home. Linda, David, and Diane would hold his hands and pull him along the sidewalks on roller skates, and on one weekend break at the height of the spectacular New York hearings, Linda got him on a pogo stick.[5]

This kind of participation brought him to grief in a midget car on Christmas Day, 1958—ironically, right after his Antitrust and Monopoly Subcommittee had published a report criticizing the automobile industry for ignoring the public demand for small automobiles. He was testing a go-kart owned by fourteen-year-old John Harrell to see if they were safe for David, who wanted one, and as David described his course down a hill in front of their home: "It's kind of a steep hill and those cars can be pretty tricky unless you're used to them. . . . His hat flew off. About halfway down, he tried

4. *Carey Estes Kefauver, Late a Senator from Tennessee*, 36.
5. Kefauver, *Crime in America*, xv.

to stop with his leg. It was going so fast he couldn't. It just bent his leg back and scraped it up."[6] Kefauver suffered a dislocated kneecap and badly pulled ligaments. He was in a cast for three weeks and was on crutches when he escourted Senator Albert Gore to the rostrum to be sworn in for a second term.

Although he usually rode to and from work in a cab or with someone else, Kefauver was in the habit of driving his family around a bit on Sundays. One Sunday, they were some distance out in the country when Diane realized it was nearly time for one of her favorite television programs. The policeman who stopped Kefauver for speeding was unimpressed with his explanation—"Well, you see, I was trying to get my daughter home in time for '*Lassie*'"—until he found out who the senator was.[7]

Kefauver was chosen national Father of the Year in 1951 and pontificated at some length for International News Service about his philosophy of parenthood: "My idea of how to be a good father is to be the friend of your children—a person the youngsters do not hesitate to come to with their problems or with their small talk. . . . I play with my children whenever I can. . . . I also think a child's reading is very important—reading inside and outside school. . . . Guidance can, I think, be given without flatly laying down rules. It can be done just by talking it over. When a child is forbidden something, he should be told why. . . . I am, I guess, a 'spare the rod' father. I don't believe in punishment if reasoning can do the trick. . . . Above all, I think that children are people, to be treated as people."[8]

Without being prohibitive about it, the Kefauvers tried to keep their children isolated from the frequent political parties and conferences at their Upton Street home during the years of Kefauver's presidential activity. When there was a party downstairs, the children ordinarily remained upstairs and sometimes would gather at the top of the stairs to peer down at the merry-making, trying to identify those present. David remembered wandering onto the back porch one summer's evening to find it crowded with practically the entire

6. Lois Laycook, *Nashville Tennessean*, Dec. 28, 1958; Isabelle Shelton, *Washington Star*, Dec. 27, 1958.
7. Personal conversation, Charles A. Caldwell, Washington, May 12, 1970.
8. Estes Kefauver, INS story, *Nashville Tennessean*, May 23, 1951.

top leadership of the Democratic party, including Adlai Stevenson.[9] The Richard Nixons lived right around the corner, and, despite their differing political philosophies, the two families were rather good friends. So were their dogs. Soon after Nixon took office as Vice President, there was a minor bipartisan flurry when it became known that his famous dog, Checkers, was "expecting." Nixon asked Mrs. Karl E. Mundt, wife of the South Dakota senator, if she minded "if Estes Kefauver's dog is the father" of the puppy she had been promised. She said she would name the pup "Coalition," but Kefauver defended the moral purity of his cocker spaniel: "So far as we can learn, Jo-Jo hasn't visited the Nixons in many months."[10]

Although he lambasted Nixon vigorously on the campaign trail, during the first Eisenhower administration Kefauver had the Vice President over for a stag party to give an off-the-cuff report on his recent Asian tour to a group of sixteen Democratic senators. And when Nixon had to take over presidential duties temporarily after Eisenhower's 1955 heart attack, Nancy made the house available to handle the overflow of officials from all over the country who descended on Nixon. The Kefauver house was so crowded for awhile that the Kefauver children slept in the attic, getting up and down by means of a pull-down ladder.

There were always a lot of visitors at the Kefauver home. In addition to old friends such as Charlie Neese, Harry Mansfield, and Noble Caudill (for whom Kefauver reserved in the refrigerator a bottle of Bristol cream sherry), Nancy got accustomed to having perfect strangers show up on Kefauver's invitation to supper or just to "drop by the house when you're in Washington." Once an entire (and rather large) family appeared on the doorstep when no one was home but the children, who entertained them creditably in the yard until their parents arrived.[11]

The sturdy health of Kefauver's father failed him at last. Cooke Kefauver died at the age of eighty-seven early in 1958. Thereafter there was only Kefauver's sister Nora at the old Kefauver town house in Madisonville, and the family did not often go back there.

By the time Kefauver relinquished his national ambition, the chil-

9. Personal conversation, David Kefauver, Knoxville, Spring 1970.
10. *Nashville Tennessean*, Feb. 26, 1953.
11. Personal conversation, David Kefauver, Knoxville, Spring 1970.

Kefauver has a friendly handshake for his 1956 adversary, Vice President Richard Nixon.

Kefauver and his junior colleague, Senator Albert Gore, greet each other in 1961.

dren were past the age of needing a "nanny," and Nanette Criper left the Kefauvers. Bobbie the cook stayed on, though. Kefauver's more consistent presence at home after 1956 meant that Nancy did not have to interrupt her painting projects to run off campaigning in some distant state. She reverted more and more to her youthful interest in her art and spent a good deal of time in an art studio she had established in 1952 with a friend, Mrs. Byrd Farioletti, in an old carriage house on the old Sumner Welles estate just behind the Cosmos Club.

Despite his individualistic role, Kefauver, like most American public figures, observed social conventions with some scrupulousness. The coonskin cap was strictly a campaign gimmick: in 1951 the American Women's Institute chose him one of the nation's ten best-dressed males for his "contemporary look": "he mirrors the average white-collar worker, neat, simple and conservative."[12] Kefauver and his family attended church with reasonable regularity, and he participated in a weekly Senate prayer breakfast session.

Except for a move from Suite 410 to Suite 443 of the Senate Office Building after Kefauver's reelection in 1954, the only major change in his office environment after Charlie Neese left was his employment of Charles Caldwell early in 1959 as his administrative assistant, succeeding Dick Wallace. Wallace had always been interested primarily in the international aspects of Kefauver's career, and he joined the staff of the Atlantic Council, an organization devoted to promoting the Atlantic Union, after Kefauver gave up his fight for membership on the Foreign Relations Committee in favor of the Appropriations Committee.

Wallace recommended Caldwell, who had been a political reporter with him on the *Press-Scimitar* in Memphis, and Caldwell was interviewed by Kefauver while the senator was still languishing in the hospital as a consequence of his entanglement with the go-kart. After asking Caldwell numerous questions, Kefauver said, "Well, Charlie, you know I'm up for election again in about a year and a half. Do you want to take a chance on that and go to work for me?"

"Well, Estes," replied Caldwell, "if you're willing to take a chance on me, I'm certainly willing to take a chance on you."[13]

12. AP story, *Nashville Tennessean*, Dec. 26, 1951.
13. Personal communication, Charles A. Caldwell, Washington, July 17, 1970.

Caldwell was an entirely different "key man" on the staff from either Neese or Wallace. Neese was very much of an easy-going politician in public and an energetic executive in the office, while Wallace was more introverted and studious, remaining largely in the background. Caldwell was a more natural socializer than either of them, a tall, solidly built man full of friendliness and good humor who dealt easily with constituents and officials alike, and was less inclined than either Neese or Wallace to proselytize his own ideas with Kefauver.

During the last years of his life, Kefauver became graver, even sombre at times, as he devoted his energies fully to the realization of a legislative program that brought him into conflict with maneuvers and manipulations fully as frustrating as those that had blocked his presidential ambition. In compensation, however, Kefauver gained many more friends and consistent allies in the Senate than he ever had before, as new liberal faces began to appear, such as Philip Hart of Michigan, Ernest Gruening of Alaska, Ralph Yarbrough of Texas, John Carroll of Colorado, William Proxmire of Wisconsin, and, shortly before Kefauver's death, George S. McGovern of South Dakota.

Kefauver was an admired figure, a hero in fact, to a substantial number of his colleagues in his later years, and he emerged as the informal leader of a rather effective minority whose activities marked its philosophy as differing considerably from the old "New Deal" liberals.

Dwight D. Eisenhower's election as President in 1952 boded ill for the Tennessee Valley Authority, which had flourished for two decades under friendly Democratic administrations. In his campaign, Eisenhower had promised that TVA "will be operated and maintained at full efficiency," but he also cited it as an example of "creeping socialism," a favorite phrase of the private power industry.[14] During World War II, TVA had used up most of its good hydroelectric sites to meet the wartime demand for power. After the war, the power demand continued to spiral, and TVA turned to construction of steam plants to supplement its hydroelectric produc-

14. Aaron Wildavsky, *Dixie-Yates: a Study in Power Politics* (New Haven: Yale Univ. Press, 1962), 12, 17, 20.

tion.[15] Retiring President Truman recommended $30 million in the 1953 budget for a new steam plant at Fulton, Tennessee, thirty miles north of Memphis, to take care of the increasing needs of that city, 100 miles from the nearest TVA power plant, but Eisenhower cut it from the budget and the Republican-controlled Congress refused to restore it.[16]

Eisenhower preferred that Memphis build its own power plant but, in the face of objections raised by the city, agreed to a suggestion by Gordon Clapp, chairman of the TVA board of directors. Clapp proposed that TVA be relieved of enough of its power commitment to the Atomic Energy Commission at Paducah, Kentucky, to supply the 600,000 kilowatts Memphis needed.[17]

Clapp's idea was that construction of another private power plant in the Paducah area would leave recognized TVA territory inviolate. But K.D. Nichols, AEC's general manager, thought it foolish to build new facilities at Paducah, 200 miles away from Memphis, where the power was needed. So Budget Director Rowland Hughes decided at the beginning of 1954 that the AEC would contract with private power to construct a plant near Memphis and feed it into the TVA system: not, theoretically, for Memphis needs but to replace power that TVA delivered to AEC at faraway Paducah.[18]

The roundabout method was designed to keep TVA from being a party to the contract because the TVA board could be expected to oppose it. It was formalized as the Dixon-Yates contract: Middle South Utilities, headed by Edgar H. Dixon, and the Southern Company, headed by Eugene A. Yates, would form a combine and contract with the AEC for twenty-five years to build a $107 million steam plant at West Memphis, Arkansas, to funnel the power into TVA installations at Memphis.[19] To overcome objections by two of his fellow commissioners, Lewis Strauss, AEC chairman, requested that Eisenhower personally order the AEC to enter into the contract, and the President did so in June 1954.[20]

Meanwhile, Walter von Tresckow, a New York financial consul-

15. Ibid., 10–11.
16. Ibid., 18–21.
17. Ibid., 33–34.
18. Ibid., 37–49.
19. Ibid., 54, 77.
20. *Nashville Tennessean*, July 13, 1954.

tant, made a counter-proposal through Kefauver's Memphis friend, attorney Lucius Burch. Von Tresckow and his associates would contract to deliver power to TVA over a thirty-year period and finance the Fulton steam plant privately on the basis of that commitment, but AEC turned him down.[21]

At the beginning of July, the Judiciary Committee's five-man Antitrust and Monopoly Subcommittee, of which Kefauver was a member, held two days of hearings on the Dixon-Yates contract. The Senate's Republican leadership refused funds for the probe, whereupon the subcommittee chairman, William Langer of North Dakota, used funds from his own office to employ New York attorney Sydney Davis as counsel to conduct it. During the subcommittee hearing, Von Tresckow testified that Dixon had pressured the New York engineering firm of Gibbs & Hill, Inc., through its customers, to withdraw from his syndicate, forcing him to turn to other designers in the midst of his negotiations with the AEC. Kefauver took time out from his Tennessee campaign for reelection to participate in the hearings. His verdict on the disclosures was that the proposed Dixon-Yates contract was "bad business, bad government and bad morals."[22]

Kefauver was campaigning against Pat Sutton while his colleague, Albert Gore, was quarterbacking an unsuccessful thirteen-day filibuster against passage of some revisions to the Atomic Energy Act without inclusion of a prohibition against the Dixon-Yates contract. Kefauver then went to Europe, visiting Nancy's family with her and attending a meeting of the Interparliamentary Union in Vienna, while Langer was struggling to get a full-fledged investigation of Dixon-Yates off the ground.

Complaining that the Republican leadership refused him any money at all, Langer said at last he would go ahead with the probe and practice a little law to finance it after Judiciary Committee funds ran out.[23] Just as the Kefauvers arrived back home, he got a big psychological boost when J.D. Stietenroth, secretary-treasurer and twenty-six-year employee of Mississippi Power & Light Company, charged that it and Middle South Utilities were dominated by "Wall Street interests" and had "coercively" imposed excessive

21. Wildavsky, *Dixon-Yates*, 207.
22. Ibid., 100, 216; *New York Times*, Aug. 17, 1954.
23. *New York Times*, July 2, 1954; Wildavsky, *Dixon-Yates*, 211.

rates on their customers to the tune of millions of dollars annually. Stietenroth was fired at once, which made him none the more loth to testify when Langer's subcommittee began its hearings. He charged that Middle South had created an "empire" covering three states, and the Dixon-Yates contract would produce a private power group "so huge it is frightening." He also charged that Mississippi Power & Light kept two sets of books, one held by Ebasco Services, Inc., in New York, implying an even vaster private power hookup.[24]

Ralph H. Demmler, chairman of the Securities and Exchange Commission, told the subcommittee that the SEC had found nothing wrong with Mississippi Power & Light's accounting standards, therefore Stietenroth's charges were groundless. But Dixon-Yates supporters were alarmed at the Democrats' recapture of congressional control. After Dixon-Yates made some contract revisions to meet objections by the General Accounting Office, Eisenhower personally asked the Joint Committee on Atomic Energy to waive a required thirty-day inspection of the contract, and it did so by a 10 to 8 party line vote.[25]

As soon as the Democrats took over in January, the committee rescinded its action by a reversed 10 to 8 party line vote and recommended that the AEC cancel the Dixon-Yates contract. The AEC refused.

Kefauver promptly made a bid for chairmanship of the Antitrust and Monopoly Subcommittee. But Senator Harley Kilgore of West Virginia, new Judiciary Committee chairman, was not especially fond of Kefauver, and the Democratic leadership reportedly was fearful that another spectacular Kefauver investigation would build him up for a 1956 presidential race.[26] Kilgore followed Langer's precedent and appropriated the subcommittee chairmanship to himself; whereupon Kefauver settled down to a persistent effort to get Kilgore to probe Dixon-Yates.

Because the Democratic margin of congressional control was too thin for effective action to reverse the AEC's commitment to the contract, the administration went ahead with it. But early in 1955, Joseph Volpe Jr., a former AEC general counsel employed by the

24. *Nashville Tennessean*, Sept. 21, 1954; Wildavsky, *Dixon-Yates*, 128–30.
25. Wildavsky, *Dixon-Yates*, 130, 136.
26. Ibid., 226, 251; Anderson and Blumenthal, *The Kefauver Story*, 218; Charles Bartlett, *Chattanooga Times*, Feb. 8, 1955.

state of Tennessee and several Tennessee Valley groups to oppose the contract in the 1954 SEC hearings, found a memorandum filed under subpoena by Ebasco Services that led him to an interesting discovery: Adolphe H. Wenzell, a vice president and director of the First Boston Corporation, a New York underwriting firm arranging the financing for Dixon-Yates, had been employed as a technical assistant to the Budget Bureau on the TVA accounting system and had attended several bureau meetings concerned with technical aspects of the Dixon-Yates plan.[27]

Senator Lister Hill of Alabama made headlines with his floor attacks on Wenzell's "dual role," and Volpe developed the matter further before SEC debt financing hearings on Dixon-Yates, which opened five days after groundbreaking ceremonies for the plant at the beginning of June. Matters got so sticky that the SEC, at the request of the White House, postponed further debt financing hearings on Dixon-Yates two days after they began.[28]

Two weeks later, the city of Memphis decided to build its own municipal power plant—to be financed, constructed, and operated by von Tresckow's group.[29] At this point, Kilgore gave in, authorizing an investigation of Dixon-Yates by a special subcommittee headed by Kefauver and including Langer and Joseph O'Mahoney of Wyoming as its other two members. Kefauver immediately zeroed in on Wenzell's mysterious role.[30]

There were obviously people in the Eisenhower administration who did not want some of the facts of Dixon-Yates to come to light. Sydney Davis, the subcommittee counsel, had been subjected to heavy pressure to drop the investigation the previous year. His career had been threatened by several senators. It had been suggested pointedly to him that he meet with Eisenhower to discuss the matter, but the suggestion was dropped when Davis said he would go to the White House only if Langer and Kefauver accompanied him.[31]

The Budget Bureau had imposed highly suspicious rules of secrecy about Wenzell's employment. Kefauver and the subcommittee developed that Wenzell, first employed by the agency in 1953,

27. Wildavsky, *Dixon-Yates*, 229.
28. Ibid., 230–31, 238, 240–42.
29. Ibid., 233–34, 247.
30. Ibid., 251, 252; *Chattanooga Times*, June 23, 1955.
31. Wildavsky, *Dixon-Yates*, 216–17.

had been called back for consultation on the possibilities of financing the Dixon-Yates plan. He was still participating in such meetings, even after Dixon had begun negotiations with First Boston about handling the financing.[32]

As the Kefauver probe began to touch sensitive areas, Eisenhower said at a press conference that "Mr. Wenzell was never called in or asked a single thing about the Yates-Dixon contract." He was irritated to learn, immediately after the conference, that he had not been told everything about the matter by his advisers. Later that afternoon, Kefauver sent the President information that Wenzell had participated in many conferences.[33]

The next day, Brigadier General Herbert D. Vogel, new TVA chairman, wrote Eisenhower that it would no longer be necessary for TVA to use Dixon-Yates power because Memphis was going to build its own power plant. Eisenhower ordered the Dixon-Yates contract cancelled less than two weeks later.[34]

Kefauver went on investigating, however, calling up both Dixon and Wenzell as witnesses. The cooperative Mr. Wenzell testified that the Dixon-Yates plan could not have been formulated without the information he supplied on the cost of financing. He admitted frankly that he considered TVA not just "creeping socialism" but "galloping socialism."[35] Kefauver said the Dixon-Yates scheme was "crudely conceived in darkness for the base and ulterior motive of destroying the Tennessee Valley Authority." The Democratic leadership called a halt to his probe at the end of 1955, while he was still trying to nose out "a case of criminal conspiracy involving a number of high-ranking persons." The AEC ruled the Dixon-Yates contract invalid on the basis of Wenzell's dual role. Dixon-Yates sued for $3½ million in damages, but the Supreme Court eventually upheld the AEC, holding that Wenzell's role represented conflict of interest.[36]

One reason the Democratic leadership was reluctant to turn over a Dixon-Yates investigation to Kefauver was that he was already

32. Ibid., 253–54.
33. Ibid., 254–55.
34. Ibid., 255, 264.
35. Ibid., 261; *New York Times*, July 9, 1955.
36. Wildavsky, *Dixon-Yates*, 288.

chairman of a Judiciary subcommittee that for two years had been making gestures toward a full-fledged investigation of juvenile delinquency. As soon as Kefauver succeeded to the chairmanship of the subcommittee in 1955, he gave indications that he hoped to turn the limping juvenile delinquency probe into a junior-grade crime investigation—and with a presidential race coming up the next year! There was no question that Kefauver was keenly aware of the publicity potential of a juvenile delinquency probe. Hennings said that "he never showed any interest in the hearings on juvenile delinquency until the witness was Mrs. Eugene Meyer, wife of the owner of the *Washington Post*. He knew he'd get a headline out of her."[37]

Langer was also a member of the Juvenile Deliquency Subcommittee and, fortunately, this was an area, like Dixon-Yates, in which the two highly independent senators saw eye-to-eye. They did not on all issues, although Langer, seventeen years older than Kefauver, was one of his closest personal friends in Congress. Langer's death in 1959 was a severe shock to Kefauver. Kefauver was in Memphis to introduce Sir Harold Caccia, the British ambassador, at a dinner. The senator was getting into his tuxedo when he received a telephone call from Washington that Langer was dead and that a group of his colleagues would accompany his body on a plane to North Dakota for the funeral the next morning. Charlie Caldwell returned from an errand to find Kefauver struggling back into his street clothes. "Call the airport, Charlie," instructed Kefauver distractedly. "I've got to get back to Washington." "But Estes!" protested the startled Caldwell. "The British ambassador!" Kefauver seemed hardly to hear him. His eyes were far away, his face set. "Charlie," he said, "Bill Langer's dead. I've got to get on that plane!" Caldwell persuaded him to telephone Sir Harold and apologize before he left.[38]

In the years before Langer's death, the two men worked together like brothers on the two Judiciary subcommittees. Their cooperation was especially painful to some of the corporation witnesses haled before the Antitrust and Monopoly Subcommittee after Kefauver became its chairman. The juvenile delinquency probe, too, though

37. See Note 1.
38. Personal conversation, Charles A. Caldwell, Washington, May 12, 1970.

Nashville Tennessean photo

Kefauver (right) and Senator William Langer, seated next to him, listen to testimony from Mrs. J. B. Bittinger before their Juvenile Delinquency Subcommittee hearing in Nashville in 1955. J. Carlton Loser, Davidson County district attorney, leans forward to listen from the jury box. Behind Langer is Peter Chambliss, associate counsel for the subcommittee. (The other man, unidentified, is probably a court reporter).

not as sensational as the crime investigation, had its highlights, particularly in the areas of obscene literature and the baby adoption racket.

After the Juvenile Delinquency Subcommittee's examination of several witnesses accused of participating in the $100 million to $300 million annual traffic in pornography to juveniles, some familiar tactics appeared. An anonymously distributed circular asked: "Are you a red dupe? There are some people in America who would *like* to censor . . . who would *like* to suppress comics. . . . The group most anxious to destroy comics are the Communists!"[39]

Had Kefauver's investigation occurred fifteen years later, it might have stirred public interest comparable to that in the crime investigation. But public awareness and concern over explicit erotica was not nearly as widespread at that time. Similarly with the matter of drug use by juveniles: the subcommittee found that juveniles were being used by drug sellers as "pushers" and were being lured into other forms of crime through their use of drugs. But, at the time, drug use by children had not penetrated noticeably into the middle class stratum of society. The public was not alarmed.

Thus none of the subcommittee's early recommendations for legislation to curb juvenile delinquency were enacted. Even so, the juvenile delinquency probe continued throughout the remainder of Kefauver's lifetime, and in 1961 Congress adopted recommendations by President Kennedy to provide grants for pilot projects, training programs, and studies on juvenile delinquency to states, cities, public agencies, and non-profit private agencies.

Kefauver had this quip he liked to repeat during his off-year report tours of Tennessee: "You know, it's the Foreign Affairs Committee in the House, but in the Senate it's called the Foreign Relations Committee. That's because, by the time you get to the Senate, you're too old for affairs—you can only have relations."[40] This levity concealed an absorbing desire to attain membership on the Foreign Relations Committee. He campaigned for it every session, as earnestly as he campaigned for office, writing letters to his colleagues and soliciting their support. He even sought the support of

39. Some of this material has been preserved in the Kefauver Collection.
40. Personal recollection. I heard Kefauver repeat this little joke a number of times during his tours of the state.

Kenneth McKellar, who was a member of the Steering Committee when he entered the Senate. McKellar replied, "Dear Senator: Your letter . . . has been received and noted, and will have proper consideration"; at the bottom of which someone in Kefauver's office, probably Charlie Neese, penned, "Translation: Blocked at all costs."[41]

Foreign Relations was Kefauver's first committee choice when he advanced to the Senate, and his persistent requests to be named to the committee might have paid off had he not entered the presidential lists. His foreign policy views, while sometimes controversial, were not highly offensive to the leadership of his own party. But the prestigious Foreign Relations Committee was generally considered a good forum for senators to promote presidential aspirations (and, in part, it is possible that Kefauver had that in mind). The 1952 presidential primaries and Democratic Convention branded him a leader of rebellion against the party hierarchy and, moreover, a dangerous challenger. Few, if any, leading Democrats doubted his intention to try for the nomination again in 1956, and there was no inclination among them to add any more weapons to his already formidable political arsenal.

After 1956, Kefauver's aspiration to the committee became entangled in a web of the personal ambition of his influential colleagues. It was apparent that Adlai Stevenson had made his last presidential race, and both Lyndon Johnson and John Kennedy already had set their sights on the 1960 nomination; perhaps Hubert Humphrey had too. The most threatening potential obstacle to any prospective Democratic candidate was Kefauver, with his extensive base of popular support and his deceptively explosive campaigning methods; and Johnson, at least, was in a strategic position to assure that the obstacle did not become any more threatening than it already was.

The retirement in 1956 of the venerable Walter F. George of Georgia, the committee's chairman, created a committee vacancy that both Kefauver and Kennedy, four years behind him in seniority, sought to fill. Johnson, chairman of the Steering Committee, threw his weight behind Kennedy, and it was agreed at a late 1956

41. This memorandum was preserved along with other intra-office correspondence in the Kefauver Collection.

meeting of party leaders at Johnson's Texas home that Kefauver was not to be given the assignment.[42] Ignoring rumors of that meeting, Kefauver placed his petition before Johnson verbally on Johnson's return and wrote letters to the other thirteen members of the Steering Committee, asking their support.

After the committee meeting, when it was announced that Kennedy had been chosen for the Foreign Relations spot, Kefauver's long face sagged even more gravely and a flush of red crept up the back of his neck. He dictated a statement for the *Congressional Record* but changed his mind, sat down, and wrote Johnson one of the bitterest letters of his career:

"I am disappointed and feel I have been done very badly. I had four years seniority over Senator Kennedy and this action indicates that Seniority Rule may or may not be applied according to personal or other considerations. . . .

"I know that argument was made that as long as some Junior members do not have a major Committee, I ought not to be allowed to transfer from one major Committee to another. Frankly, Lyndon, this looks like a rule that was specifically made for me, and has not been applied to others. . . . When you were a member of Armed Services and Interstate and Foreign Commerce, you transferred from Interstate and Foreign Commerce to Appropriations. . . . It is only fair to point out that Kennedy, Gore and Pastore were members of the Senate at that time. . . .

"I have tried, Lyndon, to cooperate with you and be helpful to you. . . . Notwithstanding all of this, I have been turned aside on every request for Committees that I have made since you became the Democratic leader. . . . I want . . . to show how keenly I feel that I have been discriminated against. . . .

"I know that rumors like this are probably not entitled to any credence, but there has been one around that you and others do not want me to have any build-up that might enable me to seek a National office in 1960. If this is in anybody's mind, I want to set the record straight that I am not and have no plans to be a candidate for any National office in 1960. . . ."[43]

42. Sorensen, *Kennedy*, 164, says Johnson's selection of Kennedy for the Foreign Relations Committee helped to establish a friendly relationship that led later to Kennedy's selection of Johnson as his vice presidential running mate.
43. Letter, Estes Kefauver to Lyndon B. Johnson, Jan. 9, 1957, Kefauver Col-

Johnson replied in a tone of offended dignity that "in addition to seniority, the Steering Committee takes into account geography, political philosophy, the current status of a member desiring a change, and sometimes the estimate of a man's own colleagues toward him." He denied making any "statement whatsoever as to my position" before the committee, said he was the last to vote, and "the decision to grant the position to Kennedy was unanimous." He concluded: "Estes, my recommendation is that you accept [the committee's] reasons in the spirit in which they are made."[44]

Later Johnson promised to keep Kefauver's application on file "where it will automatically be before the Democratic Steering Committee anytime that a vacancy occurs," and several senators promised Kefauver their support, including Humphrey. But when a Foreign Relations Committee vacancy occurred again two years later, Kefauver chose the Appropriations Committee instead, and the Foreign Relations spot went to Gore.[45]

Kefauver kept in his files a statement made once by Cordell Hull: "In a smaller and smaller world, it will soon no longer be possible for some nations to choose and follow the way of force and for other nations to follow the way of reason. All will have to go in one direction and in one way." This viewpoint underlay Kefauver's general philosophy of foreign relations.

The man whom Ed Crump had called "a darling of the Communists" was rather militant in his posture *vis-a-vis* communism in international affairs, as indicated by his agreement with General Douglas MacArthur in 1951 that Red China's Manchurian bases

lection, Ser. 1, Box 76. In the same box is an undated clipping on Kennedy's selection despite Kefauver's seniority, with the words "best news yet" written on it, purportedly from Frank J. Costello, postmarked New York, Jan. 11, 1957.

44. Letter, Lyndon B. Johnson to Estes Kefauver, Jan. 10, 1957, Kefauver Collection, VIP file. Before the meeting, however, Sen. Matthew M. Neely of West Virginia had sent Kefauver a copy of his proxy, addressed to Johnson and directing him "to cast my vote at the Steering Committee Meeting in behalf of Senator Estes Kefauver for assignment to the Senate Foreign Relations Committee, if he is the senior applicant"; it is in the Kefauver Collection, Ser. 1, Box 76. Lois Laycook, *Nashville Tennessean*, Jan. 9, 1957, reported that Johnson "reportedly blocked Senator Estes Kefauver's bid for the assignment" and that Kefauver had "substantial support in the committee."

45. AP story, *Nashville Tennessean*, Jan. 11, 1959; Frank van der Linden, *Nashville Banner*, Jan. 15, 1959.

should be bombed if Korean peace talks failed. Kefauver even proposed using atomic artillery in the Korean fighting in that event. But he desired to avoid a general world war and was concerned with maintaining congressional prerogatives against invasion by executive power in matters of war and peace. In the 1955 crisis over the Formosa Straits, Kefauver said he was convinced that certain members of the Eisenhower administration were "plotting and planning" to throw the United States into war with Communist China.[46] When, after the Red Chinese seized the offshore island of Ichiang, President Eisenhower asked Congress for specific authority to use American armed forces to protect Formosa, the adjoining Pescadores Islands and "related positions and territories," Kefauver joined Humphrey and Herbert Lehman in criticizing the administration for its ambiguity regarding the islands of Quemoy and Matsu, which they considered traditionally Chinese territory and not subject to the American agreement to defend Formosa.[47]

Kefauver's view was that Japan and India were the key Asian nations toward which American foreign policy should be directed. He recommended negotiations toward diplomatic recognition of Red China in return for settlement of the Korean, Formosan, and other Asian problems. He was one of six senators who voted against a mutual security pact with Nationalist China, saying, "I am afraid his [Chiang Kai Shek's] ambition to invade the mainland, while ours is to preserve the peace, enhances the chances of dragging us into war."[48]

In 1954, when Eisenhower was considering acceding to the French request for military help in Vietnam, Kefauver criticized the administration sharply for coming "within a hair's breadth of openly intervening in the Indochina war" and expressed opposition to unilateral American intervention. On the other hand, he called the idea "that we can abandon the area to Communism . . . unthinkable."

Dick Wallace expressed the belief that Kefauver, "had he been alive . . . would have been very doubtful about the escalation in Vietnam [in the 1960s]. He believed in strengthening the Free

46. AP story, *Nashville Tennessean*, March 31, 1955.
47. Ibid., Jan. 27, 1955.
48. *Nashville Banner*, Feb. 10, 1955.

World in its heartland. He was an internationalist, but a discriminating one."[49]

At the same time, Kefauver's belief that the President should have reasonable freedom of action in the conduct of international affairs was one of the reasons behind his fight against the Bricker Amendment in 1953 and 1954. In the beginning, he opposed it almost single-handedly, and he remained the leader of the fight against it from its inception until its very narrow defeat.

This amendment by Senator John W. Bricker of Ohio, reacting to increasing American involvement in such organizations as the United Nations and the North Atlantic Treaty Organization, would have invalidated any treaty provisions abridging rights guaranteed in the Constitution, required congressional approval before any treaty became effective as internal law in the United States, and required that Executive Agreements be ratified by the Senate in the same manner as the more formal treaties. Within a month, Bricker had enough co-sponsors to assure the necessary two-thirds vote for Senate passage of a constitutional amendment resolution, and it was supported by the American Bar Association, the U.S. Chamber of Commerce, and veterans' organizations; but the Eisenhower administration opposed it as too restrictive to permit effective presidential direction of foreign affairs.

When the Judiciary Committee approved the Bricker Resolution, Kefauver wrote the dissenting report for four of its members, declaring that such an amendment would "leave the United States only partially sovereign. . . . The President would no longer have control over foreign relations, since the Congress could regulate his conduct of such affairs down to the last detail."[50]

Early in 1954, the Eisenhower administration succeeded in getting the resolution toned down to the point of acceptability—to the administration. Kefauver still argued against any constitutional amendment at all, saying that requiring congressional approval of treaty effects on internal law would entail double congressional action because the Senate had to ratify treaties; and invalidation of treaty provisions in conflict with the Constitution he called "totally

49. Personal communication, Richard J. Wallace, Washington, July 26, 1970.
50. *Congressional Quarterly Almanac*, 1953, pp. 233–37, 258.

unnecessary" because the Constitution was overriding anyhow and would be so interpreted by the Supreme Court. Kefauver attempted to substitute a mere statement of policy for the Bricker Amendment, reaffirming the primacy of the Constitution. He failed, but the Bricker Resolution was further watered down by a substitution authored by George, and then failed by a 60 to 31 favorable vote—short of the necessary two-thirds.

Kefauver's internationalism incurred the wrath of jingoists who used it against him in his reelection campaigns even while, paradoxically, his support for a strong America defensively was winning him praise from patriotic organizations. In 1955, the Philadelphia Flag Day Association chose him for the Leopold C. Glass Founder's Award for "outstanding achievement in the support of Old Glory" and the American Defense Society of New York City awarded him its Distinguished Service Medal.

Kefauver visited Europe about as often as any member of the Senate during his career. Most of these trips were as a delegate to meetings of the Interparliamentary Union, some as a representative of the United States at meetings of NATO nations. Most of the time Nancy accompanied him, taking advantage of the trips to stop off for a visit with her parents in Scotland before joining Kefauver on the continent.

More often than not, Kefauver would tour several nations in Europe, and sometimes Asia, while he was abroad. In 1955, he went from an Interparliamentary Union meeting in Helsinki to Russia, then went on around the world on his way back to the United States. He and four other senators conferred at the Kremlin with Russia's top leaders, Nikita S. Khrushchev and Nikolai Bulganin, but it was with the "little people" of Russia that Kefauver got along famously. One of his companions, Representative J.M. Robison Jr. of Kentucky, reported that Kefauver, "here in Moscow, like back home, is going all around, shaking people's hands."[51]

When the group visited a factory on the outskirts of Moscow, they found themselves among a crowd of Russian workers, none of whom could speak English, in the courtyard. After a moment of strained silence, Kefauver smiled and waved. The Russians smiled and waved back. When they left the factory, Kefauver and all the

51. AP story, *Nashville Tennessean*, Sept. 5, 1955.

Kefauver visits Vienna during one of his European trips to attend meetings of the Interparliamentary Union.

Kefauver and Jim Bobo wait for Lucius Burch to complete a telephone conversation.

workers again exchange farewell smiles and "Kefauver waves"— friendly, half-limp flaps of the hand.

The language barrier bothered Kefauver not at all throughout the trip through a dozen countries. In Seoul, Korea, he managed to communicate to the bellhop that he wanted water and ice by pulling a bottle of Scotch from his bag and pointing to it. When the water was brought, he promptly drank it all, without touching the whiskey, and ordered three more decanters of water in the same way, without ever speaking a word.

One of Kefauver's major reasons for desiring membership on the Foreign Relations Committee was his persistent sponsorship of Atlantic Union, a plan for federal union of 15 "Atlantic democracies," organized along the lines of the original American federation of colonies, with each nation controlling its internal affairs but delegating foreign policy and defense to a joint federal government chosen by popular ballot.

When Kefauver sought the help of his Memphis friends for his Senate race early in 1948, the consensus was that Edmund Orgill filled the bill as an outstanding citizen to head a public pro-Kefauver organization. Lucius Burch told Kefauver the best way to persuade Orgill to accept the post, with its attendant risks, was through Orgill's enthusiasm for Atlantic Union, which had been fanned by a recent visit by the idea's originator, Clarence Streit, to Memphis.

Kefauver was not familiar with the Atlantic Union idea, but Burch offered him a $250 campaign contribution if he would read Streit's book, *Union Now*—no further commitments demanded. Kefauver did and agreed to support Atlantic Union in Congress.[52]

"All of us who were later on the 'Memphis Committee' had been going around talking in favor of Atlantic Union at various meetings, and we decided one man in the United States Senate was worth a whole lot of us talking to civic clubs," said Orgill. "We were impressed with Estes' House record too, but I would say it was Atlantic Union that decided us to risk Mr. Crump's displeasure by coming out publicly for him. It certainly was, in my case. And, you know, at the time of his death, Estes was still working for Atlantic Union. He was a man who never broke faith."[53]

---

52. Telephone conversation, Lucius Burch, Memphis, Spring 1970.
53. Telephone conversation, Edmund Orgill, Memphis, Spring 1970.

Some time after Kefauver took his seat in the Senate, Orgill and Burch went to Washington, and the three of them drove to the Philadelphia home of former Associate Justice Owen Roberts, who had resigned from the Supreme Court to devote much of his time to promoting Atlantic Union. The four men agreed to form the Atlantic Union Committee, with Roberts as its first president.

Kefauver introduced a resolution calling on President Truman to invite the other six sponsors of NATO to meet with American representatives "in a federal convention" to explore the possibility of "free federal union." A surprisingly large percentage of his nineteen co-sponsors were of conservative persuasion, such as Walter George, Harry P. Cain of Washington, and Joseph McCarthy, and the next year he picked up others like Richard Nixon, John Stennis, and Humphrey.

Kefauver and thirty-four others—including Streit, Roberts, Orgill, Burch, and Kefauver's Aunt Charlotte Johns—called on Truman to urge his support of Atlantic Union. Truman declined to do so, but did say he could see nothing but good in the idea. But the State Department opposed the Atlantic Union Resolution before the Foreign Relations Committee, questioning "bold proposals for a radically new international organization." Kefauver, questioning Rusk and Hickerson, attacked the department's position sharply.

"I think the State Department is assuming the prerogative of speaking for the American people," he said. "If we had had this attitude before 1787, we never would have had a federal union" in the United States.[54]

Shortly thereafter on the Senate floor, Kefauver gave the State Department a full-fledged tongue-lashing, enjoyed by all and contributed to by some, saying that the department had "brought us measures which soon turned out to be only a stopgap, and which required a greater stopgap to prop it up."

"The answer of the State Department to every proposal for peace . . . is that it needs time to consider the proposal," said Kefauver. "My heaven, Mr. President, the one thing we do not need is time to consider! We need to utilize the brief time we have . . . to quit

54. AP story, *Nashville Tennessean*, Feb. 16, 1950; *Hearings Before a Subcommittee of the Committee on Foreign Relations, U.S. Senate, 81st Congress, 2nd Session, on Resolution Relative to the Revision of the United Nations charter, Atlantic Union, World Federation, etc.*, Feb. 15, 1950, p. 446.

drifting and start moving. . . . I am afraid the hydrogen bomb wears no wristwatch."

Opposing the alternative proposed by a number of liberal senators of developing the United Nations into a world federation, Kefauver saw Atlantic Union as a foil to Communist expansion.

"The greatest possible blow that could be dealt the forces of Kremlin Communism," he said, "would be the achievement of real unity, of real union among the forces of freedom. . . . If we are to reverse the trend of the cold war, it will require a reversal of thinking on the part of our officials who refuse to recognize the genius of this method, which is peculiarly American—the method of democratic federal union."[55]

A Gallup poll about this time showed a majority of Americans in favor of an exploratory Atlantic Union meeting, and shortly afterward the Canadian Senate adopted an Atlantic Union resolution. Kefauver also gained some European support in varying degrees from people like former Premier Paul Reynard of France, M. van Cauwelaert, president of the Belgian Chambre des Députés, and Henry Usborne of the British House of Commons. But nothing could be worked out with the State Department, despite a couple of meetings of department officials—including Secretary of State Dean Acheson the first time—with Kefauver and other members of Congress.

After a four-year hiatus—largely, Kefauver said, in the interest of final action on the European Defense Community—Kefauver and fourteen co-sponsors reintroduced the Atlantic Union Resolution in 1955. He was encouraged at receiving a letter from Clement Davies, leader of the British Liberal party, that he had initiated Atlantic Union action in Parliament; but about the same time he got a telephone call from Thruston B. Morton, assistant secretary of state, to the effect that Secretary John Foster Dulles—who had endorsed Atlantic Union in his earlier unsuccessful race for reelection to the Senate—now was afraid the Atlantic Union proposal might be detrimental to diplomatic relations with France and Germany.

"Thruston," Kefauver replied, "all progress that has been made in State Department affairs in Europe was during the pendency of our resolution. We held it up two years because, according to the State Department's views, the time was inopportune. No progress

55. *Congressional Record*, vol. 95, pt. 7, July 11, 1949, pp. 9210–14.

was made, and several diplomatic defeats were suffered. . . .
"I sincerely think Mr. Dulles is taking a very short-sighted view."[56]
But Dulles continued to oppose the move and, in a statement to
the Foreign Relations Committee, suggested that "a way be found
to hold the exploratory convention under less official auspices than
is now suggested." So Kefauver obtained congressional approval of
a different proposal: a conference of legislators from NATO nations,
the NATO Parliamentarians Conference. The first one, held in Paris,
was attended by 190 legislators from all NATO nations and resulted
in establishment of a permanent conference, to meet every year.

In 1957, Kefauver used this new organization to bypass the State
Department: he gained its unanimous approval for an Atlantic
Congress of delegates from fourteen NATO nations in 1959. He was
one of sixteen members of Congress among the 130 American delegates who attended the congress in London's grey old Church
House. The delegates were guests at a reception at St. James Palace,
and Queen Elizabeth II addressed the opening session in Westminster Hall.

"The Atlantic Community," she said, "is the first real effort to
give practical form to a growing desire of the people of this part of
the world to work more closely together for their mutual security
and benefit. . . . My hope is that, when you disperse, the peoples
of the Atlantic Community will be one step nearer to a practical system of cooperation."

Addressing the final plenary session, Kefauver said it had "become increasingly apparent during the formative years of NATO that
we should strengthen our political and economic ties . . . against
our genius and our integrity, to define our honest intentions in re-
alistic terms which will be understood by all people of good will."[57]

Americans among the 650 delegates returned home to press for
administration support of an officially sponsored meeting, as proposed in the Atlantic Union plan itself. Kefauver and four co-
sponsors offered the resolution in 1960, calling for the President to
name a commission of twenty citizens to participate in an Atlantic

56. A copy of Kefauver's note to Morton, in reply to the telephone call, is in
the Kefauver Collection.
57. The quotations from Queen Elizabeth and Kefauver at the congress were
taken from the final Report of the Atlantic Congress, supplied to me by Richard J.
Wallace, Washington, July 6, 1970, and subsequently returned to him.

Kefauver (second from right) goes over the tally sheet after he succeeded in attaching a jury trial amendment to the 1957 Civil Rights Bill, with (from left) Frank Church, Joseph O'Mahoney, Lyndon Johnson, and Richard Russell.

Kefauver attends a reception for delegates to the first Atlantic Congress at St. James Palace in London in 1959.

Union meeting under U.S. government auspices, but the Foreign Relations Committee rewrote it to provide for appointment by the Vice President and Speaker of the House and to specify that the delegates would not be speaking for the government. In this form, the State Department supported the resolution, and Vice President Nixon threw his influence behind it in the Senate. Kefauver interrupted his Tennessee race for reelection to fly back to Washington and participate in the debate.

He said: "The events of the Summit Conference have convinced me that the No. 1 goal of Khrushchev is to destroy the North Atlantic alliance. . . . The nature of the Communist effort for world domination has shifted to a considerable extent to the economic, political and propaganda fields. The democracies can meet that new challenge with success only if they have workable mechanisms for consultation."[58]

Congress approved the Atlantic Union at last, after eleven years, and the twenty-member American delegation—which included no members of Congress this time—attended the Atlantic Convention in Paris in January 1962. The convention adopted a set of proposals for transforming NATO into a confederation of nations, and its members called on their governments "urgently . . . to reinforce and develop the North Atlantic Treaty Organisation as a political centre," including an Atlantic Assembly with a permanent secretariat and a High Court of Justice to settle disputes among participating nations. Implementation of these objectives would require further action by the individual governments. The Atlantic Council of the United States, with Wallace as its director general, was maintained as an informational and promotional organization. American participation in such a program would require passage of considerable enabling legislation during the ensuing years.

But a year and a half after the Atlantic Convention, Estes Kefauver was dead, and the bold idea of extending the original American principles of federation to embrace the culturally related peoples of the Atlantic community had lost its most dedicated and determined spokesman. The tide of America's fears turned from Europe westward, and the United States, under Lyndon Johnson, plunged deeper and deeper into the morass of Southeast Asia.

58. *Congressional Record*, vol. 106, pt. 10, June 15, 1960, p. 12629.

Chapter 17

We Cannot Destroy Ideas Merely by Passing Laws

Kefauver was considered by many of his admirers to be a man well ahead of his time, but it would be more accurate to look upon him as a man whose heart was in the distant past. None of his approaches was new under the sun. He was steeped in history and the values he had acquired in childhood, and the essence of his originality was his effort to adapt almost forgotten ideas to the problems of a changed society.

His remarkable campaign technique was not greatly different from that of the original hero of the coonskin cap, Davy Crockett, in his races for Congress; its uniqueness was its application in the impersonal atmosphere of a heterogeneous, machine-oriented nation. The principle of Atlantic Union was lifted *in toto* from the original American Confederation of autonomous states, and his solution to the monopoly problem was essentially that of John Sherman and Theodore Roosevelt. He always resisted more radical schemes such as world government internationally and socialism domestically.

In no field was Kefauver more a man "behind his time" than in the area of civil rights, which was just beginning to emerge as a burning issue while he was in the House and intensified during his Senate career. In this field, too, Kefauver was considered well "ahead" of other Southerners in Congress, primarily because of his consistent opposition to the poll tax and his expressed attitude on the Senate filibuster.

But nationally the question of civil rights has been essentially one of Negro rights, and Kefauver was still the man to whom a Chicago girl friend wrote in 1934, "What in the world are you Southerners going to do when you have to mix with these 'jigaboos' in Heaven?"[1]

---

1. Undated letter, [name withheld], Chicago, to Estes Kefauver, Chattanooga, Kefauver Collection, Early Personal Correspondence.

As late as 1950, he said publicly, "I am opposed to abolishing segregation." It was not until the end of his first term in the Senate that he changed his views on segregation.

Harry Truman's advocacy of a full-fledged civil rights program in 1948, the year Kefauver was elected to the Senate, was largely responsible for the party revolt against him at the Democratic National Convention and the split-off of the Dixiecrats in that year's general election. Truman's surprise victory despite a double split in his party seemed to vindicate his vigorous sponsorship of civil rights legislation. Thus, Kefauver's entry into the Senate coincided with the beginning of a sustained Democratic offensive in the civil rights field that culminated in passage of the 1957 and 1960 Civil Rights Acts.

Kefauver got off on the wrong foot with his fellow-Southerners within less than two months, when the administration attempted to change Senate rules to make limitation of debate easier and curb the filibusters that had been mounted against civil rights legislation in the past. It is apparent from some of his later stands on filibusters that Kefauver still viewed the issue from the theoretical position of the House member who had written *A 20th Century Congress*: he said, "If the Senate cannot discharge its constitutional obligations, our system of democratic government may be doomed." But, in practical fact, he and Senator Claude Pepper of Florida were the only other Southerners to vote with Vice President Alben W. Barkley on a technical challenge to one of his rulings.

Two years later, however, Kefauver was welcomed by his Dixie brethren into a strategy conference in Walter George's office against administration efforts to push through legislation for a compulsory Fair Employment Practices Commission—and voted with them twice on the floor against invoking cloture (limitation of debate). He also opposed efforts to write FEPC and anti-segregation provisions into a proposed "home rule" charter for the District of Columbia.

In *A 20th Century Congress*, Kefauver had called the filibuster "prostitution of the vital deliberative function," and his public position was that he thought cloture ought to be effective as a last resort to force eventual action on a measure when only a small minority of senators opposed it. But the realities of senatorial power politics and his opposition to most civil rights legislation caused him to hedge on that principle when the chips were down—which was most of the time. Finally, when he himself was leading a filibuster against a communications satellite bill in 1963, his disapproval of the filibuster as a legislative device reduced itself to a question of whose ox was being gored.

Kefauver, in fact, cooperated with the other Southerners on civil rights matters more often than he opposed them, even participating actively in their strategy councils both in 1950 and in 1960. Their hatred of him as a "liberal renegade" was far less justified than were the doubts of the Northern liberals, which cost him important support in his 1952 and 1956 presidential races.

He was not so much a "liberal" as he was a populist and an individualist. He wrote in 1955: "I have never felt it necessary or proper to place myself in a catagory [*sic*] of general classification, particularly one capable of numerous and divergent interpretations and definitions. It is my belief that a man in public office need only conduct himself in a manner consistent with his genuine belief in what is good for his country, regardless of what the public may see fit to classify him as. So I will only refer you to my record with a parallel to Patrick Henry's statement on treason, 'If this be liberalism, let's make the most of it.' "[2]

The U.S. Supreme Court's decision outlawing school segregation in 1954 settled, in principle, the racial question for Kefauver. With something of relief, he gave up his lifelong opposition to integration and began to adjust his thinking to consideration of how the South could convert from segregation to integration with the least possible disturbance of its living patterns.

His acceptance of integration was expressed in an interview two years later: "I think I've lived and developed with the problem in the last two or three years. I think it's been apparent that segregation couldn't be justified. One of the considerations is our position in the world. The winds of freedom and equality have encompassed the world. . . . Coming originally from the South, it takes a little time to adjust to these realities."[3]

When Eisenhower's civil rights program hit Congress in 1956 and 1957, Kefauver demonstrated at the outset that his abandonment of the segregationist cause had not been a mere political ges-

2. Letter, Estes Kefauver, Washington, to Eric F. Goldman, Princeton, N.J., Feb. 16, 1955, Kefauver Collection, Ser. 1, Box 77.
3. Irwin Ross, *New York Post*, May 11, 1956.

ture in the interest of his presidential ambition. He refused to sign the "Southern Manifesto" criticizing the Supreme Court decision and was the only Southerner voting in favor of a rules change to make cloture easier (for once), a tactic aimed at heading off a Southern filibuster against the legislation. He stayed with the civil rights proponents through most of the bill's rocky progress through the Judiciary Committee—and then pulled another unexpected switch.

The measure called for creation of a Civil Rights Division in the Justice Department and an executive Civil Rights Commission to investigate charges that Negroes were being deprived of voting rights or subjected to economic pressure, and authorized court injunctions against obstruction or deprivation of voting rights. When the Southerners succeeded in pushing through a committee amendment to assure jury trials in criminal contempt cases under the bill, they suddenly found Kefauver on their side again.

The Southerners argued that those accused of contempt for denying Negroes voting rights should have a constitutional right to trial by jury, while the bill's supporters feared that Southern juries would not convict in such cases. When the bill got bottled up in Senator James O. Eastland's Judiciary Committee and its supporters resorted to the tactic of bringing its House-passed companion to the floor, Kefauver was one of three sponsors of a jury trial amendment, which was lacking in the House bill.

His amendment provided that a judge could still try a civil contempt case without a jury, but jury trials were guaranteed in voting rights cases where the attorney general brought criminal contempt cases. Kefauver said that, while a jury trial was dispensable in civil contempt cases, "without such a jury trial amendment, we will have sacrificed a great right—the right to trial by jury for criminal acts."[4]

The bill passed with the Kefauver amendment (though it was watered down later in conference committee), and Lyndon Johnson sent him a note the next day: "Your calm, reasonable approach was one of the major factors in bridging the gap between our people. Your descendants can always be rightfully proud of the role that you played."[5]

4. Estes Kefauver, *Nashville Tennessean*, July 28, 1957; *Congressional Record*, vol. 103, pt. 9, July 25, 1957, p. 12968.
5. Letter, Lyndon B. Johnson to Estes Kefauver, Nov. 24, 1958, Kefauver Collection, Ser. 1, Box 76.

PART III: *A Senator of the People, of the Nation*

As 1960 approached, with widespread unrest over integration in the South, only Kefauver's concern about the effect of his pro-civil rights reputation on his chances for reelection could have led him to join forces with his implacable enemy, Eastland, in support of a constitutional amendment to guarantee state control of public schools and thus, in effect, prevent integration in the South. The proposal was so blatantly transparent that he and Eastland were the only subcommittee members to vote in favor of reporting it to the full Judiciary Committee.

When, after considerable intricate maneuvering, Eisenhower's new seven-point civil rights program landed in the Senate Judiciary Committee early in 1960, its most controversial provision was a section authorizing federal courts to appoint voting referees to assure that Negroes were not deprived of the right to vote. Kefauver proposed an amendment to strike out the requirement that a Negro's appearance before a voting referee be *ex parte* (without cross-examination by opponents), and to add a provision to make the hearings public and permit the appearance at them of the voting registrar or his counsel. Southerners on the committee fell upon this amendment with delight, and it was adopted 7 to 6.

The margin of victory was Senator John Albert Carroll of Colorado, a consistent Kefauver ally but an ardent civil rights advocate, who voted for it simply because he trusted Kefauver. But when the bill hit the floor, he realized his mistake, as liberals raised a howl that to make hearings public and permit the accused voting officials to face their accusers would identify the accusers and open the way to intimidation of Negro voters. Carroll promptly moved that the Senate strike out the amendment, saying that he had misunderstood it, and thought Kefauver himself "didn't know what he was doing" when he wrote it.[6] But Kefauver knew exactly what he was doing, as he evidenced by voting (unsuccessfully) to retain his amendment against all of his usual allies, and what he said on the floor in its defense.

Without his amendment, he said, the bill would lead to secret hearings "for the benefit of one side only"—"star chamber" proceedings against which the Founding Fathers of the nation had

6. Frank van der Linden, *Nashville Banner*, March 31, 1960.

fought—and he added: "I think it is simply a matter of basic right that in any proceeding the person who is being accused . . . should be able to hear the dereliction of duty of which he is charged with being guilty."[7]

Kefauver recognized, as clearly as did Eastland and Paul Douglas, that adoption of his amendment would prevent many blacks who faced discrimination in their efforts to vote from complaining about it, for fear of retribution at the hands of the dominant whites. He knew that his position would contribute to setting up what Douglas called "an elaborate obstacle course which the disenfranchised Negro in the South must successfully run before he will be permitted to vote at all." His liberal friends were inclined to excuse him (and his fortuitous conservative allies to distrust him), especially since he voted for the bill at last, on the ground of his upcoming reelection race in a Southern state.

But Kefauver looked at the matter from a different viewpoint than either Eastland or Douglas, who were on opposite sides of the simple issue of a black citizen's right to vote without interference. In the effort to protect black voting rights, he did not want to abrogate the Anglo-Saxon legal tradition that a man accused of a criminal action—in this case, the voting official charged with discrimination —has a right to face his accuser in the interest of proving his innocence. He did not want to set, in America, a precedent for the totalitarian institution of the anonymous accuser who, through sheer spite, may ruin an innocent man without fear of any repercussion, because of his anonymity.

Kefauver would not have said so in the same phraseology, but his position was not far from that of Senator Sam Ervin of North Carolina—who admired Kefauver probably as little as any man in the Senate—who protested that the bill's approach would "single out certain groups of Americans on no basis but their race, and demand that they be given rights superior to those ever sought by or granted to any other Americans."[8] Kefauver stood in the civil rights fight in that peculiar, lonesome position that ranged him sometimes against the conservatives, sometimes against the liberals: be-

7. *Congressional Record*, vol. 106, pt. 6, March 31, 1960, p. 7027.
8. Ibid., 7043ff.

hind the immediate issue, he looked back to the founding principles of the American system, as he had been taught them.

Kefauver's attitude toward women, legislatively and personally, was as old-fashioned as his attitude toward racial segregation but without the benefit of a change of heart in mid-career. Had the women's liberation movements been in full swing during his lifetime, he probably would have been anathema to them.

Even though he could be called "liberal" only in comparison to his fellow-Southerners, his liberal colleagues in the Senate liked and admired him, as the Southerners did not. Similarly, he exhibited a very "Southern" conservatism and paternalism toward women and their role in society, yet few political candidates ever were able to command anything like the enthusiastic support from women that was mobilized in Kefauver's behalf.

After a friendship of nearly two decades, during which she worked for him and his projects as often and hard as any woman in the nation, Mrs. Martha Ragland of Nashville was still surprised at the revelation of "his conservative attitude toward women" in a 1959 conversation. At the time, Mrs. Ragland had been chosen as one of twelve women on the 130-member American delegation to the first Atlantic Congress in London, the fruit of Kefauver's efforts. Holding a degree in economics from Vanderbilt University, she was delighted to be appointed to the Economic Committee of the congress. But, at lunch with Kefauver in Washington just before the delegation left, she was somewhat startled when he told her he would like for her to be on the Spiritual and Cultural Committee.

"But Estes," she protested, "I've already been appointed to the Economic Committee, and that's what I want."

Kefauver let the matter drop, "but," she related later, "you could tell he didn't like it. He just didn't think of women as being competent to deal with things like economics."[9]

It is hard to visualize Estes Kefauver's wife ever developing a public career of own, as did Eleanor Roosevelt, or for that matter, any career outside the home. Nor is it easy to see Kefauver's wife in the role of an alter ego or shadow adviser, as exceptionally capable

9. Personal conversation, Martha Ragland, Nashville, Spring 1970.

wives of some public figures have been, especially during the early parts of their careers.

Nancy helped her husband in political campaigning, and very effectively, but always, except in emergencies, in a modest supporting role. He might consult her before taking a political step but only on the basis of personal considerations. When they were together among political friends she cooperated to make him the center of attention and remained quietly in the background unless he lapsed into silence.

Kefauver did not disapprove of other women, many of them very close friends like Mrs. Ragland, participating actively and in an executive capacity in business or political affairs. Indeed, he expected them to, when they helped him in his campaign. But, in those cases, their roles served his ends; and they were other men's wives.

In later years, especially after his 1952 presidential race, Nancy was able to spend more time on her art and taught her art class for a long time before his death. But to the mind of a traditionalist Southern male, art teaching was a permissible "feminine" occupation, and it was never a career for Nancy until after Kefauver died.

Kefauver's attitude in his extramarital amours—the extent of which was as often exaggerated on the one side as mistakenly disbelieved on the other—reflected the masculine values of the late 1920s and early 1930s, when he was a young man. This attitude was substantially adventitious and led, even though unwittingly, to occasional callousness. His failure to notify the most intimate of his women friends of his engagement to Nancy in early 1935 demonstrates a remarkable lack of sensitivity.

On his brief side trip to Paris in 1938, when Nancy was in Scotland, he met an Austrian woman, a refugee from the Nazis, and they had a thoroughly good time together. Apparently she did not know he was married, and she wrote to him several times after his return to the United States. His rather unfortunate behavior in her case exemplifies his casualness in such matters: he "recommended" her to one of his friends who was going to Paris, as someone who "loved me to death."

She rebuked him in a letter: "Should you, clever and well bred as you are, have overlooked the fact that I *am* a lady? . . . Dear Estes, as I continue to believe that you are a cultivated man, I can only think you . . . had just a little too much drinks. . . . I see you sit-

Estes and Nancy Kefauver sit together at a political rally during his 1948 campaign for the U.S. Senate.

Mrs. Eleanor Roosevelt appears with Kefauver to testify before the Senate Antitrust and Monopoly Subcommittee. Behind them is Senator John Carroll.

ting in your office and saying 'a woman must not think,' but, Dear, you really have made a *faux pas.*"[10]

With such a casual masculine attitude, it is hardly surprising that some of Kefauver's transitory feminine associates could not claim, with the Austrian, to be "ladies." One of his old friends and his wife, on a Florida jaunt with Kefauver, wondered how he happened to know such a disreputable person as a woman companion with whom he showed up. And Kefauver caused a brief local scandal in a European capital on one of his Interparliamentary Union tours by appearing at a society ball, escourting the city's best-known courtesan.[11]

Such rakish adventures, however, were occasional and opportunistic. His involvements were usually more personal and discriminating, and, as in his premarital affairs, the women usually adored him. But he did not respond in kind.

"He was so kind and considerate that a good many women thought he cared more for them than he did," said his secretary, Lucile Myers, who was called on sometimes to answer love letters to him because he did not want to bother. "But there was never really anyone but Nancy for him."[12] Henrietta O'Donaghue, his receptionist, who knew him even longer than Miss Myers, agreed that "the only woman he ever really loved was Nancy. She was everything to him."[13]

Kefauver, in fact, never became involved in one of those starcrossed passions that sometimes afflict great men. He enjoyed, and perhaps needed, women's admiration—their adoration, even. Nancy's theory was that he was able to relax with women as he could not otherwise. Certainly he wasted no time in finding intimate feminine companionship on occasions when she was absent for a while. In addition to the Austrian with whom he dallied on his side trip to Paris while Nancy was in Scotland in 1938, his correspondence discloses that he became involved with at least one woman in the States while she was gone and apparently met this woman several times in different Southern cities. Their correspon-

10. Letter, [name withheld], Paris, to Estes Kefauver, Chattanooga, Sept. 15, 1938, Kefauver Collection, Early Personal Correspondence.

11. Personal conversations, Noble C. Caudill, Hendersonville, Tenn., Autumn 1970, and Bernard Fensterwald Jr., Washington, May 15, 1970.

12. Personal conversation, Lucile Myers, Washington, May 14, 1970.

13. Personal communication, Carol Harford, Washington, Oct. 17, 1970.

dence, at least, continued beyond Nancy's return. In subsequent years, there was too much talk from too many different people about his involvement with different women not to have had some basis in fact.

Nancy knew about the most blatant of his peccadilloes and sometimes was as caustic about them as any wife. She even interfered on at least one occasion: a beautiful young newcomer to his staff was separated from it abruptly and found a position in Europe.[14] But the occasional rumors that his marriage was in trouble were no more than gossip. Carol Harford, Nancy's secretary in whom she confided greatly after Kefauver's death, said that, "being Nancy, she of course handled 'the situations' well—would invite the gal of the moment over to dinner or include her in some social function they were having."[15] Kefauver was very dependent on the stability of his marriage, and Nancy was as near an ideal mate for him as he could have found. On his long trips away from home, an evening rarely passed that he did not telephone Nancy, even though an hour later he might be with some other woman, his deep, soft voice dripping with smooth Southern honey.

The claim by Bobby Baker, former aide to Lyndon Johnson, in a 1978 *Playboy* article that Kefauver often was "bribed with women" on legislative matters does not ring true. Baker cites hearsay as a major source of his claim; his statement that he procured women for Kefauver could be true, as at least one Kefauver committee staffer said he was called on occasionally to do the same thing when they were in a strange city. But that is an entirely different matter from Kefauver trading legislative action for sexual favors, an act totally out of character for him. The attitudes of Kefauver's generation were such that there was no correspondence between the morality of consorting with women of questionable character and the ethics of one's conduct in his profession, whether law or government; they were different areas of personal values. And Baker, who served a prison term for influence peddling, was a protege of Lyndon Johnson, no lover of Kefauver.[16] The last word in the matter

14. Personal conversations, Nat Caldwell, Nashville, Spring 1971, and Lois Laycook, Nashville, Nov. 6, 1978.
15. Personal communication, Carol Harford, Washington, Oct. 17, 1970.
16. AP and UPI stories, Chicago and Dallas, May 2, 1978. Both my own personal acquaintance with Kefauver and my usually frank and revealing interviews

may be Nancy's, who said once when she was asked if Kefauver was difficult to live with, "Only that his ideals and principles were so high it was hard to live up to them."[17]

Kefauver's conservative double standard was reflected legislatively in 1950, when he and four other senators offered a substitute for a proposed constitutional amendment guaranteeing equal rights for women. The amendment, which had been floating around since three years after women gained the right to vote, stated simply that "equality of rights under the law shall not be denied or abridged by the United States or by any state on account of sex." Kefauver's substitute proposed setting up a commission on the legal status of women to study discrimination against women and recommend laws to eliminate it.

Kefauver said a constitutional amendment was not needed, because "women are clearly 'persons' in the constitutional sense" and such an amendment "would be destructive of the laws which have been passed for the benefit of women." He said the amendment would nullify laws against rape and while slavery, confuse laws affecting family status and property rights, and require drafting women into the armed forces on the same basis as men.

Senator Margaret Chase Smith of Maine, who rarely spoke in the Senate and was not one of the amendment's thirty-three sponsors, took the floor to argue eloquently for it, saying it should be adopted even if it meant that "women must give up all their feminine privileges." The two of them debated the issue, not only on the Senate floor but a few days later via International News Service, and their differences were summed up more precisely in the newspaper debate.

"I think it is high time that we stopped thinking of women as being second class citizens—as people with less qualifications and second in priority," said Mrs. Smith. "I say protective legislation can be written for all people—men and children as well as women."

---

with several of his more intimate associates convince me that, whereas Kefauver was not above brief and causal involvement with women, Lucile Myers' statement in a letter to me May 24, 1978, is completely true: "There was no way Estes could have been persuaded to accept a bribe and he certainly had no need of Bobby Baker as a procurer."

17. Letter, Dorothy Holt to Lucile Myers, May 3, 1978, enclosed in a personal communication from Miss Myers, Washington, May 24, 1978.

"The Great Creator intended to augment, supplement and complement man with woman and woman with man," said Kefauver. "I think women should have equal status with men where the God-made differences, sound customs and contrary wishes of women are not in question."[18]

Despite his arguments, Kefauver voted for the equal rights amendment (he was able to gain only eighteen votes for his substitute), but by then it had been modified to provide that it would not impair any existing or subsequent rights, benefits, or exemptions conferred on women by law. In his Senate argument against the amendment, Kefauver conceded that one area in which it was "clear that no distinctions should be made" between men and women was in the right to vote. But his general attitude was such that one can but wonder what his position would have been in debate on the 19th Amendment—if he might not have argued in such a case that denial of women's right to vote was one of those "sound customs" that justified exceptions to equal status.[19]

As for the general right to vote, it was of passionate concern to him, as was to be expected in a man who evoked "the will of the people" so consistently against his political opposition. He naturally zeroed in on the indirect manner in which presidential nominees and Presidents are chosen, and—departing from his usual commitment to original constitutional principles—he followed in the footsteps of George Norris in advocating both nationwide presidential primaries and abolition of the electoral college. Calling the convention system of nominating presidential candidates "a mockery of our democratic processes," Kefauver tried for several years, beginning in 1952, to gain approval of legislation for presidential primaries in every state, at first through agreement between the U.S. attorney general and the states but subsequently through a constitutional amendment.

Major alternatives for altering the electoral college system put forward during Kefauver's Senate tenure were: (1) by Senator Henry Cabot Lodge of Massachusetts and Representative Ed Gossett of Texas, to substitute "federal votes" proportionate to the popular vote in each state for the all-or-none electoral votes; (2) by Senator

18. INS story, *Nashville Tennessean*, Jan. 30, 1950.
19. *Nashville Tennessean*, Jan. 24, 1950.

Karl Mundt of South Dakota and Representative Frederic R. Coudert of New York, to require states to use the district plan, in which a single elector was chosen in each district, similar to the election of representatives; and (3) various efforts to abolish the electoral system altogether and elect the President by direct popular vote. Kefauver preferred the Lodge-Gossett approach and supported it actively during the several successive years it was offered.

"The Founding Fathers did not anticipate political parties," he said in a floor speech in 1948, when he was still in the House. "They intended that the people of a state would elect a superior group of people known as electors, and that these electors would use their independent judgment in selecting a President. . . . There is no logic or wisdom in holding onto a system which does not represent what the people, by common practice, have decided should be done."[20]

After the Lodge-Gossett plan had had several unsuccessful runs, Kefauver and Senator Price Daniel of Texas in 1955 introduced a bill to submit a constitutional amendment containing the basic features of the Lodge-Gossett proposal. Electoral votes would be divided in each state proportionately to the popular vote, to three decimal points. The major opponent of the Kefauver-Daniel plan, when it came up for floor action in 1956, was Senator John Kennedy, who expressed himself as against any change at all in the electoral system, lest it disturb the balance of power in the "whole solar system of government." Kefauver was absent for most of the debate, on the primary campaign trail, and during his absence Senator William Langer tried unsuccessfully to amend the plan to provide for a national presidential primary.

Kennedy opposed this, too, as an impractical means of choosing presidential nominees. In support of his position, Langer cited what had happened to Kefauver at the 1952 Democratic National Convention, but Kennedy retorted shortly, "In my opinion, the convention in 1952 made the right choice."[21]

Kennedy obviously had the votes, so Daniel formed a coalition with the conservatives and was joined by Mundt and Senator Strom Thurmond of South Carolina in offering an amendment to give states a choice between the Kefauver-Daniel plan and the Mundt-

20. *Congressional Record*, vol. 94, pt. 3, March 16, 1948, p. 2949.
21. Ibid., vol. 102, pt. 4, March 21, 1956, p. 5237.

Coudert district plan. This brought Paul Douglas into the act on Kennedy's side, with the protest that the compromise "would tend to weaken the liberal elements" in both political parties.

Whether or not Kefauver would have gone along with Daniel's coalition, had he been present, the whole argument points up a basic difference between him and his liberal friends in Congress. For, aside from Douglas' opposition to the compromise, a number of organizations including the NAACP, American Jewish Congress, and several labor unions, telegraphed all senators in opposition to the Kefauver-Daniel proposal itself, charging that a vote for it would be "a vote against civil liberties." And the vote by which the whole business was dismissed saw almost all Southern Democrats and conservative Republicans ranged on Kefauver's side and most of the bipartisan liberal bloc against him.[22]

Kefauver's argument in favor of his plan, while he was still there, was that he advocated "getting as close as possible to the popular vote system," and Daniel remarked to Douglas that "it would seem to me that the liberal elements of both parties would want to see more of the people express themselves at the polls." But the political support on which the liberals depended rested in an alliance of organized minorities, concentrated largely in the big cities of pivotal states. Much of the ambivalence of Kefauver's relations with the liberals stemmed from the fact that they admired him personally and philosophically, but were often at odds with him in terms of practical politics.

Kefauver's record on civil rights could not be considered anything better than spotty, whether looked on from the liberal or the conservative viewpoint, but there was never any wavering in his stand on civil liberties, as distinguished, somewhat arbitrarily, from "civil rights" in the American political lexicon. In fact, it was his concern for civil liberties, the legal rights of the accused, that conflicted with the liberal concern for civil rights—the right of blacks to vote without intimidation—during consideration of the 1960 Civil Rights Act.

Kefauver's first major activity in this field was his long, hard but unsuccessful fight, along with a handful of colleagues, against the

22. Irwin Ross, *New York Post*, May 11, 1956.

McCarran Act in 1950. The measure, a reaction to the cold war tensions of that period, was a potpourri of anti-Communist provisions, including requirements for registration of Communist-front organizations and their officers, authorization for the Justice Department to detain or deport "subversives," and several similar features.

President Truman spoke out against the omnibus measure in a special message to Congress, calling it "so broad and vague . . . as to endanger the freedoms of speech, press and assembly protected by the First Amendment."[23] When it hit the Senate floor, Kefauver, representing a small group of administration senators, offered a series of amendments to restrict some of the bill's provisions, which he said were so broad they could sweep up the innocent with the guilty. The only one accepted specified that proposing a constitutional amendment would not constitute conspiracy to set up a totalitarian government!

The Senate similarly beat down a milder substitute sponsored by Kefauver and Senator Harley Kilgore of West Virginia with administration support. In the final debate on the McCarran bill, Kefauver charged it would permit prosecution of individuals on flimsy evidence, allow conviction of innocent persons on charges of passing confidential information when they knew nothing about it, and ignore due process of law.

"Were it not for the insidious threat of Communism, and were we not in the very shadow of World War III, no thinking American would ever consider asking Congress to enact laws to control the thoughts of any of its citizens," said Kefauver. "I do not think we should follow the philosophy of voting for a bill, regardless of whether it meets constitutional requirements, regardless of whether it is sound, just because it is called anti-Communist."[24]

Kefauver was one of only seven senators to vote against the bill. When a conference committee adjusted differences between the House and Senate versions, Kefauver fought it too, and again tried unsuccessfully to substitute a milder measure of his own.

"America is never going to find security in oppression," he said. "America is going to find strength only in free men who have the right to speak and think as they wish."[25]

23. *Congressional Record*, vol. 96, pt. 11, Sept. 22, 1950, pp. 15629–32.
24. Ibid., Sept. 12, 1950, p. 14596.
25. Ibid., Sept. 22, 1950, p. 15107.

Again, he was one of seven senators to vote against the conference version. When Truman vetoed the bill, Kefauver resorted to an all-night filibuster, along with Hubert Humphrey, Paul Douglas, Herbert Lehman, William Langer, and James E. Murray of Montana (they denied it was a filibuster, calling it an effort to give the people a chance to read the veto message and contact their senators). He was one of ten senators who voted to uphold the veto.[26]

Kefauver was philosophically at home in the realm of civil liberties, and his position was unequivocal and wholly consistent. Although he was not in a position to take a major role in the fight against the phenomenon of "McCarthyism" that hit the country that same year, he was one of the first members of Congress to speak out against it.

When a foreign relations subcommittee began investigating charges by Senator Joseph R. McCarthy of Wisconsin that a large number of State Department employees were members of the Communist party, Kefauver said McCarthy's "reckless accusations of disloyalty" gave Communist propagandists the opportunity to say that "America, the leading exponent of democracy, is unable to handle elementary problems of government at home."[27]

Kefauver itched to get into the developing fight against McCarthy, and when a furore erupted over McCarthy's charges early in 1954 that the Army sought to "blackmail" the Permanent Investigations Subcommittee, of which he had become chairman, into halting an inquiry into Communist influence in the Army, Kefauver tried repeatedly to get the Armed Services Committee, of which he was a member, to launch an investigation into the dispute. Senator John L. McClellan of Arkansas pointed out to him that the Armed Services Committee might have jurisdiction over "those aspects relating to the Army" but none at all over "the staff of the investigating subcommittee."[28] Kefauver had to satisfy himself with speaking out against McCarthy on the floor and voting with the majority when the Senate censured McCarthy for his conduct of his investigations.

The most courageous stand of Kefauver's career in the area of civil liberties was his lone vote against a Communist control bill in

26. W. McNeil Lowry, *Progressive*, June 1951.
27. *Nashville Banner*, March 29, 1950.
28. AP story, *Nashville Tennessean*, April 2, 1954.

that same year, 1954. It was, he wrote William Benton, publisher of the *Encyclopaedia Britannica*, five years later, "the case in my career in which I take the most satisfaction."[29]

The vote came two weeks after he had weathered a fight for renomination against Pat Sutton, who had patterned his campaign largely on McCarthy-type tactics and had raised the spectre of Communism all over Tennessee. Kefauver's heavy majority had discredited Sutton's strategy, but Kefauver still faced the threat of opposition in the general election from Ray Jenkins, whose reputation had skyrocketed as a consequence of his service as special counsel in the McCarthy hearings.

The Communist control bill was born in an atmosphere of political partisanship: Democrats were smarting under Republican charges of "softness" toward Communism, which some Republicans thought were largely responsible for the election of Eisenhower and a Republican-controlled Congress in 1952. The Democrats were looking for some way to turn the tables on their critics.

A number of prior efforts had been made in Congress to "control" the Communist party, which, in contrast to other political parties, advocated the overthrow of the existing democratic government by revolutionary means. The McCarran Act of 1950 was only the last of several measures that had passed Congress to that effect. But none of these earlier laws had made it a criminal offense just to be a member of the Communist party, nor had they outlawed the party outright.

The original 1954 bill, introduced by Senator John Marshall Butler of Maryland, a Republican, simply required registration and annual reports of "Communist-infiltrated" organizations, in addition to the "Communist-action" and "Communist-front" organizations specified by the McCarran Act, and prohibited federal employment of their members. The bill was directed at allegedly Communist-infiltrated labor unions.

When the bill reached the Senate floor, the Democrats "toughened" it—according to some Washington news analysts, as an object lesson to the Republicans. Humphrey offered an amendment that made membership in the Communist party a criminal offense,

29. Letter, Estes Kefauver, Washington, to William Benton, New York, Dec. 23, 1958, Kefauver Collection, Ser. 1, Box 77.

and it was adopted 85 to 1, with only Lehman voting against it. It was an election year, in which the Democrats were seeking to recapture control of Congress, and no one wanted to vote against an "anti-Communist" bill.

During all this time, Kefauver was in Tennessee, campaigning. Before he got back, the House took note of Attorney General Herbert Brownell's objection that making it a crime to belong to the Communist party would simply send the Communist movement underground, and the House modified the bill. But as soon as the measure returned to the Senate for concurrence, Humphrey got his amendment tacked back on it, over almost solid Republican opposition.

Kefauver, although back in Washington by this time, was not on the floor at the time the Humphrey amendment was readopted. "Instinctively" suspicious of it, according to Dick Wallace, he was paired against it and, meanwhile, put his staff to work on research to determine what the actual effect of the Communist control bill would be.

During this interim, one of Kefauver's more influential Tennessee supporters telephoned him and urged him to speak for the bill and vote for it, thus refuting the "soft on Communism" charges that had been hurled at him throughout the primary campaign. Well, Kefauver opined, he did not know: it seemed to him that the bill contained "some elements of thought suppression."[30] His old schoolmate, Jack Doughty, was in Washington that day, and the two men had lunch together.

"What do *you* think I ought to do, Jack?" asked Kefauver.

"It doesn't make any difference what I think, Kef," replied Doughty with a smile. "You're going to do it your own way."[31]

When he returned to the floor that afternoon, some of the Democratic party leaders urged him at least to keep his mouth shut about the bill, lest he damage the "liberal image" of some of his friends such as Humphrey and Douglas by contrast. But Kefauver just mumbled a reply about it being "a bad bill" that he would have to oppose.

"We do not have to abdicate the Constitution to catch a few Com-

30. Personal conversation, Richard J. Wallace, Washington, May 13, 1970.
31. Personal conversation, John H. Doughty, Knoxville, Autumn 1970.

munists," he said on the floor. "To do so would please the Communists greatly.

"We cannot destroy ideas merely by passing laws. I think it is always true that if we try to outlaw an idea, try to outlaw the way in which a man thinks, we are going to make a martyr of him and it will result in many vocal people coming to his defense. This would create real disunity in the nation. Communism thrives upon disunity. . . ."[32]

The Senate vote to concur in the bill, with the Humphrey amendment attached, was 81 to 1. The dissenter was Kefauver. Shortly after the vote, the Tennessee supporter telephoned again to urge that Kefauver support the bill. Wallace told him he was a little too late: the bill had just passed with but one dissenting vote, and "Estes was the one."

"My God!" the man moaned. "That really finishes Estes!"[33]

Later that day, Kefauver was telephoned from Nashville for a newspaper comment.

"Charlie, you fix me up," he said. "And take care of me. A lot of people are going to be awfully mad at me about this vote."[34]

Kefauver went home that evening and told Nancy they might be moving back to Tennessee after the first of the year because he did not know whether the voters would return him to the Senate after that vote.

"But I did what I thought was right," he said soberly. "I don't see how I could have done anything else."[35]

When the bill went to a second conference committee, it was toned down once more. Instead of making membership in the Communist party a crime, it substituted penalties for membership in "Communist-action" organizations as defined under the McCarran Act.

Both houses approved the conference report this time. Kefauver voted for the final version of the bill, though he expressed grave misgivings about it.

Because Kefauver's major legislative battle on the civil liberties issue occurred during the Communist scare of the 1950s, he was

32. *Congressional Record*, vol. 100, pt. 12, Aug. 19, 1954, p. 15107.
33. Personal conversation, Richard J. Wallace, Washington, May 13, 1970.
34. Telephone conversation, Estes Kefauver, Washington, Aug. 19, 1954.
35. Personal communication, Carol V. Harford, Washington, Aug. 29, 1970.

subjected to a great deal of criticism for his stands. But he was strongly anti-Communist and expressed his anti-Communism firmly in the positions he took on foreign affairs. Nor was he amenable to a change of opinion on Communism, as he was in the case of segregation, for example, for he considered Communism a form of totalitarianism as hostile to the American concept of government as Nazism and Fascism.

But the problem of *legislating* against home-grown Communists was complicated for him by the recognition that the United States had served historically as a battleground for diverse theories and philosophies, by his concern for constitutional guarantees, and by the conviction that totalitarianism could not be contained effectively by totalitarian methods.

Chapter 18

Out of His Mind and Out of His Heart

It was a typical August day in Washington. The superheated air shimmered above the glaring sidewalks. The newspapers were concerned with a deadlock in the Kaesong talks in Korea and speculation that Frank Sinatra and Ava Gardner might get married in Mexico, and the twenty-ninth instalment of Estes Kefauver's new book, *Crime in America*, was being serialized.

Kefauver himself had converted the Senate Chamber into something of a school room that Tuesday afternoon in 1951. A blackboard was set up by the speaker's rostrum, and the tall, bespectacled Tennessee senator stood beside it with chalk in one hand and a pointer in the other.

The role was one long familiar to him on the other side of the Capitol: Kefauver was breaking a lance against monopoly. An effort was afoot to change the Robinson-Patman Act, which prohibits discriminatory prices to retailers, and Kefauver had an amendment. The blackboard was scrawled with diagrams showing how the proposed change would permit suppliers to drive small, independent retailers out of business by favoring chain stores in pricing. The dozen or so senators present listened, more or less—some slouched sidewise in their chairs, some scribbling at their desks, some riffling through newspapers—as Kefauver tapped his blackboard with the pointer and drawled, "All of us want competition to the greatest possible extent, but we do not wish to have the kind of competition which destroys competition or creates monopoly . . ." and on and on, in his deadly monotone.

One reporter wrote of him: "For Estes Kefauver to rise and address the Senate during a legislative debate is the signal for reporters in the press gallery to rise and depart. Kefauver is a mumbler."[1]

1. Cater, "Estes Kefauver, Most Willing of the Willing."

And yet, for all of his mumbling, a colleague said of him: "Kefauver gets up with that slow drawl of his, talking so softly you can hardly hear him. You lean forward to catch his words, and you discover he's quietly beating your brains out."[2]

In this particular case, Kefauver lost his fight in the Senate but was saved by the House, which refused to pass the bill. His amendment, which would actually have strengthened the Robinson-Patman Act, was the beginning of an unsuccessful Senate fight for Kefauver over a period of years to modify a Supreme Court interpretation that a seller's reduction in prices "in good faith to meet an equally low price by a competitor" was an absolute defense against monopolistic price discrimination.

Chance, if not destiny, firmly balked Kefauver's persistent efforts to get on the Foreign Relations Committee, where he could promote more effectively his ideas for changes in American international relations and foreign policy. Chance, if not destiny, marked him for a lonelier course, on which he was able to bring to public light one of the most insidious threats to individual liberty in twentieth-century America: the spread of monopoly in the nation's economy.

Although he had been on the House Judiciary Committee for nearly a decade and it is considered one of the choicest assignments in either House, Kefauver did not list Judiciary as one of his preferences when he entered the Senate in 1949. But he was not, apparently, too happy with the assignments he received: Interstate and Foreign Commerce, his third choice; Armed Services, his fifth; and District of Columbia, for which he had not asked at all.

In mid-1949, Senator J. Howard McGrath (whom Kefauver introduced to an audience once in one of his tongue-twisted moments, when McGrath was one of his top presidential campaign officials, as "J. Hoover McGuire") resigned from the Senate to accept appointment as U.S. attorney general. Kefauver seized the opportunity, asked for the Judiciary Committee instead of Interstate and Foreign Commerce, and got it.

As a member of the Interstate and Foreign Commerce Committee, Kefauver already had plunged into one of his major antitrust fights: 1949 bills to provide a two-year moratorium on prosecutions

2. Anderson and Blumenthal, *The Kefauver Story*, 88.

of antitrust violations under the complex basing point system. Under such a system, the price to the consumer equals the factory price plus transportation costs from one or more "basing points," no matter what the actual origin of the goods shipped. Critics of the system contended that such uniform prices could be explained only by collusion among manufacturers to avoid price competition, and the U.S. Supreme Court ruled in 1948 that "concerted maintenance of the basing point delivered price system is an unfair method of competition."

During Senate consideration of the moratorium measure, Senator Joseph O'Mahoney substituted for it permanent legislation to legalize certain basing point practices, but Kefauver, Paul Douglas, and Russell Long of Louisiana succeeded in getting approval of two Kefauver amendments that banned such practices when their substantial effect would be to lessen competition. But when the basing point bill went to the House, the Judiciary Committee struck out the Kefauver amendments.

The move split the Tennessee delegation wide open. Representative Joe L. Evins of Tennessee tried to get the bill sent back to committee for further study, while two other Tennessee members, Representatives J.B. Frazier Jr. and John Jennings Jr., members of the Judiciary Committee, defended the committee's action. Kefauver's name was batted back and forth like a catchword in the debate that ensued.[3]

At last, Representative John Albert Carroll of Colorado sponsored the Kefauver amendments under his own name, and they were adopted and the bill passed. But now they were the "Carroll amendments" in the House, so a conference committee had to be named—and it threw out both Carroll amendments and one Kefauver amendment.

Kefauver and Long launched a floor attack on the conference committee action, Kefauver charging that supporters of the bill "want to change and emasculate the antitrust laws of the nation. They cannot do that by frontal attack. A bill to take away the protection of any of those antitrust laws would be defeated. But they try to do it by indirection, by writing it into this basing point bill."[4]

3. J. Lacey Reynolds, *Nashville Tennessean*, July 10, 1949.
4. *Congressional Record*, vol. 95, pt. 9, Aug. 12, 1949, p. 11336.

The Senate rejected the conference committee report, but a new conference committee took essentially the same action, and the House adopted its report. When it reached the Senate floor, Kefauver argued in vain against it: "Behind this bill lies the fundamental question of power—the power to determine . . . 'which businesses grow and which do not, which states and regions prosper and which do not.' If Senate bill 1008 becomes the law of the land, that power will be placed squarely in the hands of a few great industrial corporations and a few great railroad systems, tied together by financial interests centering in Wall Street."[5]

Although the Senate adopted the conference committee report, President Truman vetoed it. Some of Kefauver's colleagues credited his long, bitter-end fight against the bill for the fact that no effort was made to override the veto.[6]

Just before Kefauver's appointment to the Senate Judiciary Committee, the House passed a companion bill to one Kefauver and O'Mahoney had sponsored in the Senate: the familiar measure Kefauver had tried repeatedly to get passed in the House, to close a loophole in the Clayton Anti-Trust Act of 1914 by prohibiting acquisition by one firm of the assets of another "if the effect would be substantially to lessen competition or tend to create a monopoly." The House bill was sponsored by Representative Emanuel Celler, and Kefauver became a Judiciary Committee member just in time to participate in hearings on, essentially, his own bill.

When the bill reached the Senate floor late the next year, Kefauver, taking the floor in its behalf, quoted a Republican—Abraham Lincoln: "As a result of the war, corporations have been enthroned, and an era of corruption in high places will follow, and the money power in this country will endeavor to prolong its reign by working upon the prejudices of the people until the wealth is aggregated in a few hands and the country is destroyed."[7]

"Shall we permit the economy of this country to gravitate into

5. Ibid., vol. 96, pt. 6, June 1, 1950, p. 7910.
6. *Nashville Tennessean*, June 1, 1950.
7. Undated statement for Judiciary Subcommittee No. 2, in support of House Resolution 515 to amend the Clayton Act, Kefauver Collection, Ser. 10, Box 1, and Ser. 1, Box 91. From this statement by Lincoln was taken the title of Kefauver's third and last book, published posthumously: *In a Few Hands: Monopoly Power in America* (Baltimore: Penguin Books, 1965). See *Congressional Record*, vol. 96, pt. 12, Dec. 12, 1950, p. 16450.

the hands of a few corporations?" Kefauver asked. ". . . The increasing concentration of economic power is dooming free enterprise.
. . . the people are losing power to direct their own economic welfare. When they lose the power to direct their economic welfare, they also lose the means to direct their political future.

"We are rapidly reaching the point in this country where the public steps in to take over when concentration and monopoly gain too much power. The taking over by the public through its government always . . . either results in a fascist state, or the nationalization of industries and thereafter a socialist or communist state."[8]

The bill passed with some minor amendments, to which the House agreed the following day. Truman signed it into law in the waning days of 1950 with the comment: "Much of the concentration of economic power which has taken place since 1914 has been due to this gap in the law. The closing of the gap is an important step in preventing the growth of monopolies and thus assuring the survival and health of free competitive enterprise."[9]

The Kefauver-Celler bill was characterized by John Blair, a recognized authority on monopoly, as one of the only two major antitrust measures (both bearing Kefauver's name) enacted since the Clayton Act in 1914.[10]

During the same year, Kefauver was involved in a legislative battle against a bill to exempt independent natural gas producers from regulation by the Federal Power Commission, a power conferred on the FPC by Congress in 1938 to prevent excessive gas rates to consumers. The 1950 bill was sponsored by Senator Robert S. Kerr of Oklahoma, who, two years later, was to be one of Kefauver's presidential opponents.

"Regulation can only be justified in a particular industry to insure that the price will be held down to a reasonable level," Kefauver said in opposition to Kerr's bill. ". . . We maintain that there is not sufficient competition. We feel that the consumer will not be protected by the present competition, in the absence of regulation."[11]

Kefauver tried unsuccessfully to amend the bill to leave subject to FPC regulation those companies selling annually more than

8. *Congressional Record*, vol. 96, pt. 12, Dec. 12, 1950, pp. 16450, 16452.
9. *Congressional Quarterly Almanac*, vol. VI, 1950, p. 661.
10. Personal conversation, John M. Blair, Washington, May 14, 1970.
11. *Congressional Record*, vol. 96, pt. 3, March 17, 1950, p. 3588.

$250,000 worth of natural gas or producing annually more than two billion cubic feet. He said this would retain the FPC's right to regulate thirty-seven companies that, "by virtue of their large size, are in a monopolistic position and can raise prices exorbitantly." Although both houses passed Kerr's bill, once again Truman came to the rescue and prevented its enactment with a veto.

The major portion of Kefauver's antitrust activity was concerned immediately with the effect of monopolistic trends on small business and industry, rather than with their direct effect on the consumer. His legislative activity was directed toward preservation of the traditional American concept of independent, competitive enterprise against economic forces tending to centralize production and power and to freeze out smaller operators.

His struggle against monopoly caused columnist Marquis W. Childs to call him in 1952 a man of "brains and convictions and ability," who had "won the implacable hostility of some of the most powerful interests in this country."

"Here in Washington," wrote Childs, "the cynical explanation for his success is his great build-up as a crime buster on the nation's television screens. But the real reason may be the sheer novelty of a man who is saying something out of his mind and out of his heart about the basic issue of power and its use and abuse in mid-century America."[12]

Kefauver's acquisition in 1956 of the chairmanship of the Senate's Antitrust and Monopoly Subcommittee put him in the best possible strategic position to pursue his antitrust fights effectively. But he was not awarded the chairmanship by his senior colleagues in appreciative recognition of his many contributions to the battle against monopolistic trends.

In fact, had the Democrats controlled Congress when the subcommittee was formed, Kefauver might not have even been on it, for the senior Democrats on the Judiciary Committee were not famous for a hatred of big business. But, since it was a Republican Congress and Kefauver's friend, Bill Langer, an active antitruster himself, was Judiciary Committee chairman, Kefauver was appointed one of the subcommittee's two Democratic members.

12. Marquis W. Childs, column, *Nashville Tennessean*, May 11, 1952.

When the Democrats regained control of Congress two years later, it was assumed generally that Kefauver would head the subcommittee because the seniority of the other subcommittee Democrat, Harley Kilgore, elevated him to the chairmanship of the full Judiciary Committee. In anticipation of the appointment, Kefauver made public early in 1955 a full outline of his plans for probing monopoly activity.[13] But, since Kilgore, reportedly carrying out the wishes of the Democratic leadership, assumed the subcommittee chairmanship himself, it did not devolve upon Kefauver until Kilgore's death early in 1956.[14]

Senator James O. Eastland, the new Judiciary Committee chairman, despite his enmity toward Kefauver, made no immediate effort to deprive Kefauver of the subcommittee chairmanship in the face of the seniority tradition. Kefauver was duly appointed, but he was in the midst of a furious presidential campaign, and in the interim, O'Mahoney took over as acting chairman.

Kefauver and O'Mahoney talked over the arrangement in advance, and Kefauver quoted O'Mahoney as saying that "he was willing to assume the position of acting chairman until after the election was over, at which time I would be in a position to assume the responsibility of the chairmanship." Kefauver was "quite surprised and shocked," then, to learn just before Christmas 1956 that O'Mahoney expected to retain the chairmanship. O'Mahoney, in fact, had told friends privately that Eastland had assured him he would keep the chairmanship, and O'Mahoney had given instructions on that basis to subcommittee staff members. Kefauver at once wrote Eastland to protest, stressing his seniority rights.[15]

Eastland brought the matter up a few days later at the Texas home of Lyndon Johnson, where certain party leaders were gathered at the meeting in which it was decided that Kefauver was to be denied his claim to the Foreign Relations Committee vacancy. Since his claim to the Foreign Relations post also was based on seniority,

13. Letter, Estes Kefauver to Harley Kilgore, Jan. 19, 1955, Kefauver Collection, Ser. 1, Box 76.
14. Lois Laycook, *Nashville Tennessean*, Feb. 29, 1956; Drew Pearson, in a column that appeared in the *Farmers Union Herald* Oct. 24, 1955, wrote that Lyndon Johnson was opposed to Kefauver's getting the subcommittee chairmanship and was behind Kilgore's action.
15. Letter, Estes Kefauver to James O. Eastland, Dec. 20, 1956, Kefauver Collection, Ser. 1, Box 76.

it was agreed that depriving him of his clear right to the Antitrust and Monopoly Subcommittee chairmanship at the same time would be too blatantly discriminatory. Yet Eastland procrastinated, and Kefauver's efforts to get O'Mahoney to withdraw his claim were unavailing. O'Mahoney had served in the Senate for nearly twenty years before being defeated in 1952, but, by Senate tradition, he had lost all of that seniority in the two-year interim before his return to the Senate.

Eastland suggested that subcommittee responsibility be divided, one segment dealing with the Sherman Act and the other with the Clayton Act. But Kefauver responded promptly and firmly that they were one body of law, not two, and concluded: "I shall, therefore, expect to be named chairman of the Subcommittee on Antitrust and Monopoly Legislation."[16] The dispute was resolved two days later when O'Mahoney withdrew his claim.

Kefauver began by shaking up the subcommittee staff and appointing several of his friends to it (eventually the staff numbered forty-one, the largest committee staff on Capitol Hill). One of his appointees, Dr. John Blair, had been one of his closest advisers on antitrust matters since he first tackled the subject in the House. Kefauver raided the Federal Trade Commission to get Blair, and named him the subcommittee's economic consultant.

Blair was acquainted with an extraordinarily complicated and virtually unknown aspect of American economics as it had developed in the twentieth century: administered prices. He also was acquainted better than most with the idiosyncrasies of that extraordinarily complicated individual, Estes Kefauver, and he used that knowledge to convince the senator that administered prices possessed a monopolistic potential worth investigating. Because the busy Kefauver was a hard man to pin down for even a few minutes of conversation, Blair would lure him to the bar in the Senate Office Building. There, comfortably relaxed with a Scotch-and-soda in his hand, Kefauver was willing to listen to Blair's often esoteric monologues.[17]

Administered price industries, as Kefauver explained them when he announced plans in 1957 to investigate them, differ from competitive industries in having "monopoly power held by a few com-

16. Letter, Estes Kefauver to James O. Eastland, Jan. 16, 1957, Ser. 1, Box 76.
17. Personal conversation, John M. Blair, Washington, May 14, 1970.

panies which produce most of the industry's output. . . . In some of these administered price industries, increases in prices have been accompanied by decreases in production."[18]

The administered price hearings, which were to occupy a great deal of Kefauver's time for the remaining six years of his life and were recorded in twenty-nine volumes, included some of his most spectacular disclosures: notably in steel, drugs, and electrical equipment. At the time of his death, he had almost completed the first draft of a book on the subject, *In a Few Hands: Monopoly Power in America*. By far the best and most profound of his books, it was completed after his death by Dr. Irene Till of the Federal Trade Commission, who played a major role in developing some of the administered price hearings.

The administered price hearings got off to a slow start, and rocked along quietly and dully for a year and a half, nosing into pricing practices in steel, asphalt roofing, and automobile parts and building up a general picture of the forces acting to suppress competition in the nation's economy. Then, in the autumn of 1958, the subcommittee was handed a bonanza—appropriately, from the Tennessee Valley Authority.

Disturbed by rising prices of electrical equipment and an increasing number of identical bids by American manufacturers, the TVA included foreign firms in its invitation for bids on a turbogenerator for its Colbert steam plant. The bids it received from Westinghouse and General Electric, in the neighborhood of $17½ million, were only $70,000 apart—while a British firm, C.A. Parsons & Company, Ltd., bid just over $12 million. The contract was awarded to Parsons.[19]

Kefauver noted the incident and told the Senate that the near-identical domestic bids were "an unusually clear demonstration of how monopoly eliminates price competition and pushes prices ruthlessly upward." But even as he spoke, representatives of the two firms and other heavy electrical equipment manufacturers were holding a combination press conference and cocktail party at the Mayflower Hotel to launch a drive on TVA purchasing policies and demand restrictions on electrical equipment purchases from foreign

18. UP story, *Nashville Tennessean*, March 11, 1957.
19. John Herling, *The Great Price Conspiracy: the Story of the Antitrust Violations in the Electrical Industry* (Westport, Conn.: Greenwood Press, 1962), 3.

nations as "a threat to the security of the United States."[20]

A few weeks later, an anonymous public relations writer in the TVA noted parenthetically in the agency's weekly news letter that the TVA had received identical sealed bids from three companies on transformers, aluminum conductor cables, and chemicals. This coincidence with the flurry over the Parsons award excited the curiosity of Julian Granger, a reporter for the *Knoxville News-Sentinel*.[21] Granger went to Chattanooga to make an exhaustive study of TVA purchasing records and came up with the fact that the TVA had been receiving identical bids—sometimes to the hundredth of a cent—since it was established in 1933.

At this revelation, the subcommittee sent its chief counsel, Paul Rand Dixon, to Chattanooga to study the matter. Kefauver announced that an inquiry would be made, and Attorney General William P. Rogers ordered a step-up of an antitrust probe into electrical equipment manufacture that the Justice Department's Philadelphia office had been carrying on for several years.[22]

The Kefauver hearings opened in Knoxville late in September. The subcommittee heard testimony from Paul Fahey, director of the TVA's Division of Materials, and Carl Strange, purchasing agent for the Knoxville Utilities Board, about numerous cases of identical bidding, rotation patterns in bidding, and increases in prices that had to be passed on to consumers in the form of higher electric rates. After three days of hearings, Kefauver adjourned the probe upon learning that a grand jury had been convened in Philadelphia to investigate price-fixing conspiracies in the industry, lest testimony brought out in the hearings prejudice the court cases. The hearings were not resumed until April 1961.[23]

Eventually, in the Justice Department proceedings, General Electric and twenty-eight other companies were fined a total of nearly $2 million, seven company executives were sent to prison, and twenty-three others were given suspended jail sentences. Kefauver said he was reopening the hearings to publicize the facts of the case because "all of the corporations and individuals pleaded either

20. *Nashville Tennessean*, March 10, 1959.
21. Herling, *The Great Price Conspiracy*, 1.
22. Ibid., 5.
23. Ibid., 8, 313.

guilty or *nolo contendere*. There was, therefore, no public trial of the issues."[24]

The announcement brought on a clash with another subcommittee member, Alexander Wiley, who, despite his cooperation with and praise for Kefauver during the earlier crime investigation, was inclined to join the rest of the subcommittee's Republican minority in criticizing Kefauver's approach to antitrust matters.[25] Wiley remarked that a number of damage suits could be expected against the companies as a result of the Philadelphia convictions and urged that the subcommittee hold executive sessions, lest its disclosures "result in a national prejudgment of the civil cases or actions against the industry in the future."

Kefauver refused, responding that the guilt of the companies already had been established, and the resulting dispute occupied the entire first two days of the eleven-day hearing. At last, Wiley made a formal motion for executive sessions. Kefauver overruled him, and Wiley appealed the ruling to the subcommittee membership.

"I do not think the chairman of this committee is an autocrat," said Wiley. "He just puts himself in that position sometimes."

"An informed public is an essential part of any legislative process," argued Kefauver. "Any legislation, if it is going to be worth anything, has to be understood by the public. If secret sessions are held without the information being made public, the public will never know what took place, what the legislation is about, and what the need for it is."

"Do not tell me that you do not have three-ring circuses," accused Wiley. "What do you suppose these people are here for? . . . It indicates very clearly that what the Senator is after is publicity, and he is getting it."

"I resent the Senator's statement," replied Kefauver. "I am not running for any office."

"Now, you are not so naïve as that," snapped Wiley. "I know how you campaign."[26]

24. Ibid., 10, 313.
25. Wiley had walked out on a committee session in 1957 after a clash with Kefauver over what he called "improper" procedure. Robert Z. Thompson, INS story, *Nashville Tennessean*, June 28, 1957.
26. *Administered Prices: Hearings before the Subcommittee on Antitrust and*

Kefauver and Senator Alexander Wiley engage in a dispute over hearings on anti-trust violations in the electrical equipment industry.

Wiley's motion failed in a tie vote, but the argument over it illustrates the grounds of the controversy over Kefauver's use of the congressional investigation as a weapon far more potent than debate on the Senate floor or log-rolling agreements with colleagues. Relegated to the fringe of the senatorial power structure, feared for his presidential ambition, he found through the crime investigation and other probes that here he possessed a sure method of appealing to his peculiarly personal source of political power: public opinion.

Most committee work, including investigative work, does not come to public attention. It is for the information of the committee members and their legislative colleagues. But some congressmen, doubting for one reason or other the clarity of their colleagues' vision when confronted with a mere printed report, have found means of calling in the voting public as the prime arbiter.

Of those skeptical investigators, Kefauver became a model. One of the devices he used to "keep the public informed" was to have his staff present the most newsworthy facets of a probe just in time for newspaper deadlines on hearing days and keep reporters alerted to sensational developments likely to come up. Thus, Kefauver investigations received an unusual amount of publicity.

After the crime investigation revealed the power of such probes to stir public interest, there was a continuing and sometimes comical tug-of-war between Kefauver and the Democratic party leaders. Kefauver angled for the means to woo public opinion in the interest of his long-range legislative objectives, while the party leaders tried to block him from the publicity that might build him up as a presidential contender. It is in this light that one must view the maneuvers to keep him off the Foreign Relations Committee and deny him the chairmanship of the Antitrust and Monopoly Subcommittee.

The electrical industry hearings did not get much publicity but provided some interesting revelations. One of the witnesses, Clarence E. Burke, told the subcommittee that he and other General Electric officials had discussed price levels with competitors, con-

---

Monopoly of the Committee on the Judiciary, United States Senate, 87th Congress, First Session, pt. 27, "Price Fixing and Bid Rigging in the Electrical Manufacturing Industry (Washington: Government Printing Office, 1961), 16512, 16523–31.

cealing their activities from company lawyers and often falsifying travel vouchers to conceal meetings. Burke, who had been general manager of General Electric's switchgear division and was one of those convicted in Philadelphia, told of being instructed by superiors to "bring about price stabilization."

"And when they said 'price stabilization,' we knew exactly what they meant," he testified. "That meant to us the only way to stabilize prices was to contact competitors and get agreement on prices."[27]

The way this agreement was accomplished, according to the federal indictments and testimony before the Kefauver subcommittee, was often esoteric, sometimes incredible. One witness told how a group of motor experts from different companies "happened to arrive by plane at the same time," with "no particular purpose," at the Airport Motel in Pittsburgh. The switchgear market was divided up among different companies by a formula called "phases of the moon." One of the key areas of dispute among witnesses before the committee was a notorious "luncheon in Dining Room B" in Philadelphia, at which a vice president and three general managers of General Electric Company all testified that they were told by Arthur F. Vinson, apparatus and industrial group executive for GE, that a competing firm, Westinghouse, was, as one of them put it, "very much interested in stabilizing prices, and we will just have to do it." Vinson denied vigorously that he ever attended such a meeting, which led Senator Philip A. Hart of Michigan to remark that the testimony "leads more clearly than ever to the conclusion that somebody is crazy or somebody is lying."[28]

Kefauver's deadpan, apparently naïve but often effective method of questioning was exemplified near the end of testimony before the subcommittee by William S. Ginn, who had been General Electric's turbine division general manager. Ginn, one of those who had "taken the rap" for higher company executives in the price conspiracy trials, was quite frank in his testimony before the subcommittee, and Kefauver said to him: "I do not understand the holier-than-thou attitude in GE when your directions came from very high at the top. But I do not ask you to comment unless you want to." "I think it would be just as well if I don't, Senator," replied Ginn.

27. Ibid., 16741.
28. Ibid., 16951.

Then Kefauver asked, "If you did comment, what would you say?" There was laughter in the hearing room, and Ginn responded with a pertinent comment.[29]

Kefauver's real concern in his subcommittee's antitrust investigations and his preoccupation with antitrust legislation was best stated, perhaps, in a comment he made during questioning of Mark W. Cresap Jr., president of Westinghouse. "It is the job of this committee to investigate antitrust and monopoly and try to be an influence to bring about competition in American industry," Kefauver said. "Big corporations getting together and fixing prices is capitalistic socialism, which the American people would never put up with. They would turn, rather, to the other kind of socialism, governmental socialism, and we do not want that to happen."[30]

Kefauver's recommendation that the record of the hearings be used by the Justice Department as the basis for further antitrust action was ignored, and none of the proposed legislation resulting from the hearings was acted on. The electrical equipment hearings simply provided another building block in the structure of the case Kefauver and the subcommittee built up against the varied network of monopolies in America.

"Common people everywhere—and perhaps not without some justification—have the feeling that there are great and powerful forces aligned against their better interests," said Hart, who became one of Kefauver's staunchest allies in antitrust matters. "But having a man like Estes Kefauver around did a lot to relieve their feeling of helplessness . . . because he was a crusader—against crime, against monopolies, against bigotry—and when he crusaded, he crusaded because he was angry."[31]

The steel industry hearings, with which the subcommittee began its probe into administered prices in 1957, were long, ponderous, and full of figures and theory. But they were significant in their disclosure of some of the theory underlying twentieth-century business practice in America.

"If we offer to sell steel to a customer at the same price as a com-

29. Ibid., 17089.
30. Herling, *The Great Price Conspiracy*, 142.
31. Personal communication, Sen. Philip A. Hart, Washington, Sept. 24, 1970.

petitor offers to sell it to the customer, that is very definitely a competitive price," Roger M. Blough, chairman of the board of the United States Steel Corporation, told the subcommittee. "Now, it isn't a different price, and, therefore, it isn't a noncompetitive price, but it is a competitive price."

"Mr. Blough, do you regard it as true competition when another company matches your price to a thousandth of a cent per pound, or you match some other company's price to a thousandth of a cent per pound?" asked Kefauver. "I mean, what difference does it make who they buy from, if the prices are going to be identical to one-thousandth of a cent per pound?"

"Mr. Chairman . . . my concept is that a price that matches another price is a competitive price," replied Blough. "If you don't choose to accept that concept, then, of course, you don't accept it. . . . I say the buyer has more choice when the other fellow's price matches our price."

"That's a new definition of competition that I have never heard," commented Kefauver.

"Mr. Chairman," said Blough a little later, "I don't think you understand competition. I beg your pardon for saying so. . . . I think you understand the words, but you don't understand the concept."

"I am trying to understand competition, and I must say, on that kind of basis, I am having a hard time doing it," confessed Kefauver wryly.[32]

The subcommittee majority concluded in its report on the steel hearings: "Steel . . . is the underpinning of our entire economy. When the price of steel goes up, the inevitable tendency is for steel-consuming industries to raise their prices. . . .

"The higher prices will tend to reduce [the] demand for steel. Faced with a decline in demand, the steel companies can be expected to reduce their output . . . resulting in higher total unit costs. This, in turn, may provide a rationale for a still further price increase. In this way, a vicious cycle of price increases, lower demand and higher unit costs may be set in motion."[33]

32. *Administered Prices*, 85th Congress, First Session, pt. 2, 1958, pp. 310, 312, 313, 314, 315.
33. *Administered Prices: Steel, Report of the Committee on the Judiciary,*

Everett Dirksen of Illinois dissented vigorously from the majority view. He filed a minority report that "disagrees emphatically with the position taken in the majority's report that so-called administered prices are associated with monopoly power. It dissents vigorously from the attempt of the majority to raise the completely unfounded specter of future economic stagnation in America as a result of an alleged monopoly power in large segments of industry."[34]

Steel company executives contended that workers' wage increases were the biggest cost factor forcing them to raise prices. When the United Steel Workers union contract with U.S. Steel expired in 1959, Kefauver appealed to the union to limit its wage increase demands to average productivity gains of the industry, as a move to curb inflation. To which David J. McDonald, union president, retorted: "I wish Senator Kefauver would learn to keep his nose out of my business." The union struck.[35]

When union contracts in the steel industry came up for renewal again in 1962, there was a different President in the White House; and Kennedy and McDonald were old friends. When Kennedy asked that the union hold down its demands, McDonald agreed not to request a general wage increase at all, on the understanding that the industry would forego a price increase, in return. But the understanding apparently was only on one side. The very afternoon that the last major contract with the union was signed, Blough obtained an appointment with Kennedy and handed him a press release announcing a $6 a ton increase in prices by U.S. Steel.

"I think you're making a mistake," the angry young President told Blough.[36] As soon as Blough left, he telephoned his brother, Attorney General Robert Kennedy, to call for antimonopoly action by the Justice Department. Then he telephoned Kefauver at his office.

Kennedy wanted Kefauver to have the Antitrust and Monopoly Subcommittee reopen its steel hearings immediately, to bring pressure against the steel companies. Kefauver was reluctant: this was

United States Senate, made by its Subcommittee on Antitrust and Monopoly, March 13, 1958 (Washington: Government Printing Office, 1958), 129–30.

34. Ibid., 139.
35. AP story, *Nashville Tennessean*, March 1, 1959.
36. Sorenson, *Kennedy*, 448.

Kefauver is greeted by President John F. Kennedy, after Kennedy's election in 1960.

an obvious use of the legislative investigation as a weapon in the service of the Executive Department. But, on Kennedy's insistence, he agreed at last to "look into it."

Kefauver went home to dress for the annual White House reception for members of Congress. While he was dressing, he had another telephone call from the President. Kennedy wanted to emphasize, he said, that Kefauver should move "immediately" with the investigation. Kefauver said he would. Before leaving for the White House reception, Kefauver telephoned Bernard Fensterwald Jr., the subcommittee's staff director, and told him to start preparing witness lists and hearing schedules to look into the cost data of the steel companies.

"Do you want us to really dig down and get into this matter in depth, Senator," asked Fensterwald, "or just run the steel companies around the ring a couple of times for public consumption?"

Kefauver hesitated, then said: "Just run them around the ring for now, I suppose. We don't have much time."

The next morning Kennedy was on the phone again. He wanted to know what Kefauver had found out. Kefauver explained patiently to the President that it took time to get the subpoenas served and get the witnesses before the subcommittee, so he had not found out anything yet.[37]

As other steel companies began to fall in behind U.S. Steel in the price boost, one by one, Kennedy brought multiple pressures on them; and within three days the steel companies were beaten. Two major firms announced that their prices would not go up, Bethlehem Steel broke under the pressure and rescinded its price hike, and late the same day, U.S. Steel surrendered.

But the machinery of the Kefauver subcommittee already was in motion, and nothing would have been more obvious than for it to cancel its announced hearings at that point. (Nor was Robert Kennedy in a position to cancel the Justice Department probe, which

---

37. Personal conversation, Bernard Fensterwald Jr., Washington, May 15, 1970; personal communication, Charles A. Caldwell, Washington, Sept. 4, 1970. Fensterwald, an attorney from Nashville, was a good friend of Kefauver who had served as chief counsel for the Constitutional Amendments Subcommittee and had helped Kefauver on foreign policy matters during the 1956 presidential campaign. He succeeded Paul Rand Dixon on the Antitrust and Monopoly Subcommittee when Dixon was appointed chairman of the Federal Trade Commission.

resulted in seven major antitrust indictments against steel companies for secret price-fixing conspiracies during the next two years.) The day after U.S. Steel backed down, subpoenas were issued to twelve companies, including five that had not raised prices, seeking production cost data. During the next two months, eight of the companies agreed to provide the information, under protest that its disclosure would damage their competitive positions. But the other four refused.

When the deadline for responding to the subpoenas passed, the subcommittee was called together to determine whether contempt action should be taken against them. But two subcommittee Democrats, Philip Hart and Thomas J. Dodd of Connecticut, were out of town, and a third, John Carroll, was absent. Alexander Wiley was absent, too, but Kefauver found himself faced with a 2 to 2 party-line deadlock on the question: himself and Edward Long against Dirksen and Roman Hruska of Nebraska.

Stalling for time, Kefauver sent Charlie Caldwell on a hurry mission to get Carroll. Caldwell found a telephone and got in touch with Harry Schnibbe, Carroll's administrative assistant.

"Harry, you gotta get John over here!" urged Caldwell desperately. "It looks like 2 to 2."

It took Carroll five minutes to get there—Kefauver, meanwhile, delaying a decision by every means he knew. But at last the Colorado senator burst into the room, and the decision to seek contempt citations was made by a 3 to 2 vote.[38]

But Kennedy had accomplished his immediate objective with the rollback of prices, and he refused to support Kefauver now.[39] When the resolution recommending that the four companies and nine officials be cited for contempt of Congress went before the full Judiciary Committee, Southern Democrats joined Republicans in voting it down, 10 to 5. Only the Democratic members of his subcommittee voted with Kefauver.

Kennedy's generosity to the defeated steel men at the expense of

38. Harris, *The Real Voice*, 146–47, relates Carroll's breaking of the deadlock as occurring during the maneuvering over the drug control bill, but both Caldwell and Fensterwald told the sequence of events as set forth above. Personal conversation, Bernard Fensterwald, Washington, May 15, 1970, personal communication, Charles A. Caldwell, Washington, Sept. 4, 1970.

39. Sorensen, *Kennedy*, 459.

his former colleague proved somewhat shortsighted: the next year the steel companies announced another price increase. The irritated Kennedy made some preparations to repeat the previous year's pressure but decided against it. More important than the industry's backsliding was the loss to the subcommittee of the cost data, which would have given it better insight into the steel industry's effect on the national economy.

Kefauver's failure to gain cooperation from anyone—industry, labor, Congress, the White House—in his effort was very discouraging to him. At one point he commented that his attempt to halt the inflationary spiral was "a lonely road to travel."

"I never meet anyone else on the road," he said. "Everyone, from the President down, complains about inflation . . . but they don't lift a finger while the horse is walking out the barn door."[40]

The same year Kennedy slapped down the steel magnates—the year before his death and Kefauver's—marked passage of two major Kefauver-sponsored legislative measures in the antitrust field. One of them was the Kefauver-Harris Drug Control Act, and the other passed almost undetected in the hurrah over its passage: the 1962 Antitrust Civil Process Act.

Kefauver had all sorts of administration support for the Civil Process Act: Robert Kennedy wanted it. It authorized the attorney general to issue a "civil investigative demand" whenever he had reason to believe a business "under investigation" possessed documentary evidence needed in a civil antitrust case. Previously, such evidence could be obtained only by voluntary cooperation of the firm, issuance of a grand jury subpoena, or resort to an investigation by the Federal Trade Commission. The Senate passed it by voice vote, and President Kennedy signed it into law after a relatively minor House amendment was accepted.

Kefauver's success as chairman of the Antitrust and Monopoly Subcommittee was measured less in the legislation that originated in it—for that, though important, was relatively little—but in the massive documentation it built up for the case against monopolistic practices. That documentation was made possible by the working majority ranged at Kefauver's side throughout the long administered price hearings.

40. AP story, *Nashville Tennessean*, June 23, 1958.

He could depend absolutely on the support of two of the sub-committee Democrats, Carroll and Hart, and usually on that of other Democrats who were members of the subcommittee part of the time: Dodd, Long, Thomas Hennings, and Joseph O'Mahoney. The three-man Republican minority opposed him as often as not, but Wiley's opposition was qualified, for his view of the basic issue of monopoly power was not too far from Kefauver's own.

Wiley stated that position during the first days of the administered price hearings: "Where you have folks who get tremendous incomes because of the freedom of the country—let's call it the freedom, which it is—and other folks can sweat 24 hours a day and cannot get even a livelihood out of it, it is not right, and we want to know what the answer it. . . . Some can fix prices and some can't, and there are those human beings who, when they get power in their hands, exercise it to the detriment of their fellow human beings."[41]

Kefauver's cleverest and most effective adversary throughout the hearings was Dirksen, whose dissent was unrelenting. The urbane, good-humored Illinois senator seemed not disturbed at all by frequent accusations that he was on the subcommittee primarily to soften the impact of its activities upon the nation's industry and big business: a devil's advocate of a sort. Nor did his consistent opposition to Kefauver contain any element of personal antagonism, as did that of the vitriolic Eastland. Dirksen and Kefauver were rather fond of each other, and after Kefauver's death, Dirksen delivered a poignant eulogy on the Senate floor:

"What shall I say of a man, a friend, a colleague, a Senator with whom I disagreed so often, whose purposes I sought to frustrate, if possible, with whom I fought fiercely over differences in viewpoint, both in committee and on the Senate floor, year in and year out? What does one say about such an adversary?

"Outstanding was his zeal for little people, for little business, for a true competitive system under which young and old, rich and poor, might have an equal chance. His investigations in the Antitrust and Monopoly Subcommittee were a testimony to an iron determination that our competitive system must be made to work

---

41. *Administered Prices, 85th Congress, First Session*, pt. 1, "Opening Phase —Economists' Views," 1957, pp. 37, 143.

justly and equitably. Whether these investigations took place in the field of milk or bread, motor cars or steel, insurance or electrical equipment, the objective was always the same; namely, to lift the hand of monopoly from little people, that they, too, might survive and prosper."[42]

Hruska, too, treated Kefauver with generosity and respect, though he did yeoman service as Dirksen's chief lieutenant in striving to block effective antimonopoly action by the subcommittee.

In his posthumous book, *In a Few Hands*, Kefauver listed four alternative methods of meeting the monopoly problem: (1) to let matters take their course; (2) to establish government control of business and industry; (3) to depend on moral persuasion and the pressure of public opinion; and (4) to attempt to reverse the trend of concentration in industry and restore competition.[43] Almost alone on the subcommittee, he seemed to think the last alternative was possible and practical.

Major economists, such as John Kenneth Galbraith and Gardiner Means, disagreed with him. But Kefauver included in his calculations a factor that was generally overlooked: that Congress and the Executive branch encouraged monopolistic practices through governmental policies in tariffs, government procurement, patents and tax favoritism. His hope for reestablishment of a competitive economy rested ultimately in the arousal and education of public opinion to the point of forcing elected officials to resist the special interest pressures that had shaped the economic policies of government for at least a century.

Kefauver hoped to give "Joe Smith," the consumer, some representation in determining government economic policy and offered a bill in three successive Congresses to create a Cabinet-level Office of Consumers. He had reason to hope for administration support for his plan when Kennedy was elected President, but what Kennedy asked Congress for—and got—was a Consumers Advisory Council.

The Kennedy administration opposed Kefauver's stronger approach. When Phillip S. Hughes of the Budget Bureau recommended against the Office of Consumers in 1962, Fensterwald transmitted Hughes's letter to Kefauver with the appended com-

42. Sen. Everett Dirksen in *Carey Estes Kefauver, Late a Senator from Tennessee*, 20–21.

43. Kefauver, *In a Few Hands*, 196–98.

ment: "As you will note from the attached, you are receiving the usual strong White House support."

Despite all of his frustrating failures, Kefauver was successful enough in his efforts to become, as Gerald Johnson noted, "hated by every thief in the United States; and most venomously by the pious banditti who claim that they pick our pockets *pro humanitate et gloria Dei.*"[44]

44. Gerald W. Johnson, *New Republic*, Aug. 7, 1961.

Chapter 19

In the Background Was Even Senator Kefauver

The long struggle for passage of the Kefauver-Harris Drug Control Act of 1962, Kefauver's last outstanding legislative accomplishment, recapitulated all of the elements of a "typical" Kefauver battle, as though a cast gathered around a veteran protagonist for one final, spectacular showing of a familiar drama.

It was a fight for the "little people" against powerful, well-financed special interests. It had the superficial support but surreptitious obstructionism of his own party's leaders. It was a story of tactical skirmishes with the help of a handful of loyal allies, of the press to the rescue like the cavalry at the crucial moment, and of qualified success at the end.

The staff of the Antitrust and Monopoly Subcommittee had been looking into the monopolistic aspects of the drug industry for about two years when Kefauver announced in September 1959 that the subcommittee would investigate it. Although the drug bill as it was passed eventually did not reflect the fact, administered prices in the ethical (prescription) drug field were the focus of the subcommittee's interest.

Twenty of the more than 1,000 pharmaceutical firms producing ethical drugs accounted for nine-tenths of the $2 billion in annual sales, chiefly to druggists and wholesalers. The subcommittee staff had information that identical prices were being charged for the same drug by different firms and that American-made drugs in such foreign nations as France cost only 17 percent of their price in the United States.[1]

With the hearings scheduled to open in December, when Kefauver returned to Tennessee for his annual "report to the people"

1. Gardner L. Bridge, AP story, *Nashville Tennessean*, Jan. 22, 1960; *Congressional Record*, vol. 105, pt. 15, Sept. 12, 1959, p. 19217; ibid., vol. 106, pt. 5, March 22, 1960, p. 6226.

tour, Charlie Caldwell took along, for briefing purposes, a folder on cortical steroids, the subject of the first series of hearings. But Caldwell had as much difficulty getting Kefauver aside for a while as anyone else, and at 10 o'clock the night before they were to fly back to Washington, Kefauver still had not had his briefing.

Desperately, knowing Kefauver's tongue-twisting propensities, Caldwell shooed out the last of the visitors at their Jackson hotel suite and locked the front door—only to find Kefauver in the shower, head and one arm stuck out to sign autographs for three men who had slipped in the back door. Caldwell got rid of them too and the two men had their briefing session in the bathroom, one sitting on the toilet seat and the other on the edge of the bathtub. Caldwell made Kefauver repeat the names after him, over and over. It became a chant: "cortisone, hydrocortisone, prednisone, prednisolone, dexamethasone," and so on. To the surprise of Washington newsmen, Kefauver never mispronounced a drug name during the hearings.[2]

The first day of the hearings brought out two of the major points of the investigation: that some big companies were buying drugs in bulk from suppliers at very low prices, processing and packaging them, and selling the trade-name product at a very high price; and that prices for the same product sold by different companies were often identical.

"Schering does not itself make prednisolone," explained Kefauver later on the Senate floor, illustrating his points with a chart at the rear of the chamber. "Schering buys prednisolone from Upjohn. Schering obtained it for $2.37 a gram. . . . Then we added to that the cost of wastage, tableting and bottling. We arrived at a computed manufacturing cost of $1.57 per 100 tablets, or 1.6¢ per tablet. . . . We wanted the companies themselves to furnish the reasons for the difference between the production cost of $1.57 and their price to the druggist of $17.90."[3] The explanation of the drug industry representatives was that the costs of research and selling had not been included in the spread. But a "friendly witness," Seymour Blackman, executive secretary of Premo Pharmaceutical Com-

2. Harris, *The Real Voice*, 48–49; personal conversation, Charles A. Caldwell, Washington, May 12, 1970; Estes Kefauver, *San Francisco Examiner*, March 12, 1960.

3. *Congressional Record*, vol. 106, pt. 5, March 22, 1960, p. 6227.

pany, told the subcommittee that a more effective and less costly substitute for a drug on the market, when developed, was sold by the big firms at the same price per dose as the original drug. If a little firm such as his own cut its price, it would get no more of the market but would just lose money.

"From this, it is obvious that the public does not benefit by the applied research of the pharmaceutical industry," he said. "It is also obvious that the selling price for a particular ethical specialty is not predicated on the cost of the materials, but, rather, predicated on what the traffic will bear."[4]

Kefauver received immediate praise for his probe. Senator Ralph Yarborough wrote him that he had "raised the standards of the Senate in the eyes of the American people," and House Leader John McCormack telephoned to congratulate him and say "it is something the country needed." Those in the drug industry and their allies were not happy, however, and neither was Senator Everett McKinley Dirksen.

Dirksen missed the first series of hearings (he was visiting his daughter, Mrs. Howard H. Baker Jr., in Tennessee), but, after all the publicity, he was very much on hand for the second series early in 1960. Subsequently, he permitted drug industry lobbyists to use his office, to write some of his speeches, and to prepare legislation, which he offered to the Senate without alteration as his own.

Dirksen had become Senate minority leader at the beginning of 1959, and halfway through the second series of hearings he notified Kefauver that he was tied up with these duties and would object to hearings being held while the Senate was in session.[5] Then, said Kefauver, the hearings would end in the morning in time for the State session, but would resume thirty minutes after the Senate adjourned.

"Mr. Chairman, I have an idea we will run late tonight, and will probably run late every night this week," said Dirksen. ". . . I doubt very much if the members of the committee, after a long day, would have a great disposition to come to take testimony at 9 o'clock at night. I think I would rather rebel at the idea."

4. Kefauver, *In a Few Hands*, 16.
5. Lois Laycook, *Nashville Tennessean*, March 23, 1960. Under the rules, a single senator could block hearings while the Senate was in session by a simple objection.

"That is certainly your right, as I have explained," said Kefauver. "But unless we can have some night hearings, I don't know when we will ever get through."[6] The subcommittee reconvened at 10:40 o'clock that night and continued work until 1:55 o'clock in the morning. Dirksen was not there, nor did he attend the next two days' sessions. Roman Hruska had to bear the burden of the Republican viewpoint, and he protested at last that such night work would "impair the health and efficiency" of the senators.

"Well, Senator Hruska," said Kefauver, smiling, "you and I are young fellows. We're healthy."[7] But, somehow, it was found possible thereafter not to cut the hearings short in the mornings, and no more night meetings were held.

When the subcommittee reopened hearings in April, Dirksen arose to criticize at length its decision to bring in witnesses known "to be critical to the drug profession and industry and to the medical profession." The ensuing exchange was described drolly by Richard Strout in the *New Republic*:

"Alas, he [Dirksen] faced one of the most wooden antagonists in the Senate. Senator Kefauver's long equine head, owl-like glasses and invisible coonskin cap did not move. Dirksen raised his mellifluous voice and wagged the remnants of his curly hair. Kefauver sat like an absent-minded doorpost. Again and again the emotional Dirksen set lance and charged—the protector of doctors and druggists.

"Milder and more limp came Kefauver's languid response, always introduced with an infuriating pause and inquiry if the distinguished Senator from Illinois were finished. Assured by the fuming Dirksen that he was temporarily through, Kefauver deprecatingly repeated his damning statistics, his voice never changing, and continuing with the iteration of a leaky faucet. Dirksen, who has the face of a lost angel, writhed in distaste—like an alcoholic offered a bowl of warm milk.

"This continued for an hour or so, while unfortunate witnesses waited and other Senators occasionally interrupted. Finally Dirksen

6. *Administered Prices*, 86th Congress, Second Session, pt. 19, "Administered Prices in the Drug Industry (General: Pharmaceutical Manufacturers Association)," 1960, pp. 10612–13.

7. Ibid., pt. 18, "Administered Prices in the Drug Industry (General: Physicians and Other Professional Authorities), 10248.

stopped trying to fire Roman candles into this pile of damp saw-
dust. The two veterans (who had hitherto hardly exchanged glances)
softly turned at the end and grinned."[8]

The subcommittee report on the drug industry hearings, June
27, 1961, said prescription drug prices were inordinately high in re-
lation to industry costs because the market was controlled by a few
large firms. This control, it said, rested on patents, giving the holder
a "private monopoly"; on advertising and promotion, which gave
an advantage to large firms able to spend great amounts of money
for the purpose; and on the use of trade names instead of generic
names in prescriptions.[9]

Dirksen and Hruska filed a dissenting report, calling the majority report "nothing more than a calculated review of choice quips,
statements, and exhibits presented by biased witnesses whose views
were well known to the majority at the time they were called to testify." Alexander Wiley filed a separate dissent in somewhat milder
tone, in which he attacked the majority's concept of "reasonableness" in drug prices.[10]

In its dissent, the Republican minority overlooked a twenty-five-
page section of the majority report dealing with an aspect of the
hearings that eventually altered the approach to the Drug Control
Act substantially, and had a good deal to do with its passage: the
question of adverse effects of drugs on patients. In fact, both the
majority and minority were oriented primarily to the issue of monopolistic conditions and excessive prices. The question of drug
safety developed incidentally in testimony. The report said side
effects of drugs on patients were ignored or played down in the advertisements for the drugs that reached the doctors who had to pre-
scribe them. Testimony was cited that "the overall incidence of
adverse reactions from dexamethasone (Decadron)," used for the
relief of arthritis, was not negligible. It included easy bruising of
the skin, rounding of the face, severe mental disorders, and spread-

---

8. Richard Strout, "Two Old Pros," in the column, "T.R.B. from Washington," April 25, 1960. Reprinted by permission of *The New Republic*, © 1960,
Harrison-Blaine of New Jersey, Inc.
9. *Administered Prices: Drugs, Report of the Committee on the Judiciary,
United States Senate, made by its Subcommittee on Antitrust and Monopoly*,
June 27, 1961 (Washington: Government Printing Office, 1961), 1–253.
10. Ibid., 263–78, 396–74.

ing of infection throughout the body as a result of the suppression of inflammation. But, the report said, advertising to doctors stated that "no worrisome side effects attributable to Decadron have occurred as yet." As for Diabinese, used in treating diabetes, the subcommittee cited testimony that six of 400 patients treated with it developed disabling jaundice, one of them dying, whereas advertising to doctors claimed an "almost complete absence of unfavorable side effects."[11]

Two months before the subcommittee report, Kefauver introduced an omnibus drug control bill, aimed at both price reduction and safety requirements for drugs. It would reduce a patent holder's exclusive control of a drug from seventeen years to three, require that generic names be displayed on labels and in advertising, require federal licensing of drug firms, and require firms offering new drugs to demonstrate both effectiveness and safety before putting them on the market.

Abraham Ribicoff, secretary of Health, Education and Welfare, endorsed the bill strongly, saying it would "give American men, women and children the same protection we have been giving hogs, sheep and cattle since 1913."[12] Former Vice President Richard Nixon, on the other hand, denounced Kefauver's bill as "definitely punitive," and said it foreshadowed "increasing central control, increasing bureaucratic conformity and decreasing individual freedom."[13] When no action was taken on the bill in 1961, Kefauver reintroduced it in March 1962.

Three nights later, accompanied by Charlie Caldwell, Bernard Fensterwald, and John Blair, Kefauver went to the White House to ask that President Kennedy's forthcoming Consumer Protection Message contain an endorsement of the bill and that the administration not introduce its own drug bill but support his. They talked with Myer Feldman, Kennedy's deputy special counsel, who would go only so far as to promise to transmit both requests to the President. Wilbur Cohen of HEW was also present, and Caldwell said he "did a lot of the hatchet work on us then and there."

"We were told not to expect any overt support," said Caldwell. "The conversation was very evasive and noncommital."

11. Ibid., 210–22.
12. Lois Laycook, *Nashville Tennessean*, Oct. 1, 1961.
13. UPI story, *Nashville Banner*, June 27, 1961.

"Estes was trying to secure some support from the White House . . . ," said Blair. "I found the whole episode incredible, and was not hesitant in making known my own views at the meeting. Although, of course, more quiet and restrained in his expression, the Senator was, if anything, more indignant than I."[14]

When Kennedy's Consumer Protection Message came out March 15, it included a recommendation for better federal controls over the sale of dangerous drugs but did not mention either Kefauver or his bill. Kefauver telephoned Feldman and told him rather sternly that he planned to put out a press release expressing his disappointment at the failure of the message to deal with reduction of drug prices (he did).

Feldman assured Kefauver that the Kennedy administration approved of the principles of his bill and would support it. Kefauver retorted sharply that it would have been nice if that fact had been made clear in the Consumer Protection Message, and then he hung up.[15] Dirksen got the Judiciary Committee to sidetrack Kefauver's bill to John McClellan's Patents Subcommittee, where several provisions were struck out, including the one to require federal licensing of drug firms.

The next day Kennedy endorsed Kefauver's bill, for the most part, in a letter to Eastland. But he did not ask that the compulsory licensing feature be restored, nor did he mention Kefauver's treasured patent-reduction provision. Most of his letter dealt with drug quality and protection from adverse effects, with little reference to prices.[16]

Then, less than two weeks later, the Kennedy administration introduced its own drug bill through Representative Oren Harris of Arkansas—and it contained no price control provisions at all. Feldman's explanation was: "We're backing Kefauver. In the Senate, we're using his bill, and in the House, the Harris bill."[17]

But Representative Emanuel Celler had already introduced a companion measure to Kefauver's in the House. Now Celler held

---

14. Harris, *The Real Voice*, 146; personal communications, Charles A. Caldwell, Washington, Sept. 4, 1970, Bernard Fensterwald Jr., Washington, Sept. 11, 1970, John M. Blair, La Plata, Md., Sept. 14, 1970.
15. Harris, *The Real Voice*, 148.
16. Ibid., 153.
17. Ibid., 155.

four days of hearings on his own bill, stirring up considerable agony among drug industry spokesmen with his sharp questioning—and bringing out for the first time, in testimony by Dr. Helen B. Taussig of Johns Hopkins University, the crippling effects of the German drug, thalidomide, on unborn babies.[18]

On the morning of June 8, Eastland arranged a meeting in the Judiciary Committee conference room, at which the Kefauver drug bill was rewritten by staff representatives of the Kennedy administration and of Eastland, Dirksen, and Hruska, plus three drug industry representatives, Edward H. Foley, Lloyd N. Cutler, and Marshall Hornblower.[19] Only 55 lines of the 35-page bill were left untouched, leaving it "a mere shadow of the one approved by the Antitrust and Monopoly Subcommittee," as Kefauver said later. The new bill eliminated the patent provisions and watered down or deleted altogether most of the safety provisions.

Kefauver did not know what had happened until the Judiciary Committee met three days later. He went to the meeting to argue for his bill's patent provisions, to find Jerome Sonosky of HEW, who had drawn up the Harris bill, present. Eastland explained that Sonosky was present because he (Eastland) had asked HEW to send over a technical adviser. The committee, with Eastland and McClellan joining the Republicans, voted down Kefauver's plea for his patent provisions. Then Dirksen brought forth the substitute bill, written in the secret meeting, to the astonishment of Kefauver, John Carroll, and Philip Hart.

Kefauver demanded, and was given, time to look over the new bill. Under intensive questioning from Carroll, Sonosky disclosed the activities of the secret meeting. But every time Carroll demanded to know if he was representing the Kennedy administration, Sonosky replied that he was representing HEW, and that only as a technical adviser. Kefauver went out to telephone Feldman at the White House. Feldman said the White House knew nothing about the revision and was behind Kefauver. Then Kefauver telephoned Cohen. Cohen said he had been asked to send someone to the secret meeting but contended that he knew nothing about the changes in the bill.

18. Ibid., 160–61.
19. Harris, *The Real Voice*, 164, names all three; Drew Pearson and Jack Anderson, *The Case Against Congress* (New York: Simon & Schuster, 1968), 326, name only Cutler and Hornblower.

"It looks to me as though you were working both sides of the street," retorted Kefauver. "This is the first time in my 23 years in Congress that an administration has emasculated a bill without letting its sponsor and chairman know."

When Kefauver returned to the committee room, Eastland attempted to substitute the new bill for Kefauver's, but Carroll promptly got the floor and filibustered until noon, when the Senate convened. Then, citing Senate rules, Carroll objected to continuing the committee meeting while the Senate was in session, and it was forced to adjourn. Kefauver left the conference room as near in a cold fury as ever in his life. He returned to Suite 443 and sent Blair and Horace Flurry, the subcommittee's senior counsel, to study the new bill. Then, trailed by Fensterwald, he retired to his inner office and sank disconsolately into the big red leather swivel chair behind his desk. For a time, there was silence. Then Kefauver arose, with determination.

"I'm going to the floor and have this out," he said.

"You'd better cool off first, boss," said Fensterwald. "Anyway, we should have whatever you're going to say down on paper."

"Okay, let's put something together," agreed Kefauver.

The two of them, with Caldwell, arrived at the Capitol about 2 o'clock right after a quorum call, when a majority of the senators were present. Kefauver notified Mike Mansfield of Montana, the majority leader, that he wanted to make a statement. Mansfield asked him to wait until the conclusion of the vote on the annual appropriation bill for the Interior Department, for which the quorum call had been sounded.

"No," said Kefauver, "I want to do it now."

Feldman, notified at the White House that Kefauver was about to speak, telephoned him at the Senate, and was alarmed at Kefauver's outline of what he planned to say. He protested.

"I haven't been so shoddily treated in 23 years in Congress," retorted Kefauver, and hung up. Robert G. Baker, secretary to the majority leader, had no better luck in trying to dissuade him.[20]

"Most of the drug manufacturing industry and its acolytes," said Kefauver, when he had the floor, "have been punching away for

20. The story of the secret meeting and Kefauver's reaction to it is told in detail by Harris, *The Real Voice*, 166–70.

some time at S. 1552, which is designed to make vital prescription drugs available to the people at reasonable prices. Today, they swung a haymaker, and just about knocked this bill right out of the ring."

He read Kennedy's letter to Eastland into the record, described the secret meeting, and concluded: "In view of the fact that representatives of the Department of Health, Education and Welfare participated in secret meetings to damage this bill seriously, I think the people are now entitled to know just how they happened to be there, and what the Administration's present position is."

Senators listening in fascinated interest to a colleague's rare disclosure of the legislative intrigues of his own party hierarchy witnessed a furious squabble. Eastland and Hruska defended the rewritten bill, Eastland accepting "full responsibility for the alleged secret meeting," and Carroll leaped angrily to Kefauver's defense.

"I believe the Senator from Tennessee is fully justified in asking the President where he stands and asking HEW where they stand," snapped Carroll. "We are hitting into one of the biggest industries of the nation, one with the highest prices, and one that is subject to the least regulation. . . . From what we have heard today, with this sort of procedure, it is a helluva way to run a railroad."

"The point is that it is being run," retorted Eastland, ". . . and we are not going to argue about it."

"I suggest to the distinguished Senator from Tennessee that he have a talk with the President," said Hart. "It seems so simple."

"I have talked with the President," replied Kefauver. "I have talked with those who are advising him as to what they want in the bill. The bill as amended in the subcommittee follows the President's recommendations. Of course, I want to know how the administration stands now."[21]

There were reports that the Kennedy administration was being ambiguous about the drug bill to put pressure on Kefauver to drop his opposition to an administration measure for a commercial communications satellite system. Ribicoff remained staunchly behind

21. *Congressional Record*, vol. 108, pt. 8, June 11, 1962, pp. 10105ff. There is no record of Kefauver having talked directly with President Kennedy about the drug bill before this time, but Charles A. Caldwell, in a personal conversation in Washington, May 12, 1970, said it is entirely possible that Kefauver had seen the President without members of his staff having knowledge of the meeting.

the Kefauver approach and told the House Interstate and Foreign Commerce Committee at hearings on the Harris bill that the administration was "quite unhappy" about the substitute drawn in the secret session. But more than a week after the spectacular Senate squabble, the President had said nothing, either personally or through his subordinates, to clarify his position, and the Senate Judiciary Committee voted out the emasculated substitute.

The situation by then was thoroughly confused. S. 1552 was a bill completely different from and weaker than the original Kefauver bill. The original remained extant in the form of Celler's House bill, but Celler expressed the view that "without the support of the administration, it's hopeless." And the administration-offered Harris bill differed from both of them. Not without justification, the periodical, *Chemical & Engineering News*, led off an article with the words: "For all practical purposes, the Kefauver drug bill is dead."

The obituary was somewhat premature; but no thanks to the Kennedy administration. In mid-July, a story by Morton Mintz, following a tip from Blair, appeared in the *Washington Post*, telling how babies without arms and legs had been born to numerous European mothers who had used the drug thalidomide as a tranquillizer during pregnancy. The story had been told three months earlier before Celler's committee but had not made the newspapers then.

A Food and Drug Administration scientist, Dr. Frances O. Kelsey, single-handedly had kept the William S. Merrell Company from putting the same drug on the American market without further testing for side effects. Kefauver urged, on the Senate floor and in a letter to President Kennedy, that Dr. Kelsey be awarded the Distinguished Federal Civilian Service Medal.[22]

Kennedy followed the recommendation—after Kefauver made his letter to the President public six days later—but did not mention Kefauver, attributing the recommendation to the HEW secretary. The White House remembered to invite Kefauver to the awards ceremony at the last minute, but, as columnist Doris Fleeson wrote of it: "Dr. Kelsey wore a radiant smile as the President paid her honor. . . . The President smiled, too, and so did Majority Whip

22. AP story, *Nashville Tennessean*, July 29, 1962.

Kefauver (in background at right) attends the ceremony as President Kennedy presents Dr. Frances Kelsey the Distinguished Federal Civil Service Medal in 1962.

Humphrey. . . . In the background, somewhere, there was even Senator Kefauver, who first suggested the medal to the President, though he did not seem to make the pictures."[23]

The thalidomide story caught the horrified fascination of the public, and all at once, the Kennedy administration developed a strong interest in seeing most of the original Kefauver provisions dealing with drug safety restored to the drug bill. The word was passed to Eastland through Sonosky and Theodore Sorensen, Kennedy's special counsel. The Judiciary Committee held a series of meetings in which it, in effect, retraced all of its steps since the secret meeting, adopted the administration's recommendations, and reported the bill to the floor.

Late in August, the Senate passed the drug bill. Kefauver attempted to amend it from the floor to restore his patent provision, altered to require that, three years after winning a patent, a manufacturer whose price to druggists was more than 500 percent of the production cost, including research, would have to license a "qualified applicant" to use the patent. This, Kefauver said, would reduce the price of drugs by breaking up the monopolistic hold of giant drug companies on medicines needed by the public.

"There is no reason or justification for the excessive prices paid by Americans" for drugs, he said.

Eastland took the floor to oppose the amendment, arguing that it would reduce drug research by taking away patent protection and reducing profits, but in the end it was not the unremitting effort of Eastland and the Republicans that killed Kefauver's antimonopoly effort; it was the Kennedy administration. Without warning, Mike Mansfield, the majority leader, moved to table Kefauver's amendment. Kefauver was taken by surprise, for he had been expecting support from that quarter.

"Hell, Mike," protested Kefauver to Mansfield privately, "if anybody's going to do that, let it be Dirksen. Why not let us vote on the merits of it?"

Mansfield replied simply that he had been instructed by the White House to make the motion. The amendment was tabled by a 53 to 28 vote, though even Humphrey, the majority whip, voted with Kefauver, remarking to a colleague that he hated "to go against

23. Harris, *The Real Voice*, 201.

the leadership" but could not ignore Kefauver's argument.[24]

After that was done, the senators relaxed, and the bill passed, 78 to 0. The House made a few changes in the measure—actually strengthening it—and, after agreement was reached in conference, Kennedy signed the bill into law October 10, 1962.

Kefauver, Hart, and Dr. Kelsey were among those present for the White House ceremony. After writing part of his signature, as is customary on such occasions, Kennedy stopped and handed the pen to Kefauver.

"Here," said Kennedy, "You played the most important part, Estes, so you get the first pen."

With an uncertain smile, Kefauver took the pen and murmured: "Thank you, Mr. President."[25]

During the final oratory over adoption of the conference committee report, Hruska called the bill "sound and workable" and praised Eastland and Dirksen for their "steadying influence" in the legislative maneuvering.

This encomium was a bit too much for Tom Dodd, who, as a subcommittee member, had seen the "steadying influence" of Eastland and Dirksen in operation at first hand. He arose to rectify the record.

"I have an idea," he said, "that the Senator from Tennessee will be remembered long after all of us in this chamber at this hour are gone, for many great things he has accomplished. . . . But, I think, perhaps, in the long run, a grateful nation will revere his memory most for the passage of this particular piece of legislation."[26]

Kefauver, being Kefauver, got to thinking, after the drug bill was enacted; and, from the standpoint of smart investment, ethical drugs were still a good thing. So he went down and, on the open market, without any maneuvering or secrecy, bought fifty-one shares of stock in Charles Pfizer and Company and 200 shares in the Rexall Drug and Chemical Company, two of the nation's leading drug firms. The total worth of the stock was about $13,000.

"My God!" moaned Fensterwald later. "What if a hostile newspaper had gotten wind of *that*?"[27]

24. Ibid., 214–15.
25. Ibid., 245.
26. *Congressional Record*, vol. 108, pt. 16, Oct. 3, 1962, p. 22052.
27. Personal conversation, Bernard Fensterwald Jr., Washington, May 14,

In the Background Was Even Senator Kefauver

But it did not become known until after Kefauver's death, when his will was probated—nor, Kefauver being Kefauver, did it prevent his reopening the drug hearings and trying to restore his lost patent provisions to the Drug Control Act, until death wrote an end to his efforts.

1970. Kefauver did not escape rumors spread by political enemies that he used his position for personal gain, and fifteen years after his death, Bobby Baker, Lyndon Johnson's ex-aide, was quoted in *Playboy* magazine as listing Kefauver as "among those senators who willingly put themselves up for sale." Baker said he delivered a $25,000 bribe "earmarked" for Kefauver to thwart the opposition of George P. Marshall, owner of the Washington Redskins football team, to a National Football League franchise for the Dallas Cowboys, by declaring through Antitrust and Monopoly Subcommittee findings that Marshall held an illegal monopoly with his Redskin Television Network. Clint Murchison, owner of the Dallas Cowboys, called Baker's story "not true" and "libelous," in an AP story from Dallas May 2, 1978. Lucile Myers stated in a letter to me May 24, 1978, "Estes was meticulous about the source of gifts and contributions. Even Christmas gifts were returned." My own information during Kefauver's early years in the Senate was that he would resort to the lecture circuit and writing articles to pay off campaign debts and, though he might accept small, edible gifts such as hams and fruitcakes at Christmas time, he would not accept substantial gifts, such as a television set. I know, and Miss Myers confirms, that he refused an automobile his Tennessee supporters had bought to replace the family Chrysler, after it burned at the end of the 1948 campaign.

Chapter 20

Mr. President, I Yield the Floor

The black bears snuffled among the eons-old rocks of Yellowstone Park, and the waters sparkled down the eternal falls of its canyons. At the park's center, amid the unperturbed heirs of geologic ages, the proud Lake Hotel was but an artifact of man's brief passage.

In its vast lobby in July 1963, among a group of his friends, stood a tall man who, in three weeks, would be dead. Already his fatality puffed his face with a ruddy flush and slackened its long lines. As he stood there, recalled one of his companions, Senator Gale Mc-Gee, "all of America seemed to recognize at once the presence of Estes. They said: 'Hi, Estes. Hello, Estes. I last saw you, Estes, in Minnesota'—or 'Alabama'—or 'New Hampshire.'"[1]

In his fourteen and a half years in the Senate, Kefauver had become a phenomenon unmatched in his lifetime in a nation that likes to take its public figures on a personal basis. Other names were more widely known, perhaps, and certainly others of his contemporaries possessed more outright charisma. But no one else in his time did so many thousands of people feel that they *knew*, familiarly and personally.

"I shall remember him best," said Abraham Ribicoff, who had been elected senator from Connecticut in 1962, "as a Senator of the people—not just of the people of Tennessee, but of the nation. . . . He dedicated his life to their interests. He was of them, by choice, and for the common good of all."[2]

"When Hawaii was not yet a full-fledged member of the Union, Senator Kefauver was often referred to with the term of endearment, 'the Senator from Hawaii,'" Representative Mark M. Matsunaga said of him. "It was he to whom many of us addressed our

1. Sen. McGee in *Carey Estes Kefauver, Late a Senator from Tennessee*, 57–58.
2. Sen. Ribicoff in ibid., 88.

problems; and he gave us unstintingly of his time and services, just as if we had been his valued voting constituents."[3]

Kefauver's health had not been really good for several years before 1963. The iron constitution that was the despair of those who tried to keep up with him had been undermined by the short sleep, the irregular meals, the exhausting 18-to-21-hour days of his campaigns and the long grind of his legislative work in committee and on the floor.

At least once annually during the immediately preceding years, he had been hospitalized for a few days with influenza. It happened to him twice in the spring of 1963, once after he took off his raincoat to put it around Dinah Shore's shoulders at the Ramp Festival and again on his return from a trip to Paris, where he looked into European Common Market operations for the Antitrust and Monopoly Subcommittee.

Kefauver was a heavy cigaret smoker. He tried repeatedly to stop smoking but never succeeded for longer than six months. Once when he and Nancy were in Germany, he bought some varicolored pills that were supposed to dull the desire to smoke, but the pills had to be taken in a certain order—and the direction on the vial were in German. When the desire for a smoke overcame him, Kefauver fumed in frustration until he could find a translator.

Of course he did not carry cigarets with him during his no-smoking periods—and also of course he was perpetually bumming a smoke from someone else. Everard K. Smith, a member of the Senate Aeronautical and Space Sciences Committee staff, during its long discussions of the communications satellite bill, would look up occasionally to catch Kefauver looking at him, intently and wistfully but silently. Without a word, Smith would offer his pack of cigarets and Kefauver would take one, with a murmured word of thanks.

Because Kefauver developed high blood pressure in his later years, his heavy smoking did his health no good; nor did his propensity for ingesting large amounts of Scotch whiskey, which he maintained until his death. He loved the liquor, and was considerably more than a moderate drinker. He could usually drink all afternoon and evening without staggering or even getting a thick tongue, since he was in the habit of sipping rather slowly, but as he

3. Rep. Matsunaga in ibid., 128.

grew older he sometimes swam in a mild alcoholic haze. Occasionally he did drink too much, even for him. Once during his final years, when he was on a political tour of Tennessee, Nancy sought out Noble Caudill, who was traveling with them, one evening in a West Tennessee town, and told him, "Noble, you'd better come and get Estes." Caudill found Kefauver well under the influence. After helping him to bed, Caudill arranged to interrupt the tour the next day and flew Kefauver to Florida for a few days of rest in the sunshine.[4]

The last few months of Kefauver's life were a happy time for him and his family. "It was as if, that last year, Estes knew he had to wind things up," said Nancy. "He spent a last weekend in New York with Lynda. He and David went fishing together. He took us West for a vacation."[5]

Kefauver utilized the 1963 Easter recess of Congress to go to Europe with Senator Thomas Dodd, FTC Chairman Paul Rand Dixon, and three subcommittee staff members to study European methods of combating monopoly and Common Market proposals. He told the subcommittee on his return that Europeans had stricter antitrust laws in some respects than the United States, but their penalties were not as severe. He never got the chance to put into practice the ideas he gained from the trip. About the same time, Kefauver opened a subcommittee probe into evidence that some large American drug companies had conspired to block a program by McKesson & Robbins to sell drugs under generic names in Latin America at prices far below the trade name prices. But John Carroll left the Senate at the end of 1962, and Eastland appointed John McClellan to the subcommittee to replace him. With this Democratic reinforcement, Dirksen was able to block the move.

Not many days before Kefauver's death, Mrs. Martha Ragland was at lunch with him in Washington, waxing indignant over some of the cynicism and obstructionism she had encountered in dealings with the Labor Department. "I just come to Washington every now and then, but you're here all the time," she said. "I just don't see how you can stand to see the way they erode and tear down everything democracy is supposed to stand for." "Well, Martha," an-

4. Personal conversation, Noble C. Caudill, Hendersonville, Tenn., Autumn 1970.

5. Personal communication, Carol Harford, Washington, Oct. 17, 1970.

Less than two months before Kefauver's death, he and his friend Noble C.
Caudill, an official of Genesco, the shoe-manufacturing firm, look over
an exhibit on legislation dealing with foreign shoe imports.

swered Kefauver wearily, "I don't know how much longer I can."[6]

One of several instances of apparent premonitions Kefauver had of his approaching death was attributed to Jowanda Shelton, a secretary on his staff, who said that a few days before his death he remarked that "if there is anything to religion, I ought to see my brother Robert again."[7]

One of the last letters Kefauver wrote was to Adlai Stevenson, to tell him that Kefauver had had "so many favorable comments about your visit to Tennessee. Perhaps you'd better come down and run for the Senate one of these days. I'll be your campaign manager."[8] His last letter, a week later, was to his daughter, Lynda (she adopted the "Y" spelling in college), who was working as a hostess on the liner *SS President Polk* in the Caribbean Sea. It was full of family chatter and references to friends, and concluded: "Be sure and write me a little card at all the ports. We are thinking of you and love you."

It was written the day of his fatal heart attack—and his twenty-eighth wedding anniversary. After their Western vacation in Santa Fe, Nancy and the two younger daughters had gone to the Cherokee Ranch at Sedalia, Colorado, to visit a friend, "Tweet" Kimball. Kefauver visited McGee in Wyoming and then returned to Washington. He dictated the letter, left his office, and rode the subway to the Capitol for the last time.

"His was a battle casualty," said Ernest Gruening of Alaska. "He was fatally wounded in action. It was on the floor of the Senate late one afternoon, toward the close of a grueling day, while engaged in one of his monumental battles—and leading that battle—that he was stricken."[9]

It was a battle, in Gruening's words, "against a monopoly, an unregulated monopoly . . . a monopoly in a vast new and unexplored cosmic field." The battle was over the communications satellite bill.

Kennedy had proposed that Congress create a profit-making cor-

---

6. Personal conversation, Martha Ragland, Nashville, Spring 1970.

7. Swados, *Standing Up for the People*, 3.

8. Letter, Estes Kefauver, Washington, to Adlai Stevenson, Chicago, Aug. 1, 1963, Kefauver Collection, Ser. 1, Box 71.

9. Sen. Gruening in *Carey Estes Kefauver, Late a Senator from Tennessee*, 45. Gruening used much the same language in an expanded tribute to Kefauver in

poration to own and operate a commercial satellite system, in lieu of a plan advocated by American Telephone & Telegraph Company and other carriers to give the task to a non-profit corporation wholly controlled by international carriers of which AT&T was the largest. Kefauver held no brief for the original AT&T plan, but he and two dozen other members of Congress wrote Kennedy that AT&T also would eventually come to dominate the private, profit-making corporation that the administration proposed.[10]

Kefauver and Wayne Morse introduced a bill to turn over space communications to a government-owned system but drew little support. The Republicans and conservative Democrats were against it in principle, and the liberal bloc had enjoyed its alliance with the administration on civil rights legislation too successfully to be critical of Kennedy proposals now.

When floor debate began, Kefauver led a group of ten Democratic senators in an outright filibuster against the bill for five days. They succeeded in getting the bill sent to the Foreign Relations Committee, but that committee reported it back to the floor without amendments; and the great public outcry against the bill they had hoped to generate with the filibuster did not materialize. The filibuster was resumed, but, for the first time in thirty-five years, the Senate voted cloture, shutting off debate. Among those voting for cloture were twenty-two Republicans and Southern Democrats who had always opposed it in filibusters on civil rights. The Senate passed the bill after tabling 122 amendments and accepting one minor one, and Kennedy signed it into law.

When the Senate received a House-passed bill in 1963 to authorize $5.5 billion in appropriations for the National Aeronautics and Space Administration, Kefauver noted that it contained some $50 million for Comsat, the communications satellite corporation set up under the Kennedy administration bill the previous year. On August 8, 1963, he offered an amendment to require that Comsat reimburse NASA for any research from which it would benefit. The Senate did not get around to the NASA appropriation until about 5 o'clock in the afternoon. While Kefauver was explaining his amend-

---

the manuscript of his autobiography, 1456, excerpts of which he sent to me as an enclosure in a personal communication from Washington, Jan. 12, 1971.

10. Lois Laycook, *Nashville Tennessean*, Feb. 27, 1962.

ment, Senator John O. Pastore of Rhode Island entered the chamber, returning from Moscow, where the United States, Great Britain, and Russia had signed a treaty to ban all but underground atomic tests.

Interrupting his discourse, Kefauver commented, "I am glad to see that the distinguished Senator from Rhode Island has returned, looking so well, from a most important mission."

"And feeling better than I look," said Pastore.

"I commend the Senator," said Kefauver. "He must be feeling very well, since he looks so well."

Returning to the amendment, Kefauver explained that, although government-financed research was in the public domain, the 1962 act prohibited anyone from going into satellite communications except Comsat, and therefore research in this area would be for the sole benefit of that corporation.

"It follows," he said, "that corporation should pay for the research and development. That is all the amendment seeks to do, to try and say that the corporation which is to make the profit shall pay a reasonable, fair, proportionate share of the cost of research and development which is done by the U.S. government."[11]

Albert Gore and Frank J. Lausche of Ohio were assisting Kefauver with leading questions, and Clinton P. Anderson of New Mexico and Stuart Symington of Missouri were arguing with him in opposition to the amendment. While Symington was talking at one point, Lausche saw Kefauver turn white and break out into perspiration.

"Are you all right, Estes?" asked Lausche.

"I'll be all right," said Kefauver weakly, but he yielded the argument for the amendment to Lausche and sat down. Lausche suggested the absence of a quorum, to give Kefauver a chance to rest for a few moments.

Joseph Clark of Pennsylvania hurried to Kefauver's side. Kefauver said he had "a stomach ache." Clark urged him to leave the floor and get medical attention.

"No, I've got to keep going, said Kefauver.[12] When the roll call on the quorum call was completed, he took the floor again and talked on the amendment for some minutes.

11. *Congressional Record*, vol. 109, pt. 11, Aug. 8, 1963, p. 14555.
12. Details of Kefauver's heart attack on the Senate floor were related principally by Charles A. Caldwell in personal conversation in Washington May 12, 1970, and supplemented in a letter from him Sept. 4, 1970.

At last, still feeling ill, he asked Ralph Yarborough, a cosponsor of the amendment, to take over for him.

"Mr. President, I yield the floor," he said.[13]

He sat at his desk, his big hands folded, his lips pursed, staring straight ahead, and pain tormented him as the argument raged over his amendment. At last, Mike Mansfield agreed to two hours of debate on the amendment the next day. Kefauver pulled himself to his feet.

"I spoke to the Majority Leader about having a yea-and-nay vote on the amendment," he reminded.[14]

They were his last words on the Senate floor. When Mansfield assured him that such a vote would be taken at the end of the debate, Kefauver left the Senate Chamber, to return no more.

He went into the nearby office of Zeake W. (Skeeter) Johnson Jr., Senate sergeant-at-arms, and sat down. Bob Perry, chief pharmacist's mate, gave him some antacid pills for indigestion, and Kefauver relaxed with a drink.

There he was found by Charlie Caldwell, who hurried to the Capitol when he was notified at last of the senator's illness. Kefauver explained that he had eaten some Mexican food at a party at Trader Vic's the night before and had an attack of heartburn.

At first, Kefauver turned down Caldwell's urging that he see a doctor or go to Bethesda Naval Hospital for a checkup, but he finally agreed to see his doctor. Caldwell called back to the office and had one of the secretaries, Jowanda Shelton, drive to the archway entrance of the Capitol to pick him up. Kefauver walked to the elevator, rode it down, and left in the car with Miss Shelton.

Caldwell was entertaining Ed Meeman, editor of the *Press-Scimitar*, at a dinner party at his home in McLean, Virginia, that evening. Fairly late in the evening, Caldwell telephoned Kefauver at his home to ask what the doctor had said. Miss Shelton answered. Kefauver had not seen the doctor, she said, but had insisted on being driven straight home and had had a bowl of soup. He was still feeling uncomfortable.

Caldwell had her get Kefauver to the telephone and prevailed on him to let Miss Shelton drive him to Bethesda and check in. He

---

13. *Congressional Record*, vol. 109, pt. 11, Aug. 8, 1963, p. 14555.
14. Ibid., 14570.

checked in about 11:30 P.M., by which time all the doctors had gone, and only interns and corpsmen were on duty. When Caldwell could get away from his party, he drove to the hospital and found Kefauver sitting up in bed in his room on the sixteenth floor, still uncomfortable but still insisting he had nothing but heartburn. Caldwell asked the intern on duty what had been done for the senator. He was told that nothing had been done.

Caldwell insisted that an electrocardiogram be run on Kefauver, but it showed nothing. He got Kefauver to promise to lie down and rest, and left about 1:30 A.M.

"Thanks for coming by, old buddy," said Kefauver.

The next day, doctors at Bethesda diagnosed Kefauver's ailment as "a mild heart attack," and ordered him to bed for "at least three weeks of complete rest." But, that night, Kefauver exhibited further symptoms, and it was decided that he had suffered "dissecting aneurism of the wall of the ascending aorta"—a breakdown of the inner wall of the main artery from the heart, causing it to balloon outward dangerously under pressure. Open heart surgery was advised. Caldwell telephoned Nancy in Colorado.

"Charlie, I want you to get the best heart surgeon in the United States, and get him there as fast as you can," instructed Nancy, and she began packing to return on the first available flight with Diane and Gail.

Caldwell determined that the best surgeon for the job was Dr. Charles Hufnagel of nearby Georgetown, Maryland. But Hufnagel was even then making a speech in Toledo, Ohio. He was called out of the meeting and flown back to Washington in an Air Force plane.

Since Kefauver wanted Nancy present for his open heart surgery, the operation was scheduled for 10 o'clock the next morning. Caldwell was told that the operation required a standby mechanical heart and lengthy technical arrangements. Since the apparatus had just been used for similar surgery, it would take several hours to prepare it for reuse.

Doctors at Bethesda told Caldwell that Kefauver had only one chance in fifty of survival with the surgery, but virtually none at all without it.[15]

15. Although most details of Kefauver's last illness and death were related by Charles A. Caldwell (see note 12 above), Bernard Fensterwald Jr. supplemented some material in personal conversation in Washington May 15, 1970.

Seventeen-year-old David, not realizing how serious his father's illness was, went to the hospital to visit Kefauver late Friday night, after a date. Kefauver talked soberly with him for a while about what David wanted to be when he grew up.

"I thought it was awfully strange," said David, "because he never talked seriously with me that way. But he was in a good frame of mind, and seemed to be feeling all right when I left him."[16]

Bernard Fensterwald remained on vigil with Kefauver.

At 3:33 o'clock the morning of Saturday, August 10, 1963, the ballooning wall of the aorta ruptured, and Kefauver's overworked heart gave way. He died, quietly and peacefully, fifteen days past his sixtieth birthday.

The plane bearing Nancy and their daughters was even then touching earth at Friendship Airport, and Nancy said later that she sensed her husband's death at that moment.[17] Caldwell was waiting for them at the airport and drove them at once to the hospital. As they drove up, Fensterwald came to the car and told them Kefauver had been dead for about an hour.[18]

"Like a giant tree that has come crashing down to earth, his passing leaves a great void," said Tom Dodd in the Senate.[19]

In Nashville, Noble Caudill entered the Third National Bank office of Sam M. Fleming to speak to him about their annual underwriting of Kefauver's personal expenses. Fleming looked at him without expression and said: "The king is dead."[20]

So he was. As he lay dying at Bethesda on Friday, his colleagues dealt him his last defeat. The Senate threw out his amendment to the NASA bill by a 60 to 11 vote.

When the senators came together again at Monday noon, their chaplain, the Reverend Frederick Brown Harris, reminded them that Kefauver "lifted up his voice for measures his conscience told him were in the best interests of the Republic. Now that voice is stilled." They adopted a resolution of regret, agreed to set aside a day for eulogies, and adjourned after seven minutes.

16. Personal conversation, David Kefauver, Knoxville, Spring 1970.
17. Personal communication, Carol Harford, Washington, Oct. 17, 1970.
18. Personal conversation, Bernard Fensterwald Jr., Washington, May 15, 1970.
19. *Congressional Record*, vol. 109, pt. 15, Oct. 24, 1963, p. 20195.
20. Personal conversation, Noble C. Caudill, Hendersonville, Autumn 1970.

In the House that day, they spoke of their memories of him: James Roosevelt, Wayne Hays, "Mannie" Celler, Wright Patman—eighteen of them, all told.[21]

"The people have lost a gallant champion, and I have lost an old friend and a companion-in-arms," said Adlai Stevenson.[22] It was, probably, one of the sincerest expressions of regret that multiplied across the country that August weekend, from President Kennedy and Vice President Johnson to the Michigan telephone repairman who said to Philip Hart, "What a shame. He was such a good man."[23]

They took his body home to Madisonville on Monday, and to Madisonville the nation's leaders followed him Tuesday for the funeral: Lyndon Johnson, Stevenson, a thirty-one-member congressional delegation including some of his good friends. Nancy and the children were flown to Tennessee aboard a presidential jet with Vice President and Mrs. Johnson, and Ward King, a staunch East Tennessee Republican, flew the nineteen members of Kefauver's staff down in a Southeast Airlines plane.

The great and the near-great mingled with Kefauver's own "little people," for a little while, that lowering day in Madisonville—but not as he had.

"That's the difference between Kefauver and the rest of the politicians," said Harry Mansfield bitterly, gesturing toward a group eating fried chicken and ham in the basement of the First Baptist Church. "Kefauver said those things, but he meant it. They don't mean a word they're saying, and we can see it."[24]

They buried Estes from Aunt Lottie's front porch. Nancy sat on the porch beside the casket, with David, Diane, and Gail. Lynda was just inside the house, watching and listening from a window. All of the important visitors sat on folding chairs on the lawn of the century-old mansion, and the townspeople crowded around the edges.

The sun beamed from the threatening clouds for just a few moments during the brief service. Then Air Force servicemen lifted the casket, stepped down the three steps to the lawn, and walked with

21. *Congressional Record*, vol. 109, pt. 11, Aug. 12, 1963, pp. 14716–26.
22. *Nashville Tennessean*, Aug. 11, 1963.
23. Personal communication, Sen. Philip A. Hart, Washington, Sept. 24, 1970.
24. *New York Herald-Tribune*, Aug. 14, 1963.

it down the road between the cornfields and the grape arbor to the open grave beside the mounds that covered the remains of Kefauver's parents. A pink rosebush bloomed beside it.

The flag was lifted from the coffin, and as the casket was lowered into the earth the thunder rolled with a crash and the rain poured down upon them all. Nancy turned away sadly, clutching the folded flag, and walked back through the rain to the house, followed by the children.

For the inscription on his tombstone, Nancy chose the words, *Courage, Justice, and Loving Kindness.*

Kefauver's sister, Nora, spent some time in Washington after his death, investigating the entire sequence of events that surrounded his fatal heart attack and what was done for him at Bethesda. She expressed the suspicion that he did not get the proper care due him because of the enmity he had stirred up in the medical profession with his drug probe. She gave Bethesda officials an uncomfortable time until Caldwell and others close to Kefauver convinced her that the senator himself, by his delay in seeking treatment, was responsible for losing the slender chance he had of living through the attack.

Miss Nora was not the only one dissatisfied with the events surrounding Kefauver's death. Gruening said that "the operation is not a tremendously difficult one, but someone was guilty of poor judgment, according to the information I have, for not operating immediately."[25]

Kefauver left to his wife and children, in a hand-written will, an estate of about $300,000, mostly in small stock holdings, but approximately half of it went for payment of his debts.[26] President Kennedy appointed Nancy the State Department's first Advisor on Fine Arts and director of the Art in the Embassies program a few days before his own death, and she and Mrs. Byrd Farioletti continued their art teaching partnership until late 1966.

Nancy died November 20, 1967, of a heart attack at a dinner party

25. Personal conversation, Charles A. Caldwell, Washington, May 12, 1970; personal communication, Ernest Gruening, Washington, Aug. 14, 1970.
26. *Chattanooga News-Free Press*, Aug. 26, 1963. Although this was substantially more than the "estate of $20,000" reported a few weeks later by columnist Marquis W. Childs (*Nashville Tennessean*, Sept. 26, 1963), it was small enough to justify Child's conclusion in his "melancholy footnote to the Kefauver career": "Honesty, as Lincoln said, may be the best policy. But in an era when money values are supreme, it can impose heavy penalties."

honoring Everett Dirksen at the Mayflower Hotel, and her ashes were returned to her native Scotland.

One of Kefauver's friends, reporter Charles Bartlett, wrote that Kefauver had laid careful plans to open an Antitrust and Monopoly Subcommittee probe of monopolistic aspects of organized labor in September 1963. Bartlett said Kefauver had mentioned the plans to only one of his employees and kept the papers on it at home. Caldwell called the Bartlett story "as wrong as it can be . . . a rumor, nothing more,"[27] but Bartlett said his source for the story was an "extremely close" friend of Kefauver, whom he would not identify.[28]

Provisions for breaking up monopolistic practices by organized labor, dealing especially with the effects of collective bargaining on competition, were included in the first major antitrust legislation proposed after Kefauver's death by Hart, who succeeded him as subcommittee chairman. Hart said they were a product of Kefauver's investigations as well as his own hearings after Kefauver's death.[29]

Hart continued Kefauver's fight against monopoly until his own death in 1976 and achieved some substantial legislation, but he never had the working majority in the Antitrust and Monopoly Subcommittee that Kefauver enjoyed during the administered price investigations.

In a very real sense, a "Kefauver era" died with the man. It was an era symbolized by the tall, bespectacled figure, sometimes in coonskin cap but more often in conservative business suit, slow of smile and soft of voice, to whom the handshake was a token of the common bond of mankind. It was an era of a few spectacular, hard-won successes and many hard-lost failures that constituted the visible surface of his long, intricate effort to bring the American ideal of government by and for the people, as he saw it, closer to realization.

He came so close to the presidential nomination—with a good chance of election—in 1952 that the second-guessing is inevitable: would it not have been better for him to have accepted a relatively minor compromise, like an "open" stance on tidelands oil, to achieve a position from which he could have accomplished goals of

27. Telephone conversation, Charles A. Caldwell, Washington, Spring 1972.
28. Telephone conversation, Charles L. Bartlett, Washington, Spring 1972.
29. Personal communication, Sen. Philip A. Hart, Sept. 24, 1970.

profound consequence to the nation's future, such as Atlantic Union and a reversal of the monopolistic trend?

That is essentially an ethical question, which Kefauver answered in his own way, by his actions. He chose to play it straight.

Bibliography

(Newspaper and periodical sources are cited, where pertinent, in the body of the text or in the notes.)

Administered Prices: Report of the Committee on the Judiciary, United States Senate, made by its Subcommittee on Antitust and Monopoly. 29 volumes. Washington: Government Printing Office, 1957–63.

Allen, Frederick Lewis. *Only Yesterday*. New York: Harper, 1931.

————. *Since Yesterday*. New York: Harper, 1940.

————. *The Big Change*. New York: Harper, 1952.

Anderson, Jack, and Fred Blumenthal. *The Kefauver Story*. New York: Dial, 1956.

Bailey, Thomas A. *The American Pageant*. Boston: D.C. Heath, 1956.

Barth, Alan. *Government by Investigation*. New York: Viking, 1955.

Bolling, Richard. *House Out of Order*. New York: Dutton, 1965.

Burnham, James. *Congress and the American Tradition*. Chicago: Regnery, 1959.

Burns, James MacGregor, *Congress on Trial*. New York: Harper, 1949.

————. *Roosevelt: the Lion and the Fox*. New York: Harcourt, Brace, 1956.

————. *John Kennedy*. New York: Harcourt, Brace & Co., 1959.

Caldwell, Mary French. *The Duck's Back*. N.p.: The author, 1952.

Carey Estes Kefauver, Late a Senator from Tennessee: Memorial Addresses Delivered in Congress. Washington: Government Printing Office, 1964.

Congress and the Nation, 1945-64. Washington: Congressional Quarterly Service, 1965.

Congressional Quarterly Almanac. Vols. i–xix. Washington: Congressional Quarterly Service, 1945–63.

Congressional Record. Washington: Government Printing Office, 1939–63.

Cook, Fred J. *The Warfare State*. New York: Macmillan, 1962.

David, Paul T., Malcolm Moos, and Ralph M. Goldman. *Presidential Nominating Politics in 1952*. 5 vols. Baltimore: Johns Hopkins Univ. Press, 1954.

Davidson, Donald. *The Tennessee.* 2 vols. New York: Rinehart, 1946; Vol. I rpt. Knoxville: Univ. of Tennessee Press, 1979.

Donald, David. *Charles Sumner & the Rights of Man.* New York: Knopf, 1970.

Flynn, John T. *The Roosevelt Myth.* New York: Devin-Adair, 1948.

Folmsbee, Stanley J., Robert E. Corlew, and Enoch L. Mitchell. *History of Tennessee.* 4 vols. New York: Lewis Historical Co., 1960.

Galloway, George B. *History of the House of Representatives.* New York: Crowell, 1962.

Gorman, Joseph Bruce. *Kefauver: a Political Biography.* New York: Oxford Univ. Press, 1971.

Grazia, Alfred de. *The Western Public, 1952 and Beyond.* Stanford, Calif.: Stanford Univ. Press, 1954.

Gruening, Ernest, and Herbert W. Beaser. *Vietnam Folly.* Washington: National Press, 1968.

Gunther, John. *Inside U.S.A.* New York: Harper, 1947.

Hamer, Philip M. *Tennessee—A History.* 4 vols. New York: American Historical Society, 1933.

Harris, Richard. *The Real Voice.* New York: Macmillan, 1964.

Heard, Alexander. *The Costs of Democracy.* Chapel Hill: Univ. of North Carolina Press, 1960.

Herling, John. *The Great Price Conspiracy: The Story of the Antitrust Violations in the Electrical Industry.* Westport, Conn.: Greenwood Press, 1962.

Hicks, John D., and George E. Mowry. *A Short History of American Democracy.* Boston: Houghton Mifflin, 1956.

Hixson, Fred. *The Age of Will Cummings.* N.p.: The author, 1962.

Howard, W.V. *Authority in TVA Land.* Kansas City: Frank Glenn Co., 1948.

Hubbard, Preston J. *Origins of the TVA.* Nashville: Vanderbilt Univ. Press, 1961.

Karanikas, Alexander. *Tillers of a Myth.* Madison: Univ. of Wisconsin Press, 1969.

Kefauver, Estes. *Crime in America.* Garden City, N.Y.: Doubleday, 1951.

————. *In a Few Hands: Monopoly Power in America.* New York: Pantheon, 1965.

————, and Jack Levin. *A 20th Century Congress.* New York: Duell Sloan, 1947.

Kerr, W.S. *John Sherman, His Life and Public Service.* 2 vols. Boston: Sherman, French, 1908.

Kirwin, Harry W. *The Inevitable Success: Herbert R. O'Conor.* Westminster, Md.: Newman Press, 1962.

Krock, Arthur. *Memoirs.* New York: Funk & Wagnalls, 1968.

Lundberg, Ferdinand. *The Rich and the Super-Rich*. New York: Lyle Stuart, 1968.

Martin, Ralph G. *Ballots & Bandwagons*. Chicago: Rand McNally, 1964.

Martin, Roscoe C., ed. *TVA, the First Twenty Years*. University, Ala., and Knoxville, Tenn.: Univ. of Alabama Press and Univ. of Tennessee Press, 1956.

Miller, William D. *Mr. Crump of Memphis*. Baton Rouge: Louisiana State Univ. Press, 1964.

Moore, William Howard, *The Kefauver Committee and the Politics of Crime, 1950-1952*. Columbia: Univ. of Missouri Press, 1974.

O'Brien, P.J. *Forward with Roosevelt!* Chicago: Winston, 1936.

Pearson, Drew, and Jack Anderson. *The Case Against Congress*. New York: Simon and Schuster, 1968.

Randall, J.G. *The Civil War and Reconstruction*. Boston: D.C. Heath, 1937.

Riencourt, Amaury de. *The Coming Caesars*. New York: Capricorn, 1964.

Roper, Elmo. *You and Your Leaders*. New York: William Morrow, 1957.

Schriftgiesser, Karl, *The Lobbyists*. Boston: Little, Brown, 1951.

Sherman, John. *Recollections of Forty Years in the House, Senate and Cabinet*. 2 vols. New York: Werner, 1895.

Sherwood, Robert E. *Roosevelt and Hopkins*. New York: Harper, 1948.

Sorenson, Theodore C. *Kennedy*. New York: Harper, 1965.

Swados, Harvey. *Standing Up for the People: the Life and Work of Estes Kefauver*. New York: Dutton, 1972.

Swaney, W.B. *Safeguards of Liberty*. New York: Oxford Univ. Press, 1920.

Thomson, Charles A.H., and Frances M. Shattuck. *The 1956 Presidential Campaign*. Washington: Brookings, 1960.

Webb, May Folk, and Patrick Mann Estes. *Carey-Estes Genealogy*. Rutland, Vt.: Tuttle, 1939.

White, Robert H. *Tennessee, Its Growth and Progress*. N.p.: The author, 1947.

White, Williams S. *The Taft Story*. New York: Harper, 1954.

_____. *Citadel*. New York: Harper, 1956.

Wildavsky, Aaron. *Dixon-Yates: a Study in Power Politics*. New Haven: Yale Univ. Press, 1962.

Index